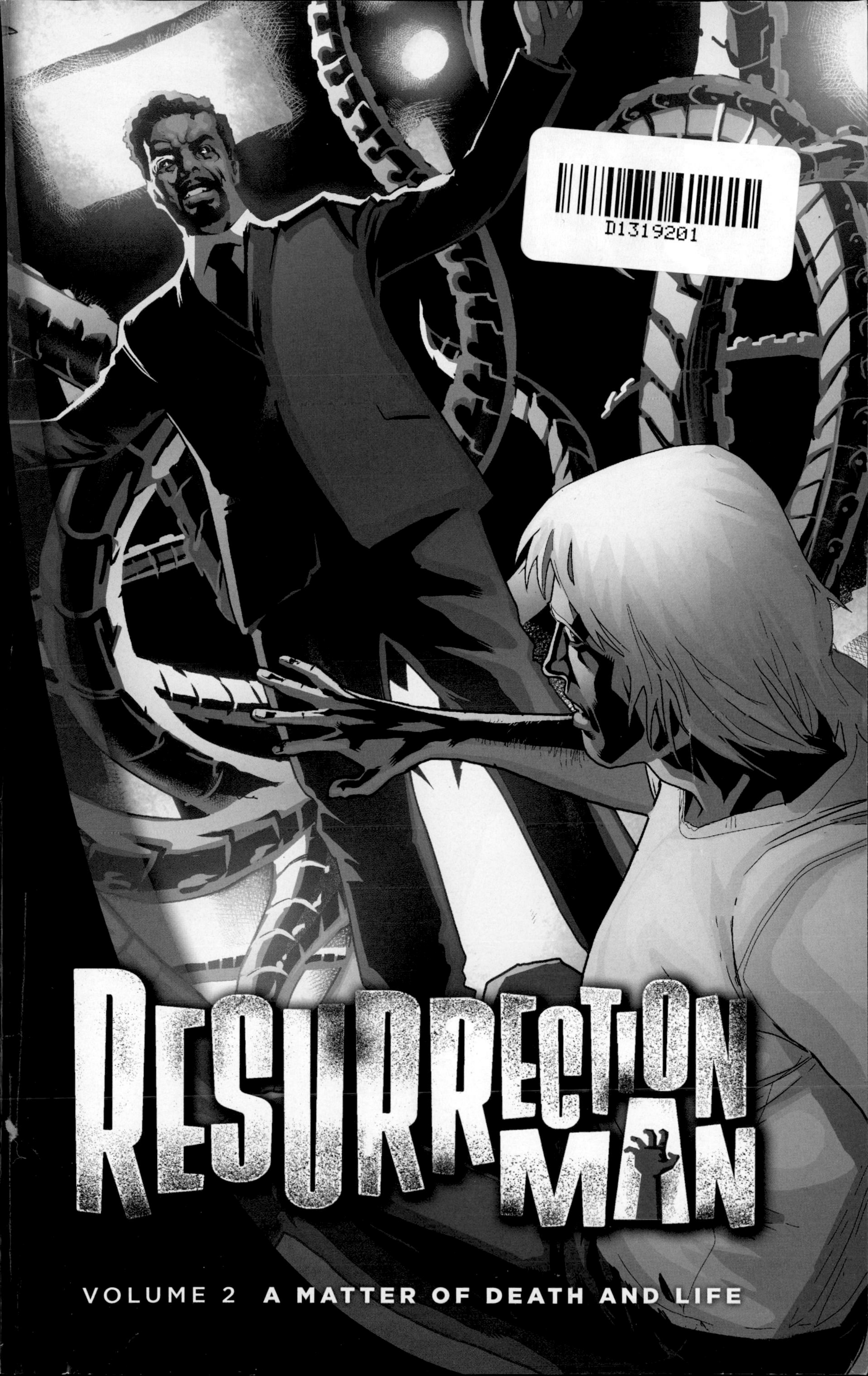

RESURRECTION MAN

VOLUME 2 A MATTER OF DEATH AND LIFE

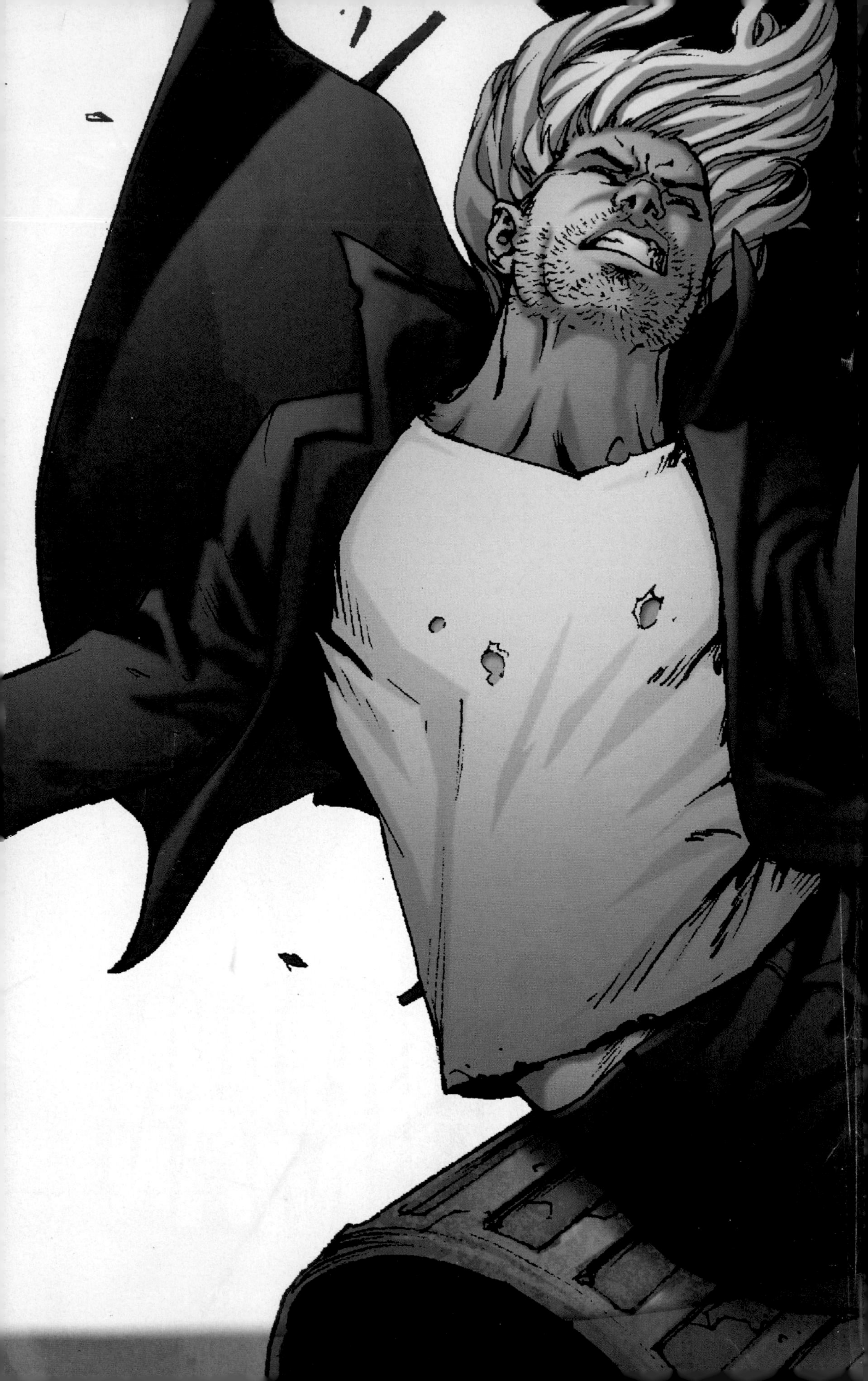

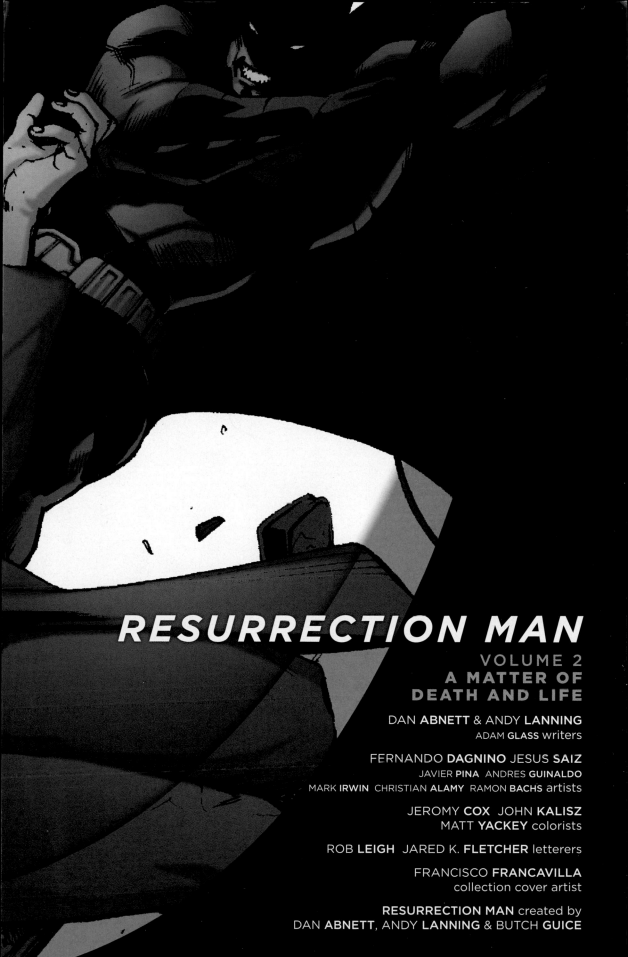

RESURRECTION MAN

VOLUME 2
A MATTER OF
DEATH AND LIFE

DAN **ABNETT** & ANDY **LANNING**
ADAM **GLASS** writers

FERNANDO **DAGNINO** JESUS **SAIZ**
JAVIER **PINA** ANDRES **GUINALDO**
MARK **IRWIN** CHRISTIAN **ALAMY** RAMON **BACHS** artists

JEROMY **COX** JOHN **KALISZ**
MATT **YACKEY** colorists

ROB **LEIGH** JARED K. **FLETCHER** letterers

FRANCISCO **FRANCAVILLA**
collection cover artist

RESURRECTION MAN created by
DAN **ABNETT**, ANDY **LANNING** & BUTCH **GUICE**

BRIAN CUNNINGHAM Editor – Original Series DARREN SHAN KATIE KUBERT Assistant Editors – Original Series
RACHEL PINNELAS Editor ROBBIN BROSTERMAN Design Director – Books ROBBIE BIEDERMAN Publication Design

BOB HARRAS Senior VP – Editor-in-Chief, DC Comics

DIANE NELSON President DAN DIDIO and JIM LEE Co-Publishers GEOFF JOHNS Chief Creative Officer
JOHN ROOD Executive VP – Sales, Marketing and Business Development AMY GENKINS Senior VP – Business and Legal Affairs
NAIRI GARDINER Senior VP – Finance JEFF BOISON VP – Publishing Planning
MARK CHIARELLO VP – Art Direction and Design JOHN CUNNINGHAM VP – Marketing
TERRI CUNNINGHAM VP – Talent Relations and Services ALISON GILL Senior VP – Manufacturing and Operations
HANK KANALZ Senior VP – Vertigo & Integrated Publishing JAY KOGAN VP – Business and Legal Affairs, Publishing
JACK MAHAN VP – Business Affairs, Talent NICK NAPOLITANO VP – Manufacturing Administration
SUE POHJA VP – Book Sales COURTNEY SIMMONS Senior VP – Publicity BOB WAYNE Senior VP – Sales

RESURRECTION MAN VOLUME 2: A MATTER OF DEATH AND LIFE

DC Comics, 1700 Broadway, New York, NY 10019
A Warner Bros. Entertainment Company.
Printed by RR Donnelley, Salem, VA, USA. 5/13/13. First Printing.

ISBN: 978-1-4012-3866-7

Library of Congress Cataloging-in-Publication Data

Abnett, Dan, author.
Resurrection man. Vol. 2, A matter of death and life / Dan Abnett, Andy Lanning, Jesús Saiz.
pages cm
"Originally published in single magazine form in Resurrection Man 8-12, 0; Suicide Squad 9."
ISBN 978-1-4012-3866-7
1. Graphic novels. I. Lanning, Andy, author. II. Saiz, Jesús, illustrator. III. Title. IV. Title: Matter of death and life.
PN6728.R478A27 2013
741.5'973—dc23
2013003529

SUSTAINABLE
FORESTRY
INITIATIVE

Certified Chain of Custody
At Least 20% Certified Forest Content
www.sfiprogram.org
SFI-01042
APPLIES TO TEXT STOCK ONLY

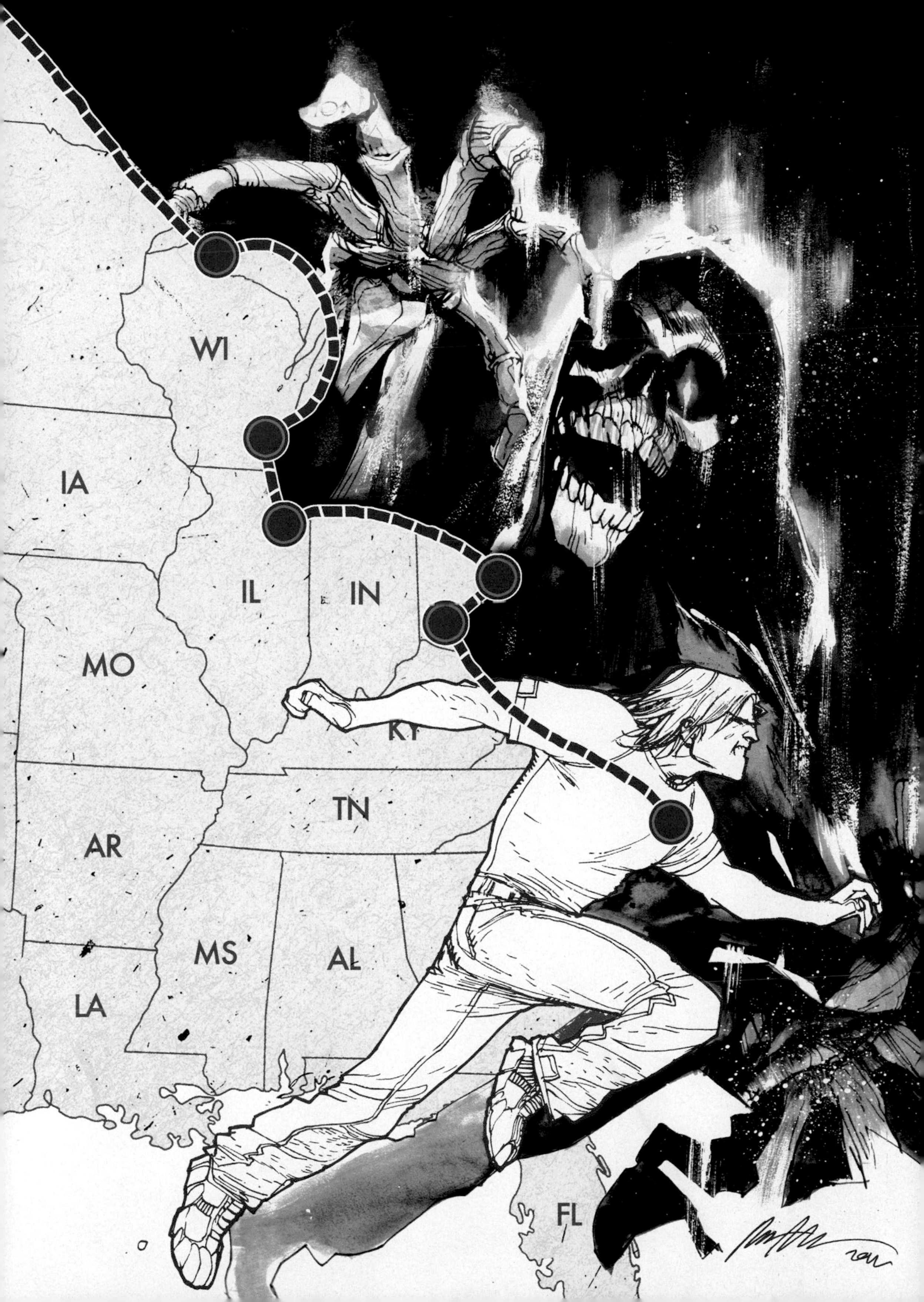
WI
IA
IL
IN
MO
KY
TN
AR
MS
AL
LA
FL

MANHUNT

DAN ABNETT & ANDY LANNING
writers

FERNANDO DAGNINO
artist

cover art by
RAFAEL ALBUQUERQUE

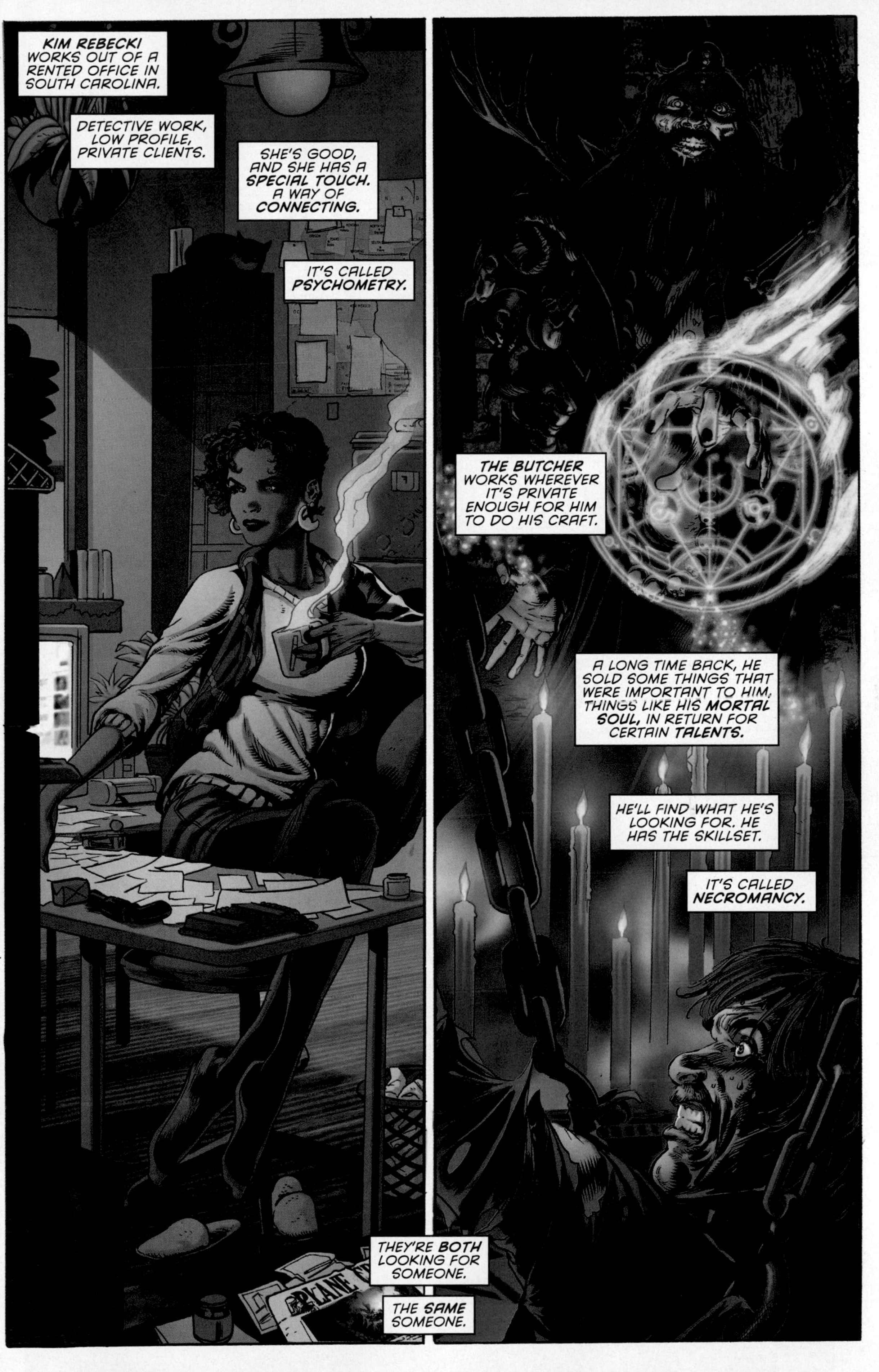
KIM REBECKI WORKS OUT OF A RENTED OFFICE IN SOUTH CAROLINA.
DETECTIVE WORK, LOW PROFILE, PRIVATE CLIENTS.
SHE'S GOOD, AND SHE HAS A SPECIAL TOUCH. A WAY OF CONNECTING.
IT'S CALLED PSYCHOMETRY.
THE BUTCHER WORKS WHEREVER IT'S PRIVATE ENOUGH FOR HIM TO DO HIS CRAFT.
A LONG TIME BACK, HE SOLD SOME THINGS THAT WERE IMPORTANT TO HIM, THINGS LIKE HIS MORTAL SOUL, IN RETURN FOR CERTAIN TALENTS.
HE'LL FIND WHAT HE'S LOOKING FOR. HE HAS THE SKILLSET.
IT'S CALLED NECROMANCY.
THEY'RE BOTH LOOKING FOR SOMEONE.
THE SAME SOMEONE.

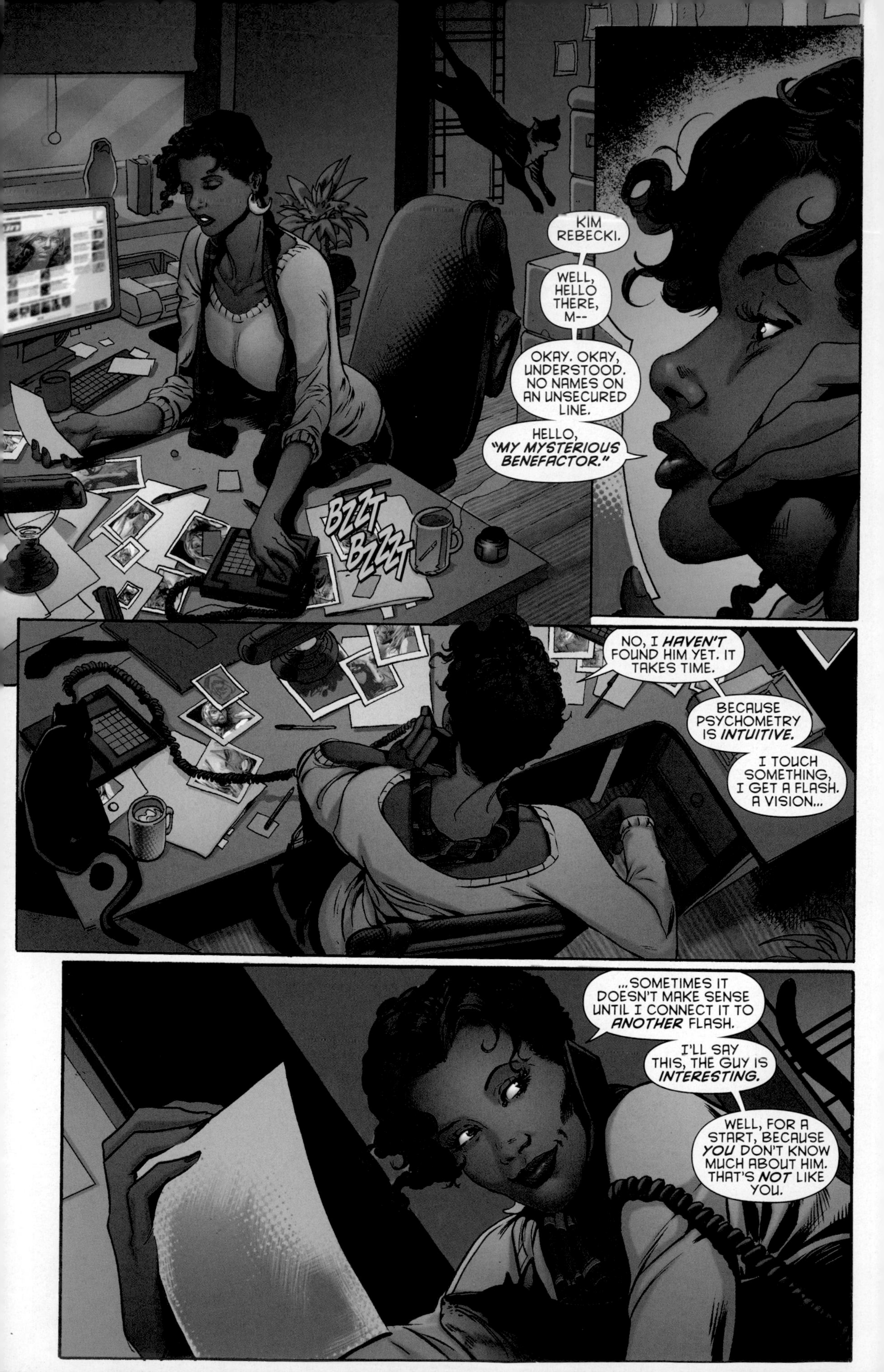

KIM REBECKI.
WELL, HELLO THERE, M--
OKAY. OKAY, UNDERSTOOD. NO NAMES ON AN UNSECURED LINE.
HELLO, *"MY MYSTERIOUS BENEFACTOR."*
BZZZT BZZZT
NO, I ***HAVEN'T*** FOUND HIM YET. IT TAKES TIME.
BECAUSE PSYCHOMETRY IS ***INTUITIVE.***
I TOUCH SOMETHING, I GET A FLASH. A VISION...
...SOMETIMES IT DOESN'T MAKE SENSE UNTIL I CONNECT IT TO ***ANOTHER*** FLASH.
I'LL SAY THIS, THE GUY IS ***INTERESTING.***
WELL, FOR A START, BECAUSE ***YOU*** DON'T KNOW MUCH ABOUT HIM. THAT'S ***NOT*** LIKE YOU.

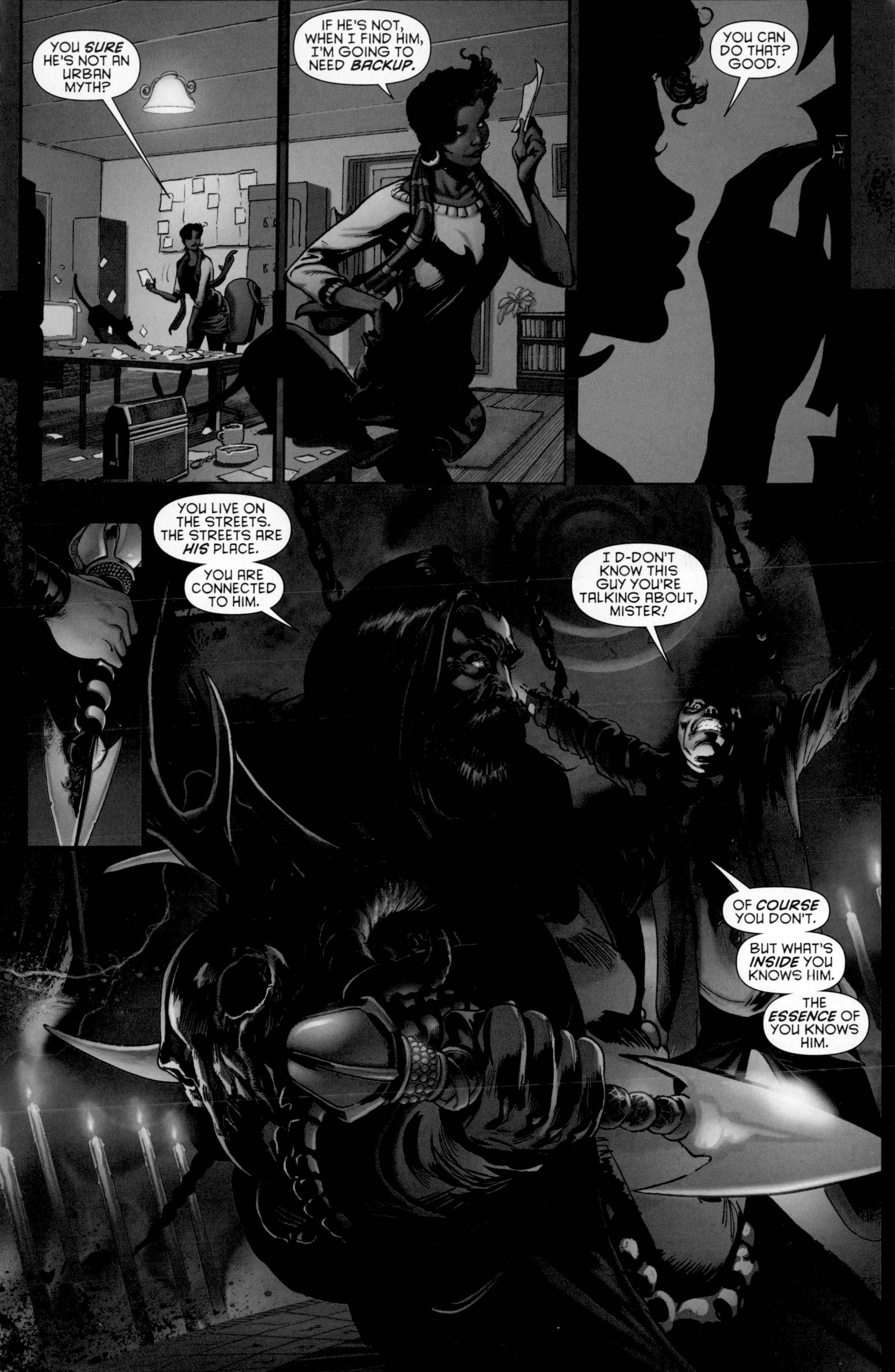
YOU SURE HE'S NOT AN URBAN MYTH?
IF HE'S NOT, WHEN I FIND HIM, I'M GOING TO NEED BACKUP.
YOU CAN DO THAT? GOOD.
YOU LIVE ON THE STREETS. THE STREETS ARE HIS PLACE.
YOU ARE CONNECTED TO HIM.
I D-DON'T KNOW THIS GUY YOU'RE TALKING ABOUT, MISTER!
OF COURSE YOU DON'T.
BUT WHAT'S INSIDE YOU KNOWS HIM.
THE ESSENCE OF YOU KNOWS HIM.

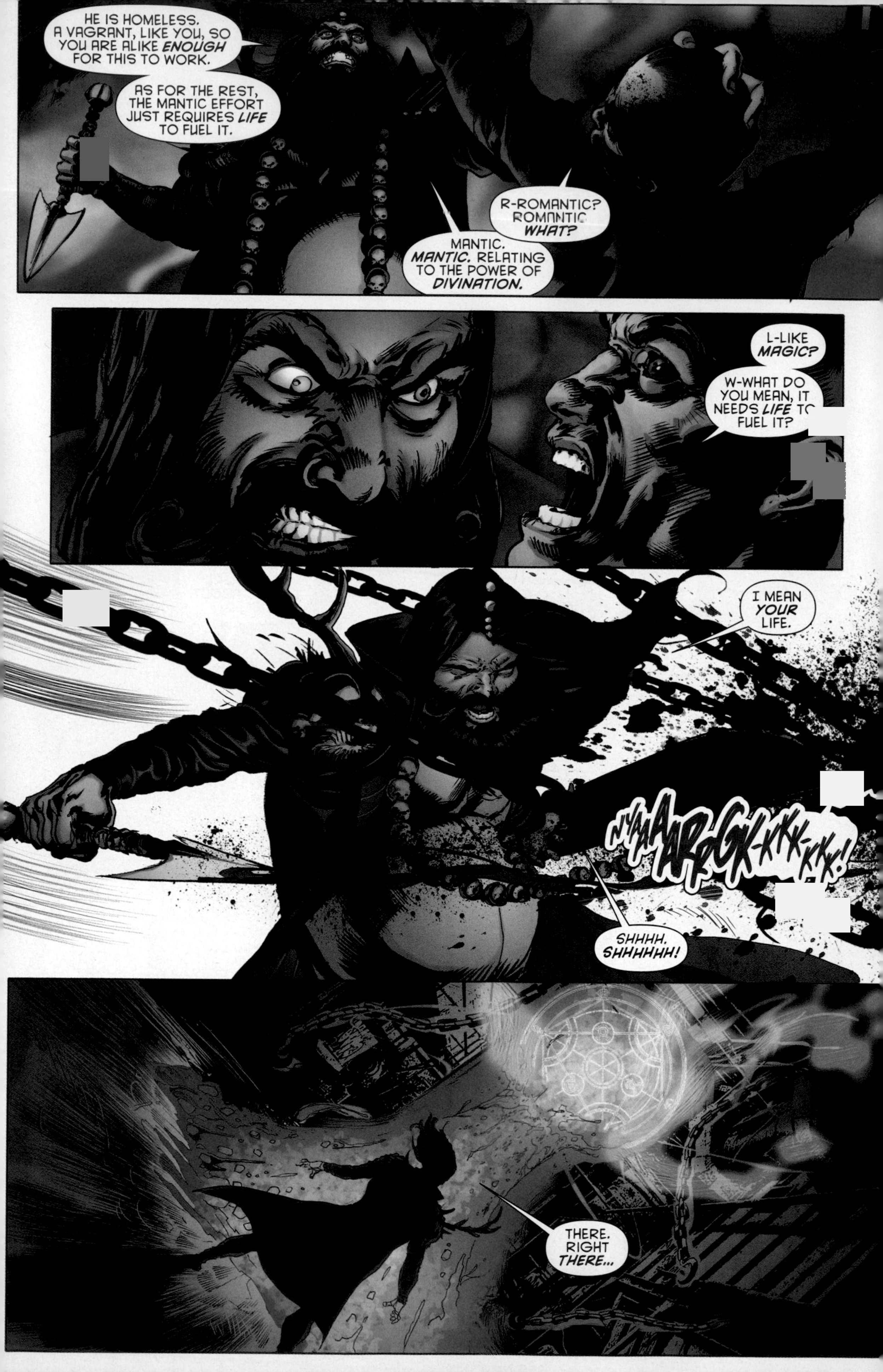
HE IS HOMELESS. A VAGRANT, LIKE YOU, SO YOU ARE ALIKE ENOUGH FOR THIS TO WORK.
AS FOR THE REST, THE MANTIC EFFORT JUST REQUIRES LIFE TO FUEL IT.
R-ROMANTIC? ROMANTIC WHAT?
MANTIC. MANTIC. RELATING TO THE POWER OF DIVINATION.
L-LIKE MAGIC?
W-WHAT DO YOU MEAN, IT NEEDS LIFE TO FUEL IT?
I MEAN YOUR LIFE.
NYAAAARRGK-KKK-KKK!
SHHHH. SHHHHHH!
THERE. RIGHT THERE...

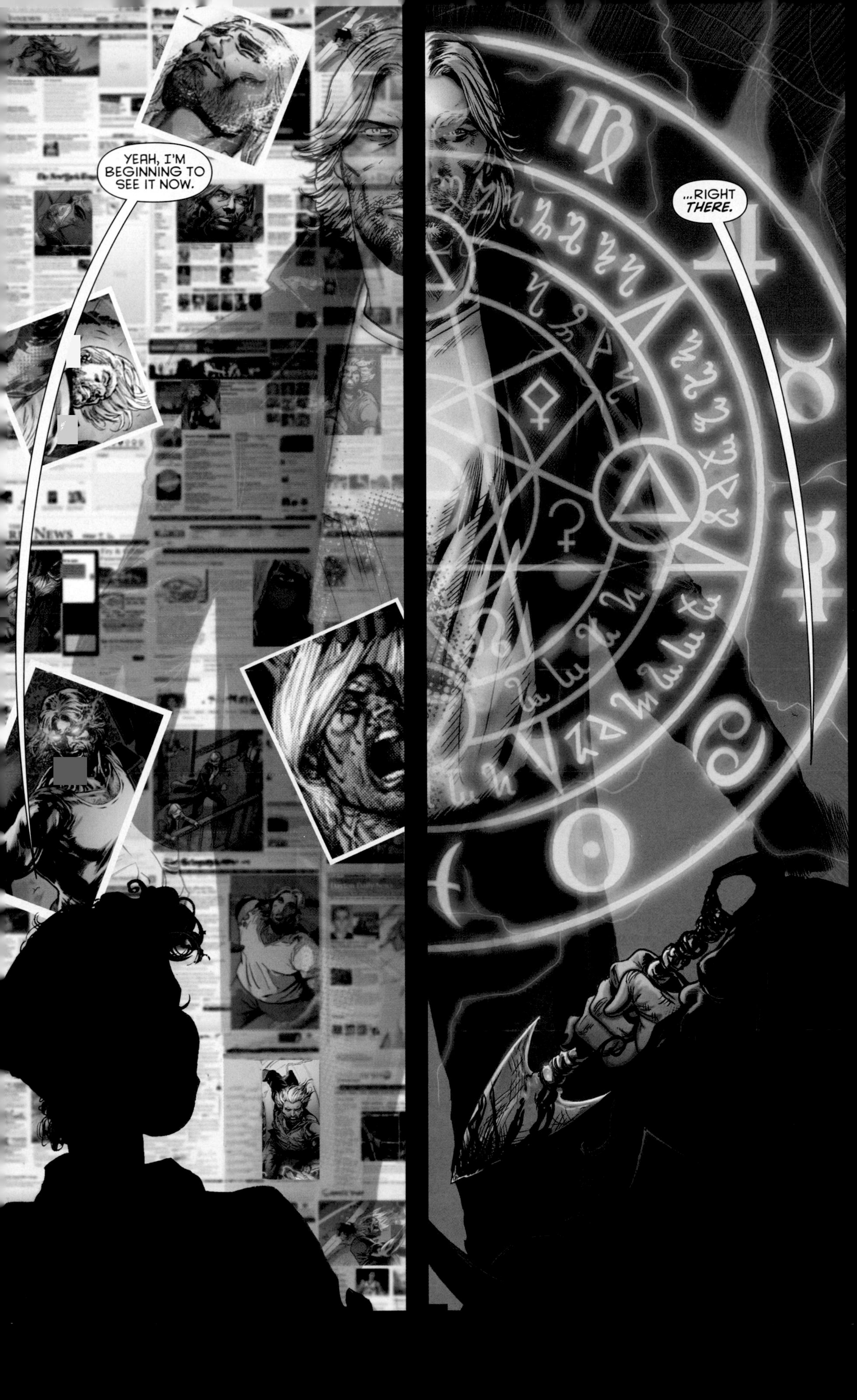
YEAH, I'M BEGINNING TO SEE IT NOW.
...RIGHT THERE.

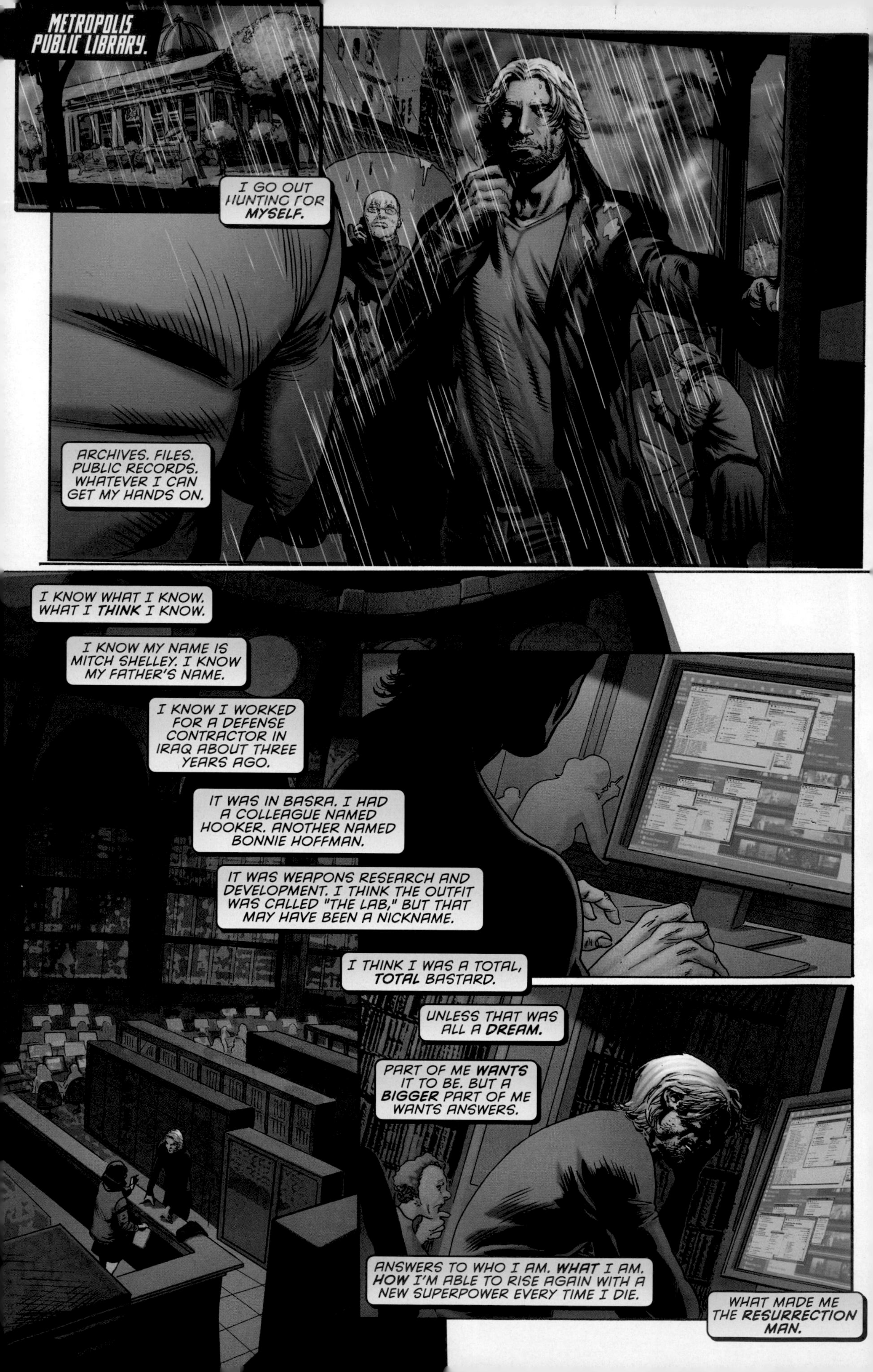
METROPOLIS PUBLIC LIBRARY.
I GO OUT HUNTING FOR MYSELF.
ARCHIVES. FILES. PUBLIC RECORDS. WHATEVER I CAN GET MY HANDS ON.
I KNOW WHAT I KNOW. WHAT I THINK I KNOW.
I KNOW MY NAME IS MITCH SHELLEY. I KNOW MY FATHER'S NAME.
I KNOW I WORKED FOR A DEFENSE CONTRACTOR IN IRAQ ABOUT THREE YEARS AGO.
IT WAS IN BASRA. I HAD A COLLEAGUE NAMED HOOKER. ANOTHER NAMED BONNIE HOFFMAN.
IT WAS WEAPONS RESEARCH AND DEVELOPMENT. I THINK THE OUTFIT WAS CALLED "THE LAB," BUT THAT MAY HAVE BEEN A NICKNAME.
I THINK I WAS A TOTAL, TOTAL BASTARD.
UNLESS THAT WAS ALL A DREAM.
PART OF ME WANTS IT TO BE. BUT A BIGGER PART OF ME WANTS ANSWERS.
ANSWERS TO WHO I AM. WHAT I AM. HOW I'M ABLE TO RISE AGAIN WITH A NEW SUPERPOWER EVERY TIME I DIE.
WHAT MADE ME THE RESURRECTION MAN.

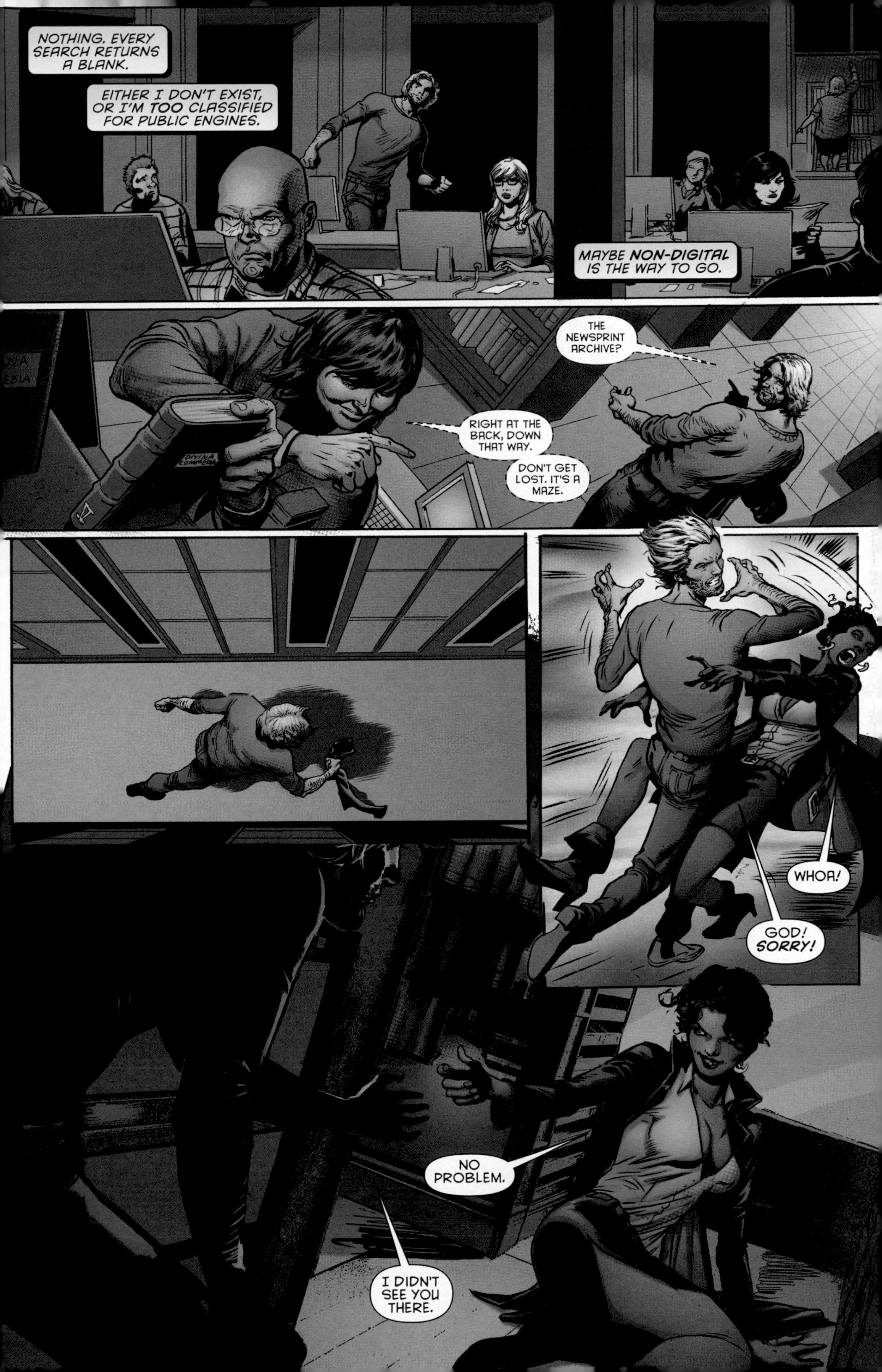
NOTHING. EVERY SEARCH RETURNS A BLANK.
EITHER I DON'T EXIST, OR I'M TOO CLASSIFIED FOR PUBLIC ENGINES.
MAYBE NON-DIGITAL IS THE WAY TO GO.
THE NEWSPRINT ARCHIVE?
RIGHT AT THE BACK, DOWN THAT WAY.
DON'T GET LOST. IT'S A MAZE.
WHOA!
GOD! SORRY!
NO PROBLEM.
I DIDN'T SEE YOU THERE.

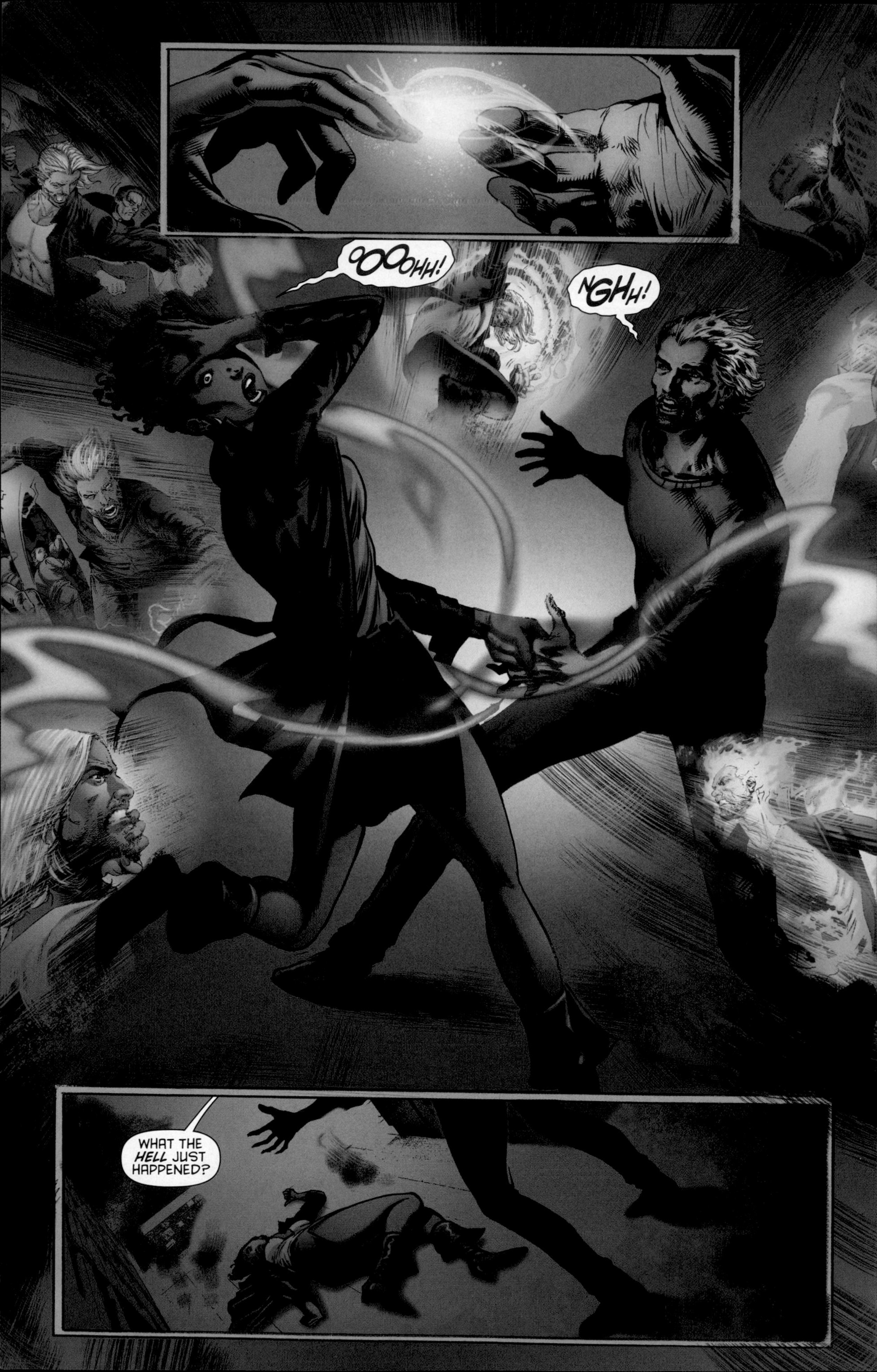
OOOOHH!
NGHH!
WHAT THE *HELL* JUST HAPPENED?

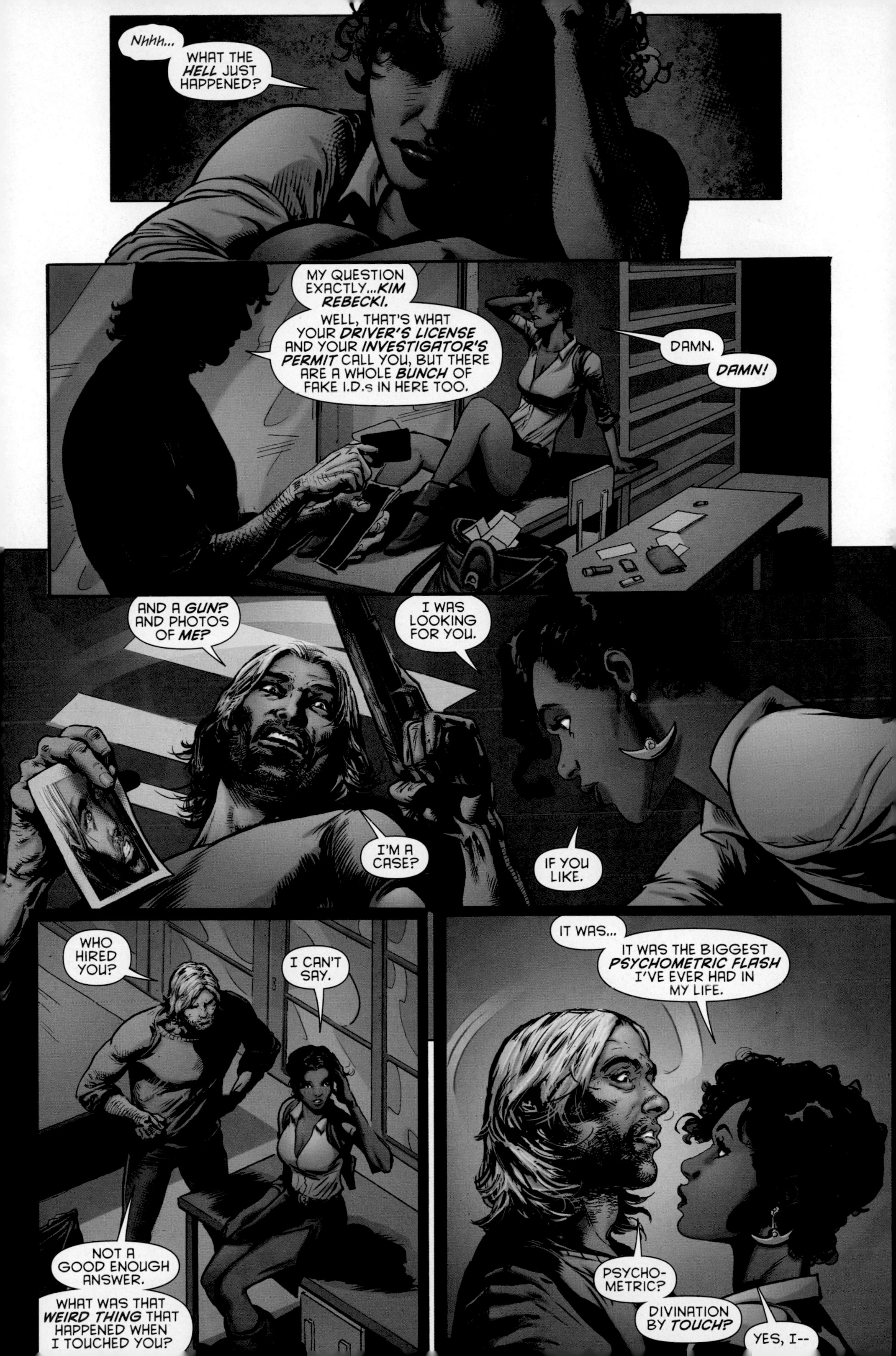
Nhhh...
WHAT THE HELL JUST HAPPENED?
MY QUESTION EXACTLY...KIM REBECKI.
WELL, THAT'S WHAT YOUR DRIVER'S LICENSE AND YOUR INVESTIGATOR'S PERMIT CALL YOU, BUT THERE ARE A WHOLE BUNCH OF FAKE I.D.s IN HERE TOO.
DAMN.
DAMN!
AND A GUN? AND PHOTOS OF ME?
I WAS LOOKING FOR YOU.
I'M A CASE?
IF YOU LIKE.
WHO HIRED YOU?
I CAN'T SAY.
NOT A GOOD ENOUGH ANSWER.
WHAT WAS THAT WEIRD THING THAT HAPPENED WHEN I TOUCHED YOU?
IT WAS...
IT WAS THE BIGGEST PSYCHOMETRIC FLASH I'VE EVER HAD IN MY LIFE.
PSYCHO-METRIC?
DIVINATION BY TOUCH?
YES, I--

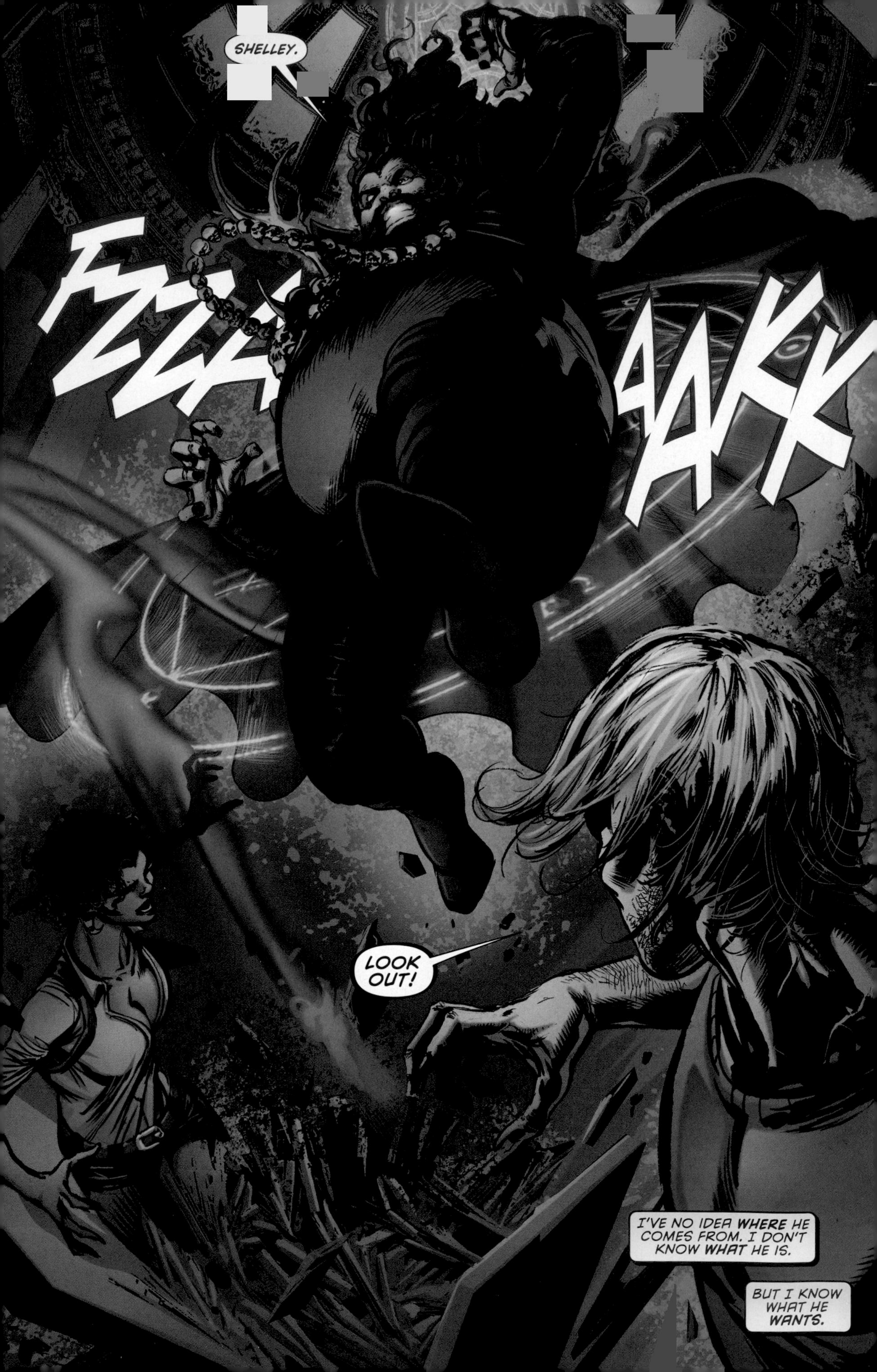
SHELLEY.
FZZAAAKK
LOOK OUT!
I'VE NO IDEA WHERE HE COMES FROM. I DON'T KNOW WHAT HE IS.
BUT I KNOW WHAT HE WANTS.

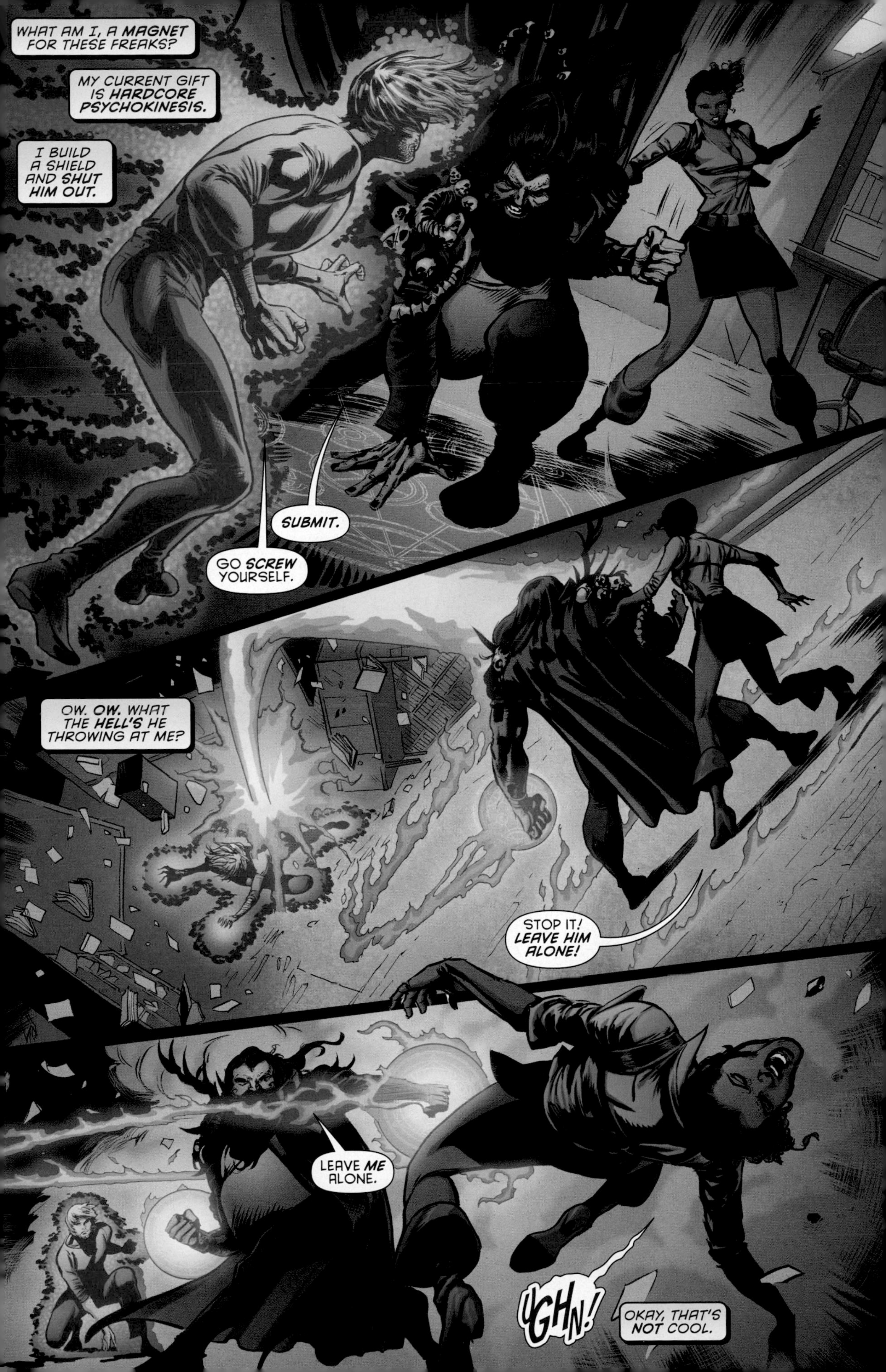
WHAT AM I, A MAGNET FOR THESE FREAKS?
MY CURRENT GIFT IS HARDCORE PSYCHOKINESIS.
I BUILD A SHIELD AND SHUT HIM OUT.
SUBMIT.
GO SCREW YOURSELF.
OW. OW. WHAT THE HELL'S HE THROWING AT ME?
STOP IT! LEAVE HIM ALONE!
LEAVE ME ALONE.
UGHN!
OKAY, THAT'S NOT COOL.

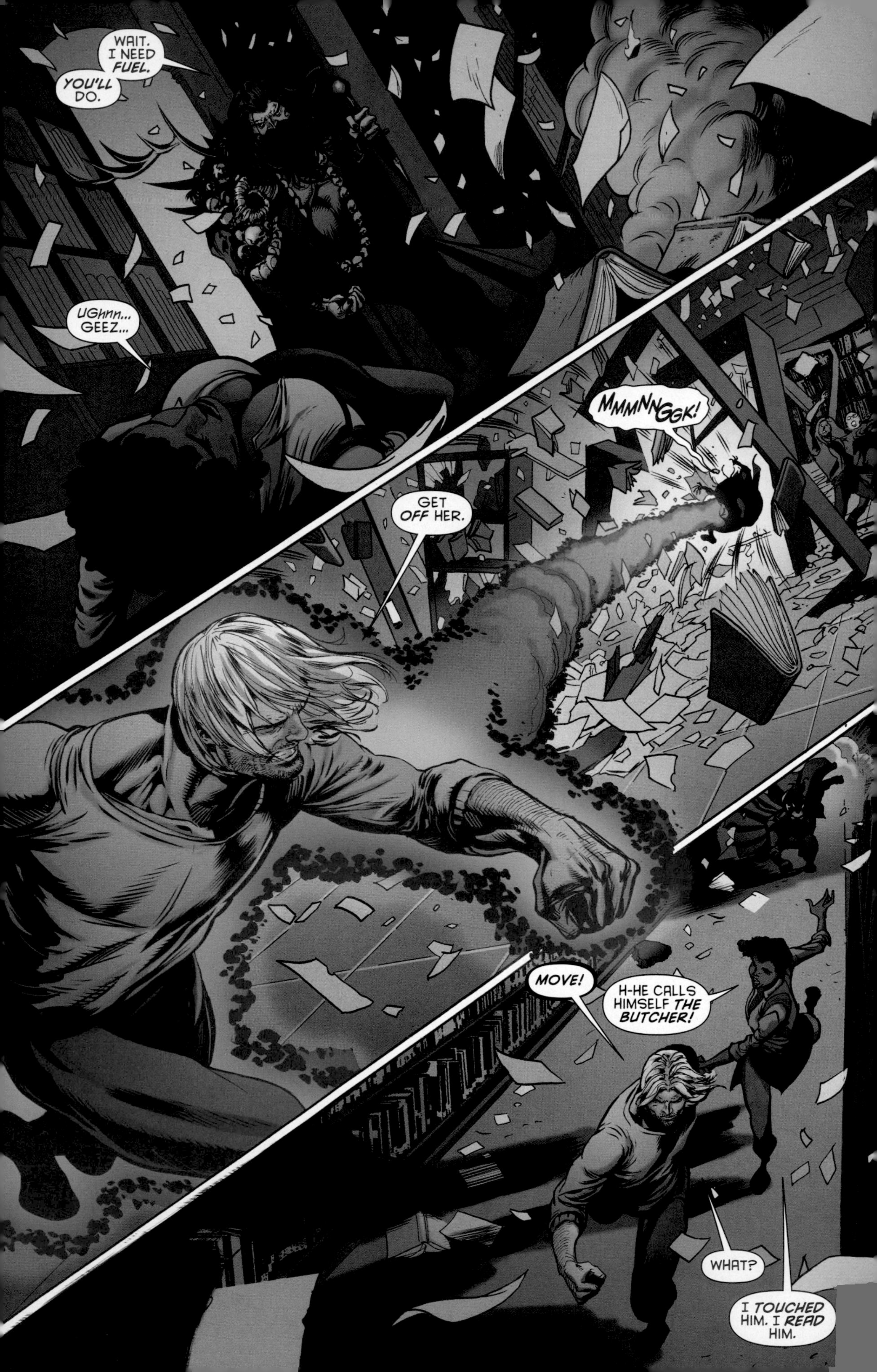
WAIT. I NEED FUEL.
YOU'LL DO.
UGhnn... GEEZ...
MMMNNGGK!
GET OFF HER.
MOVE!
H-HE CALLS HIMSELF THE BUTCHER!
WHAT?
I TOUCHED HIM. I READ HIM.

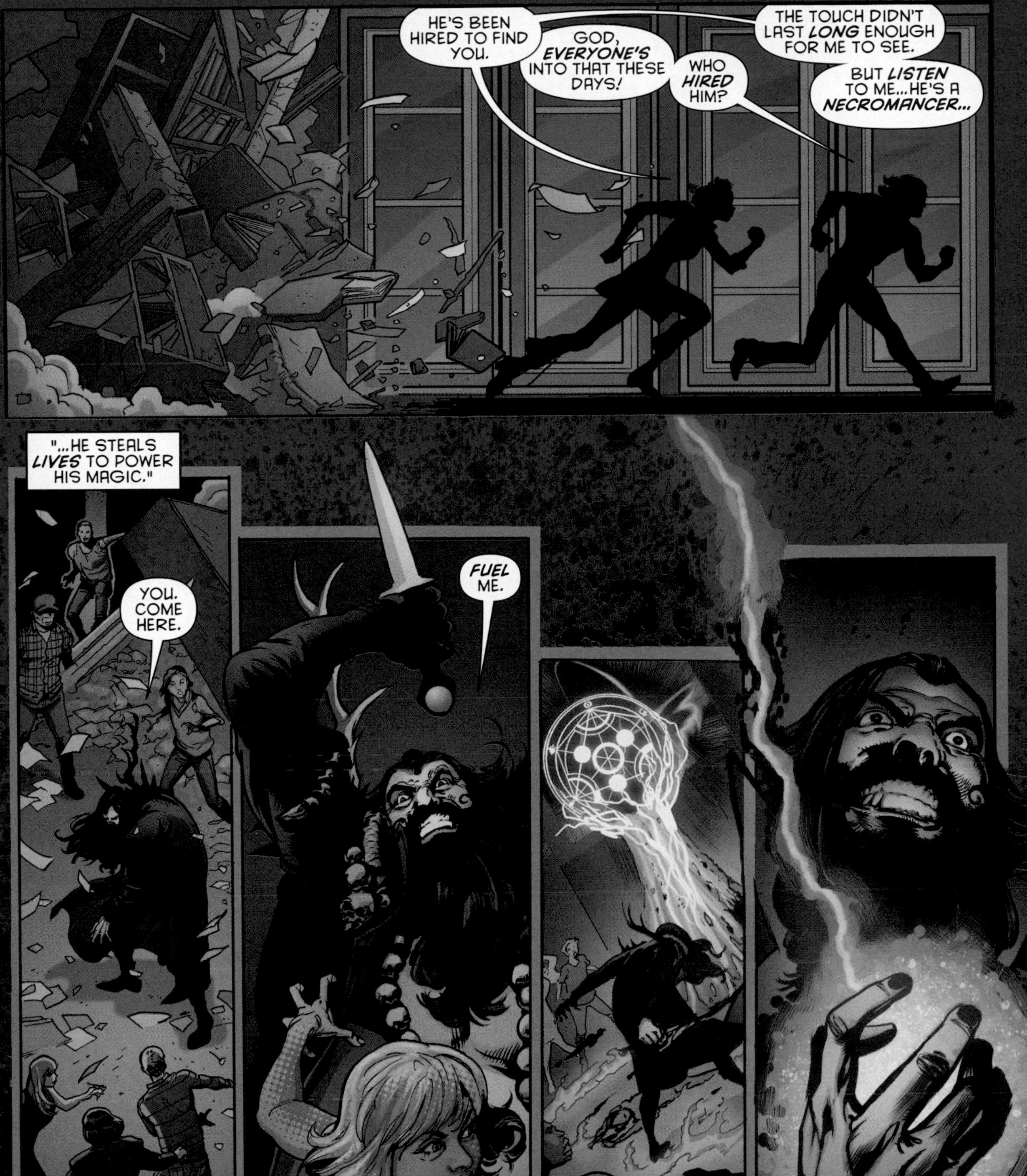
HE'S BEEN HIRED TO FIND YOU.
GOD, *EVERYONE'S* INTO THAT THESE DAYS!
WHO *HIRED* HIM?
THE TOUCH DIDN'T LAST *LONG* ENOUGH FOR ME TO SEE.
BUT *LISTEN* TO ME...HE'S A *NECROMANCER*...
"...HE STEALS *LIVES* TO POWER HIS MAGIC."
YOU. COME HERE.
WHAT THE HELL *ARE* YOU? WHAT *IS* THIS?
FUEL ME.
AAIIEEE!
RUN! *RUN!*
HE'S *CRAZY!*
SHELLEY.
YOU CAN'T HIDE.

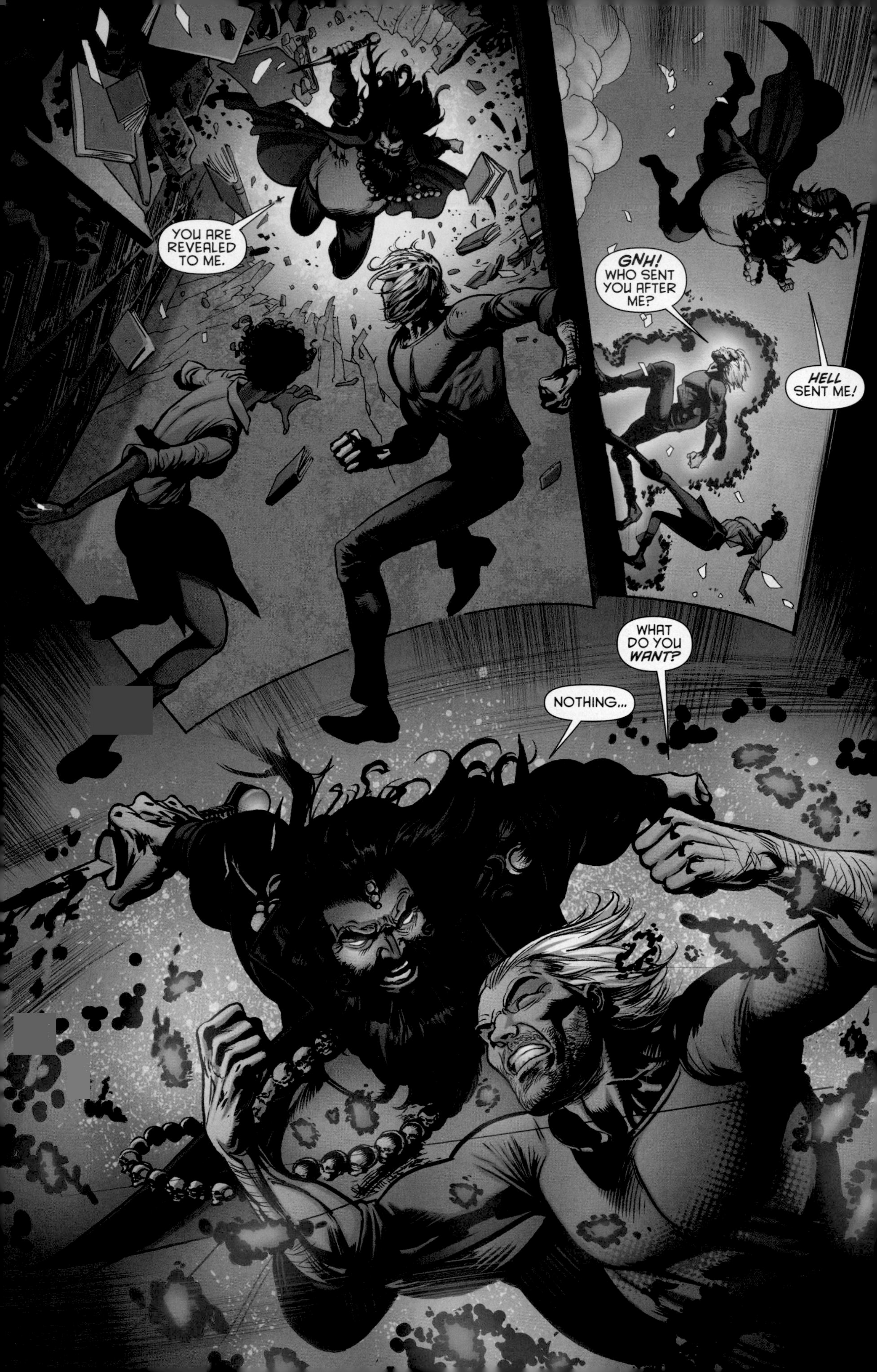
YOU ARE REVEALED TO ME.
GNH! WHO SENT YOU AFTER ME?
HELL SENT ME!
WHAT DO YOU WANT?
NOTHING...

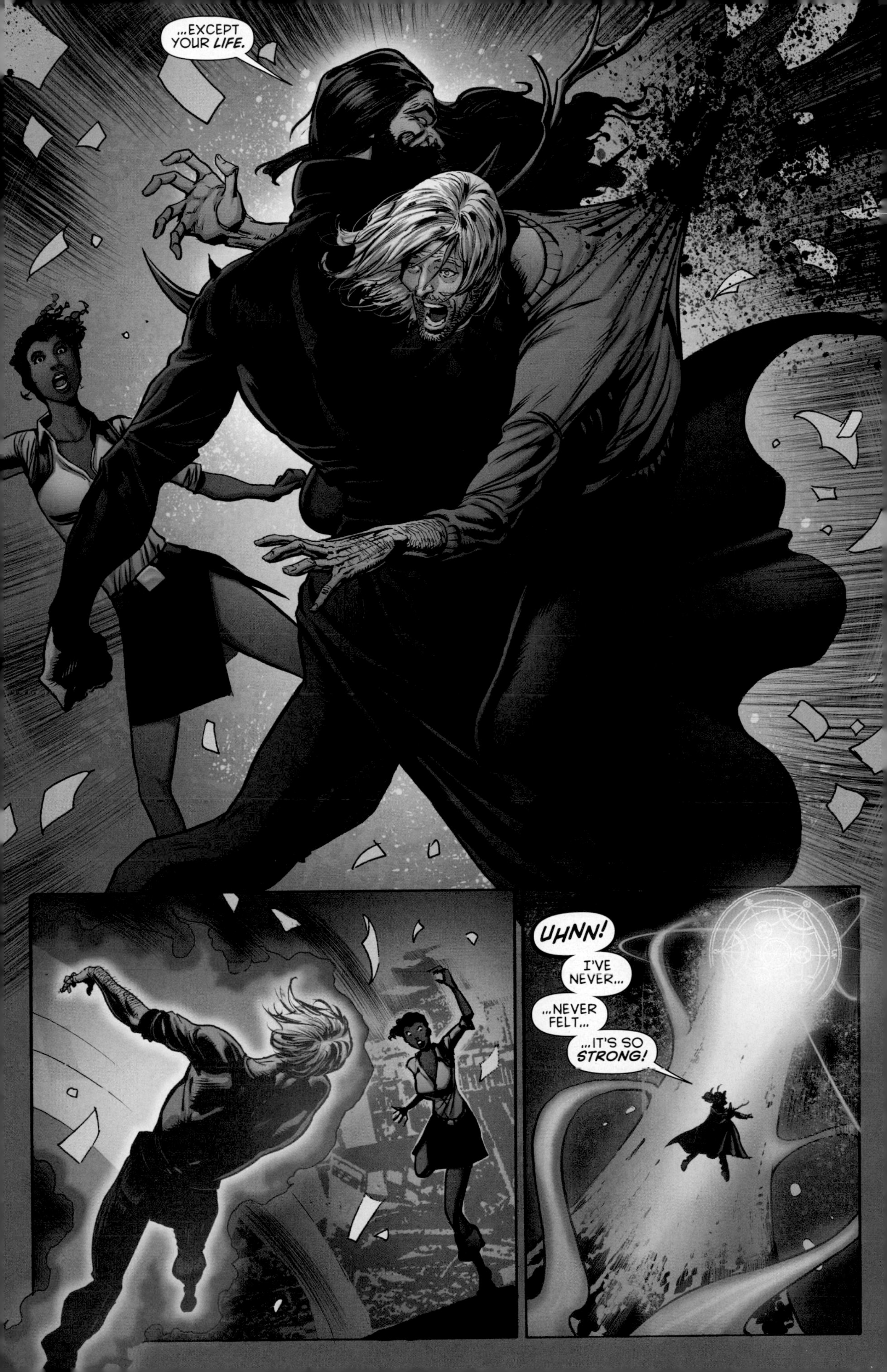
...EXCEPT YOUR *LIFE.*
UHNN!
I'VE NEVER...
...NEVER FELT...
...IT'S SO *STRONG!*

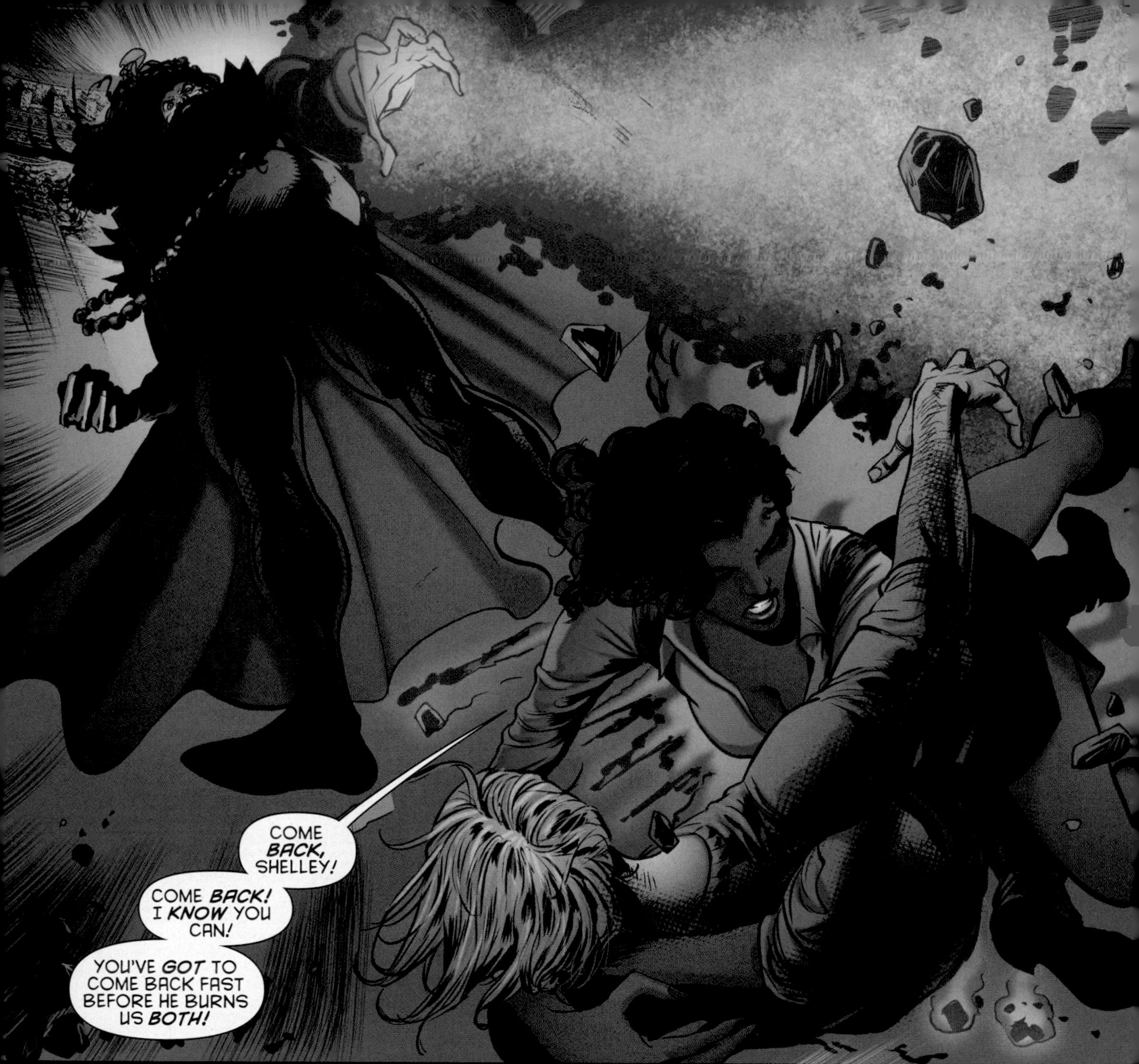
COME BACK, SHELLEY!
COME BACK! I KNOW YOU CAN!
YOU'VE GOT TO COME BACK FAST BEFORE HE BURNS US BOTH!

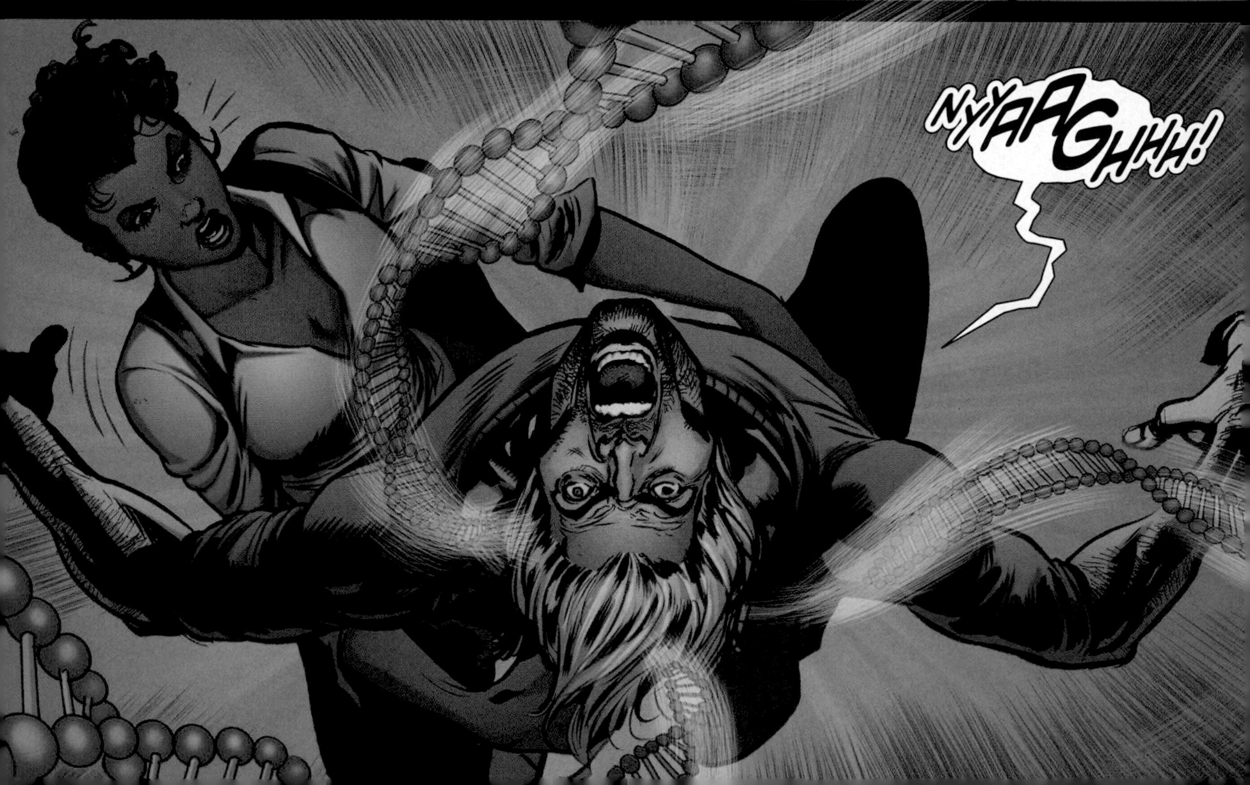
NYYAAGHHH!

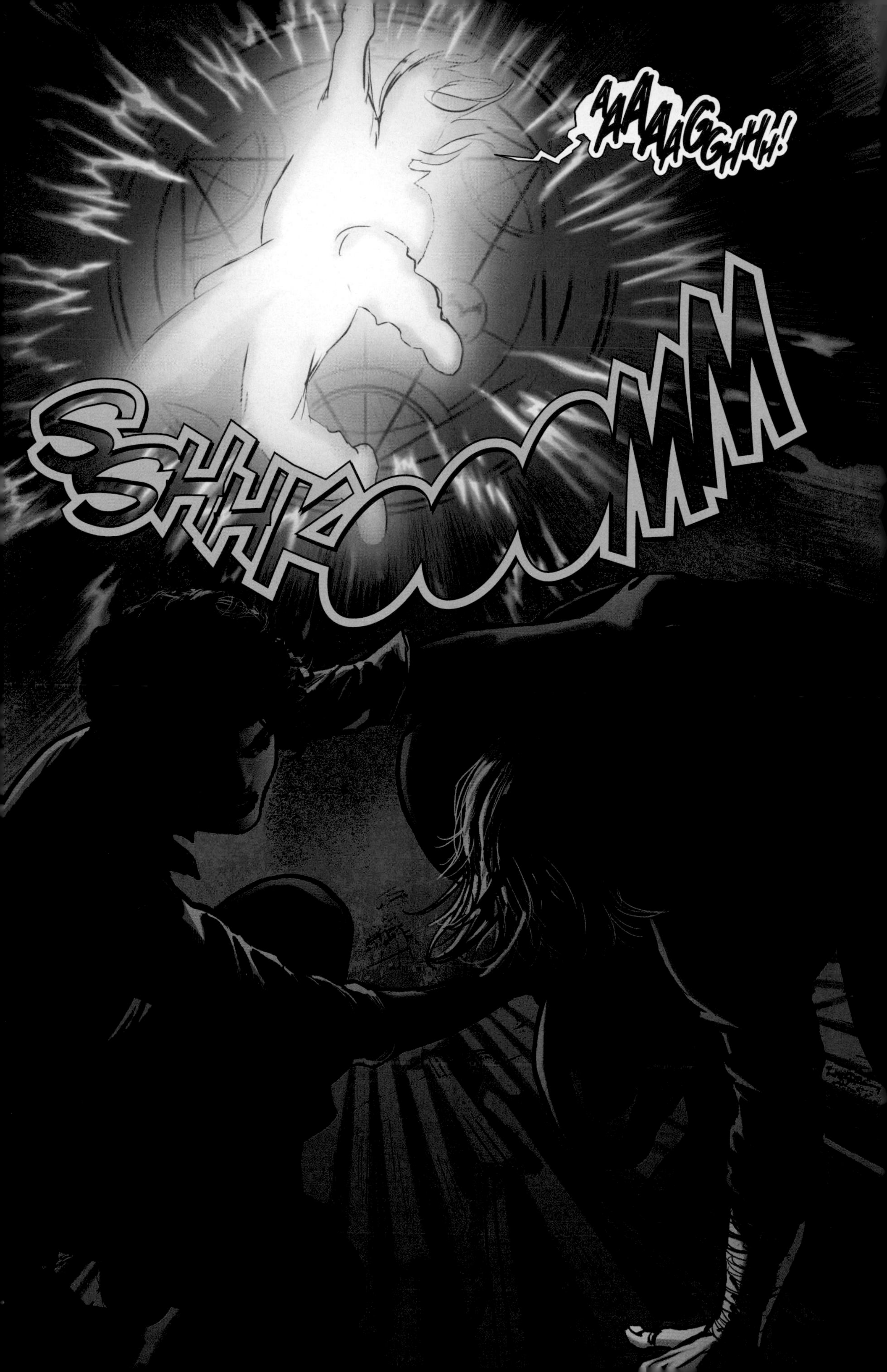
AAAAAAGGHHH!
SSHHAOOOMM

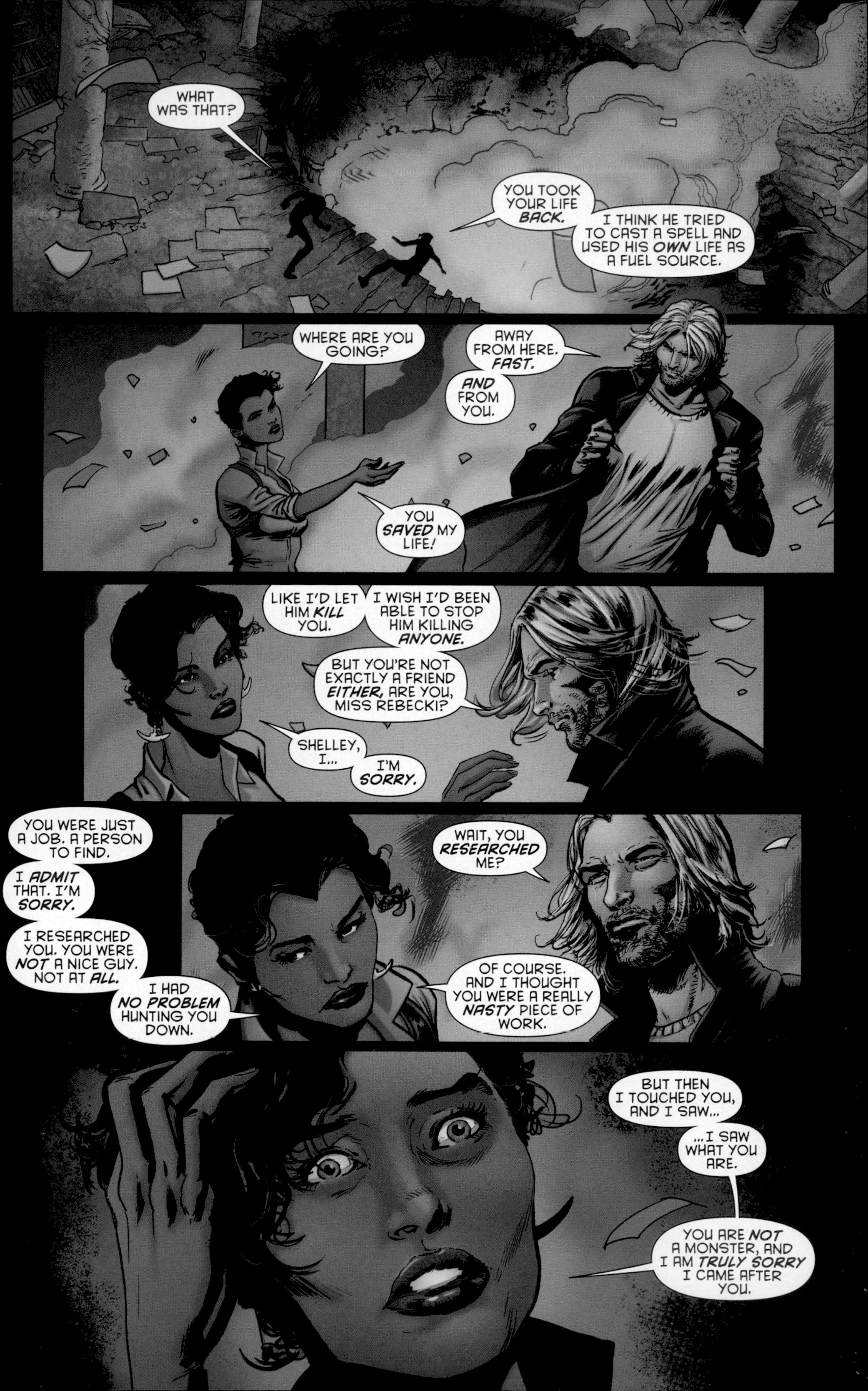
WHAT WAS THAT?
YOU TOOK YOUR LIFE BACK.
I THINK HE TRIED TO CAST A SPELL AND USED HIS OWN LIFE AS A FUEL SOURCE.
WHERE ARE YOU GOING?
AWAY FROM HERE. FAST.
AND FROM YOU.
YOU SAVED MY LIFE!
LIKE I'D LET HIM KILL YOU.
I WISH I'D BEEN ABLE TO STOP HIM KILLING ANYONE.
BUT YOU'RE NOT EXACTLY A FRIEND EITHER, ARE YOU, MISS REBECKI?
SHELLEY, I...
I'M SORRY.
YOU WERE JUST A JOB. A PERSON TO FIND.
I ADMIT THAT. I'M SORRY.
I RESEARCHED YOU. YOU WERE NOT A NICE GUY. NOT AT ALL.
I HAD NO PROBLEM HUNTING YOU DOWN.
WAIT, YOU RESEARCHED ME?
OF COURSE. AND I THOUGHT YOU WERE A REALLY NASTY PIECE OF WORK.
BUT THEN I TOUCHED YOU, AND I SAW...
...I SAW WHAT YOU ARE.
YOU ARE NOT A MONSTER, AND I AM TRULY SORRY I CAME AFTER YOU.

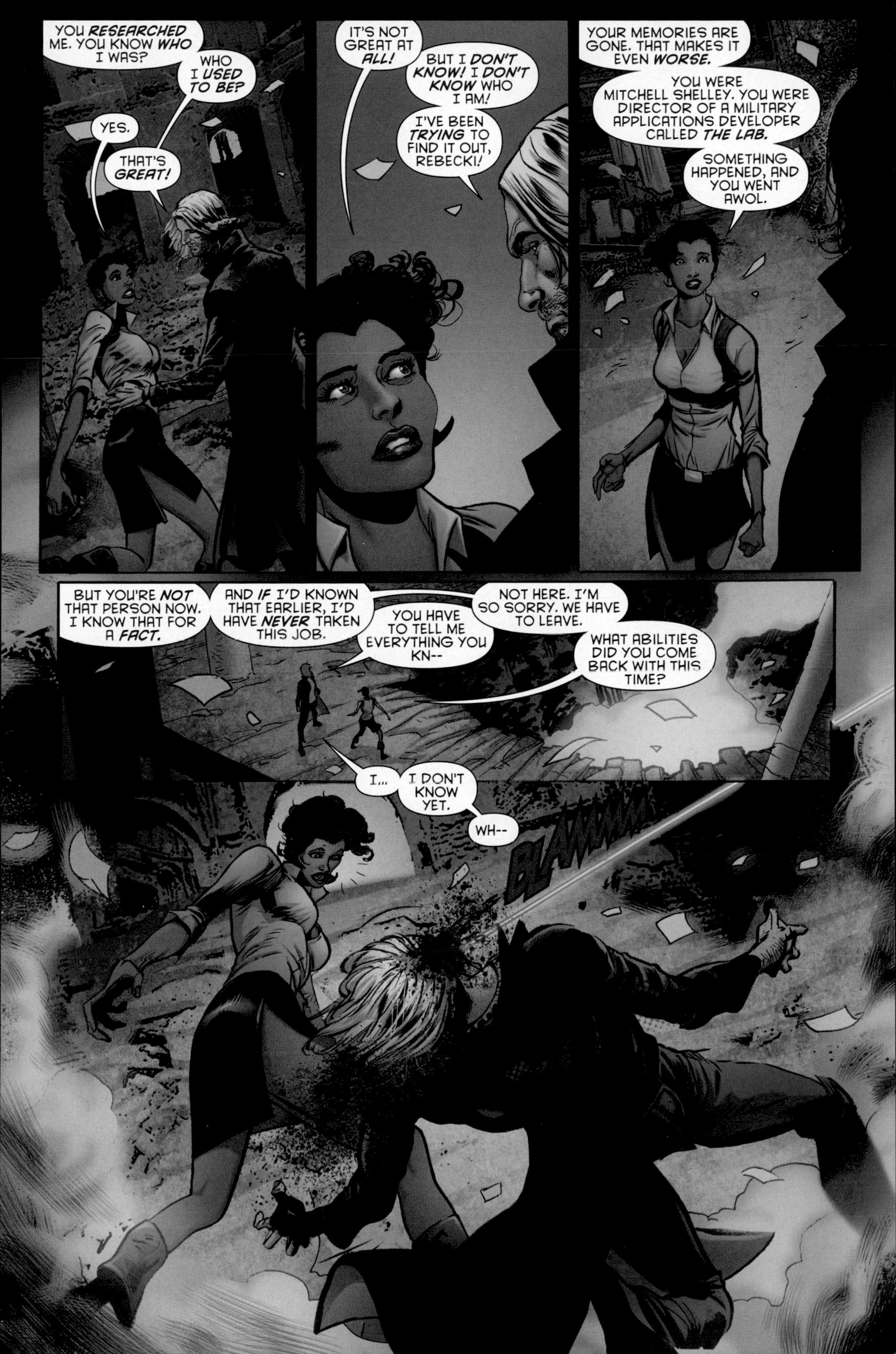

YOU RESEARCHED ME. YOU KNOW WHO I WAS?
WHO I USED TO BE?
YES.
THAT'S GREAT!
IT'S NOT GREAT AT ALL!
BUT I DON'T KNOW! I DON'T KNOW WHO I AM!
I'VE BEEN TRYING TO FIND IT OUT, REBECK!
YOUR MEMORIES ARE GONE. THAT MAKES IT EVEN WORSE.
YOU WERE MITCHELL SHELLEY. YOU WERE DIRECTOR OF A MILITARY APPLICATIONS DEVELOPER CALLED THE LAB.
SOMETHING HAPPENED, AND YOU WENT AWOL.
BUT YOU'RE NOT THAT PERSON NOW. I KNOW THAT FOR A FACT.
AND IF I'D KNOWN THAT EARLIER, I'D HAVE NEVER TAKEN THIS JOB.
YOU HAVE TO TELL ME EVERYTHING YOU KN--
NOT HERE. I'M SO SORRY. WE HAVE TO LEAVE.
WHAT ABILITIES DID YOU COME BACK WITH THIS TIME?
I...
I DON'T KNOW YET.
WH--

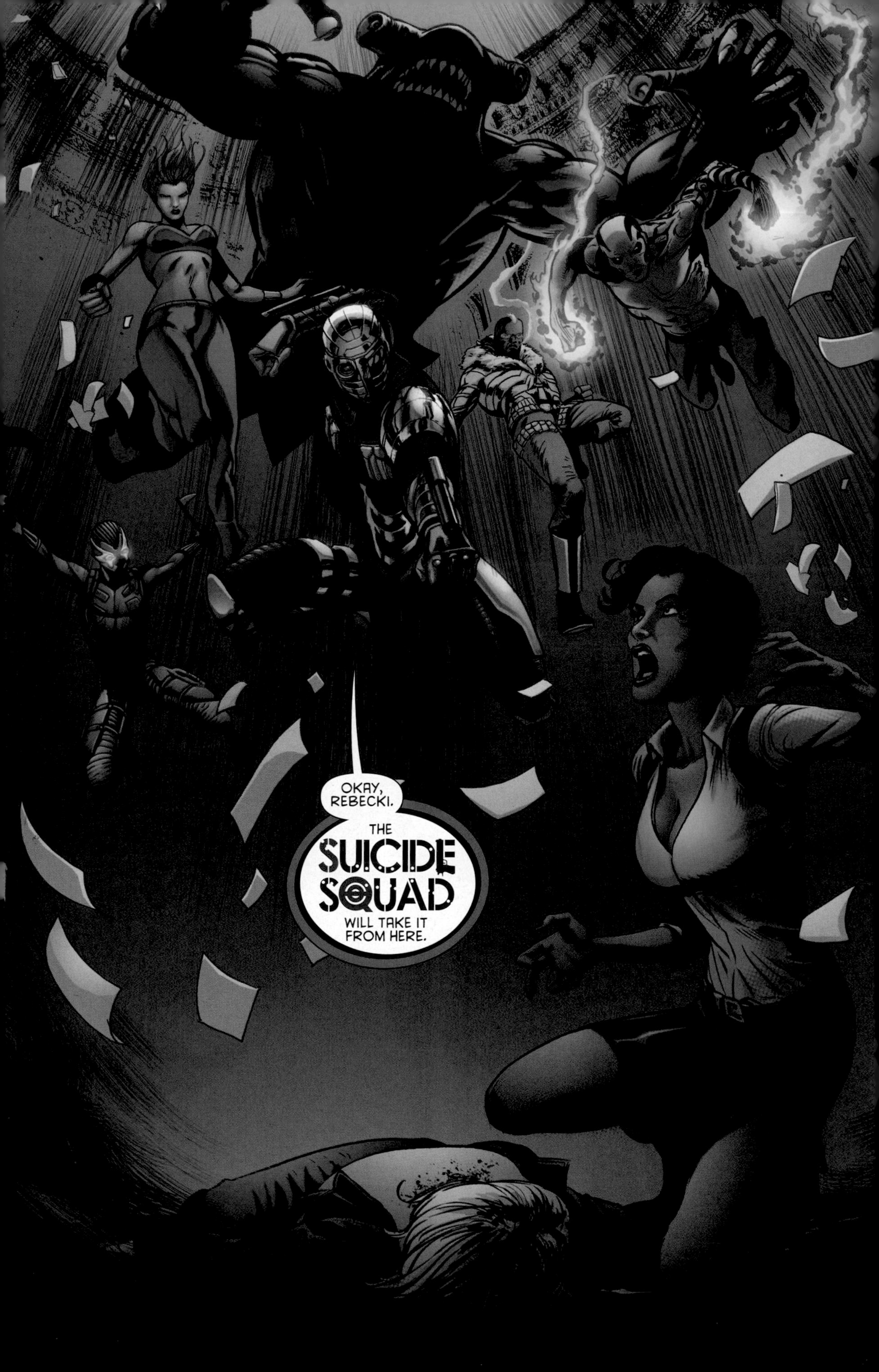
OKAY, REBECKI.
THE SUICIDE SQUAD WILL TAKE IT FROM HERE.

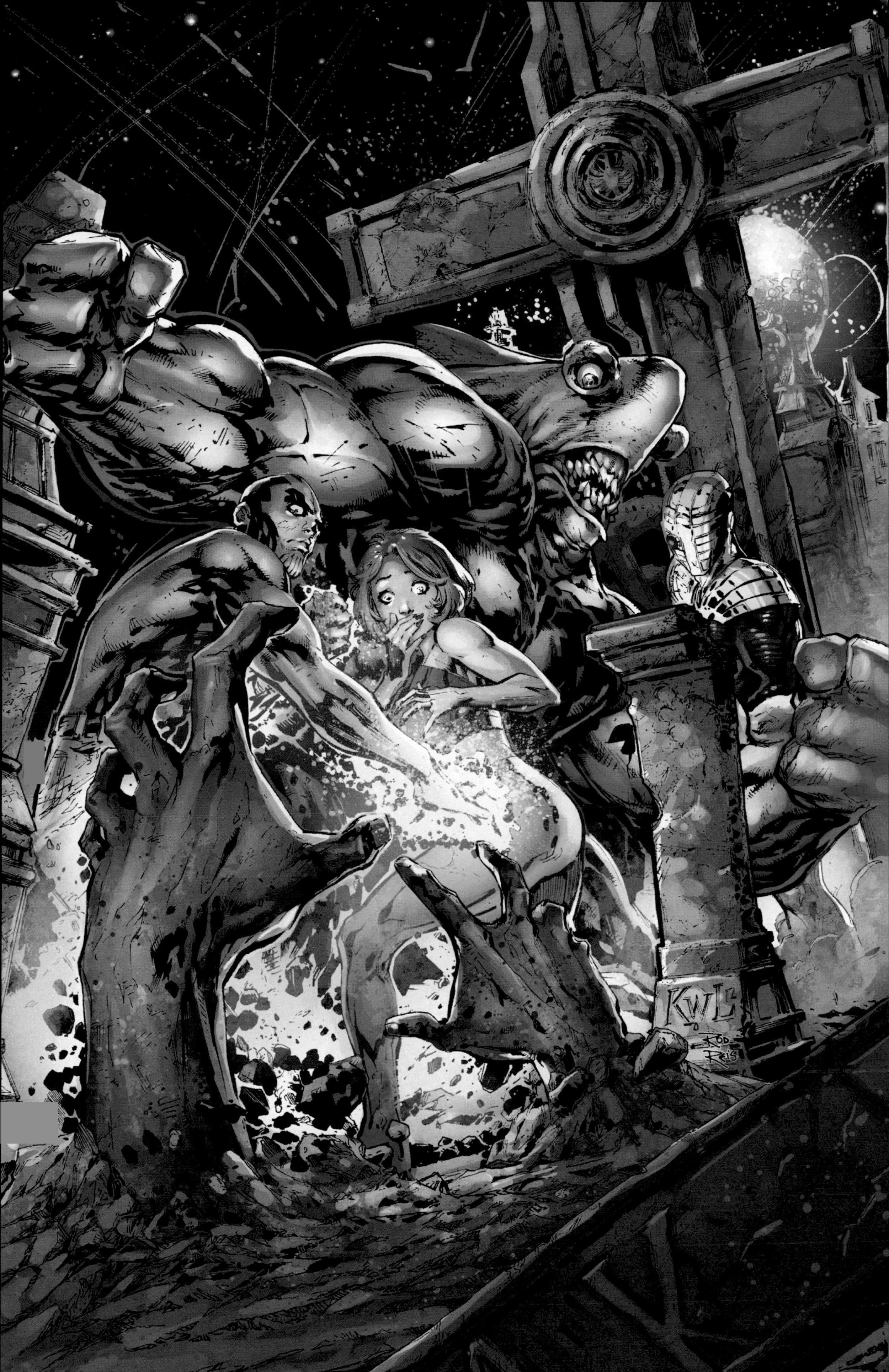

KWL
ROD REIS

DEAD MAN WALKING

ADAM GLASS
writer

FERNANDO DAGNINO
artist

cover art by
KEN LASHLEY with ROD REIS

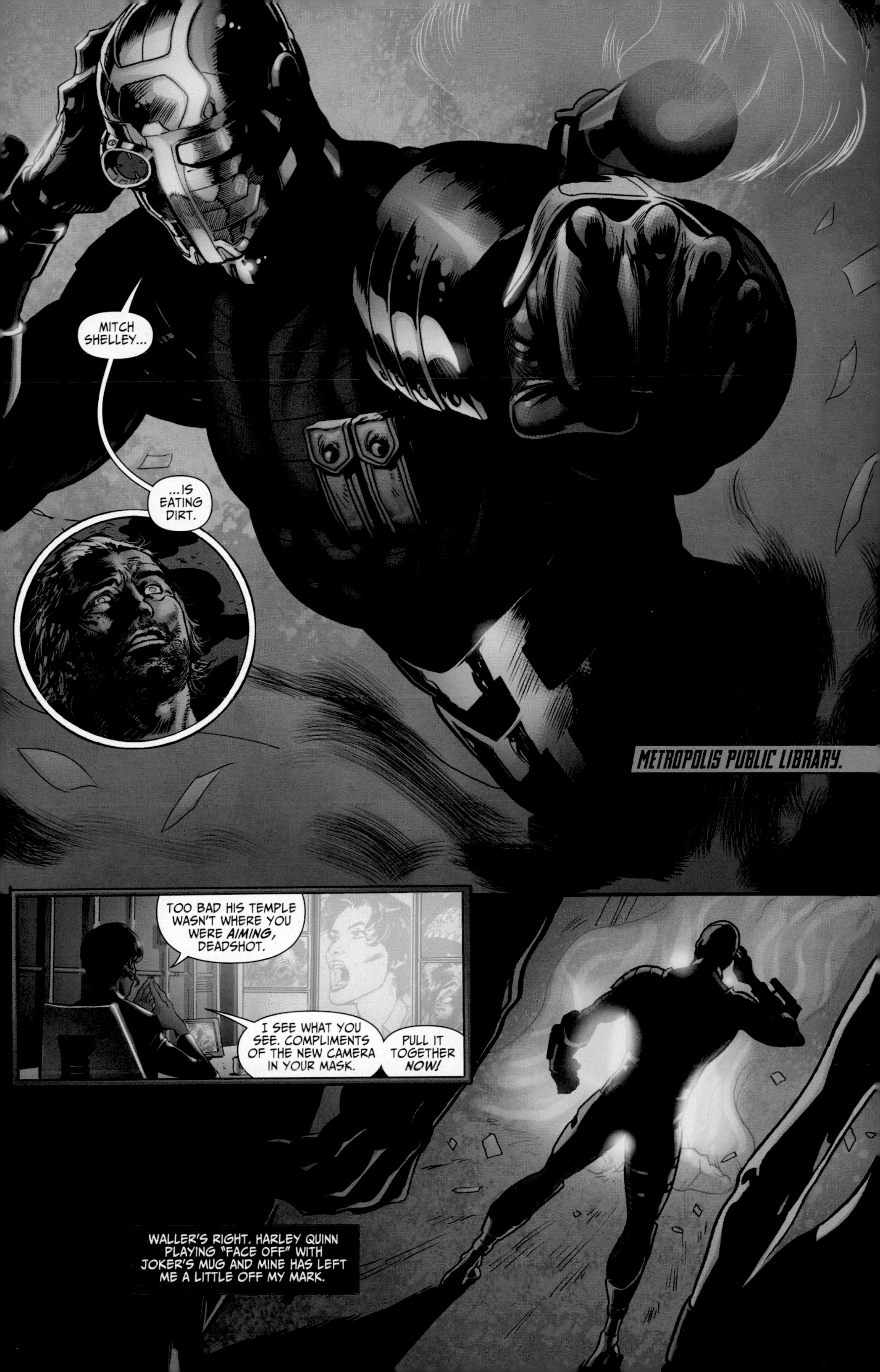
MITCH SHELLEY...
...IS EATING DIRT.
METROPOLIS PUBLIC LIBRARY.
TOO BAD HIS TEMPLE WASN'T WHERE YOU WERE AIMING, DEADSHOT.
I SEE WHAT YOU SEE. COMPLIMENTS OF THE NEW CAMERA IN YOUR MASK.
PULL IT TOGETHER NOW!
WALLER'S RIGHT. HARLEY QUINN PLAYING "FACE OFF" WITH JOKER'S MUG AND MINE HAS LEFT ME A LITTLE OFF MY MARK.

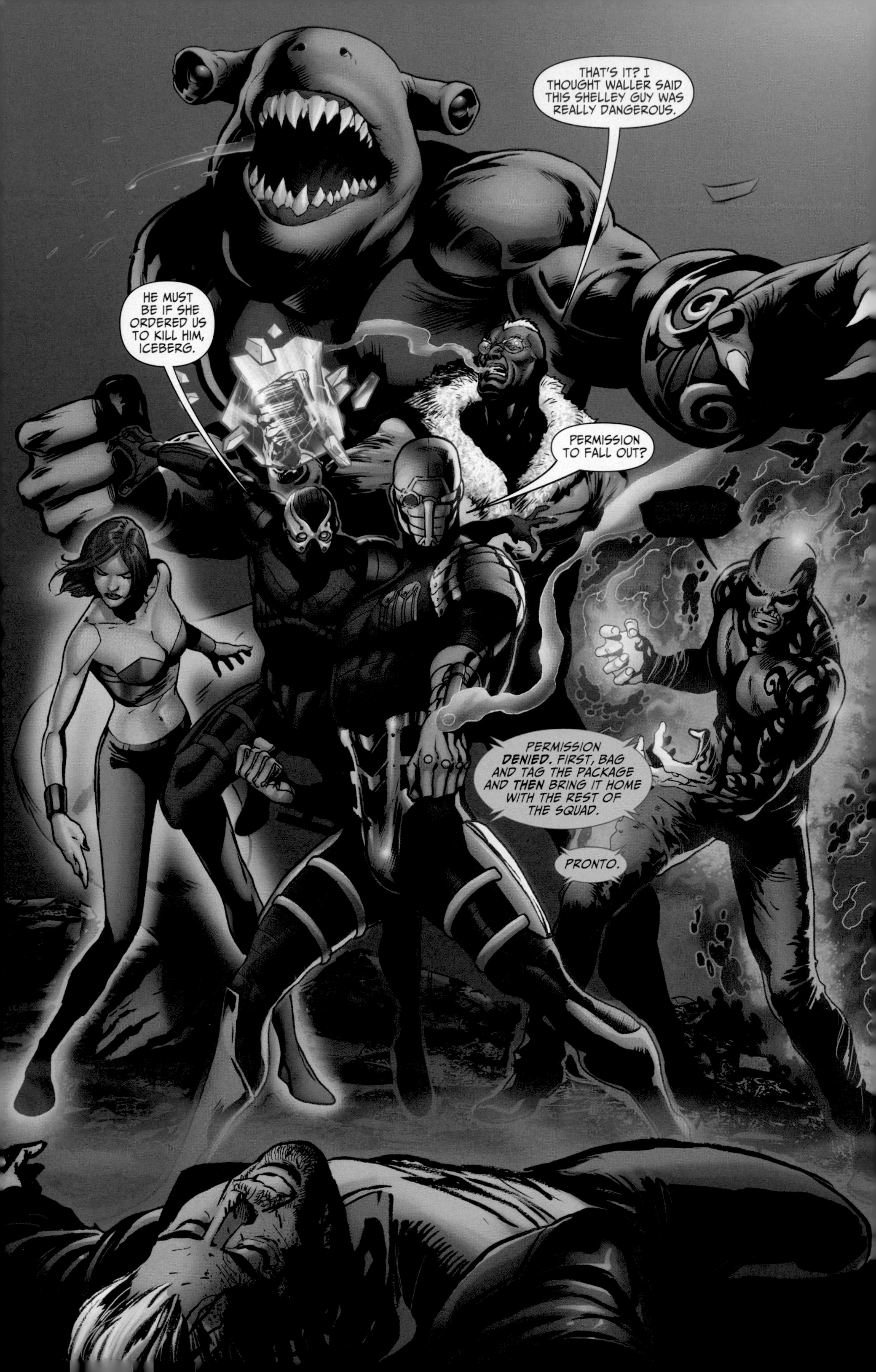
THAT'S IT? I THOUGHT WALLER SAID THIS SHELLEY GUY WAS REALLY DANGEROUS.
HE MUST BE IF SHE ORDERED US TO KILL HIM, ICEBERG.
PERMISSION TO FALL OUT?
PERMISSION DENIED. FIRST, BAG AND TAG THE PACKAGE AND THEN BRING IT HOME WITH THE REST OF THE SQUAD.
PRONTO.

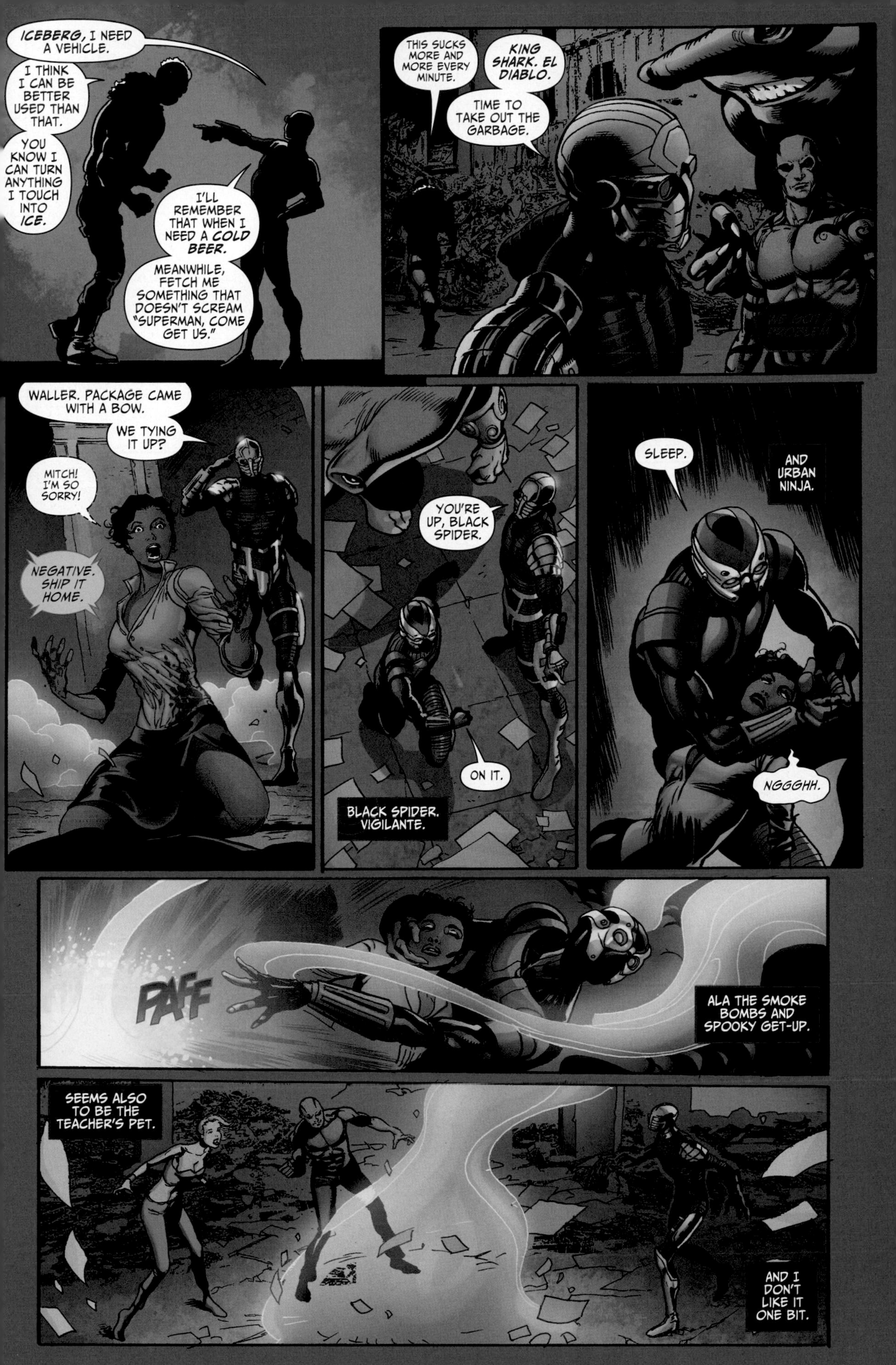
ICEBERG, I NEED A VEHICLE.
I THINK I CAN BE BETTER USED THAN THAT.
YOU KNOW I CAN TURN ANYTHING I TOUCH INTO ICE.
I'LL REMEMBER THAT WHEN I NEED A COLD BEER.
MEANWHILE, FETCH ME SOMETHING THAT DOESN'T SCREAM "SUPERMAN, COME GET US."
THIS SUCKS MORE AND MORE EVERY MINUTE.
KING SHARK. EL DIABLO.
TIME TO TAKE OUT THE GARBAGE.
WALLER. PACKAGE CAME WITH A BOW.
WE TYING IT UP?
MITCH! I'M SO SORRY!
NEGATIVE. SHIP IT HOME.
YOU'RE UP, BLACK SPIDER.
ON IT.
BLACK SPIDER. VIGILANTE.
SLEEP.
AND URBAN NINJA.
NGGGHH.
PAFF
ALA THE SMOKE BOMBS AND SPOOKY GET-UP.
SEEMS ALSO TO BE THE TEACHER'S PET.
AND I DON'T LIKE IT ONE BIT.

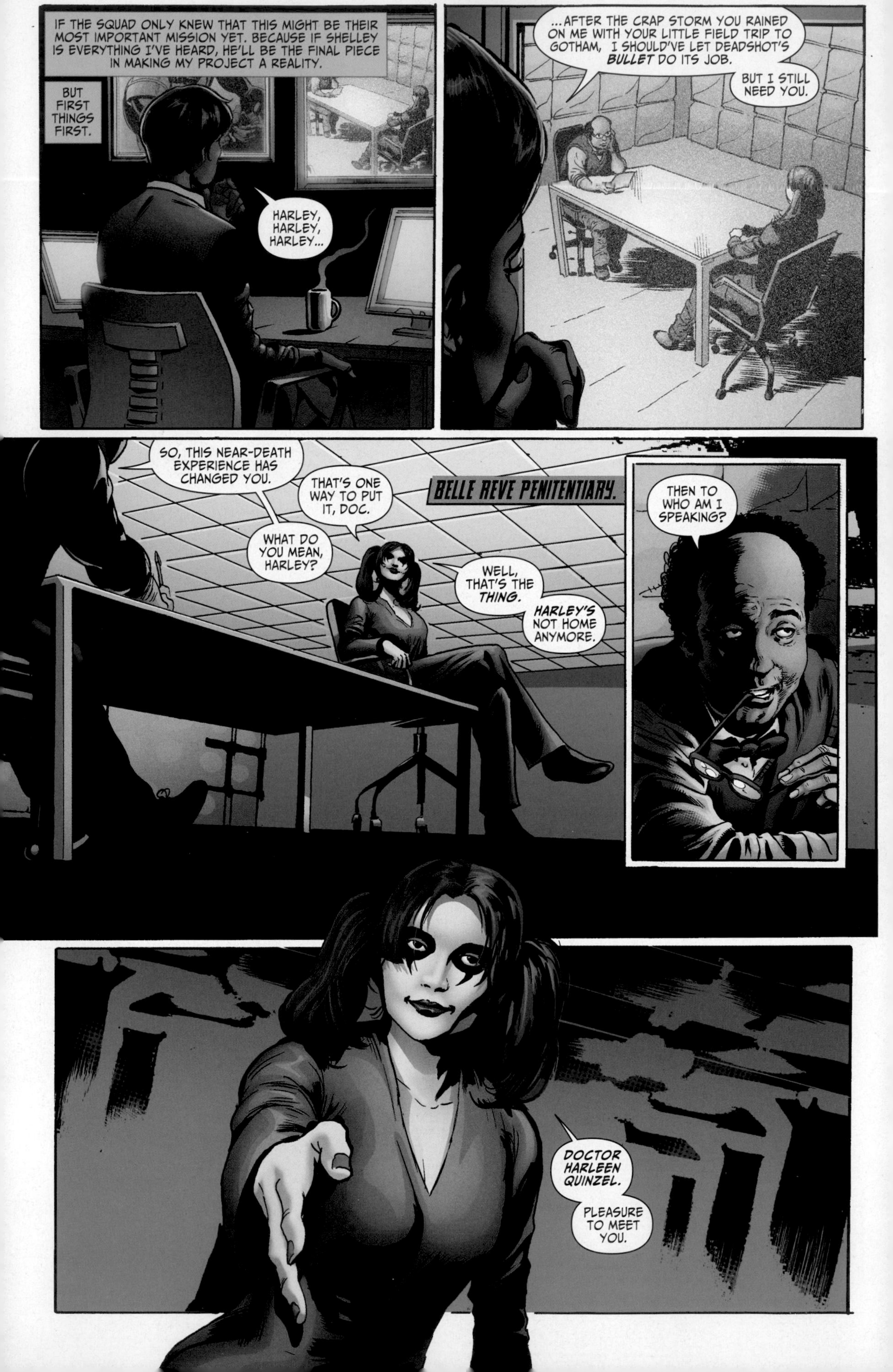

IF THE SQUAD ONLY KNEW THAT THIS MIGHT BE THEIR MOST IMPORTANT MISSION YET. BECAUSE IF SHELLEY IS EVERYTHING I'VE HEARD, HE'LL BE THE FINAL PIECE IN MAKING MY PROJECT A REALITY.
BUT FIRST THINGS FIRST.
HARLEY, HARLEY, HARLEY...
...AFTER THE CRAP STORM YOU RAINED ON ME WITH YOUR LITTLE FIELD TRIP TO GOTHAM, I SHOULD'VE LET DEADSHOT'S BULLET DO ITS JOB.
BUT I STILL NEED YOU.
BELLE REVE PENITENTIARY.
SO, THIS NEAR-DEATH EXPERIENCE HAS CHANGED YOU.
THAT'S ONE WAY TO PUT IT, DOC.
WHAT DO YOU MEAN, HARLEY?
WELL, THAT'S THE THING.
HARLEY'S NOT HOME ANYMORE.
THEN TO WHO AM I SPEAKING?
DOCTOR HARLEEN QUINZEL.
PLEASURE TO MEET YOU.

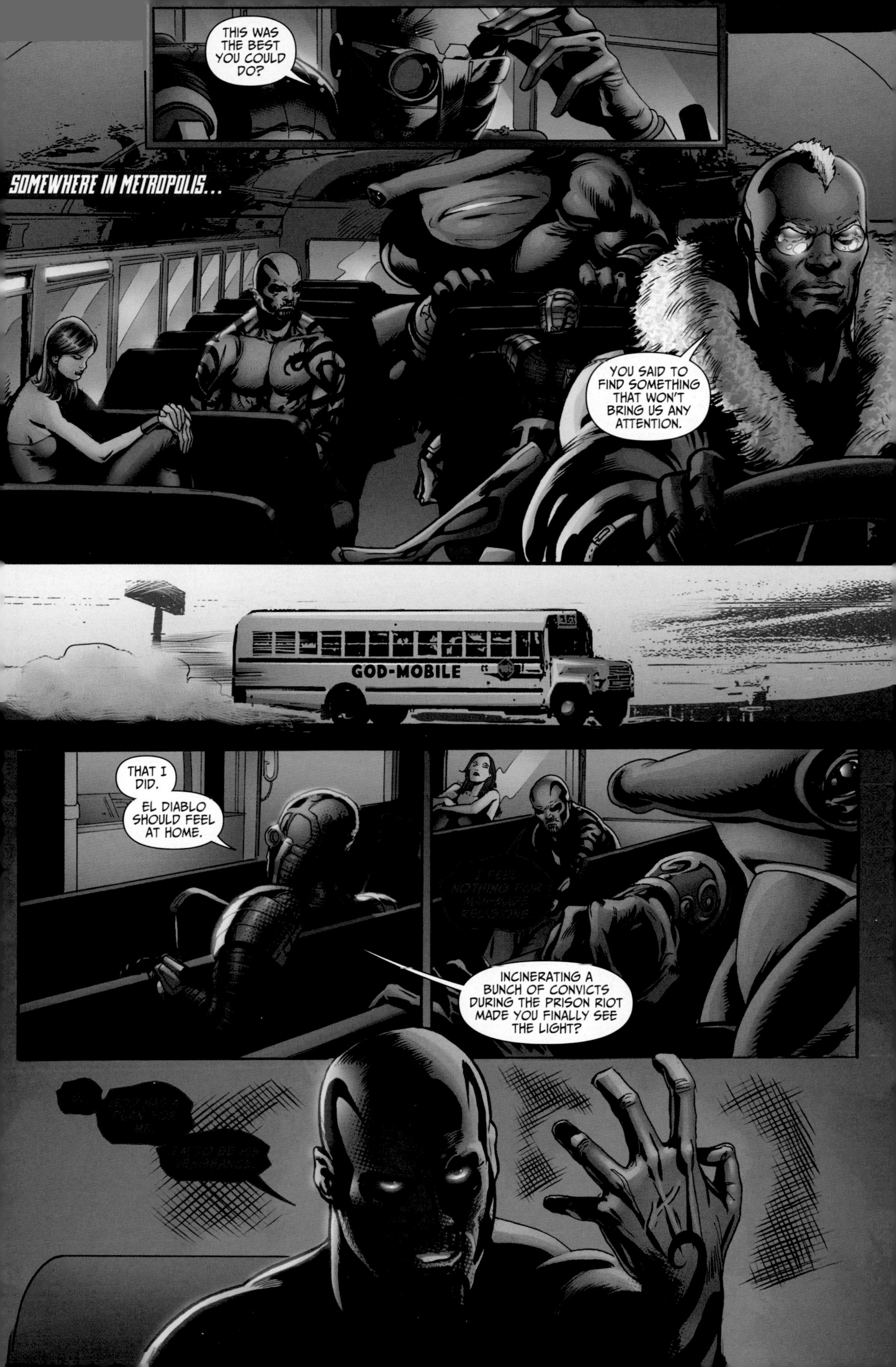
THIS WAS THE BEST YOU COULD DO?
SOMEWHERE IN METROPOLIS...
YOU SAID TO FIND SOMETHING THAT WON'T BRING US ANY ATTENTION.
GOD-MOBILE
THAT I DID.
EL DIABLO SHOULD FEEL AT HOME.
I FEEL NOTHING FOR MAN-MADE RELIGIONS.
INCINERATING A BUNCH OF CONVICTS DURING THE PRISON RIOT MADE YOU FINALLY SEE THE LIGHT?

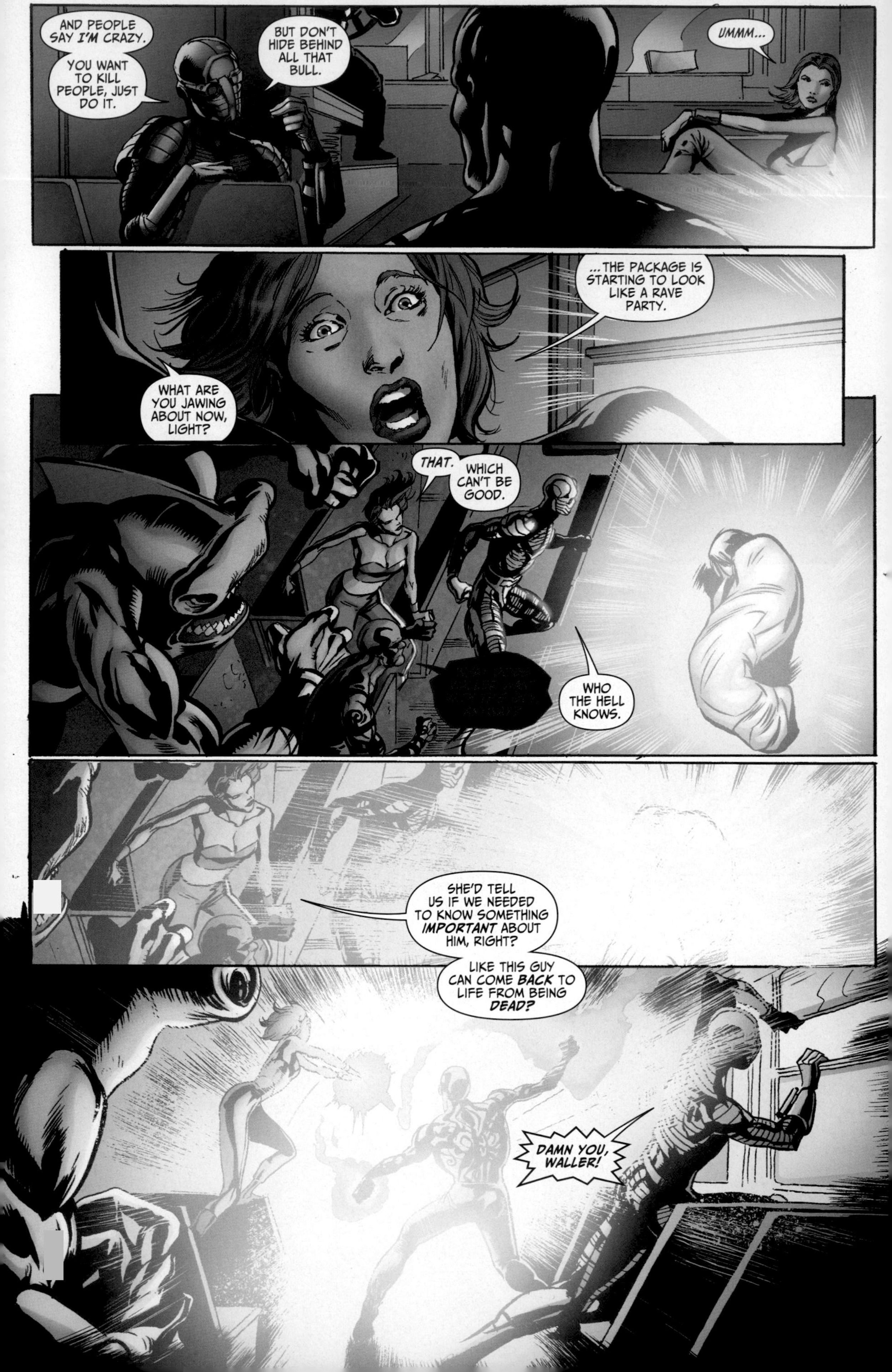
AND PEOPLE SAY I'M CRAZY.
YOU WANT TO KILL PEOPLE, JUST DO IT.
BUT DON'T HIDE BEHIND ALL THAT BULL.
UMMM...
...THE PACKAGE IS STARTING TO LOOK LIKE A RAVE PARTY.
WHAT ARE YOU JAWING ABOUT NOW, LIGHT?
THAT. WHICH CAN'T BE GOOD.
WHO THE HELL KNOWS.
SHE'D TELL US IF WE NEEDED TO KNOW SOMETHING IMPORTANT ABOUT HIM, RIGHT?
LIKE THIS GUY CAN COME BACK TO LIFE FROM BEING DEAD?
DAMN YOU, WALLER!

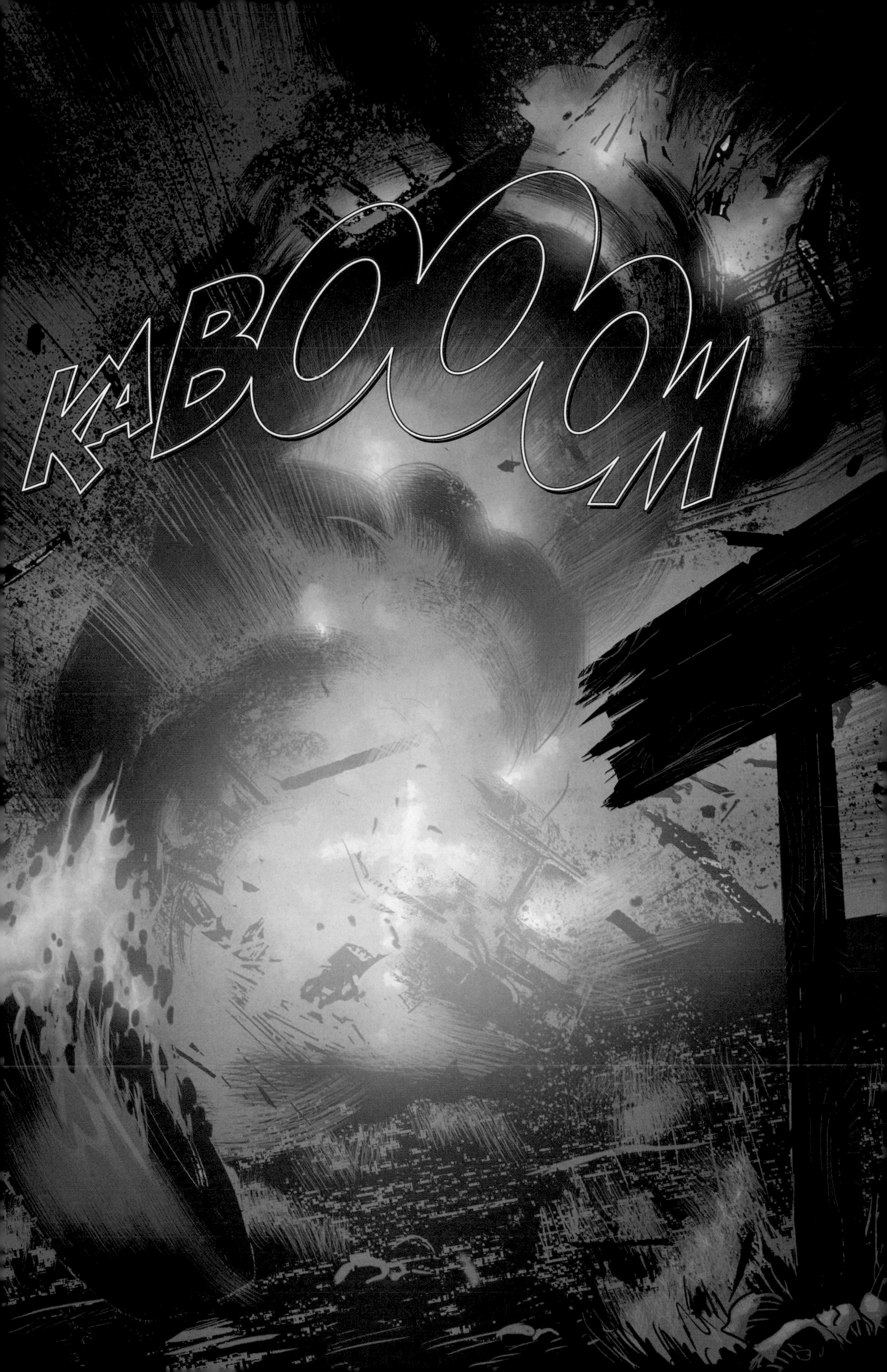
KABOOOM

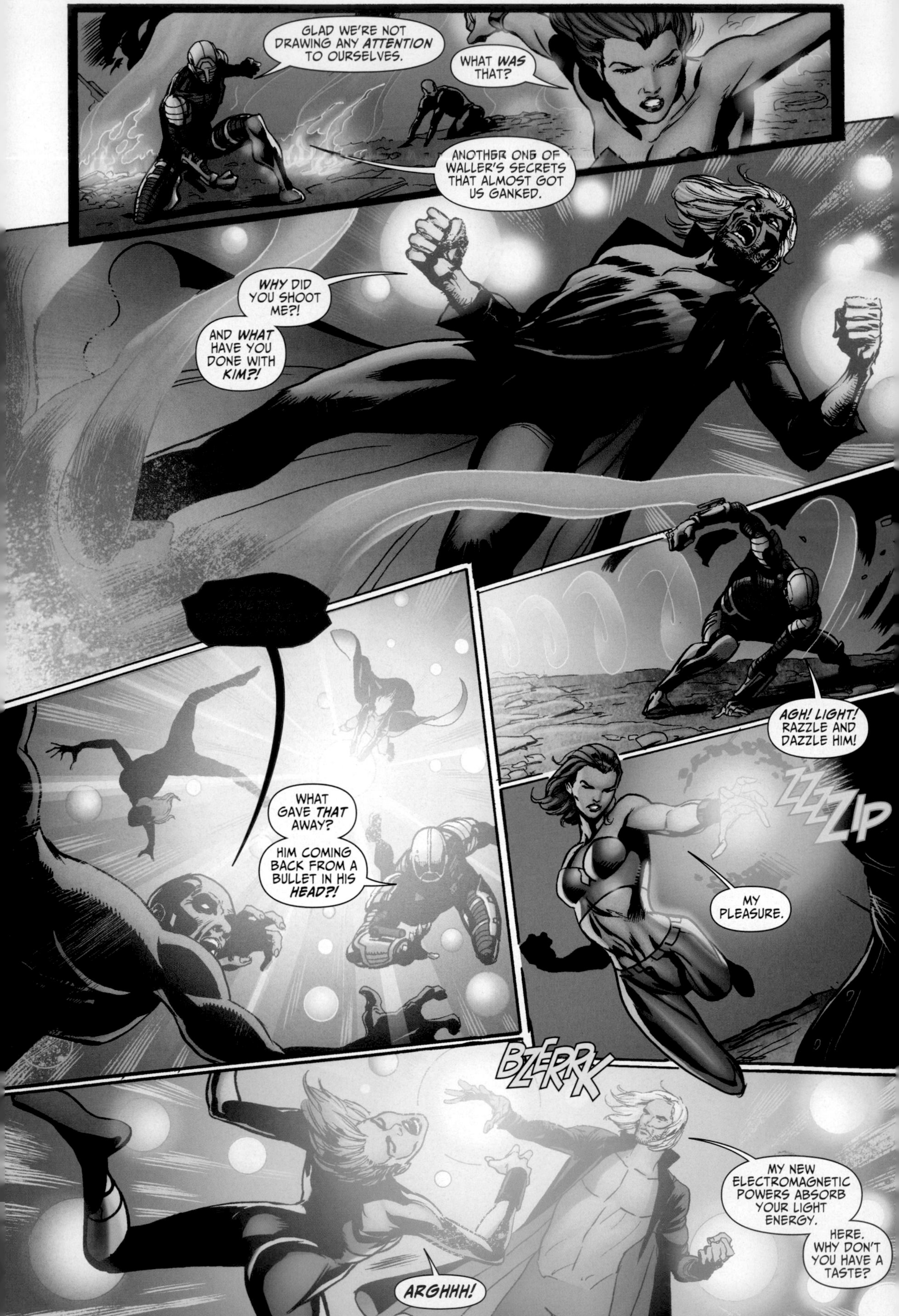
GLAD WE'RE NOT DRAWING ANY *ATTENTION* TO OURSELVES.
WHAT *WAS* THAT?
ANOTHER ONE OF WALLER'S SECRETS THAT ALMOST GOT US GANKED.
WHY DID YOU SHOOT ME?!
AND *WHAT* HAVE YOU DONE WITH *KIM?!*
WHAT GAVE *THAT* AWAY?
HIM COMING BACK FROM A BULLET IN HIS *HEAD?!*
AGH! LIGHT! RAZZLE AND DAZZLE HIM!
ZZZZIP
MY PLEASURE.
BZERRK
MY NEW ELECTROMAGNETIC POWERS ABSORB YOUR LIGHT ENERGY.
HERE. WHY DON'T YOU HAVE A TASTE?
ARGHHH!

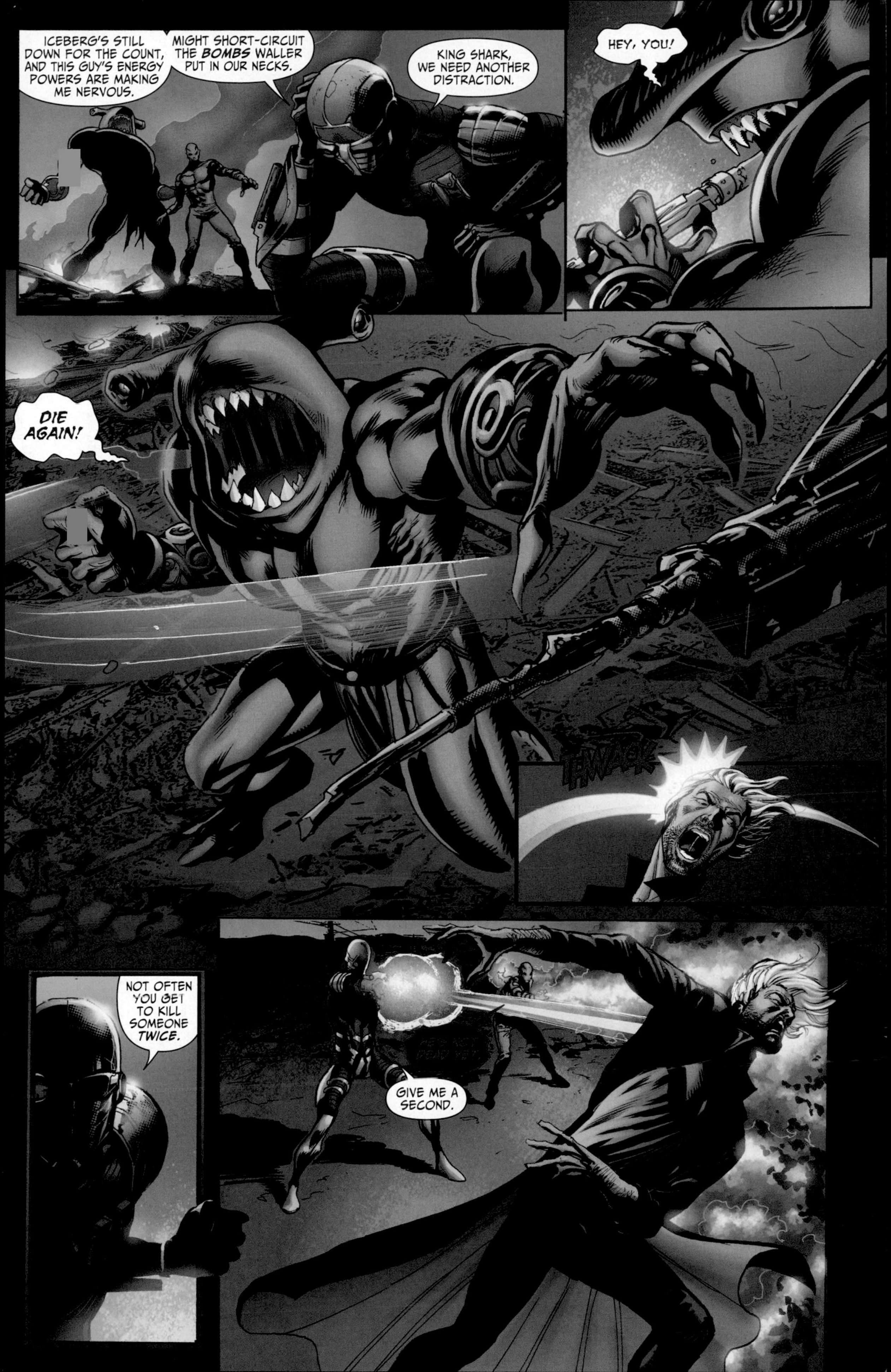
ICEBERG'S STILL DOWN FOR THE COUNT, AND THIS GUY'S ENERGY POWERS ARE MAKING ME NERVOUS.
MIGHT SHORT-CIRCUIT THE BOMBS WALLER PUT IN OUR NECKS.
KING SHARK, WE NEED ANOTHER DISTRACTION.
HEY, YOU!
DIE AGAIN!
THWACK
NOT OFTEN YOU GET TO KILL SOMEONE TWICE.
GIVE ME A SECOND.

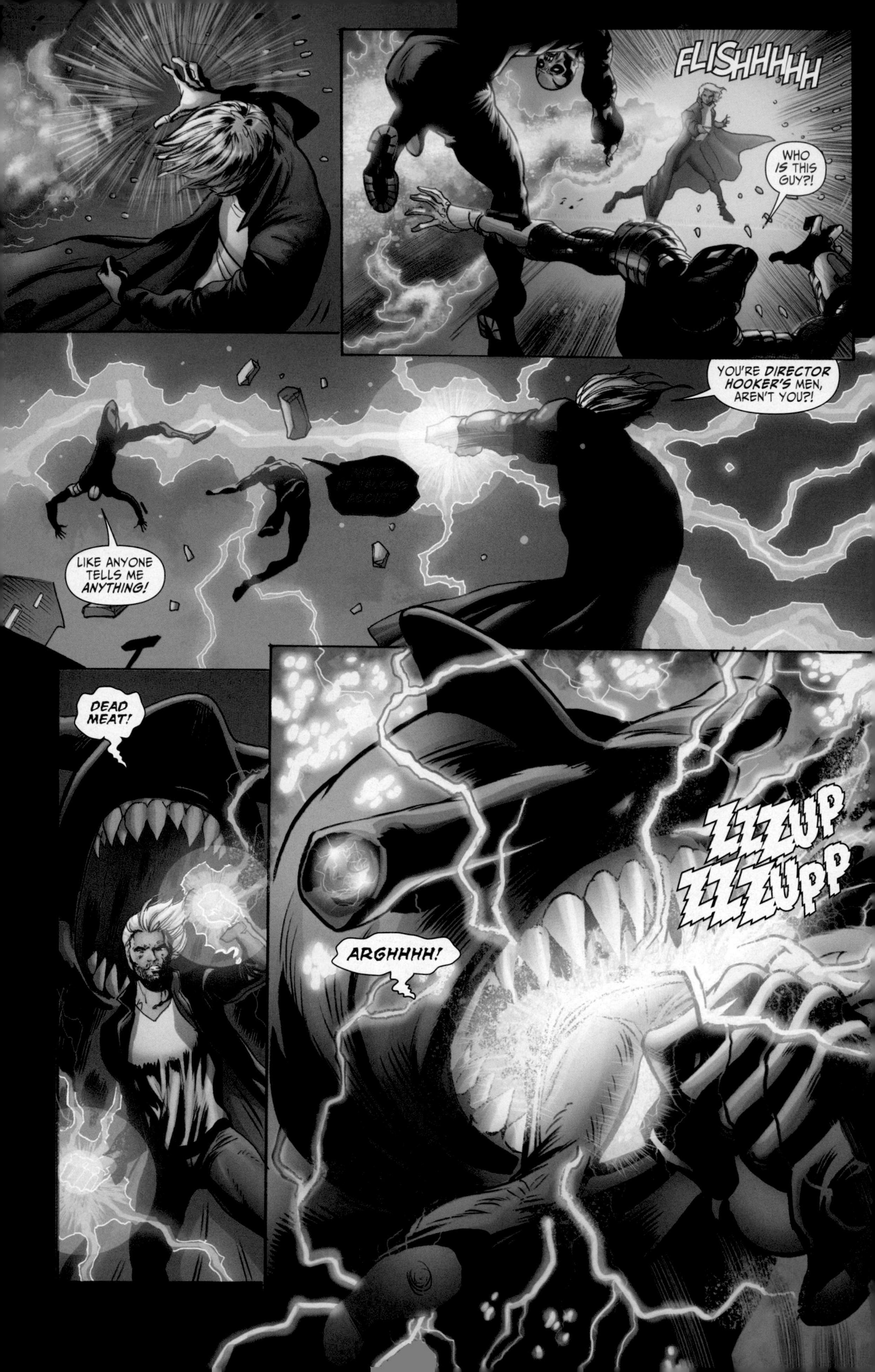
FLISHHHHH
WHO IS THIS GUY?!
YOU'RE DIRECTOR HOOKER'S MEN, AREN'T YOU?!
LIKE ANYONE TELLS ME ANYTHING!
DEAD MEAT!
ZZZUP ZZZUPP
ARGHHHH!

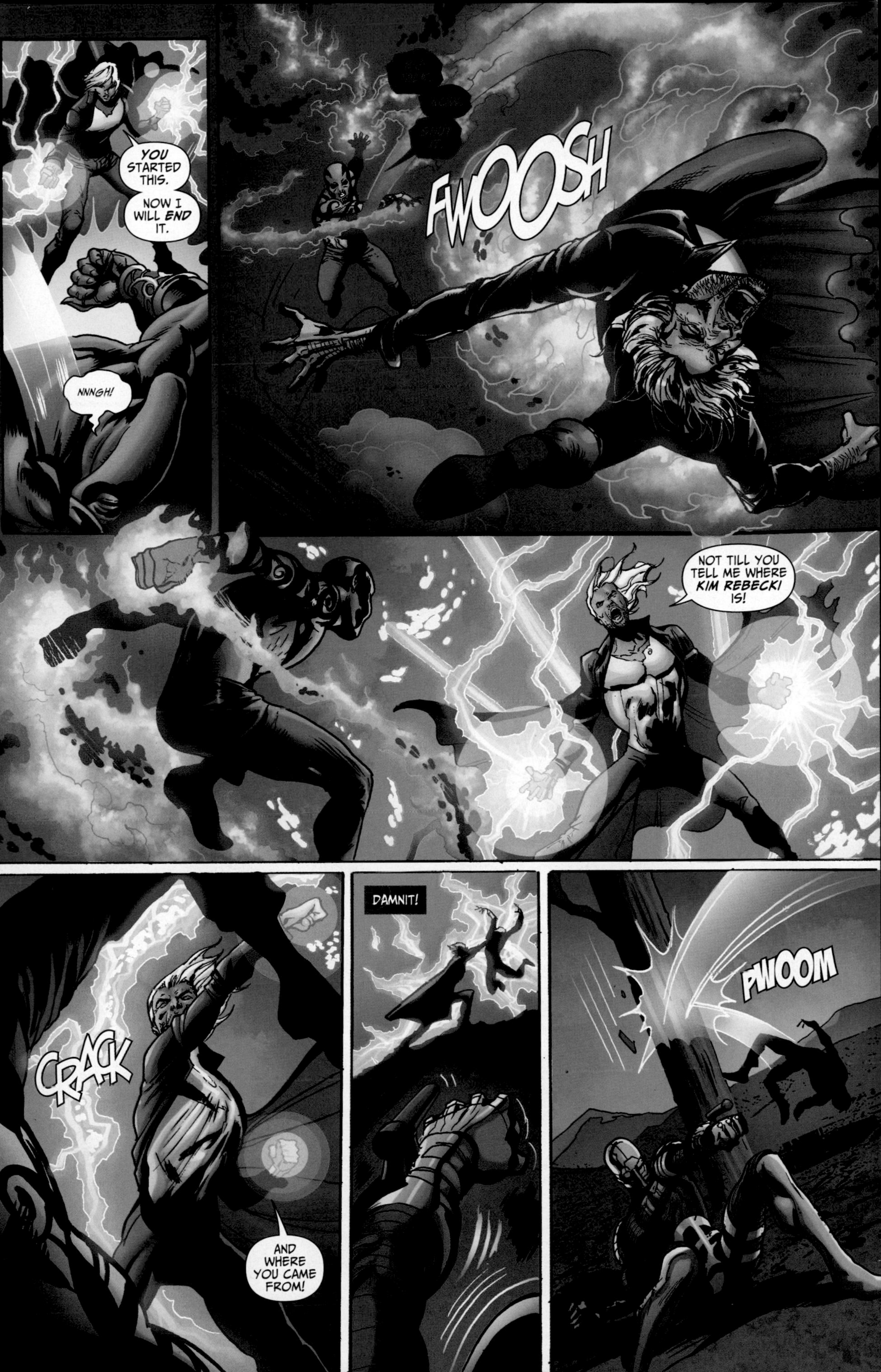
YOU STARTED THIS.
NOW I WILL END IT.
NNNGH!
FWOOSH
NOT TILL YOU TELL ME WHERE KIM REBECKI IS!
CRACK
AND WHERE YOU CAME FROM!
DAMNIT!
PWOOM

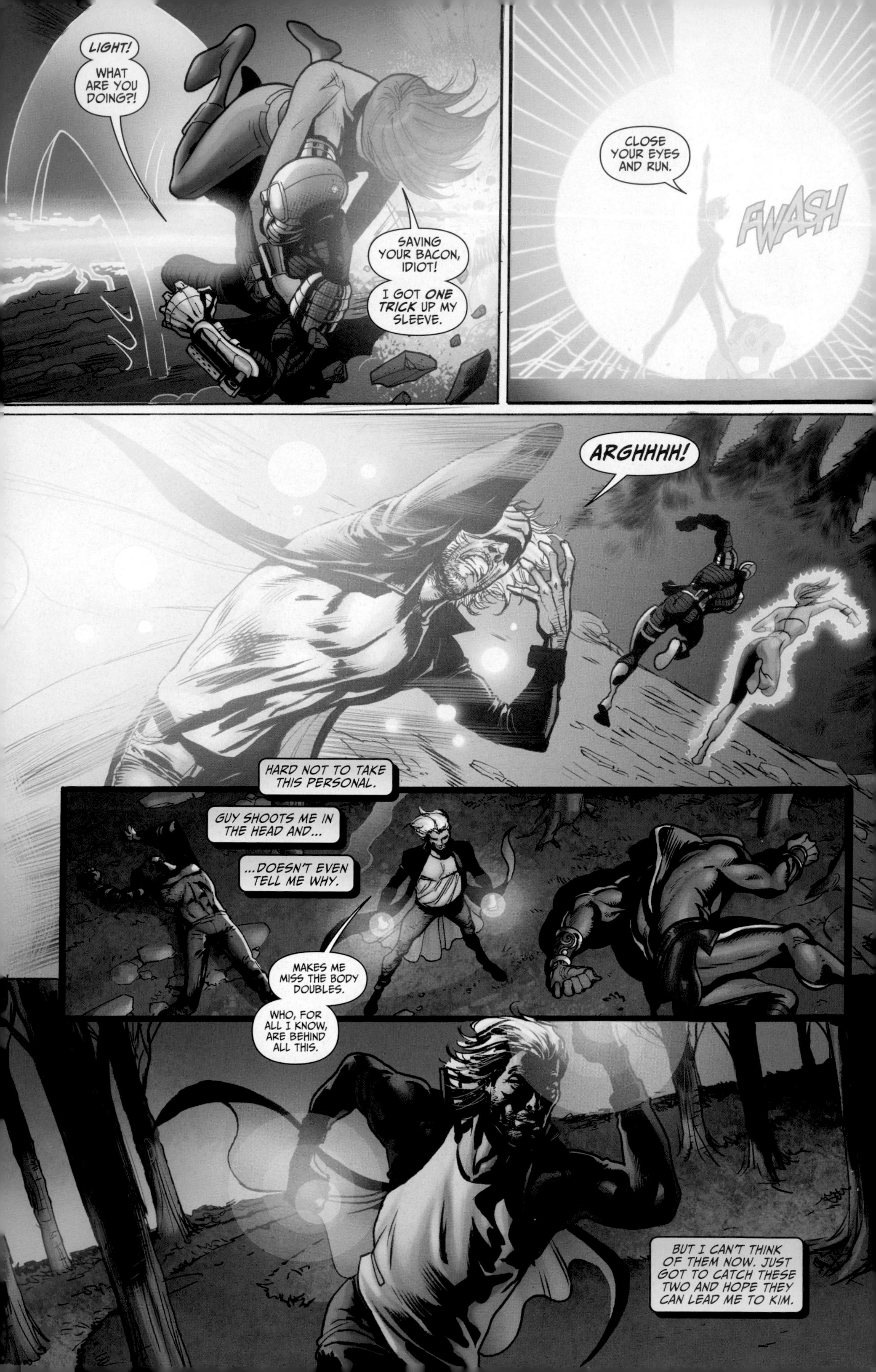
LIGHT!
WHAT ARE YOU DOING?!
SAVING YOUR BACON, IDIOT!
I GOT ONE TRICK UP MY SLEEVE.
CLOSE YOUR EYES AND RUN.
FWASH
ARGHHHH!
HARD NOT TO TAKE THIS PERSONAL.
GUY SHOOTS ME IN THE HEAD AND...
...DOESN'T EVEN TELL ME WHY.
MAKES ME MISS THE BODY DOUBLES.
WHO, FOR ALL I KNOW, ARE BEHIND ALL THIS.
BUT I CAN'T THINK OF THEM NOW. JUST GOT TO CATCH THESE TWO AND HOPE THEY CAN LEAD ME TO KIM.

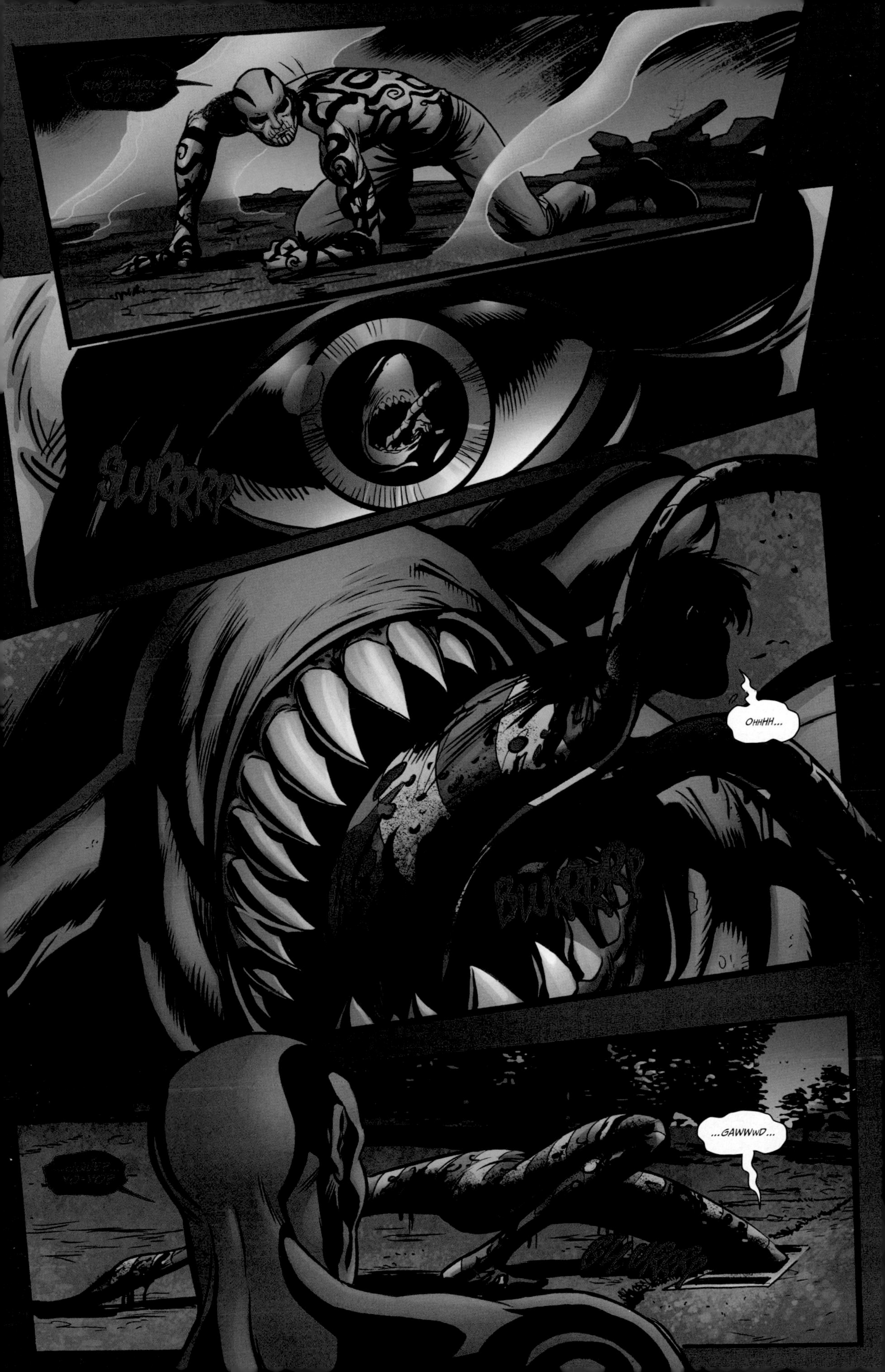
UHHH... KING SHARK? YOU OK?
SLURRRP
OHHHH...
BLURRRP
...GAWWWD...

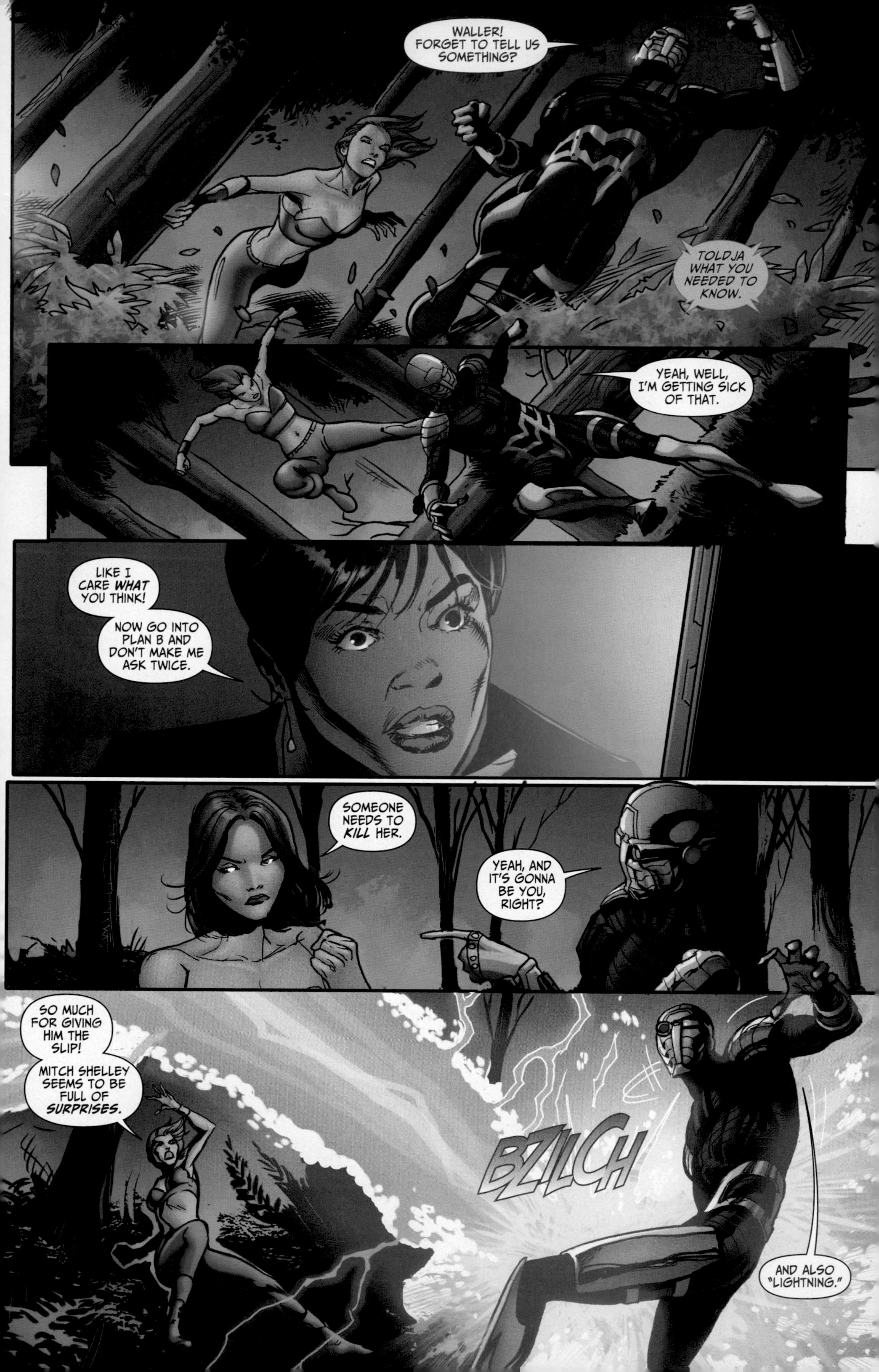
WALLER! FORGET TO TELL US SOMETHING?
TOLDJA WHAT YOU NEEDED TO KNOW.
YEAH, WELL, I'M GETTING SICK OF THAT.
LIKE I CARE WHAT YOU THINK!
NOW GO INTO PLAN B AND DON'T MAKE ME ASK TWICE.
SOMEONE NEEDS TO KILL HER.
YEAH, AND IT'S GONNA BE YOU, RIGHT?
SO MUCH FOR GIVING HIM THE SLIP!
MITCH SHELLEY SEEMS TO BE FULL OF SURPRISES.
BZLCH
AND ALSO "LIGHTNING."

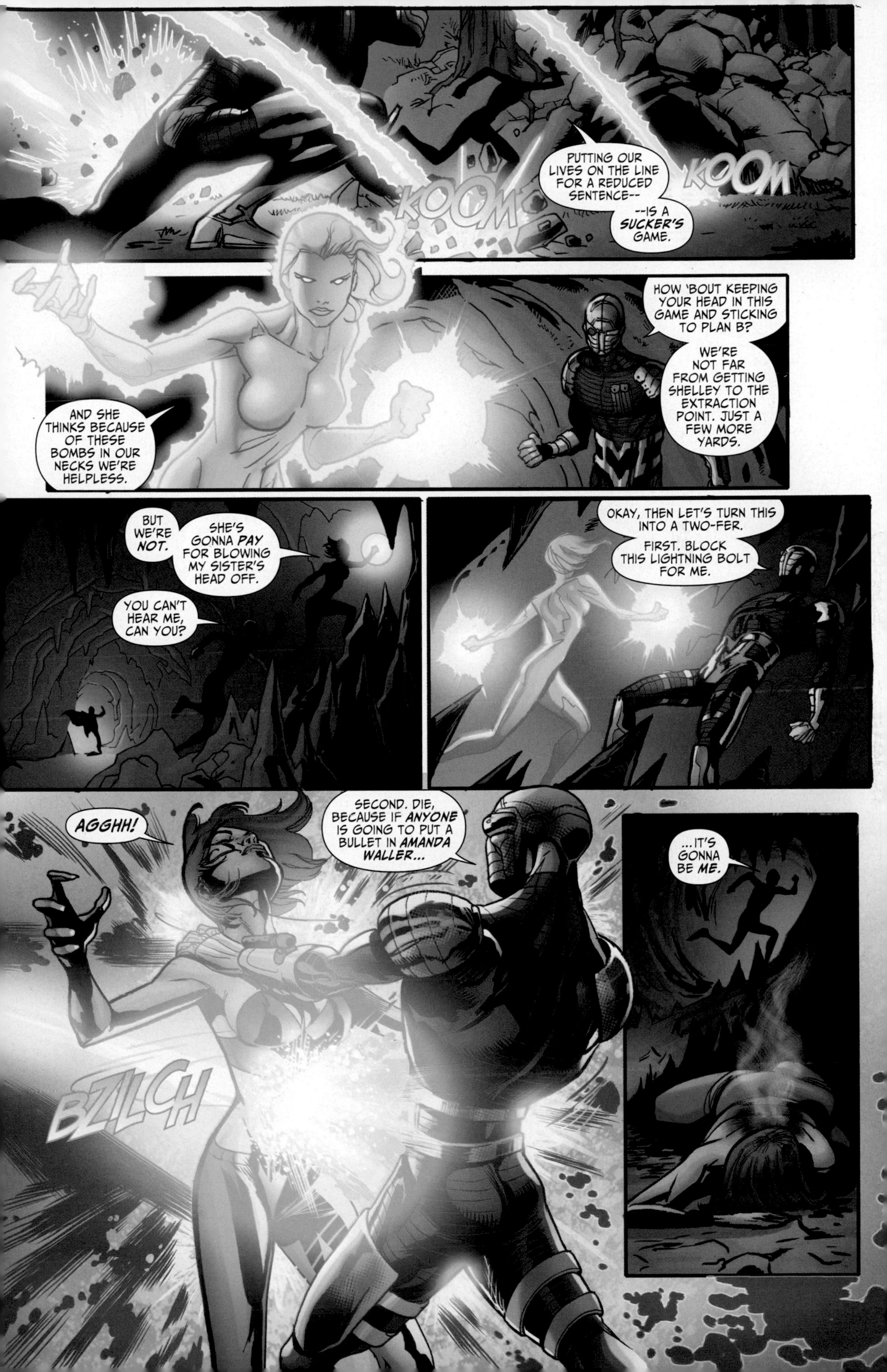

PUTTING OUR LIVES ON THE LINE FOR A REDUCED SENTENCE--
--IS A SUCKER'S GAME.
KOOM
KOOM
HOW 'BOUT KEEPING YOUR HEAD IN THIS GAME AND STICKING TO PLAN B?
WE'RE NOT FAR FROM GETTING SHELLEY TO THE EXTRACTION POINT. JUST A FEW MORE YARDS.
AND SHE THINKS BECAUSE OF THESE BOMBS IN OUR NECKS WE'RE HELPLESS.
BUT WE'RE NOT.
SHE'S GONNA PAY FOR BLOWING MY SISTER'S HEAD OFF.
YOU CAN'T HEAR ME, CAN YOU?
OKAY, THEN LET'S TURN THIS INTO A TWO-FER.
FIRST. BLOCK THIS LIGHTNING BOLT FOR ME.
AGGHH!
SECOND. DIE, BECAUSE IF ANYONE IS GOING TO PUT A BULLET IN AMANDA WALLER...
...IT'S GONNA BE ME.
BZLCH

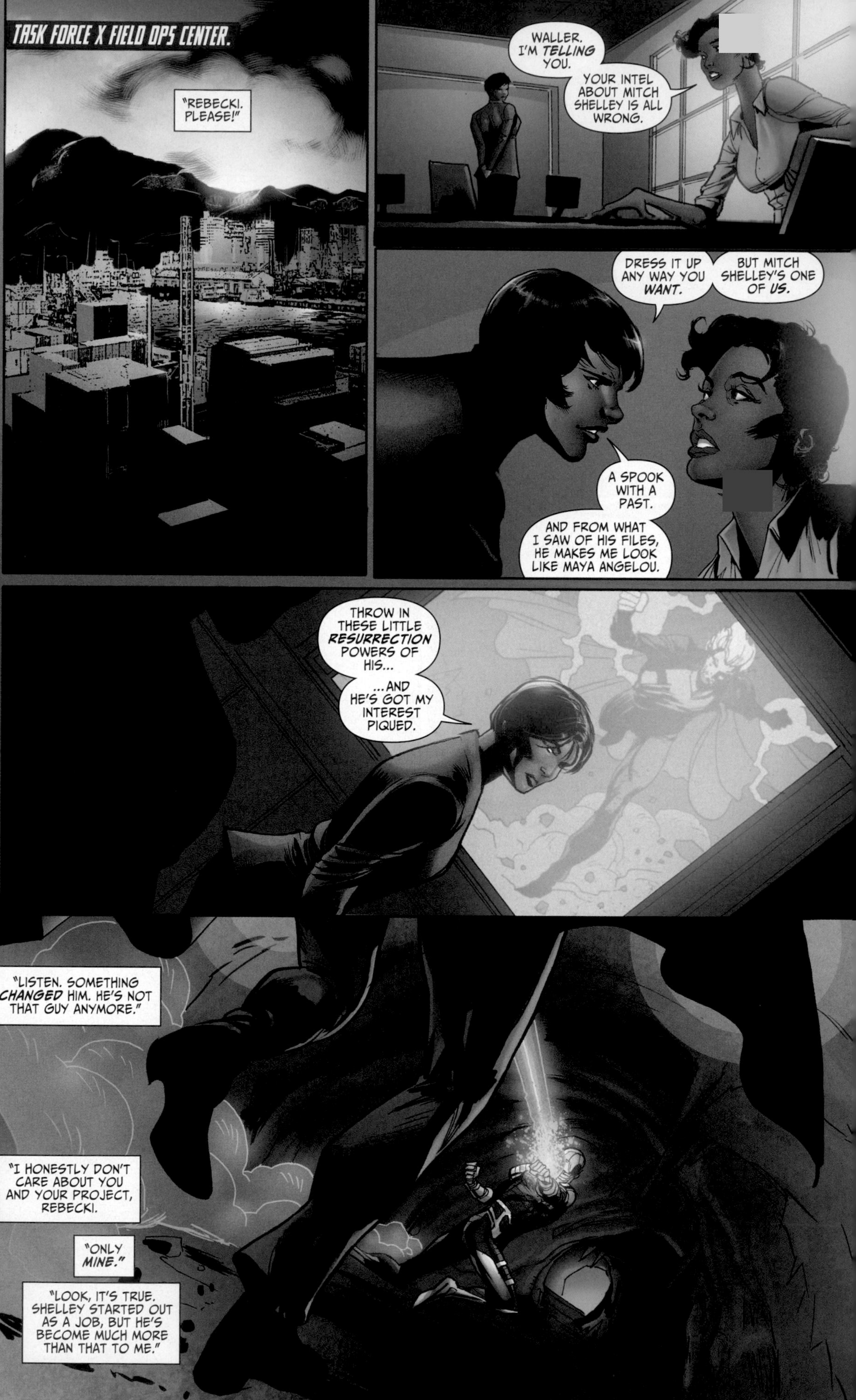
TASK FORCE X FIELD OPS CENTER.
"REBECKI. PLEASE!"
WALLER. I'M TELLING YOU.
YOUR INTEL ABOUT MITCH SHELLEY IS ALL WRONG.
DRESS IT UP ANY WAY YOU WANT.
BUT MITCH SHELLEY'S ONE OF US.
A SPOOK WITH A PAST.
AND FROM WHAT I SAW OF HIS FILES, HE MAKES ME LOOK LIKE MAYA ANGELOU.
THROW IN THESE LITTLE RESURRECTION POWERS OF HIS...
...AND HE'S GOT MY INTEREST PIQUED.
"LISTEN. SOMETHING CHANGED HIM. HE'S NOT THAT GUY ANYMORE."
"I HONESTLY DON'T CARE ABOUT YOU AND YOUR PROJECT, REBECKI.
"ONLY MINE."
"LOOK, IT'S TRUE. SHELLEY STARTED OUT AS A JOB, BUT HE'S BECOME MUCH MORE THAN THAT TO ME."

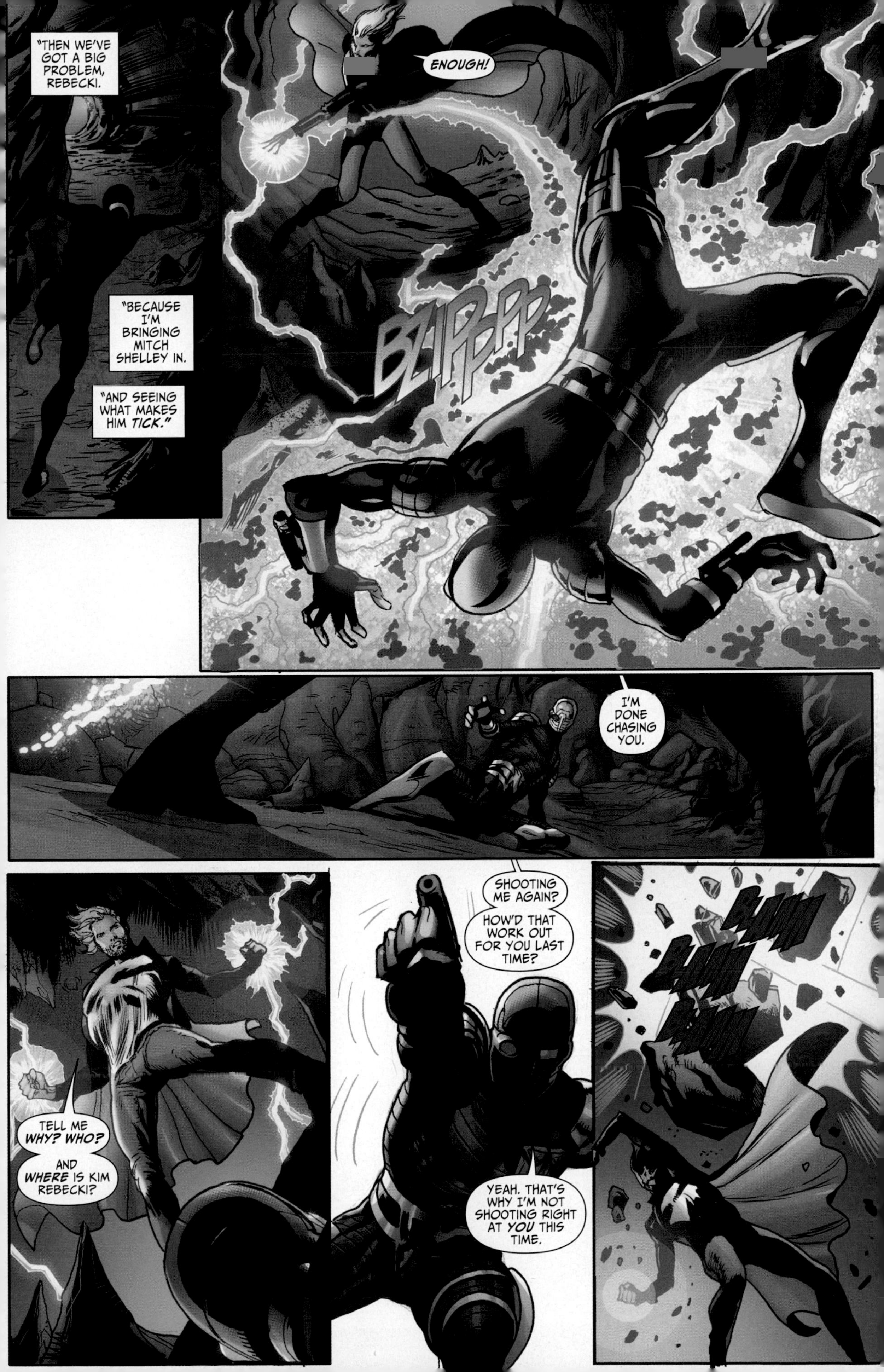
"THEN WE'VE GOT A BIG PROBLEM, REBECKI.
"BECAUSE I'M BRINGING MITCH SHELLEY IN.
"AND SEEING WHAT MAKES HIM *TICK.*"
ENOUGH!
BZIPPPP
I'M DONE CHASING YOU.
TELL ME *WHY? WHO?*
AND *WHERE* IS KIM REBECKI?
SHOOTING ME AGAIN?
HOW'D THAT WORK OUT FOR YOU LAST TIME?
YEAH. THAT'S WHY I'M NOT SHOOTING RIGHT AT *YOU* THIS TIME.

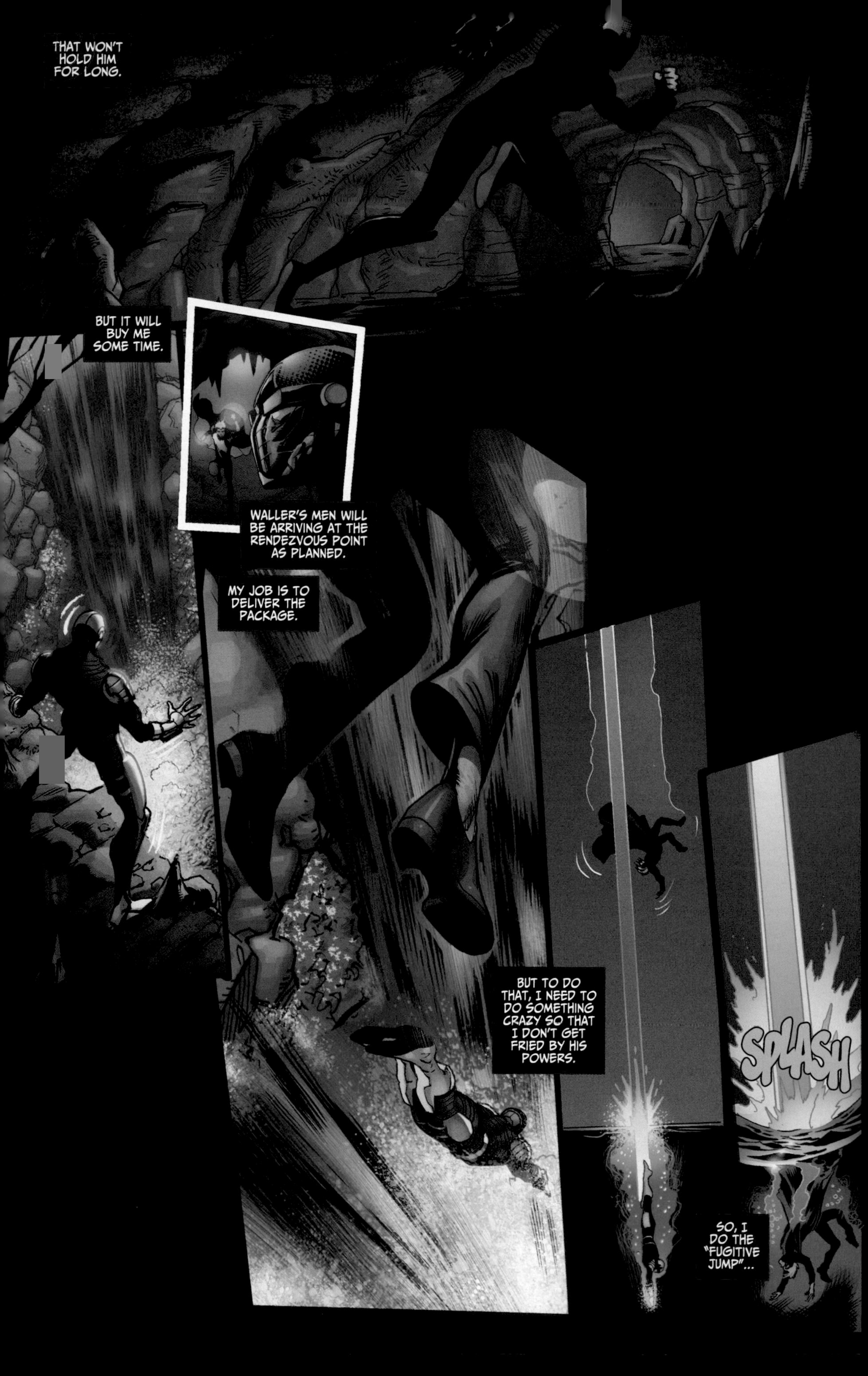
THAT WON'T HOLD HIM FOR LONG.
BUT IT WILL BUY ME SOME TIME.
WALLER'S MEN WILL BE ARRIVING AT THE RENDEZVOUS POINT AS PLANNED.
MY JOB IS TO DELIVER THE PACKAGE.
BUT TO DO THAT, I NEED TO DO SOMETHING CRAZY SO THAT I DON'T GET FRIED BY HIS POWERS.
SPLASH
SO, I DO THE "FUGITIVE JUMP"...

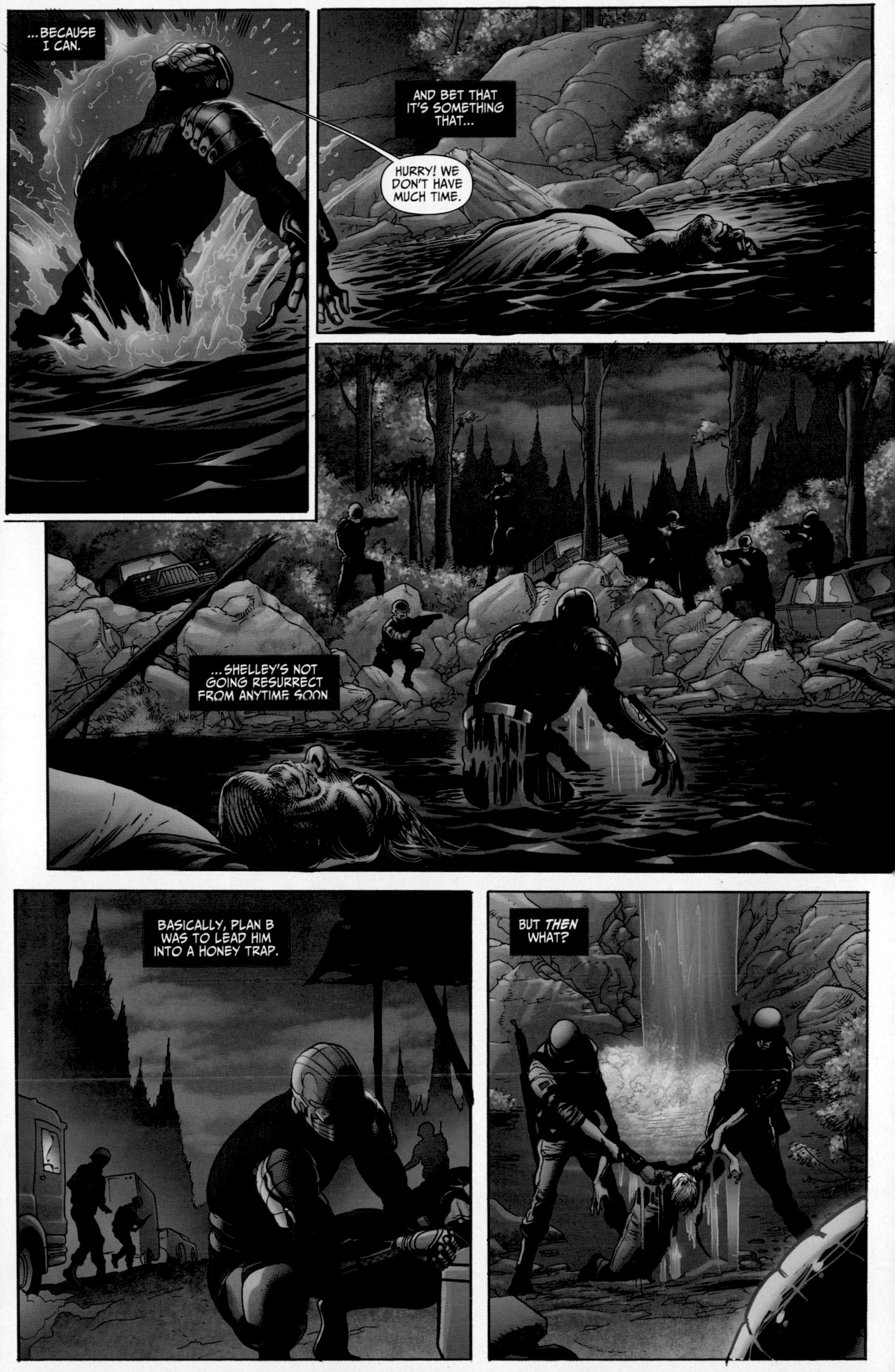
...BECAUSE I CAN.
AND BET THAT IT'S SOMETHING THAT...
HURRY! WE DON'T HAVE MUCH TIME.
...SHELLEY'S NOT GOING RESURRECT FROM ANYTIME SOON.
BASICALLY, PLAN B WAS TO LEAD HIM INTO A HONEY TRAP.
BUT *THEN* WHAT?

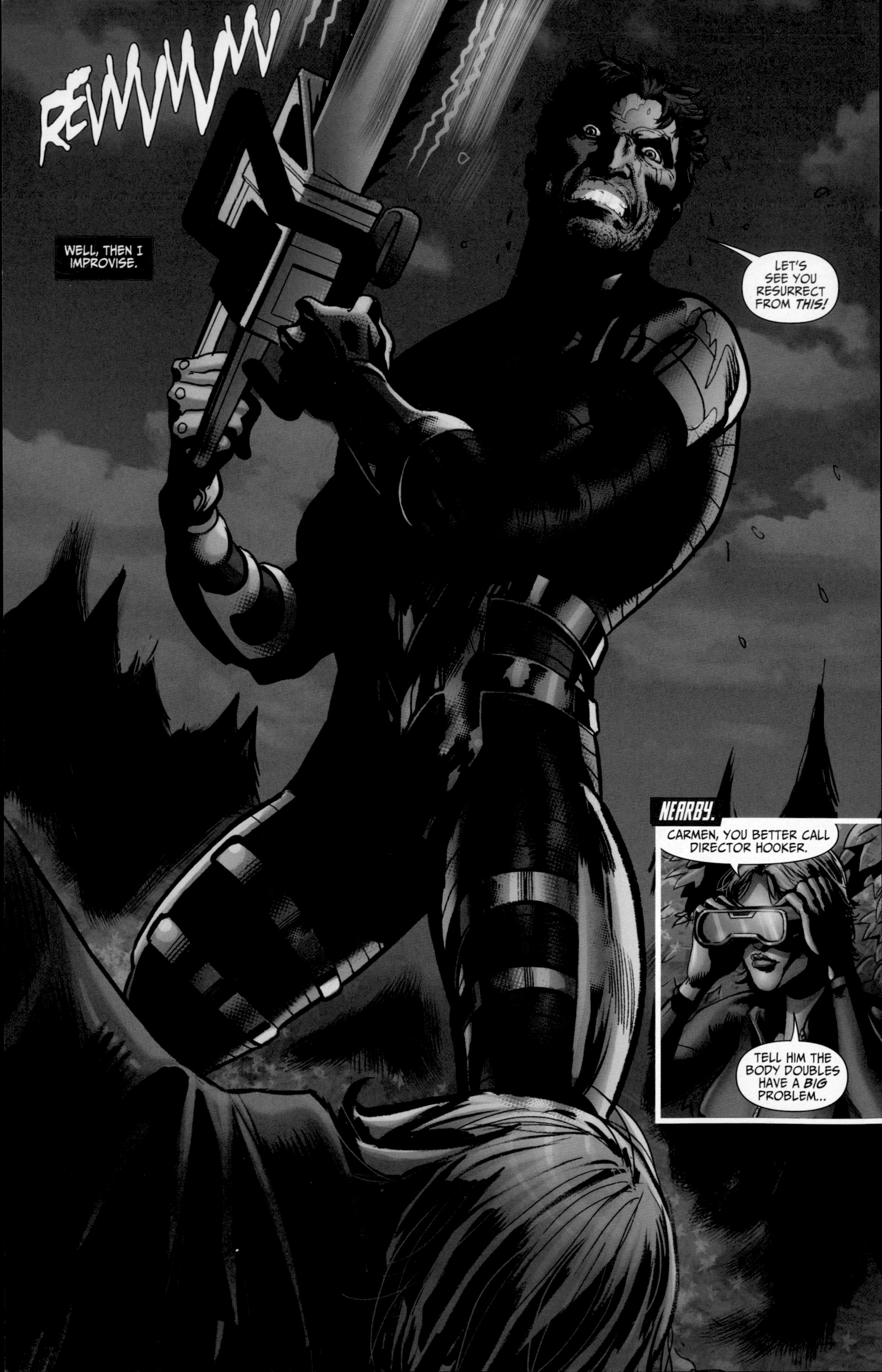
REVVVVVVV
WELL, THEN I IMPROVISE.
LET'S SEE YOU RESURRECT FROM *THIS!*
NEARBY.
CARMEN, YOU BETTER CALL DIRECTOR HOOKER.
TELL HIM THE BODY DOUBLES HAVE A *BIG* PROBLEM...

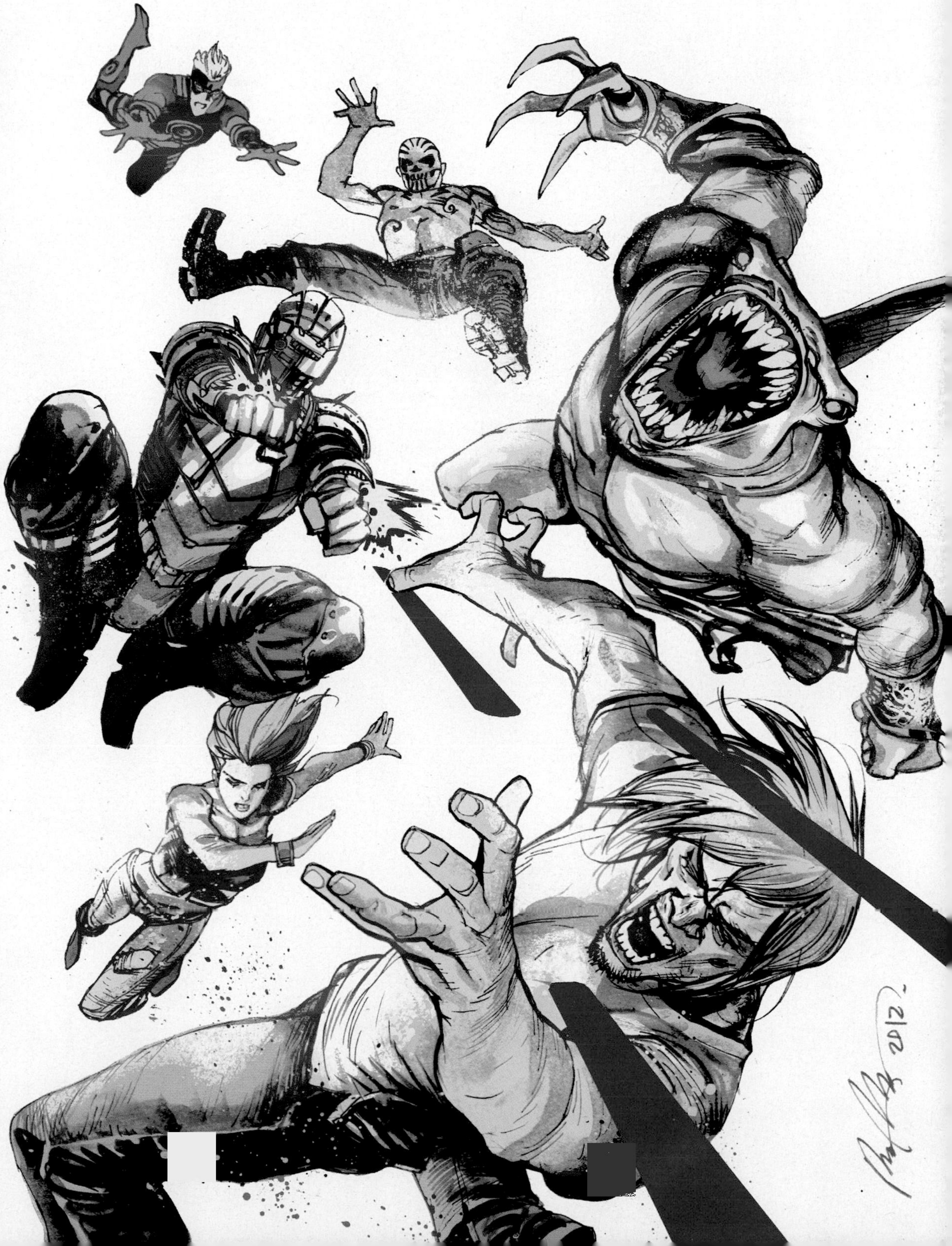

DEAD HEAT

DAN ABNETT & ANDY LANNING
writers

JESUS SAIZ & ANDRES GUINALDO
pencillers

JESUS SAIZ, MARK IRWIN & CHRISTIAN ALAMY
inkers

cover art by
RAFAEL ALBUQUERQUE

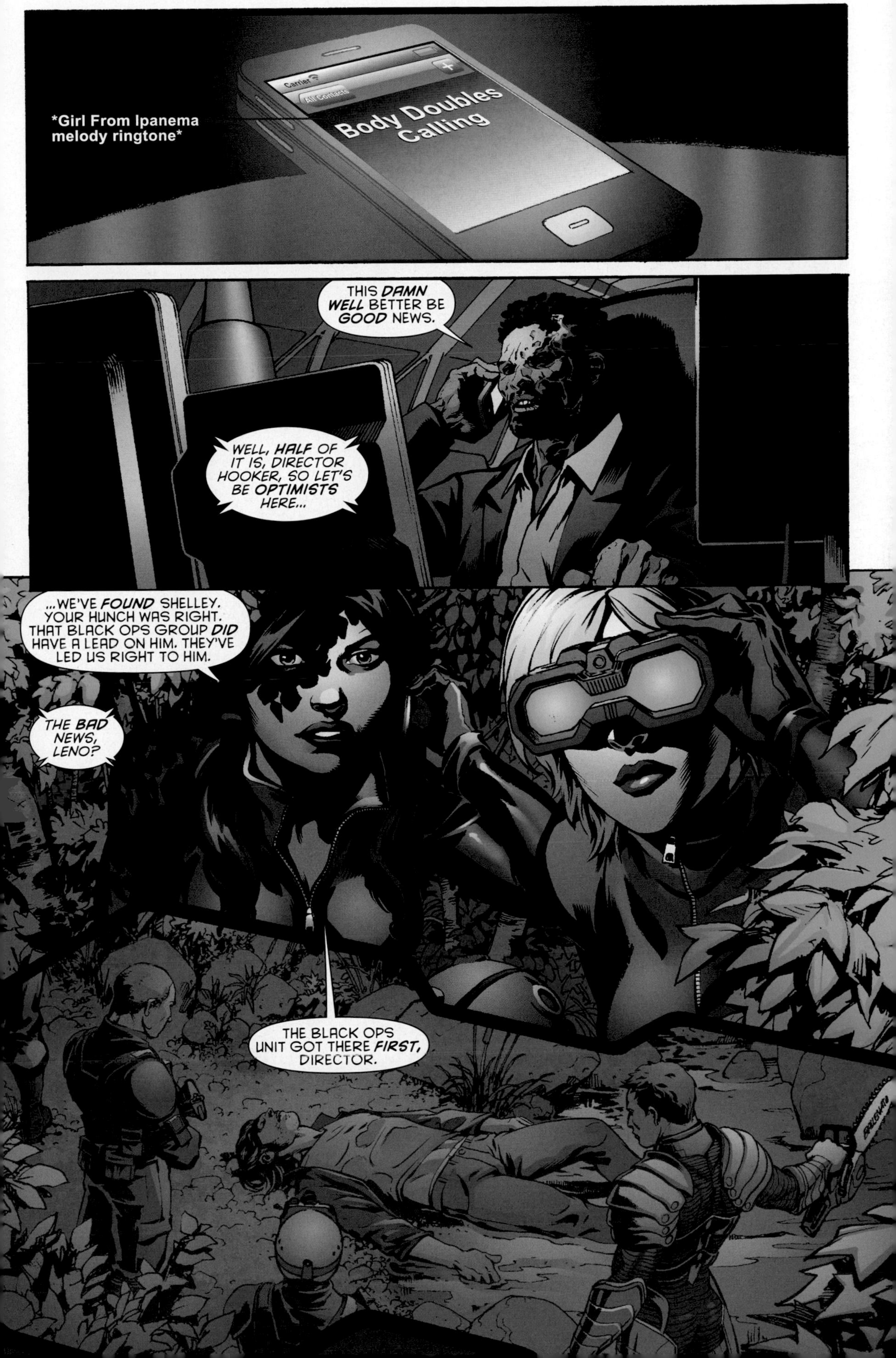

Girl From Ipanema melody ringtone
Carrier
All Contacts
Body Doubles Calling
THIS DAMN WELL BETTER BE GOOD NEWS.
WELL, HALF OF IT IS, DIRECTOR HOOKER, SO LET'S BE OPTIMISTS HERE...
...WE'VE FOUND SHELLEY. YOUR HUNCH WAS RIGHT. THAT BLACK OPS GROUP DID HAVE A LEAD ON HIM. THEY'VE LED US RIGHT TO HIM.
THE BAD NEWS, LENO?
THE BLACK OPS UNIT GOT THERE FIRST, DIRECTOR.

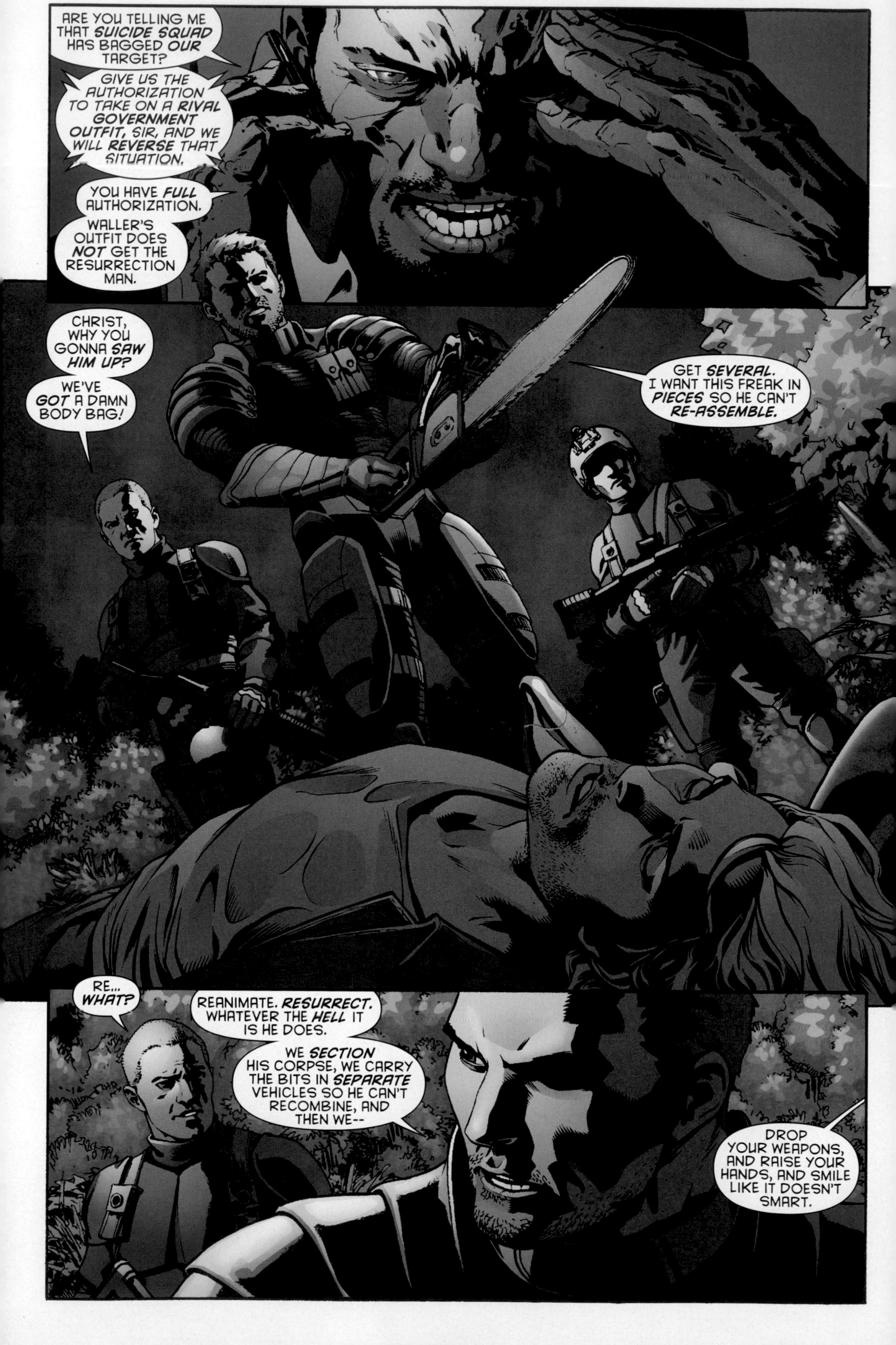
ARE YOU TELLING ME THAT SUICIDE SQUAD HAS BAGGED OUR TARGET?
GIVE US THE AUTHORIZATION TO TAKE ON A RIVAL GOVERNMENT OUTFIT, SIR, AND WE WILL REVERSE THAT SITUATION.
YOU HAVE FULL AUTHORIZATION.
WALLER'S OUTFIT DOES NOT GET THE RESURRECTION MAN.
CHRIST, WHY YOU GONNA SAW HIM UP?
WE'VE GOT A DAMN BODY BAG!
GET SEVERAL. I WANT THIS FREAK IN PIECES SO HE CAN'T RE-ASSEMBLE.
RE... WHAT?
REANIMATE. RESURRECT. WHATEVER THE HELL IT IS HE DOES.
WE SECTION HIS CORPSE, WE CARRY THE BITS IN SEPARATE VEHICLES SO HE CAN'T RECOMBINE, AND THEN WE--
DROP YOUR WEAPONS, AND RAISE YOUR HANDS, AND SMILE LIKE IT DOESN'T SMART.

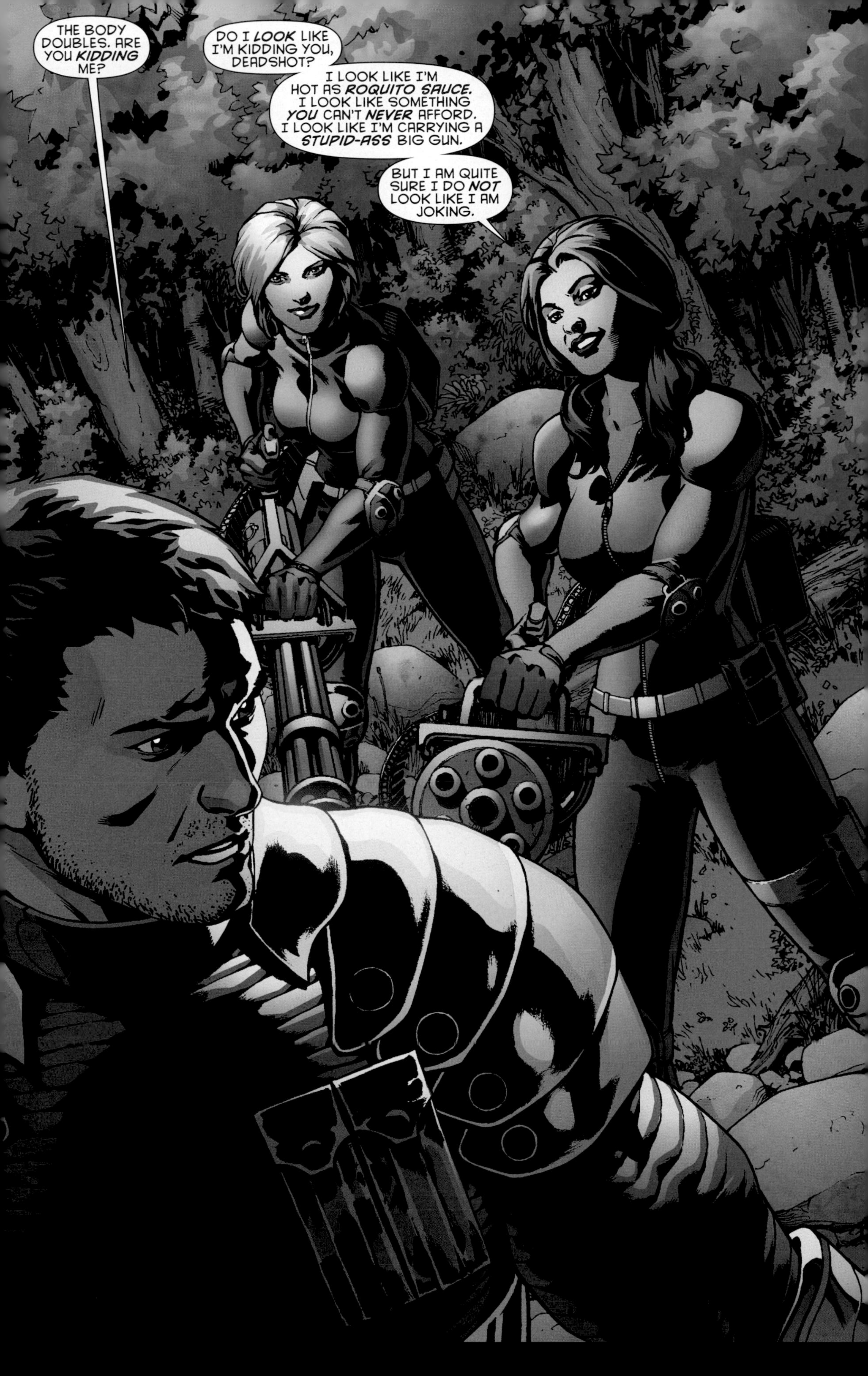
THE BODY DOUBLES. ARE YOU KIDDING ME?
DO I LOOK LIKE I'M KIDDING YOU, DEADSHOT?
I LOOK LIKE I'M HOT AS ROQUITO SAUCE. I LOOK LIKE SOMETHING YOU CAN'T NEVER AFFORD. I LOOK LIKE I'M CARRYING A STUPID-ASS BIG GUN.
BUT I AM QUITE SURE I DO NOT LOOK LIKE I AM JOKING.

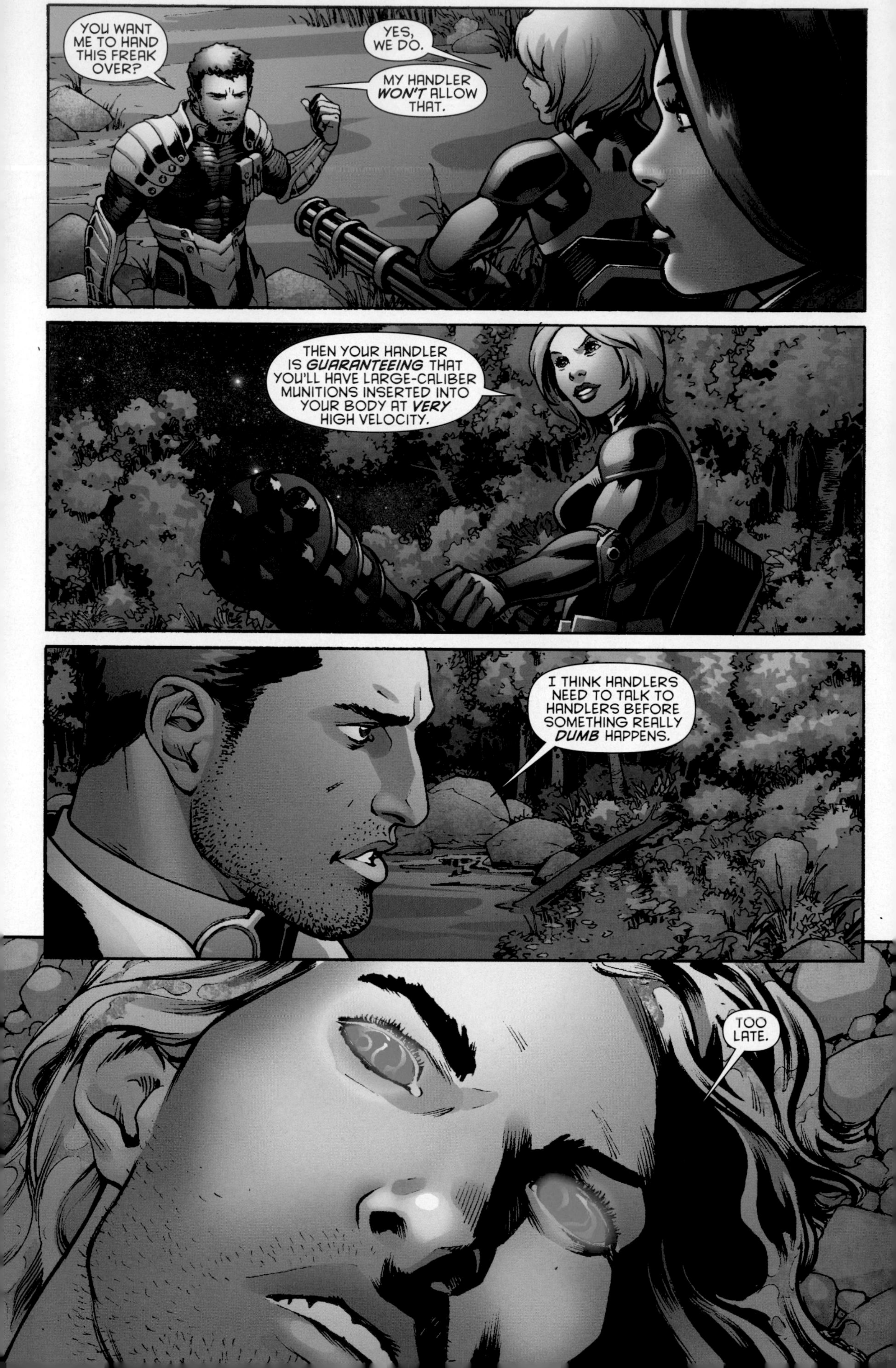

YOU WANT ME TO HAND THIS FREAK OVER?
YES, WE DO.
MY HANDLER WON'T ALLOW THAT.
THEN YOUR HANDLER IS GUARANTEEING THAT YOU'LL HAVE LARGE-CALIBER MUNITIONS INSERTED INTO YOUR BODY AT VERY HIGH VELOCITY.
I THINK HANDLERS NEED TO TALK TO HANDLERS BEFORE SOMETHING REALLY DUMB HAPPENS.
TOO LATE.

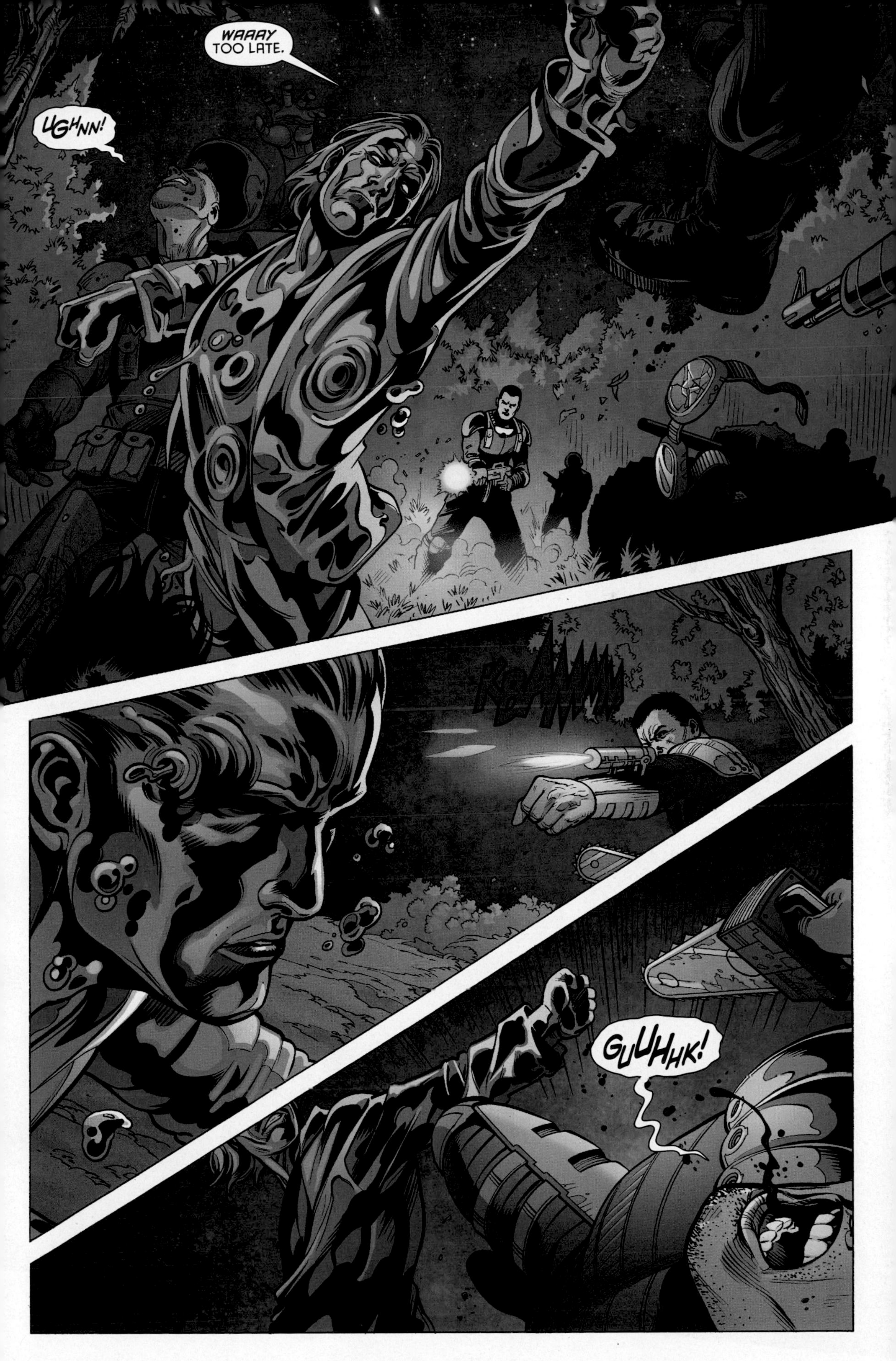

UGHNN!
WAAAY TOO LATE.
RRAAMM
GUUHHK!

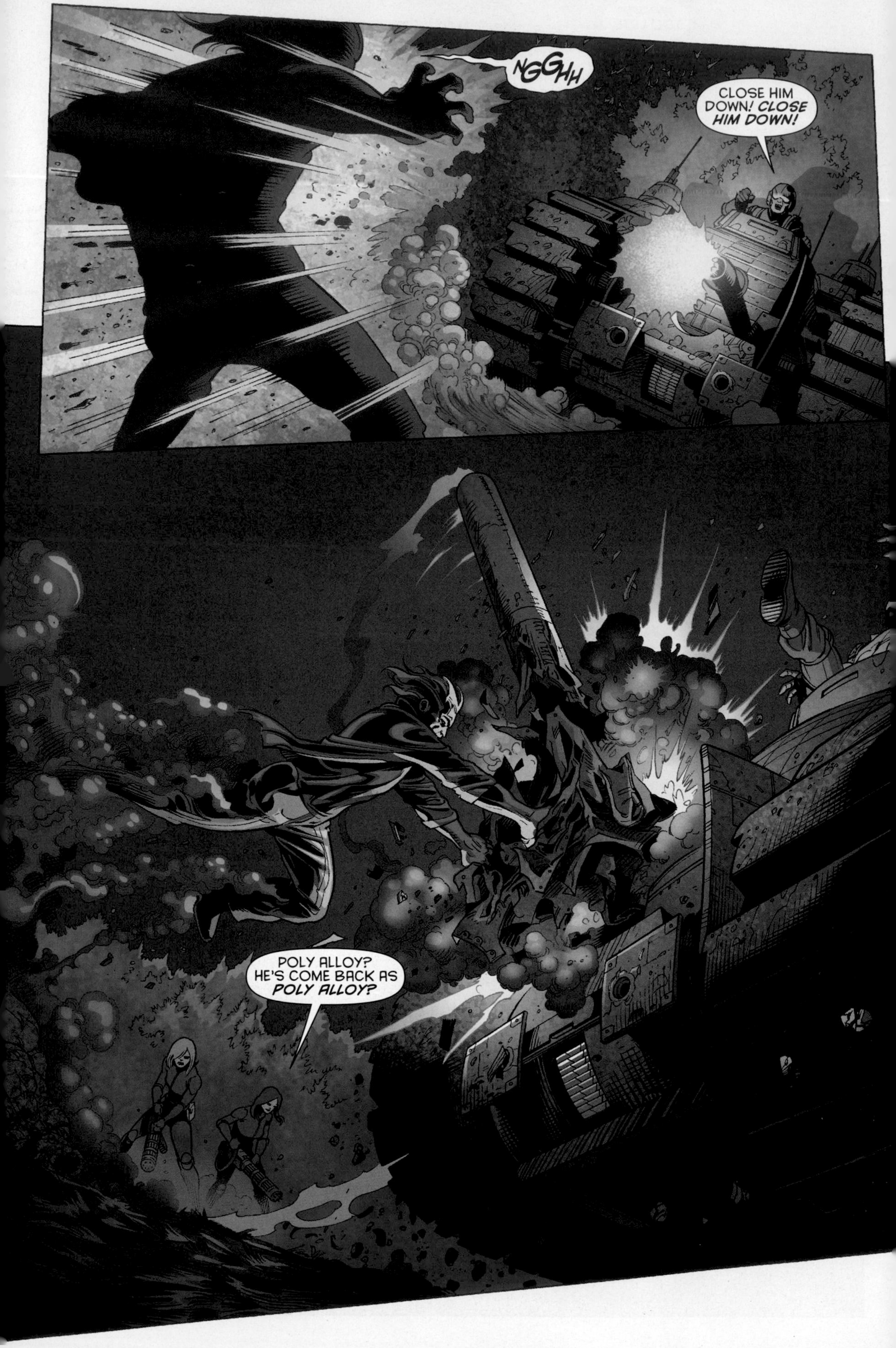
NGGHH
CLOSE HIM DOWN! *CLOSE HIM DOWN!*
POLY ALLOY? HE'S COME BACK AS *POLY ALLOY?*

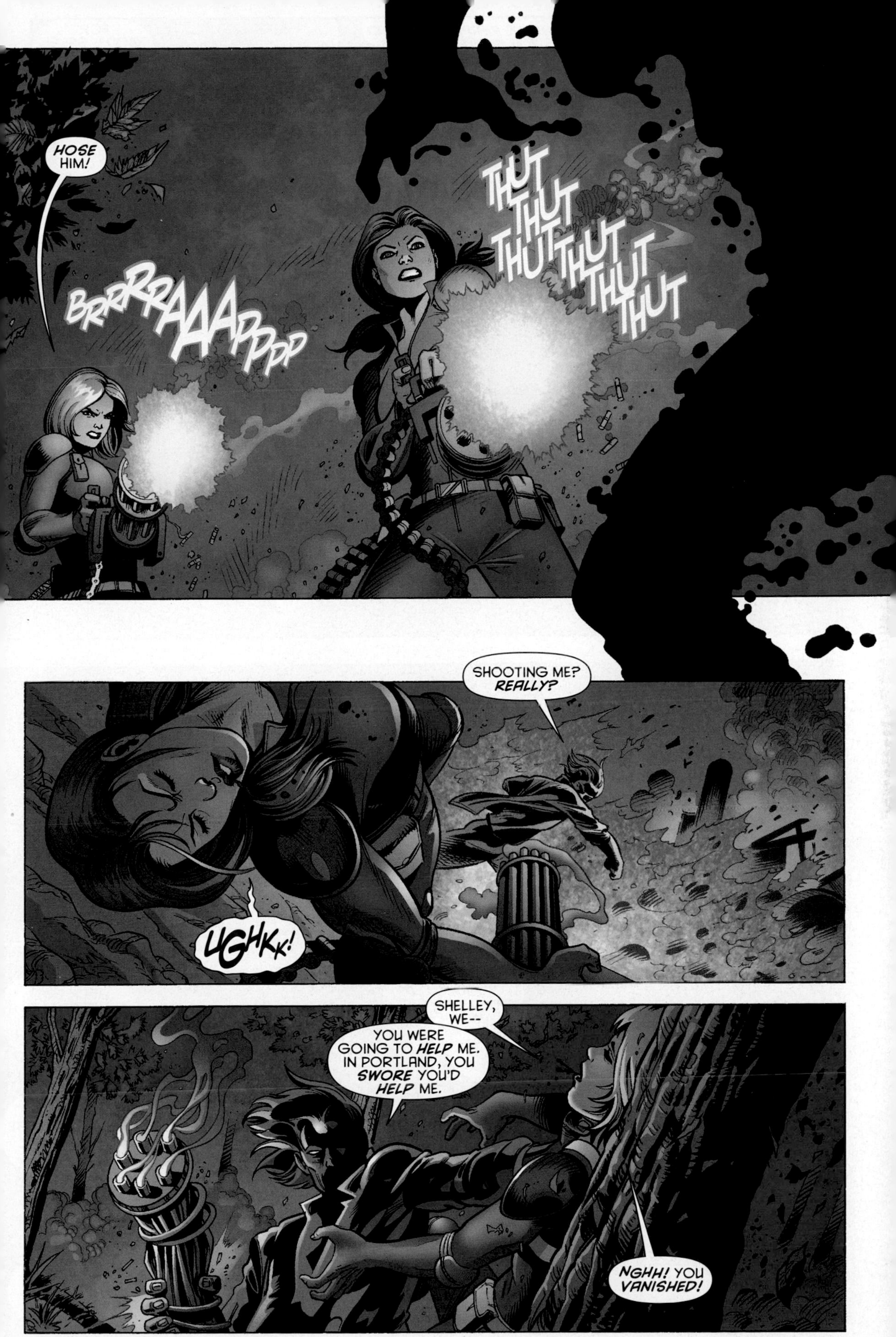
HOSE HIM!
BRRRRAAAAPPPP
THUT THUT THUT THUT THUT THUT
SHOOTING ME? REALLY?
UGHKK!
SHELLEY, WE--
YOU WERE GOING TO HELP ME. IN PORTLAND, YOU SWORE YOU'D HELP ME.
NGHH! YOU VANISHED!

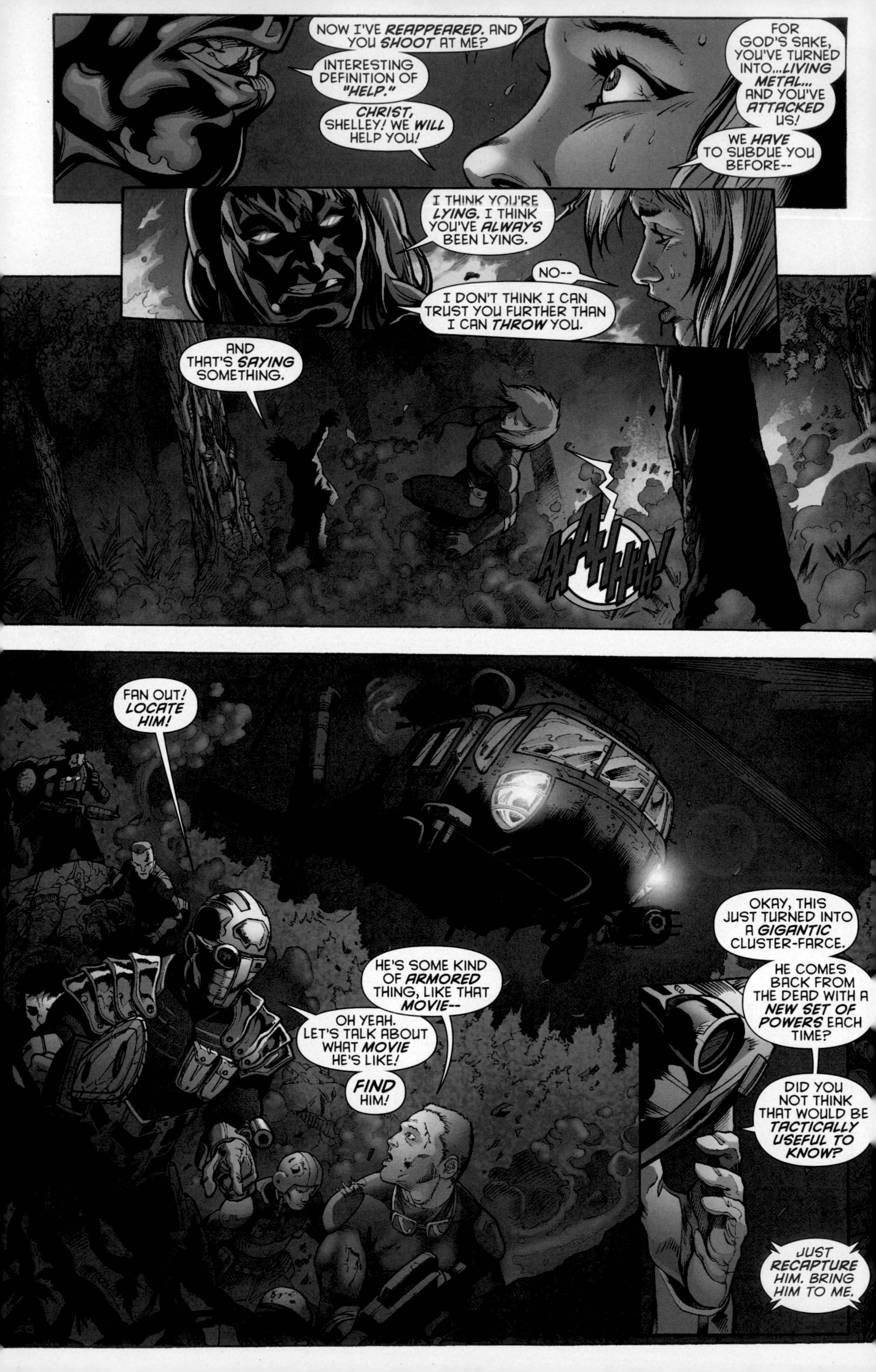
NOW I'VE REAPPEARED, AND YOU SHOOT AT ME?
INTERESTING DEFINITION OF "HELP."
CHRIST, SHELLEY! WE WILL HELP YOU!
FOR GOD'S SAKE, YOU'VE TURNED INTO...LIVING METAL... AND YOU'VE ATTACKED US!
WE HAVE TO SUBDUE YOU BEFORE--
I THINK YOU'RE LYING. I THINK YOU'VE ALWAYS BEEN LYING.
NO--
I DON'T THINK I CAN TRUST YOU FURTHER THAN I CAN THROW YOU.
AND THAT'S SAYING SOMETHING.
AAAHHHH!
FAN OUT! LOCATE HIM!
HE'S SOME KIND OF ARMORED THING, LIKE THAT MOVIE--
OH YEAH. LET'S TALK ABOUT WHAT MOVIE HE'S LIKE!
FIND HIM!
OKAY, THIS JUST TURNED INTO A GIGANTIC CLUSTER-FARCE.
HE COMES BACK FROM THE DEAD WITH A NEW SET OF POWERS EACH TIME?
DID YOU NOT THINK THAT WOULD BE TACTICALLY USEFUL TO KNOW?
JUST RECAPTURE HIM. BRING HIM TO ME.

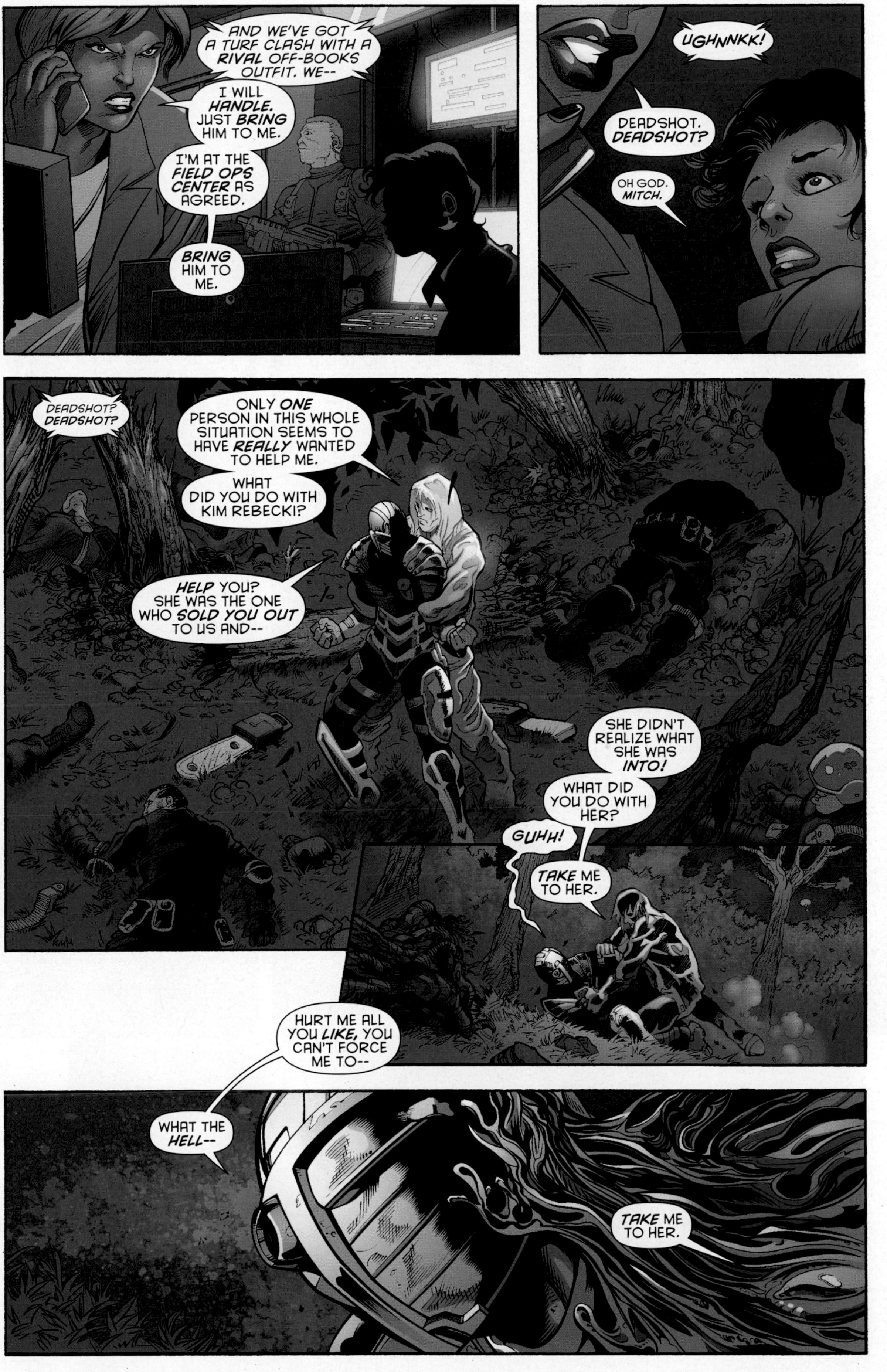
AND WE'VE GOT A TURF CLASH WITH A RIVAL OFF-BOOKS OUTFIT. WE--
I WILL HANDLE. JUST BRING HIM TO ME.
I'M AT THE FIELD OPS CENTER AS AGREED.
BRING HIM TO ME.
UGHNNKK!
DEADSHOT. DEADSHOT?
OH GOD. MITCH.
DEADSHOT? DEADSHOT?
ONLY ONE PERSON IN THIS WHOLE SITUATION SEEMS TO HAVE REALLY WANTED TO HELP ME.
WHAT DID YOU DO WITH KIM REBECKI?
HELP YOU? SHE WAS THE ONE WHO SOLD YOU OUT TO US AND--
SHE DIDN'T REALIZE WHAT SHE WAS INTO!
WHAT DID YOU DO WITH HER?
GUHH!
TAKE ME TO HER.
HURT ME ALL YOU LIKE, YOU CAN'T FORCE ME TO--
WHAT THE HELL--
TAKE ME TO HER.

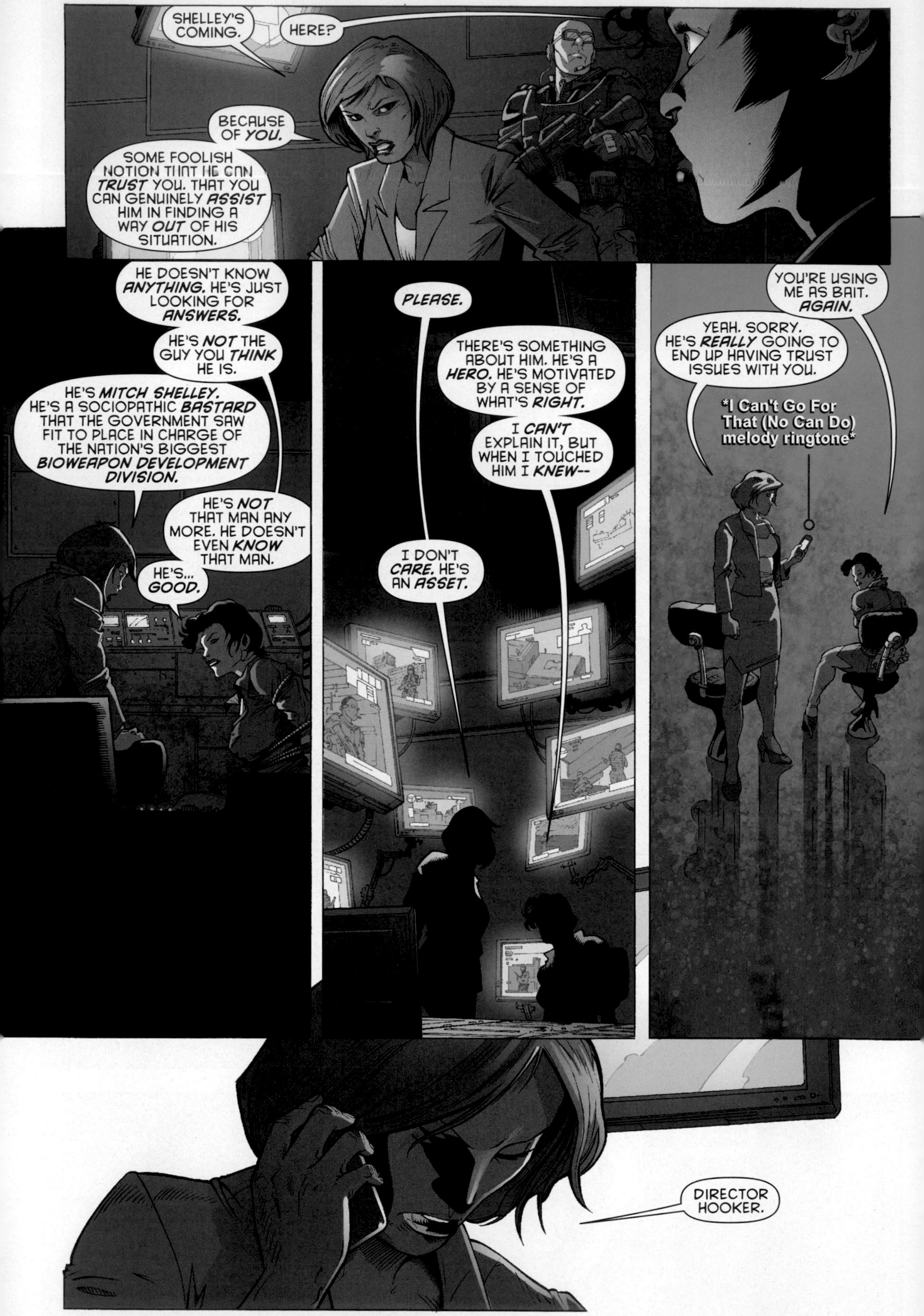
SHELLEY'S COMING.
HERE?
BECAUSE OF YOU.
SOME FOOLISH NOTION THAT HE CAN TRUST YOU. THAT YOU CAN GENUINELY ASSIST HIM IN FINDING A WAY OUT OF HIS SITUATION.
HE DOESN'T KNOW ANYTHING. HE'S JUST LOOKING FOR ANSWERS.
HE'S NOT THE GUY YOU THINK HE IS.
HE'S MITCH SHELLEY. HE'S A SOCIOPATHIC BASTARD THAT THE GOVERNMENT SAW FIT TO PLACE IN CHARGE OF THE NATION'S BIGGEST BIOWEAPON DEVELOPMENT DIVISION.
HE'S NOT THAT MAN ANY MORE. HE DOESN'T EVEN KNOW THAT MAN.
HE'S... GOOD.
PLEASE.
THERE'S SOMETHING ABOUT HIM. HE'S A HERO. HE'S MOTIVATED BY A SENSE OF WHAT'S RIGHT.
I CAN'T EXPLAIN IT, BUT WHEN I TOUCHED HIM I KNEW--
I DON'T CARE. HE'S AN ASSET.
YOU'RE USING ME AS BAIT. AGAIN.
YEAH. SORRY. HE'S REALLY GOING TO END UP HAVING TRUST ISSUES WITH YOU.
I Can't Go For That (No Can Do) melody ringtone
DIRECTOR HOOKER.

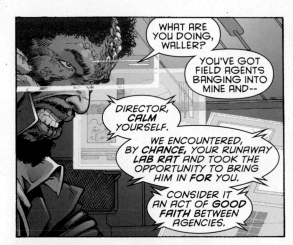

WHAT ARE YOU DOING, WALLER?

YOU'VE GOT FIELD AGENTS BANGING INTO MINE AND--

DIRECTOR, *CALM* YOURSELF.

WE ENCOUNTERED, BY *CHANCE*, YOUR RUNAWAY *LAB RAT* AND TOOK THE OPPORTUNITY TO BRING HIM IN *FOR* YOU.

CONSIDER IT AN ACT OF *GOOD FAITH* BETWEEN AGENCIES.

YOU'RE NOT EVEN CONVINCING *YOURSELF.*

AU CONTRAIRE. WE'RE *RETURNING* YOUR ASSET TO YOU. WE'RE DOING *YOUR* DIRTY WORK FOR YOU.

YOU OUGHT TO BE *GRATEFUL.*

AND *YET...*

CALL YOUR *GIRLS* OFF, DIRECTOR. I WILL DELIVER MITCHELL SHELLEY TO YOU BEFORE *DAY'S END.*

Call ended

Girl From Ipanema melody ringtone

Carrier

All Contacts

Body Doubles Calling

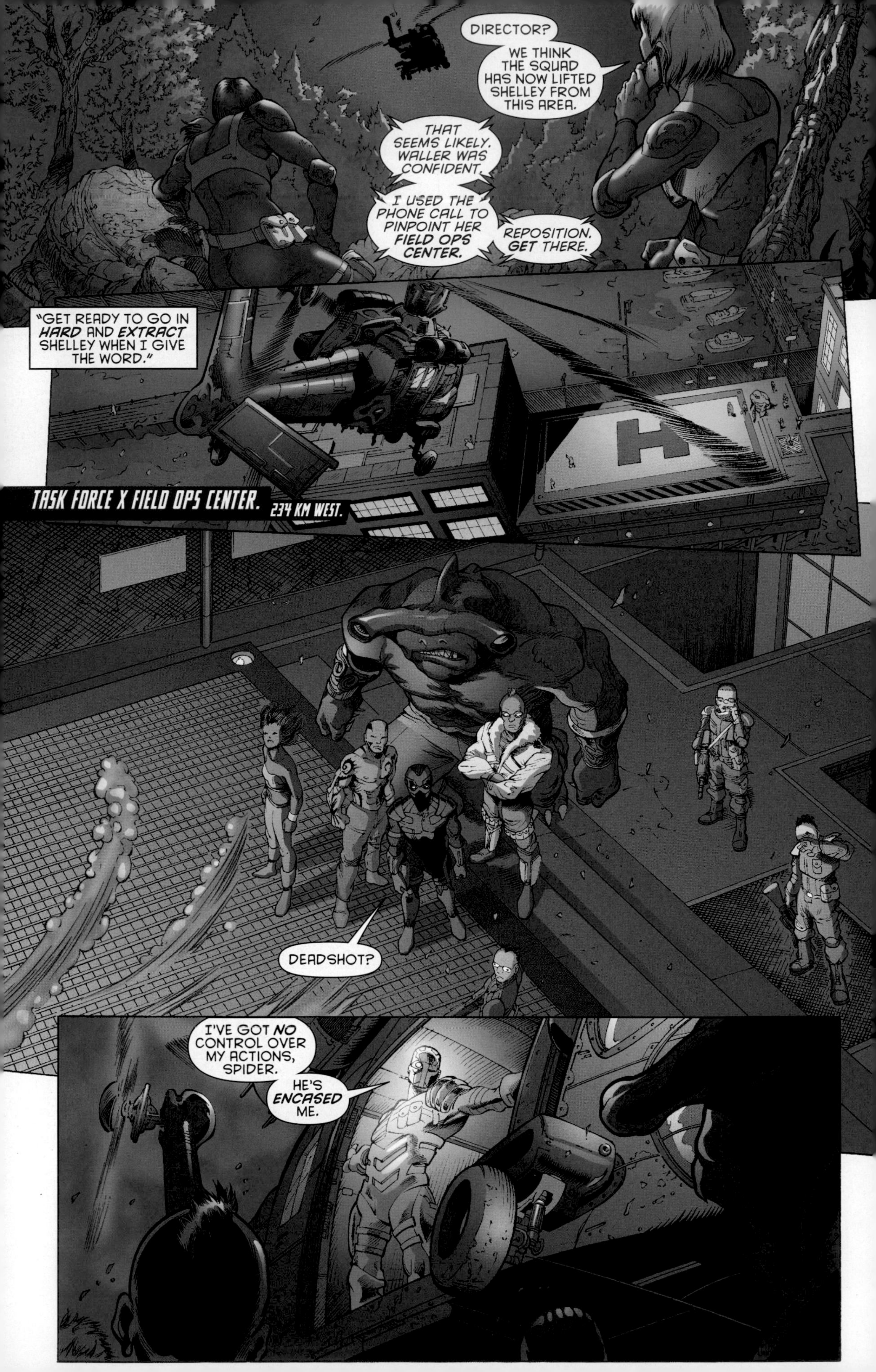
DIRECTOR?
WE THINK THE SQUAD HAS NOW LIFTED SHELLEY FROM THIS AREA.
THAT SEEMS LIKELY. WALLER WAS CONFIDENT.
I USED THE PHONE CALL TO PINPOINT HER FIELD OPS CENTER.
REPOSITION. GET THERE.
"GET READY TO GO IN HARD AND EXTRACT SHELLEY WHEN I GIVE THE WORD."
TASK FORCE X FIELD OPS CENTER. 234 KM WEST.
DEADSHOT?
I'VE GOT NO CONTROL OVER MY ACTIONS, SPIDER.
HE'S ENCASED ME.

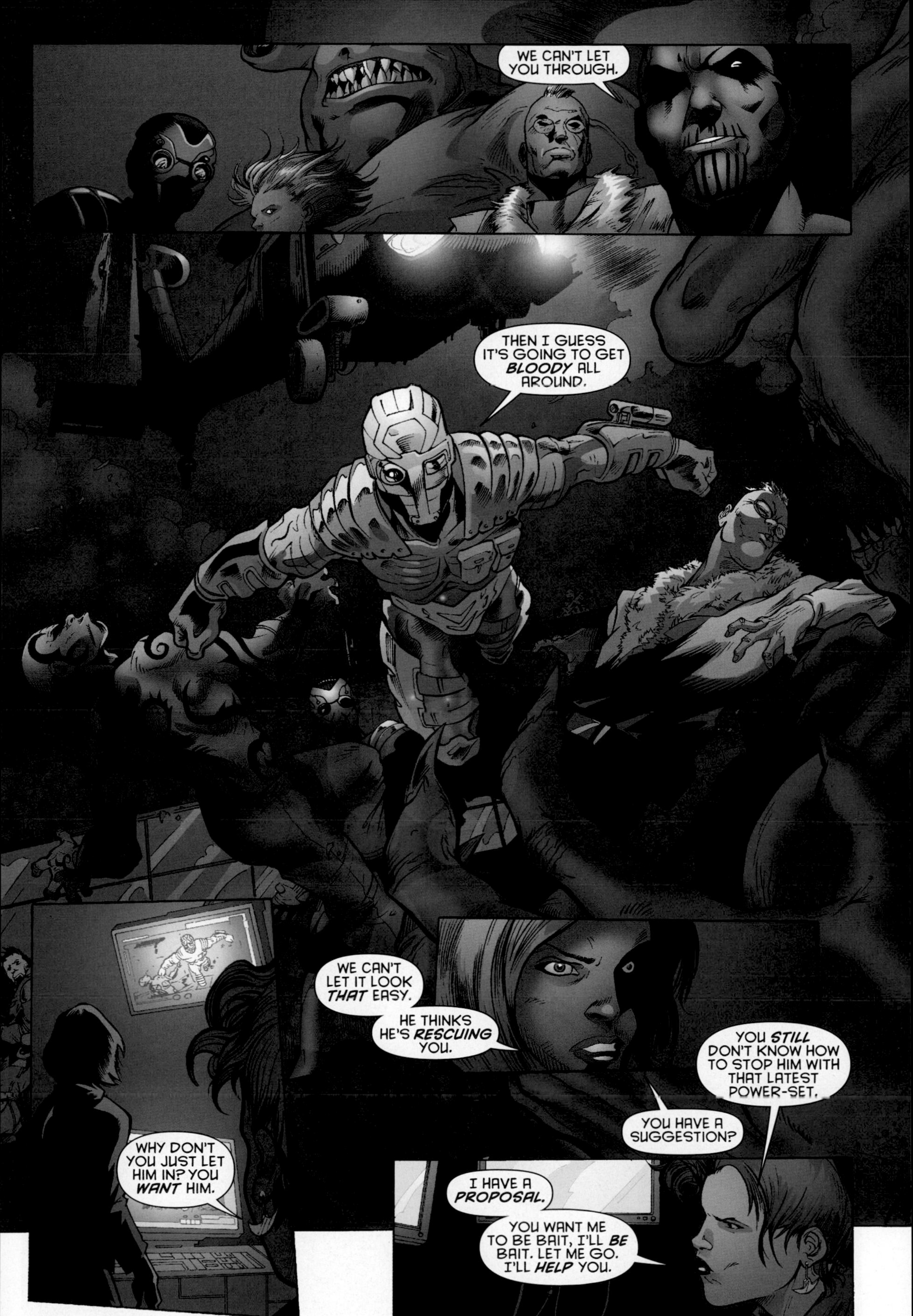
WE CAN'T LET YOU THROUGH.
THEN I GUESS IT'S GOING TO GET BLOODY ALL AROUND.
WHY DON'T YOU JUST LET HIM IN? YOU WANT HIM.
WE CAN'T LET IT LOOK THAT EASY.
HE THINKS HE'S RESCUING YOU.
YOU STILL DON'T KNOW HOW TO STOP HIM WITH THAT LATEST POWER-SET.
YOU HAVE A SUGGESTION?
I HAVE A PROPOSAL.
YOU WANT ME TO BE BAIT, I'LL BE BAIT. LET ME GO. I'LL HELP YOU.

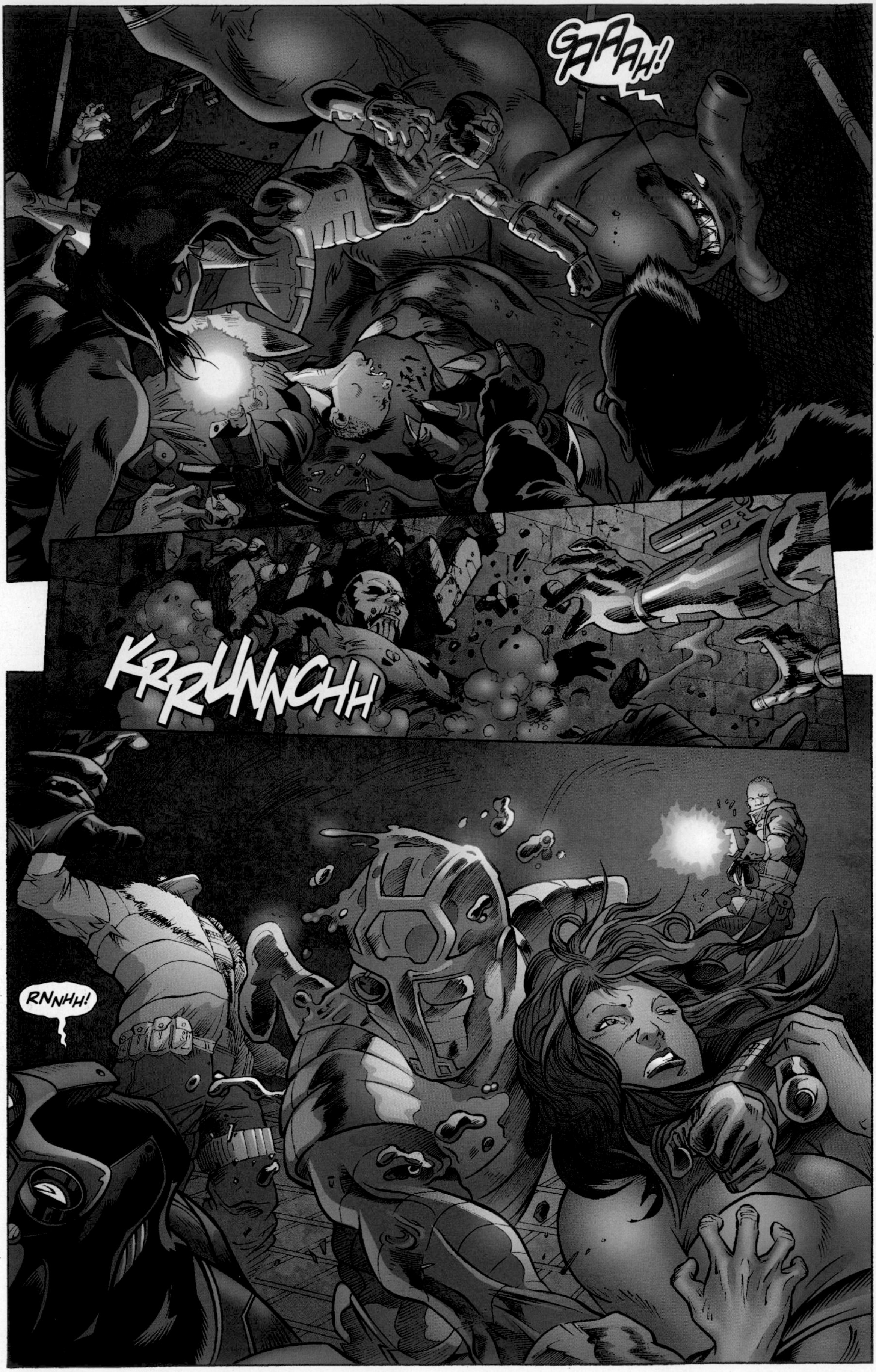
GAAAH!
KRRUNNCHH
RNNHH!

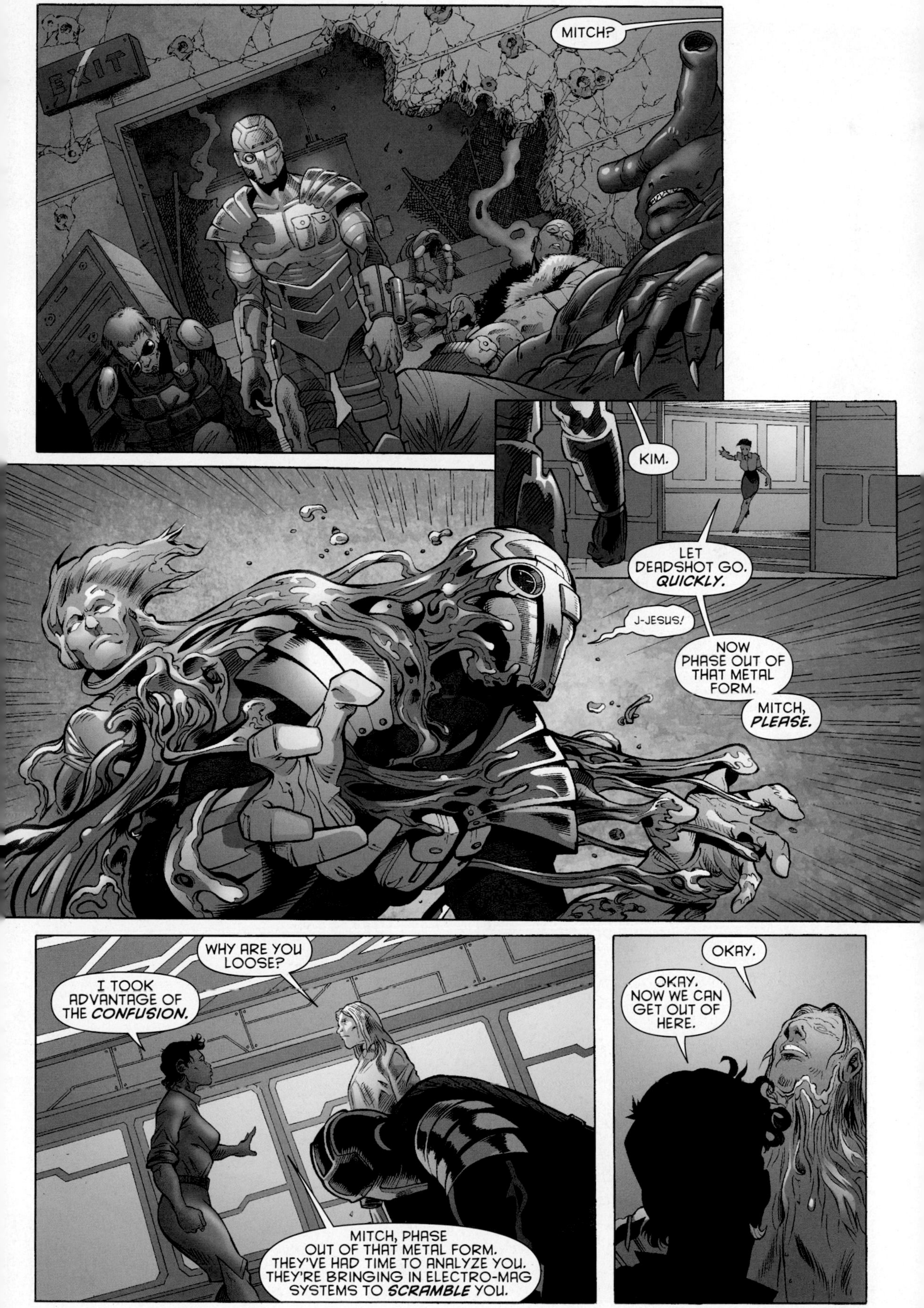

MITCH?
KIM.
LET DEADSHOT GO. *QUICKLY.*
J-JESUS!
NOW PHASE OUT OF THAT METAL FORM.
MITCH, *PLEASE.*
WHY ARE YOU LOOSE?
I TOOK ADVANTAGE OF THE *CONFUSION.*
MITCH, PHASE OUT OF THAT METAL FORM. THEY'VE HAD TIME TO ANALYZE YOU. THEY'RE BRINGING IN ELECTRO-MAG SYSTEMS TO *SCRAMBLE* YOU.
OKAY.
OKAY. NOW WE CAN GET OUT OF HERE.

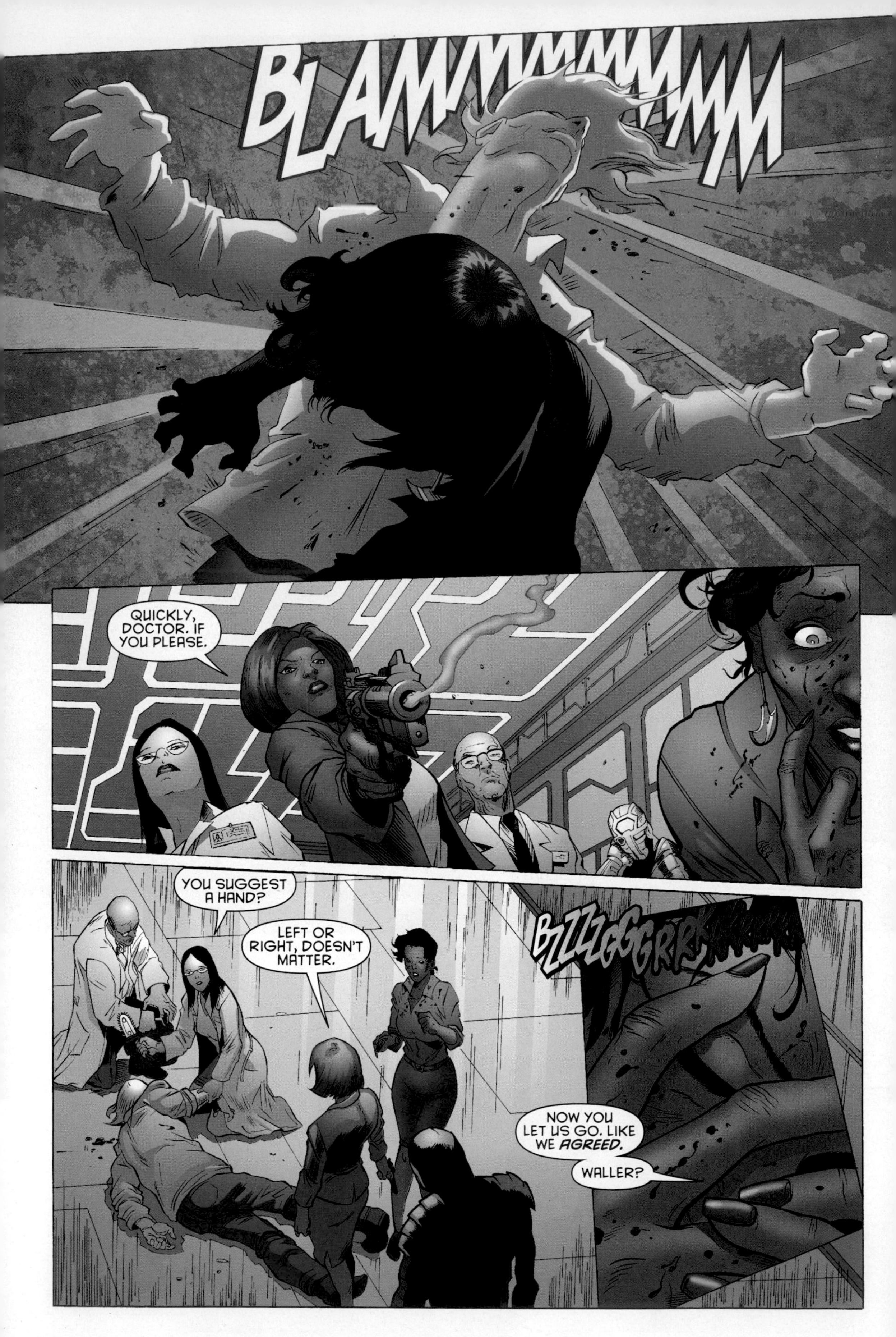
BLAMMMMMMM
QUICKLY, DOCTOR. IF YOU PLEASE.
YOU SUGGEST A HAND?
LEFT OR RIGHT, DOESN'T MATTER.
BZZZGGGRRRRRRR
NOW YOU LET US GO. LIKE WE AGREED.
WALLER?

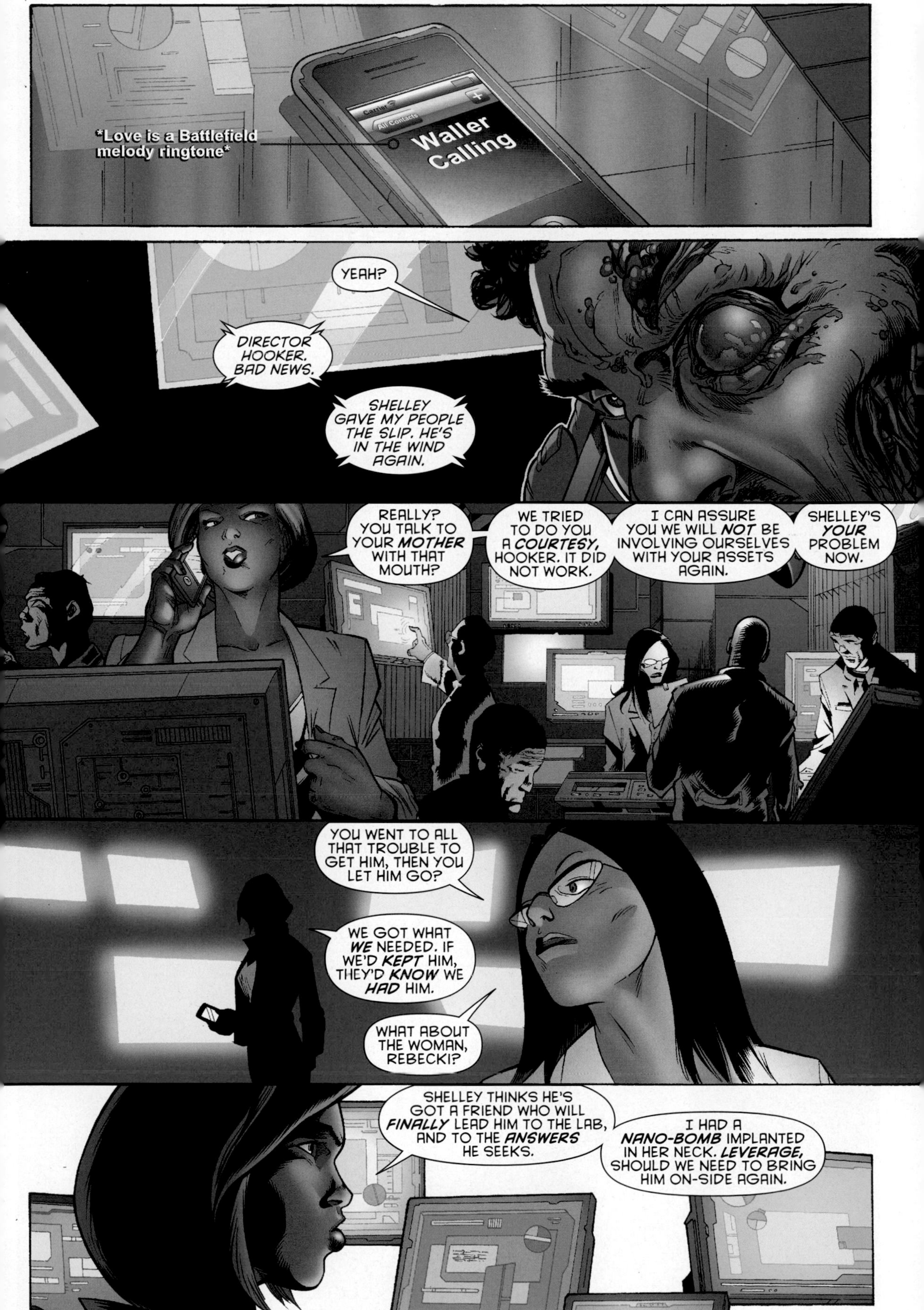
Love is a Battlefield melody ringtone
Carrier
All Contacts
Waller Calling
YEAH?
DIRECTOR HOOKER. BAD NEWS.
SHELLEY GAVE MY PEOPLE THE SLIP. HE'S IN THE WIND AGAIN.
REALLY? YOU TALK TO YOUR MOTHER WITH THAT MOUTH?
WE TRIED TO DO YOU A COURTESY, HOOKER. IT DID NOT WORK.
I CAN ASSURE YOU WE WILL NOT BE INVOLVING OURSELVES WITH YOUR ASSETS AGAIN.
SHELLEY'S YOUR PROBLEM NOW.
YOU WENT TO ALL THAT TROUBLE TO GET HIM, THEN YOU LET HIM GO?
WE GOT WHAT WE NEEDED. IF WE'D KEPT HIM, THEY'D KNOW WE HAD HIM.
WHAT ABOUT THE WOMAN, REBECKI?
SHELLEY THINKS HE'S GOT A FRIEND WHO WILL FINALLY LEAD HIM TO THE LAB, AND TO THE ANSWERS HE SEEKS.
I HAD A NANO-BOMB IMPLANTED IN HER NECK. LEVERAGE, SHOULD WE NEED TO BRING HIM ON-SIDE AGAIN.

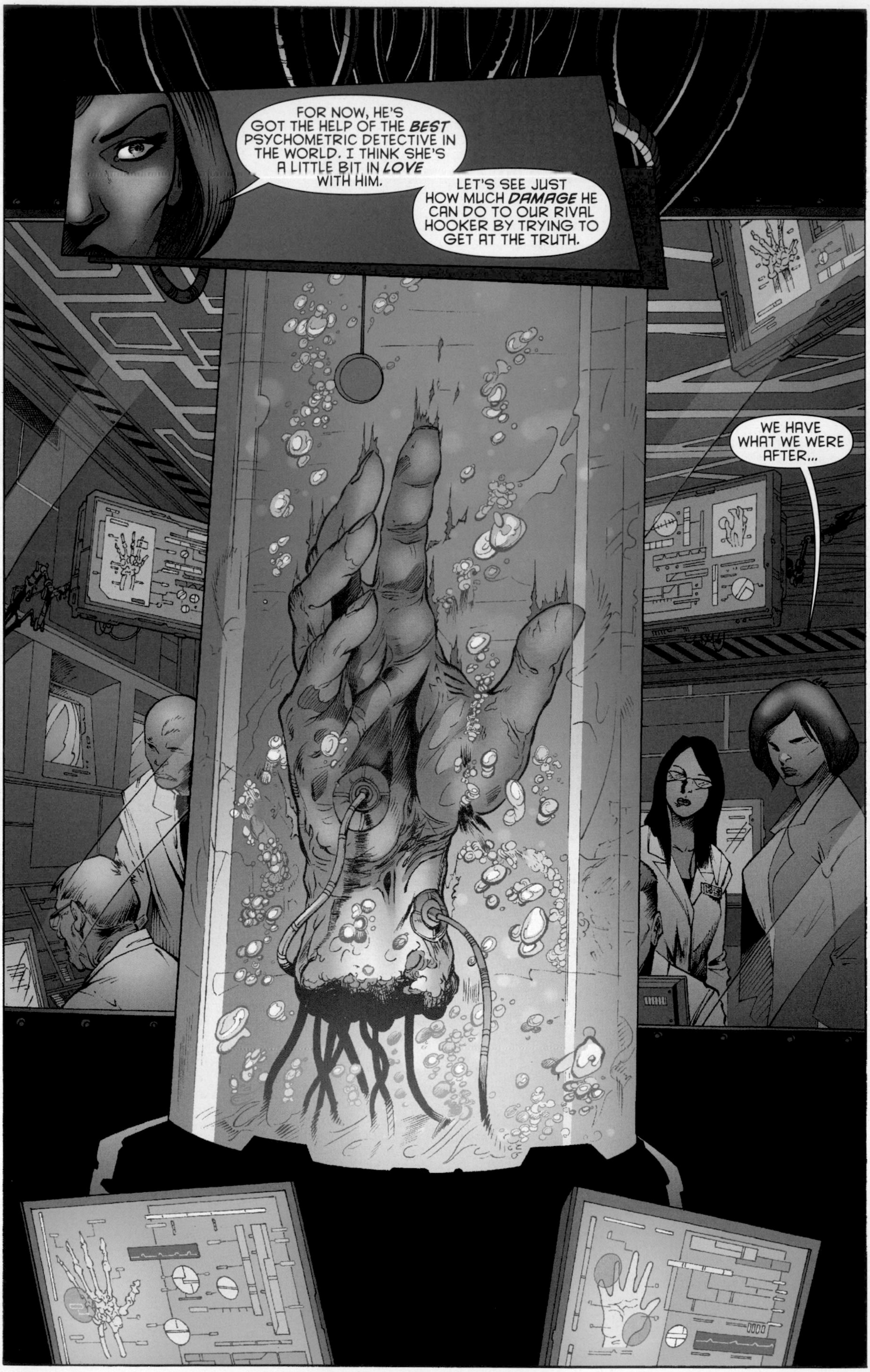
FOR NOW, HE'S GOT THE HELP OF THE BEST PSYCHOMETRIC DETECTIVE IN THE WORLD. I THINK SHE'S A LITTLE BIT IN LOVE WITH HIM.
LET'S SEE JUST HOW MUCH DAMAGE HE CAN DO TO OUR RIVAL HOOKER BY TRYING TO GET AT THE TRUTH.
WE HAVE WHAT WE WERE AFTER...

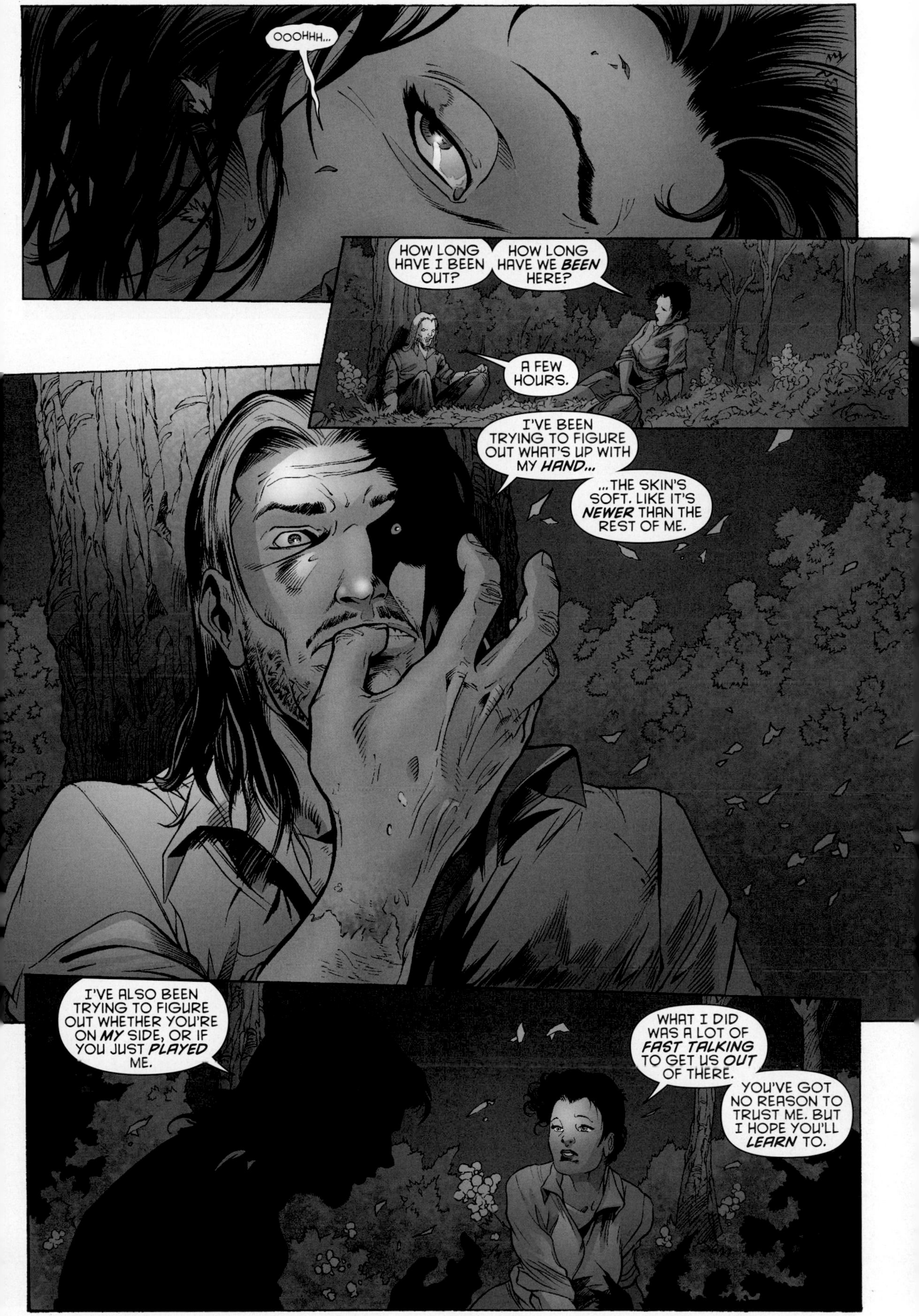

OOOHHH...
HOW LONG HAVE I BEEN OUT?
HOW LONG HAVE WE *BEEN* HERE?
A FEW HOURS.
I'VE BEEN TRYING TO FIGURE OUT WHAT'S UP WITH MY *HAND*...
...THE SKIN'S SOFT. LIKE IT'S *NEWER* THAN THE REST OF ME.
I'VE ALSO BEEN TRYING TO FIGURE OUT WHETHER YOU'RE ON *MY* SIDE, OR IF YOU JUST *PLAYED* ME.
WHAT I DID WAS A LOT OF *FAST TALKING* TO GET US *OUT* OF THERE.
YOU'VE GOT NO REASON TO TRUST ME. BUT I HOPE YOU'LL *LEARN* TO.

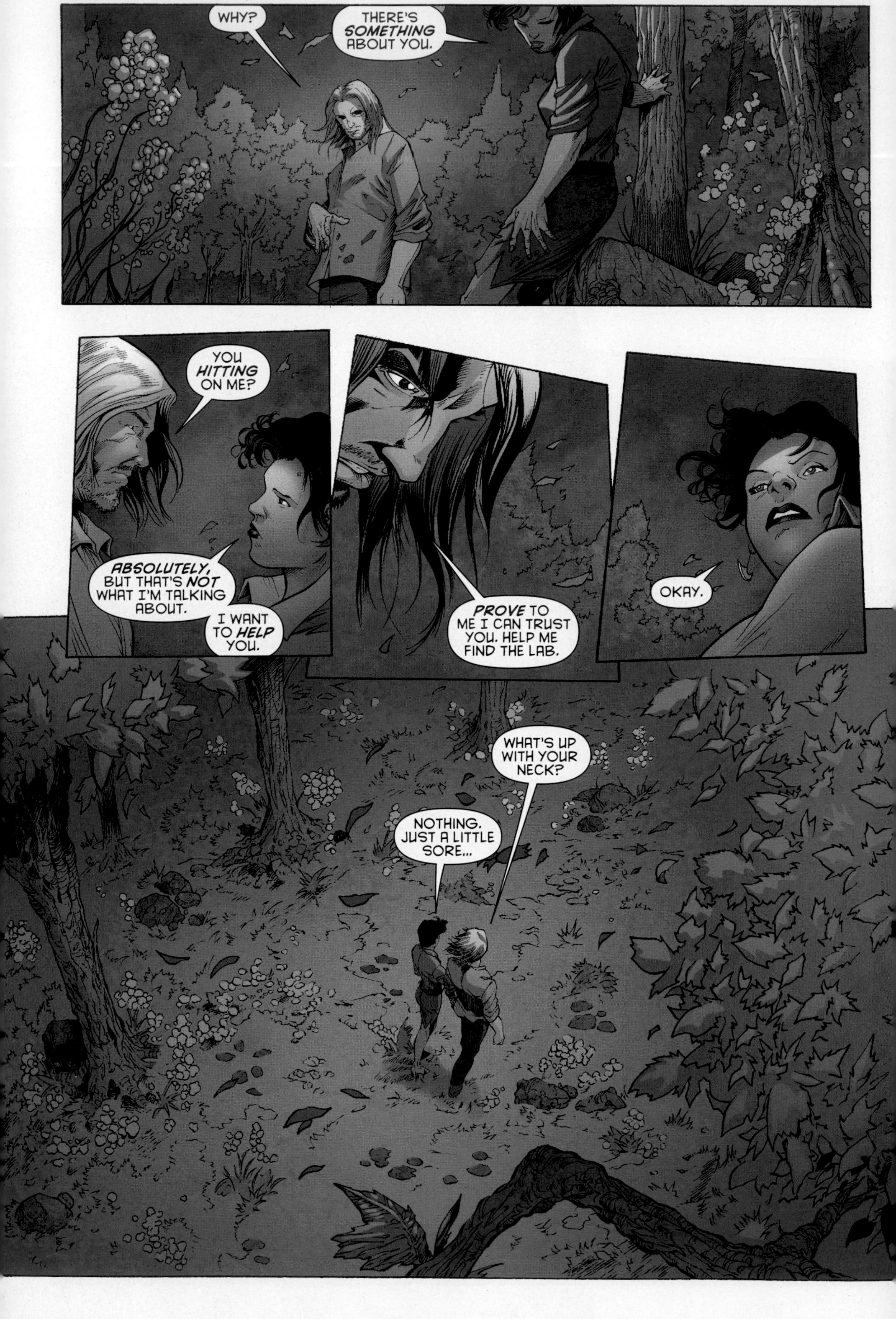
WHY?
THERE'S SOMETHING ABOUT YOU.
YOU HITTING ON ME?
ABSOLUTELY, BUT THAT'S NOT WHAT I'M TALKING ABOUT.
I WANT TO HELP YOU.
PROVE TO ME I CAN TRUST YOU. HELP ME FIND THE LAB.
OKAY.
WHAT'S UP WITH YOUR NECK?
NOTHING. JUST A LITTLE SORE...

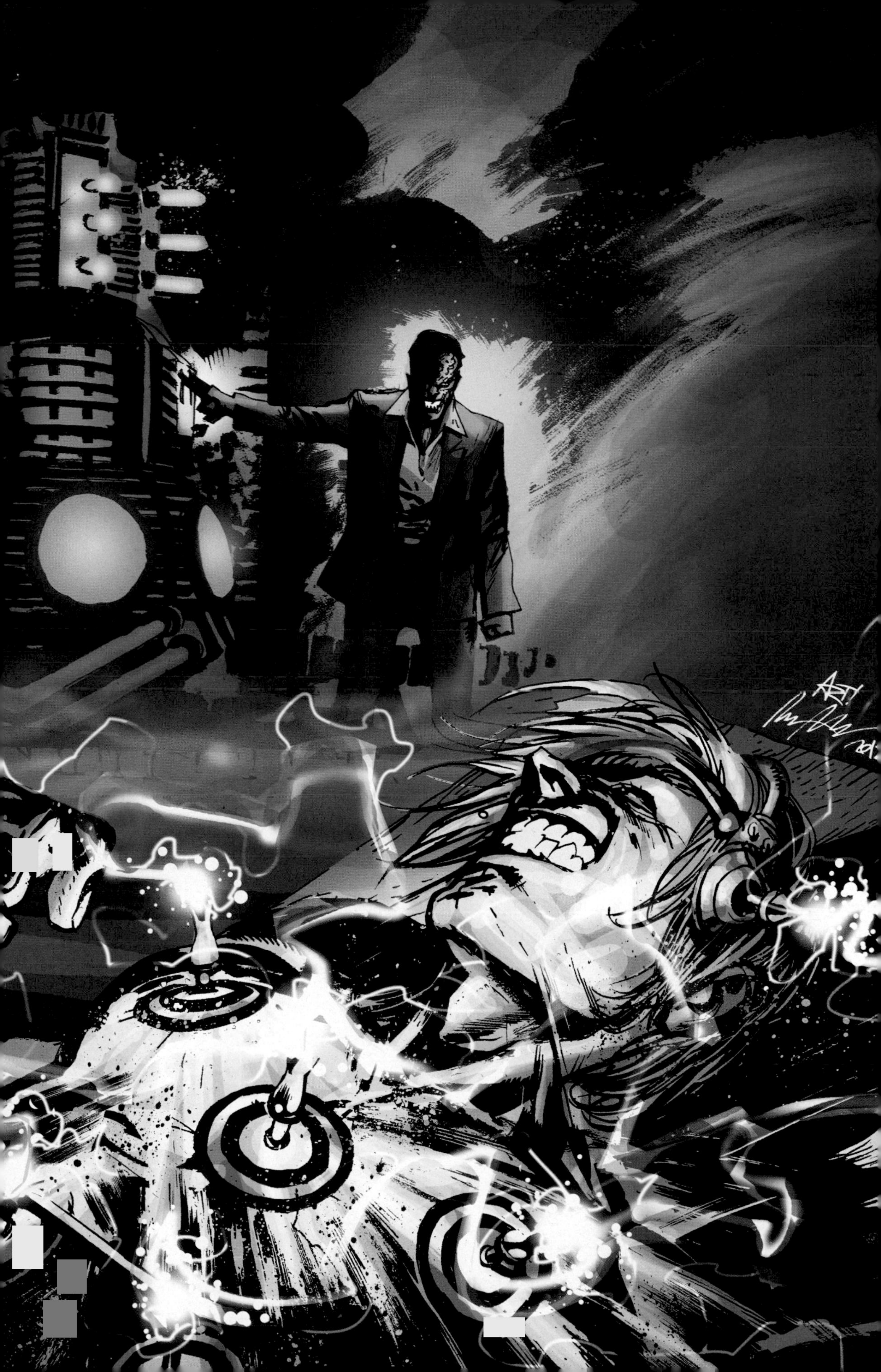

HEAVEN CAN WAIT

DAN ABNETT & ANDY LANNING
writers

JESUS SAIZ
artist

cover art by
RAFAEL ALBUQUERQUE with ART LYON

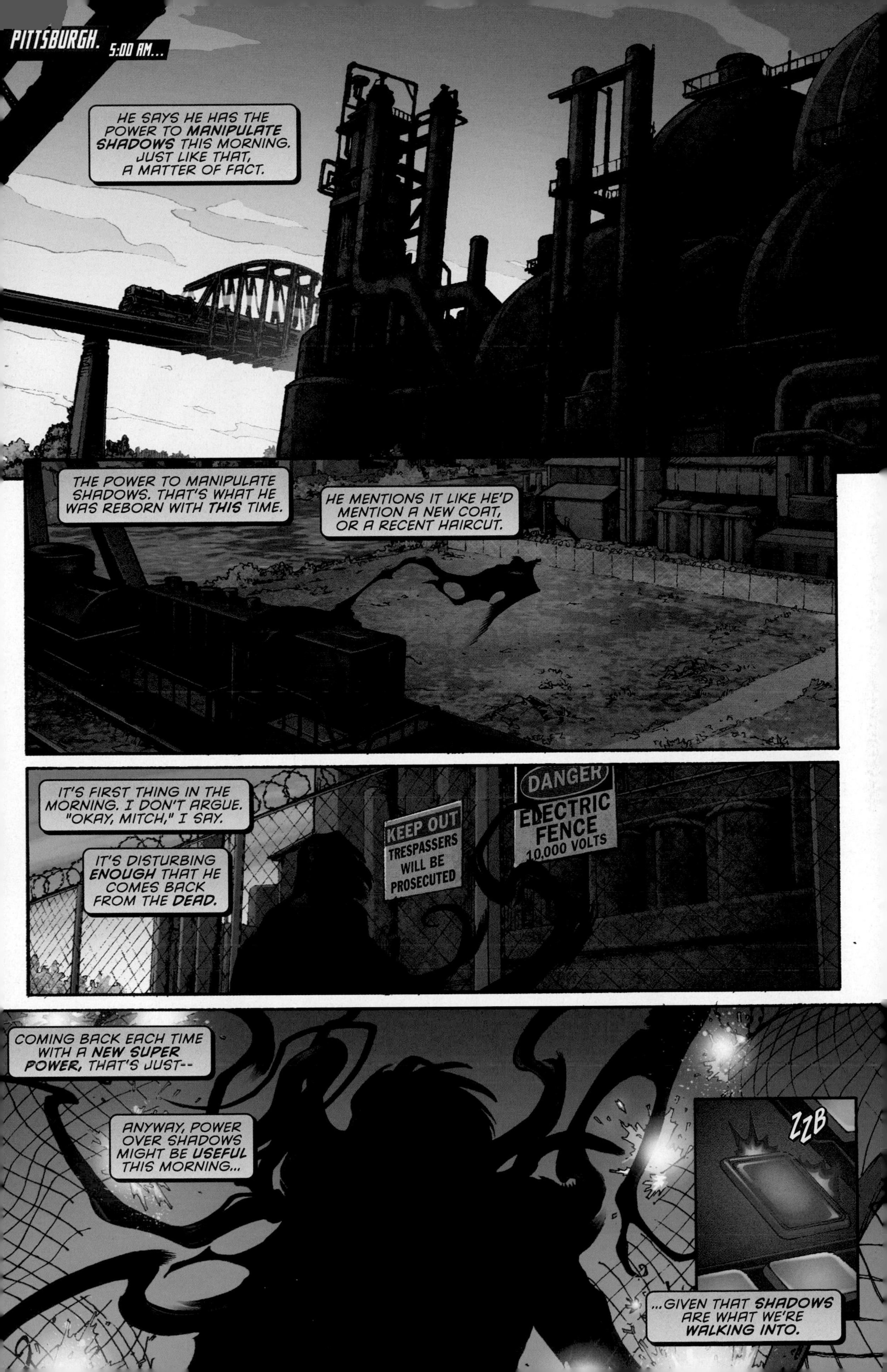
PITTSBURGH. 5:00 AM...
HE SAYS HE HAS THE POWER TO MANIPULATE SHADOWS THIS MORNING. JUST LIKE THAT, A MATTER OF FACT.
THE POWER TO MANIPULATE SHADOWS. THAT'S WHAT HE WAS REBORN WITH THIS TIME.
HE MENTIONS IT LIKE HE'D MENTION A NEW COAT, OR A RECENT HAIRCUT.
IT'S FIRST THING IN THE MORNING. I DON'T ARGUE. "OKAY, MITCH," I SAY.
IT'S DISTURBING ENOUGH THAT HE COMES BACK FROM THE DEAD.
KEEP OUT
TRESPASSERS WILL BE PROSECUTED
DANGER
ELECTRIC FENCE
10,000 VOLTS
COMING BACK EACH TIME WITH A NEW SUPER POWER, THAT'S JUST--
ANYWAY, POWER OVER SHADOWS MIGHT BE USEFUL THIS MORNING...
ZZB
...GIVEN THAT SHADOWS ARE WHAT WE'RE WALKING INTO.

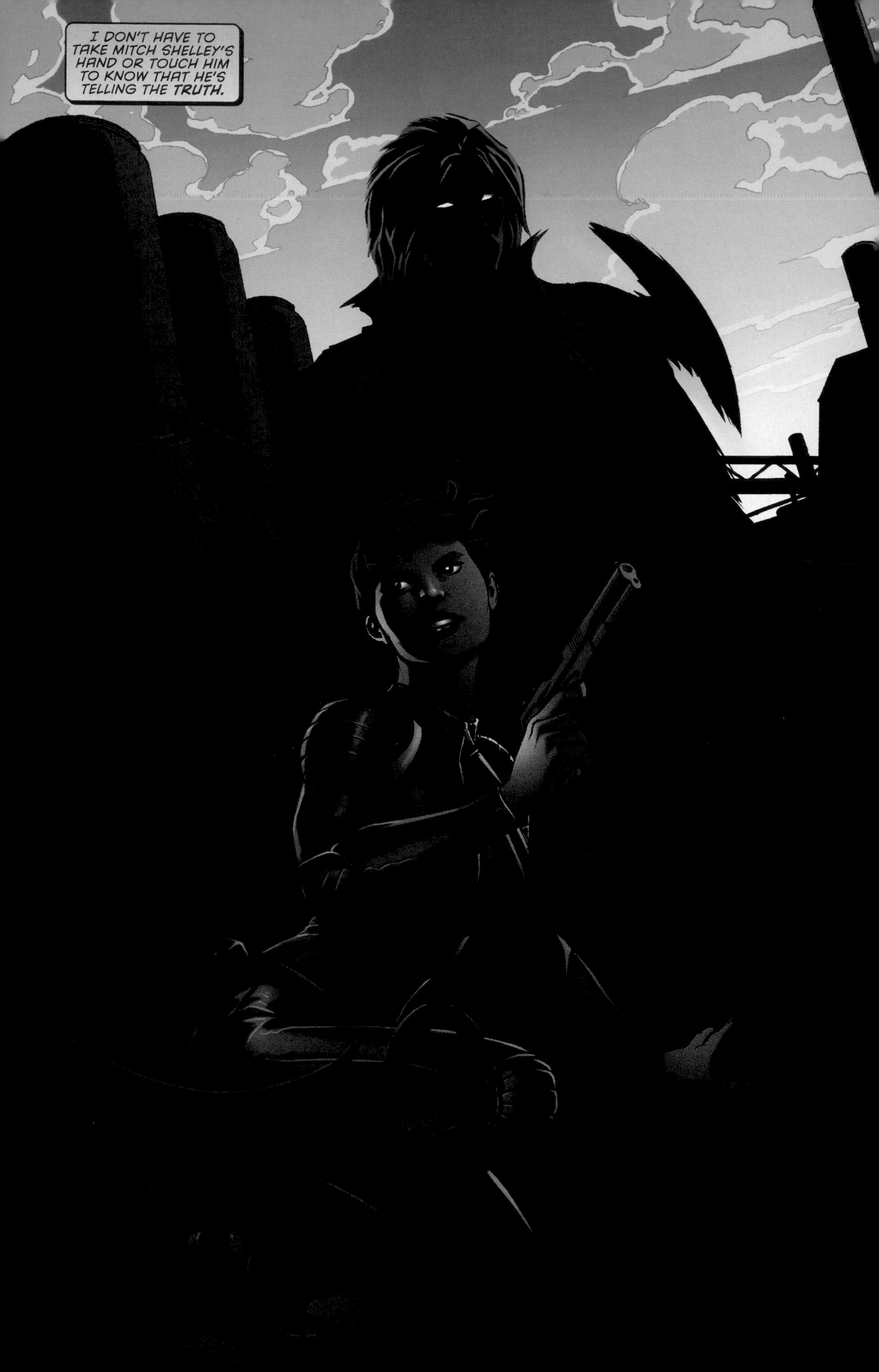
I DON'T HAVE TO TAKE MITCH SHELLEY'S HAND OR TOUCH HIM TO KNOW THAT HE'S TELLING THE TRUTH.

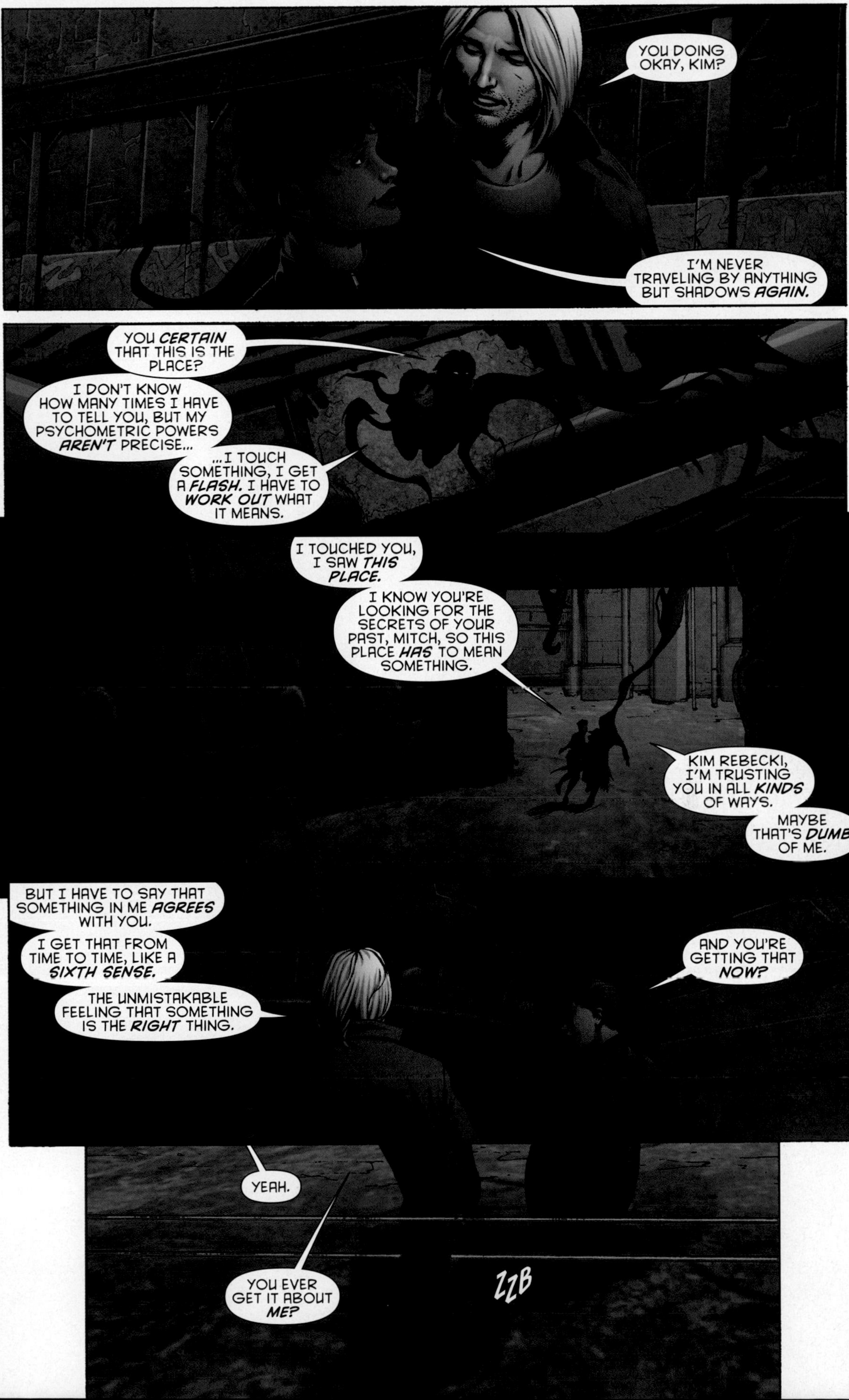
YOU DOING OKAY, KIM?
I'M NEVER TRAVELING BY ANYTHING BUT SHADOWS AGAIN.
YOU CERTAIN THAT THIS IS THE PLACE?
I DON'T KNOW HOW MANY TIMES I HAVE TO TELL YOU, BUT MY PSYCHOMETRIC POWERS AREN'T PRECISE...
...I TOUCH SOMETHING, I GET A FLASH. I HAVE TO WORK OUT WHAT IT MEANS.
I TOUCHED YOU, I SAW THIS PLACE.
I KNOW YOU'RE LOOKING FOR THE SECRETS OF YOUR PAST, MITCH, SO THIS PLACE HAS TO MEAN SOMETHING.
KIM REBECKI, I'M TRUSTING YOU IN ALL KINDS OF WAYS.
MAYBE THAT'S DUMB OF ME.
BUT I HAVE TO SAY THAT SOMETHING IN ME AGREES WITH YOU.
I GET THAT FROM TIME TO TIME, LIKE A SIXTH SENSE.
THE UNMISTAKABLE FEELING THAT SOMETHING IS THE RIGHT THING.
AND YOU'RE GETTING THAT NOW?
YEAH.
YOU EVER GET IT ABOUT ME?
ZZB

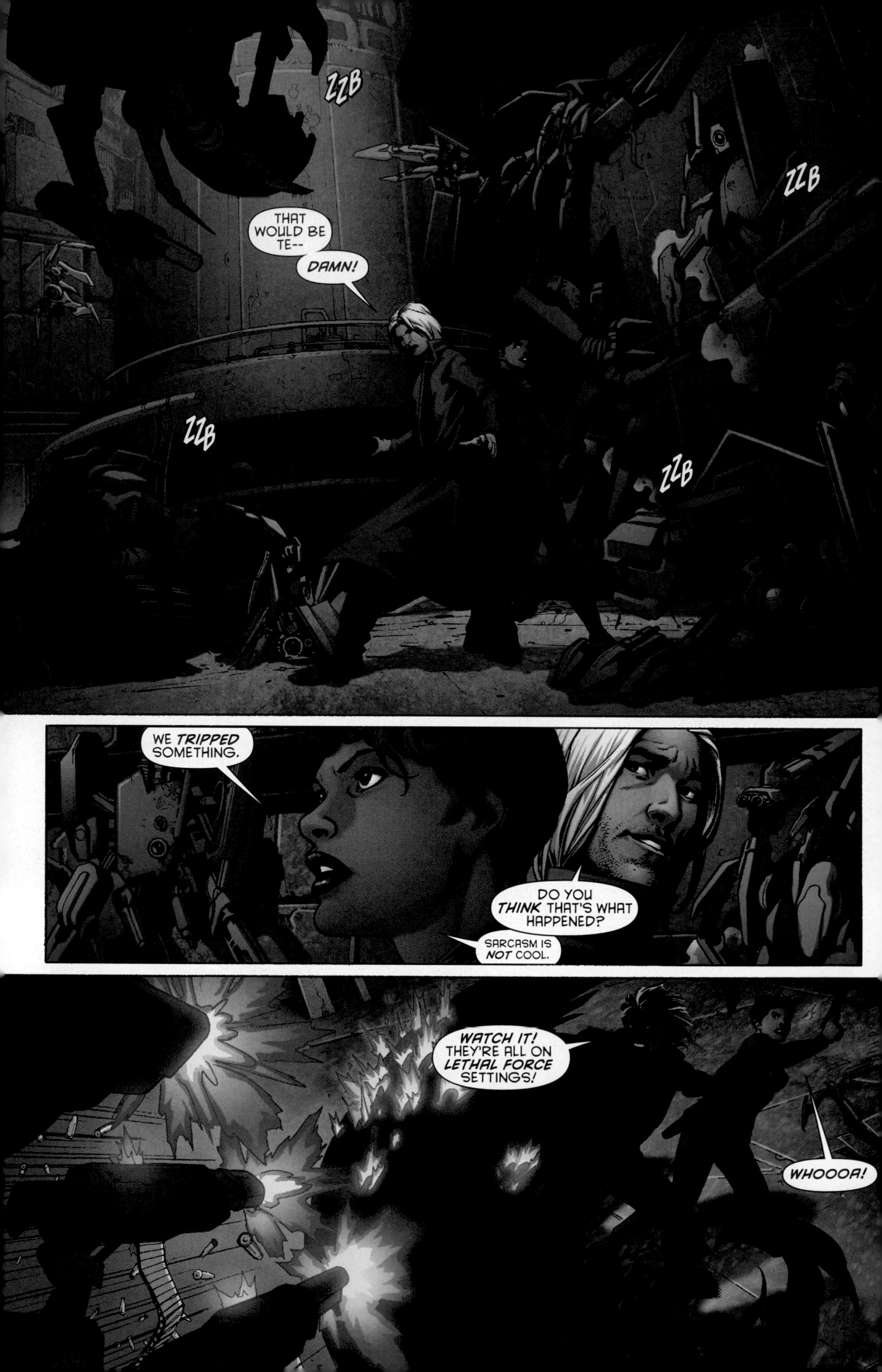
ZZB
THAT WOULD BE TE--
DAMN!
ZZB
ZZB
ZZB
WE TRIPPED SOMETHING.
DO YOU THINK THAT'S WHAT HAPPENED?
SARCASM IS NOT COOL.
WATCH IT! THEY'RE ALL ON LETHAL FORCE SETTINGS!
WHOOOA!

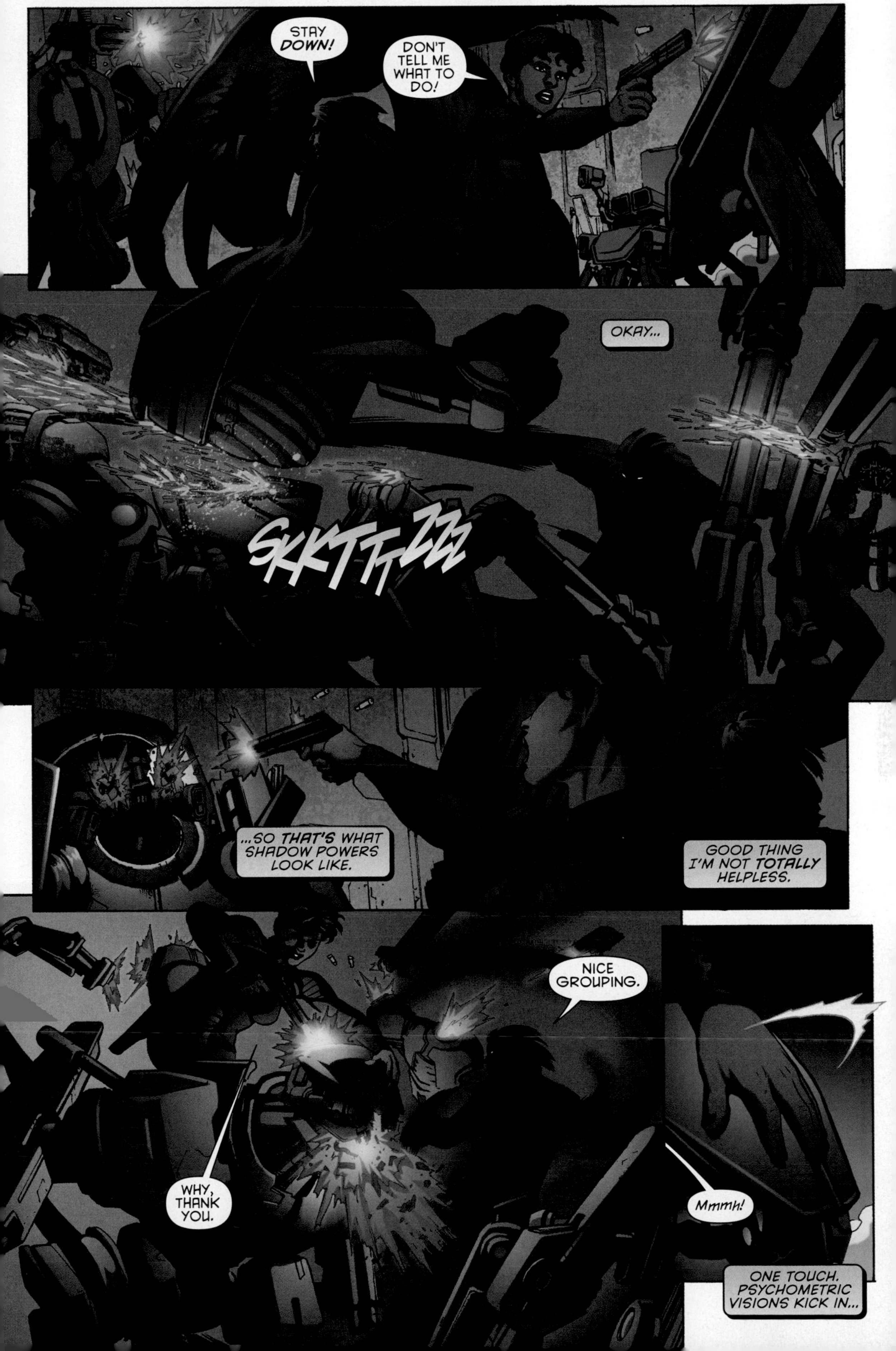
STAY DOWN!
DON'T TELL ME WHAT TO DO!
OKAY...
SKKTTTZZZ
...SO THAT'S WHAT SHADOW POWERS LOOK LIKE.
GOOD THING I'M NOT TOTALLY HELPLESS.
NICE GROUPING.
WHY, THANK YOU.
Mmmh!
ONE TOUCH. PSYCHOMETRIC VISIONS KICK IN...

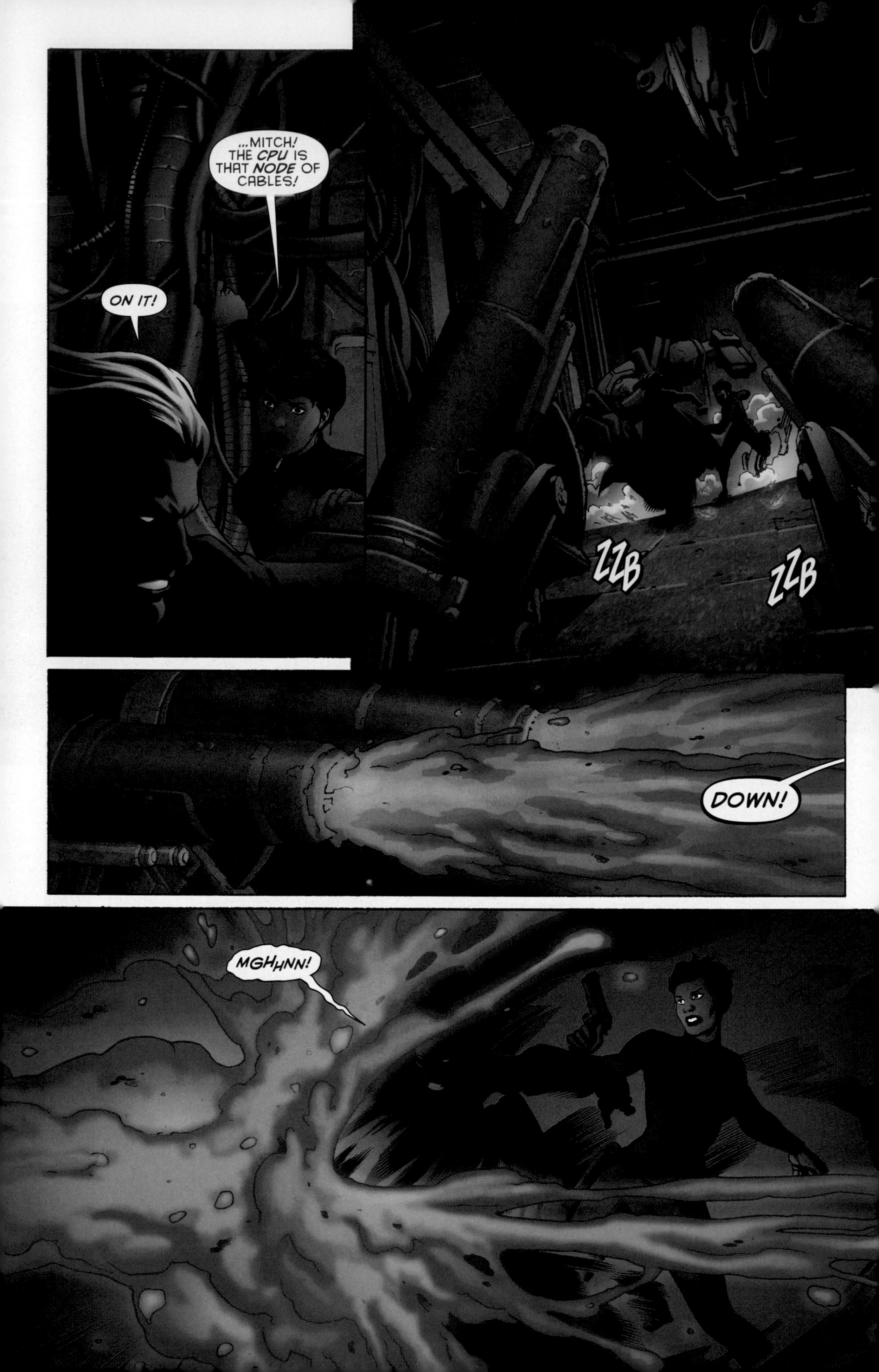
...MITCH! THE CPU IS THAT NODE OF CABLES!
ON IT!
ZZB
ZZB
DOWN!
MGHHNN!

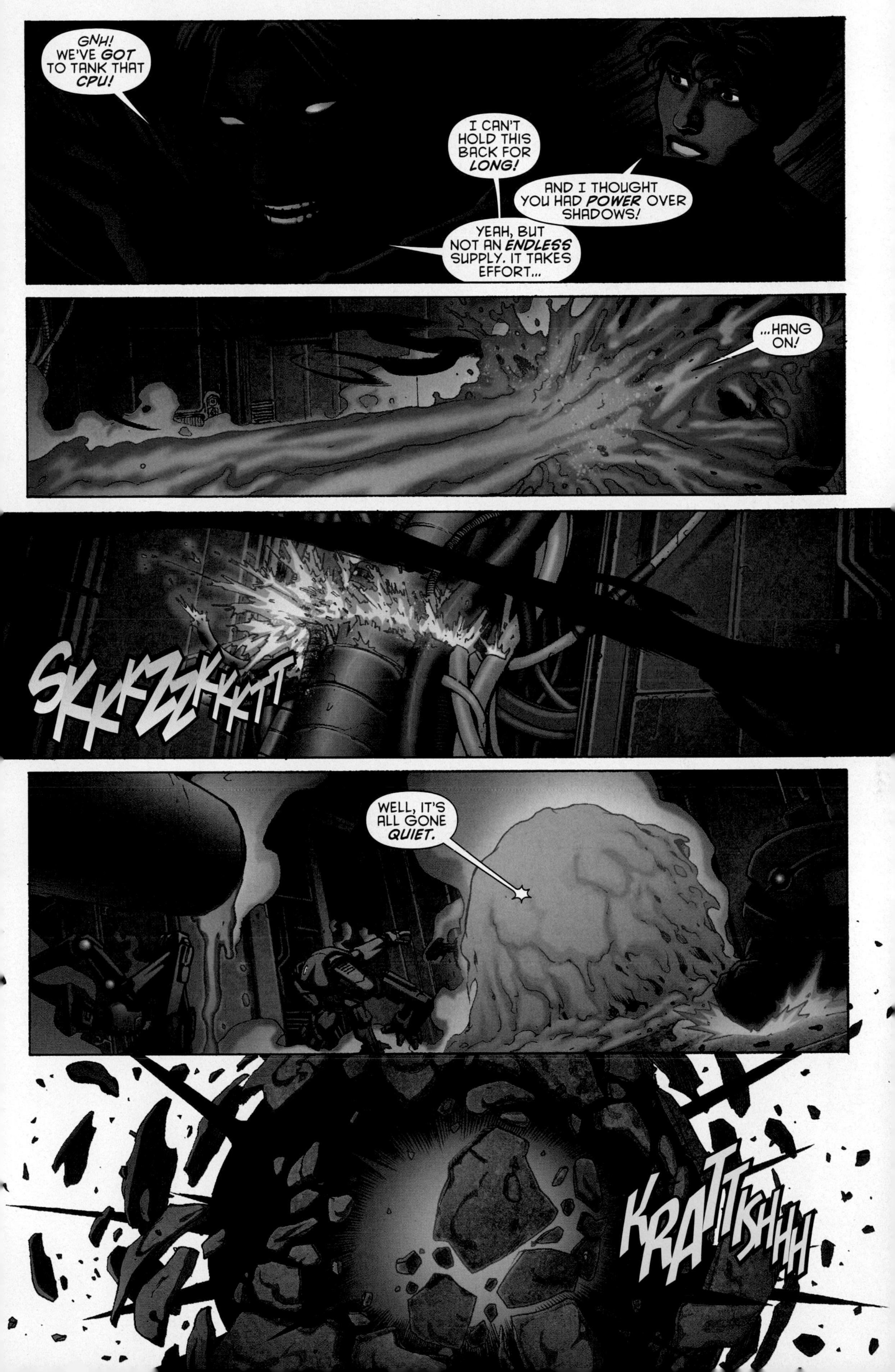
GNH! WE'VE GOT TO TANK THAT CPU!
I CAN'T HOLD THIS BACK FOR LONG!
AND I THOUGHT YOU HAD POWER OVER SHADOWS!
YEAH, BUT NOT AN ENDLESS SUPPLY. IT TAKES EFFORT...
...HANG ON!
SKKKZZKKKTT
WELL, IT'S ALL GONE QUIET.
KRATTTSHHH

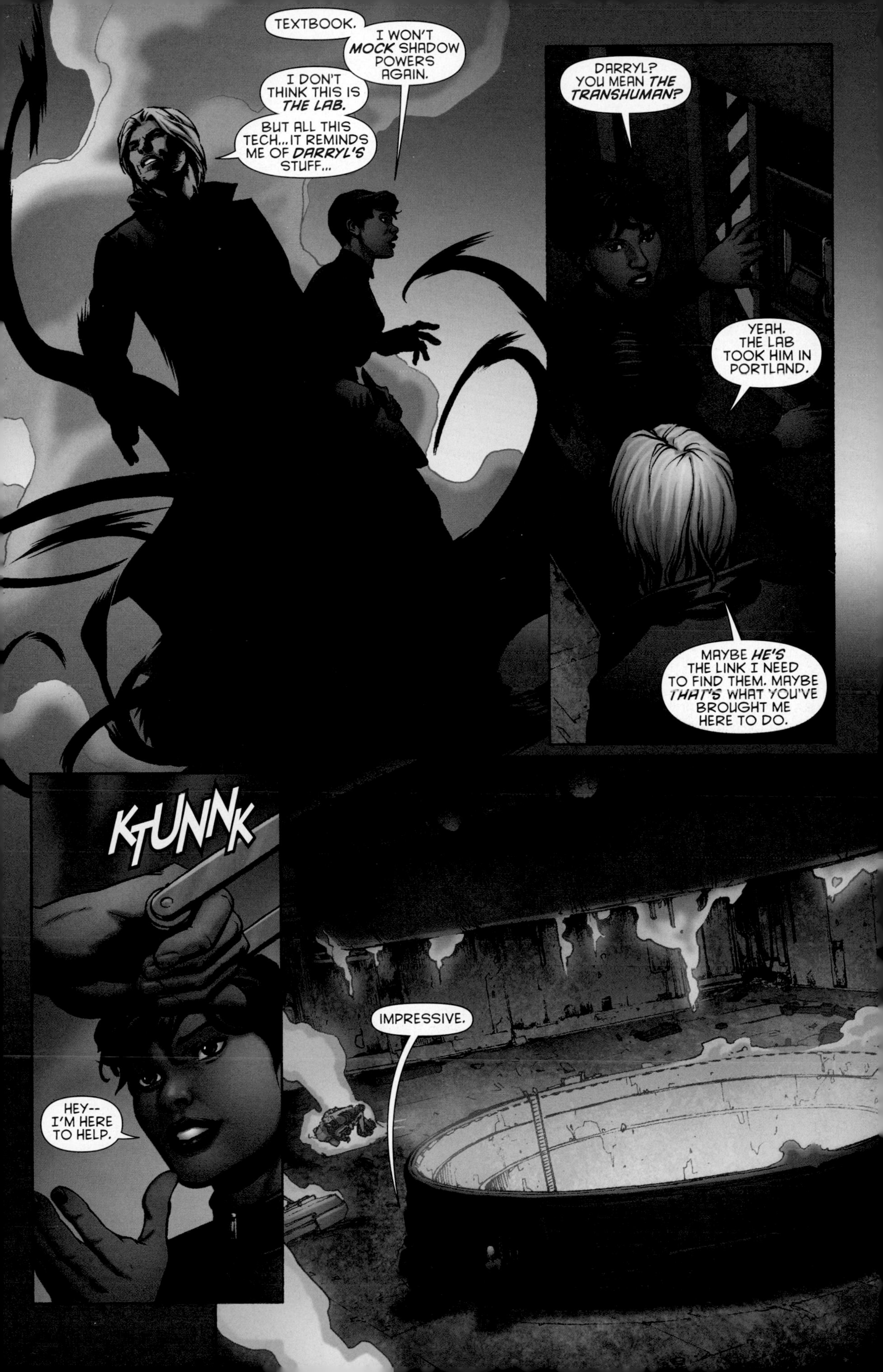

TEXTBOOK.
I WON'T *MOCK* SHADOW POWERS AGAIN.
I DON'T THINK THIS IS *THE LAB.*
BUT ALL THIS TECH...IT REMINDS ME OF *DARRYL'S* STUFF...
DARRYL? YOU MEAN *THE TRANSHUMAN?*
YEAH. THE LAB TOOK HIM IN PORTLAND.
MAYBE *HE'S* THE LINK I NEED TO FIND THEM. MAYBE *THAT'S* WHAT YOU'VE BROUGHT ME HERE TO DO.
KTUNNK
HEY-- I'M HERE TO HELP.
IMPRESSIVE.

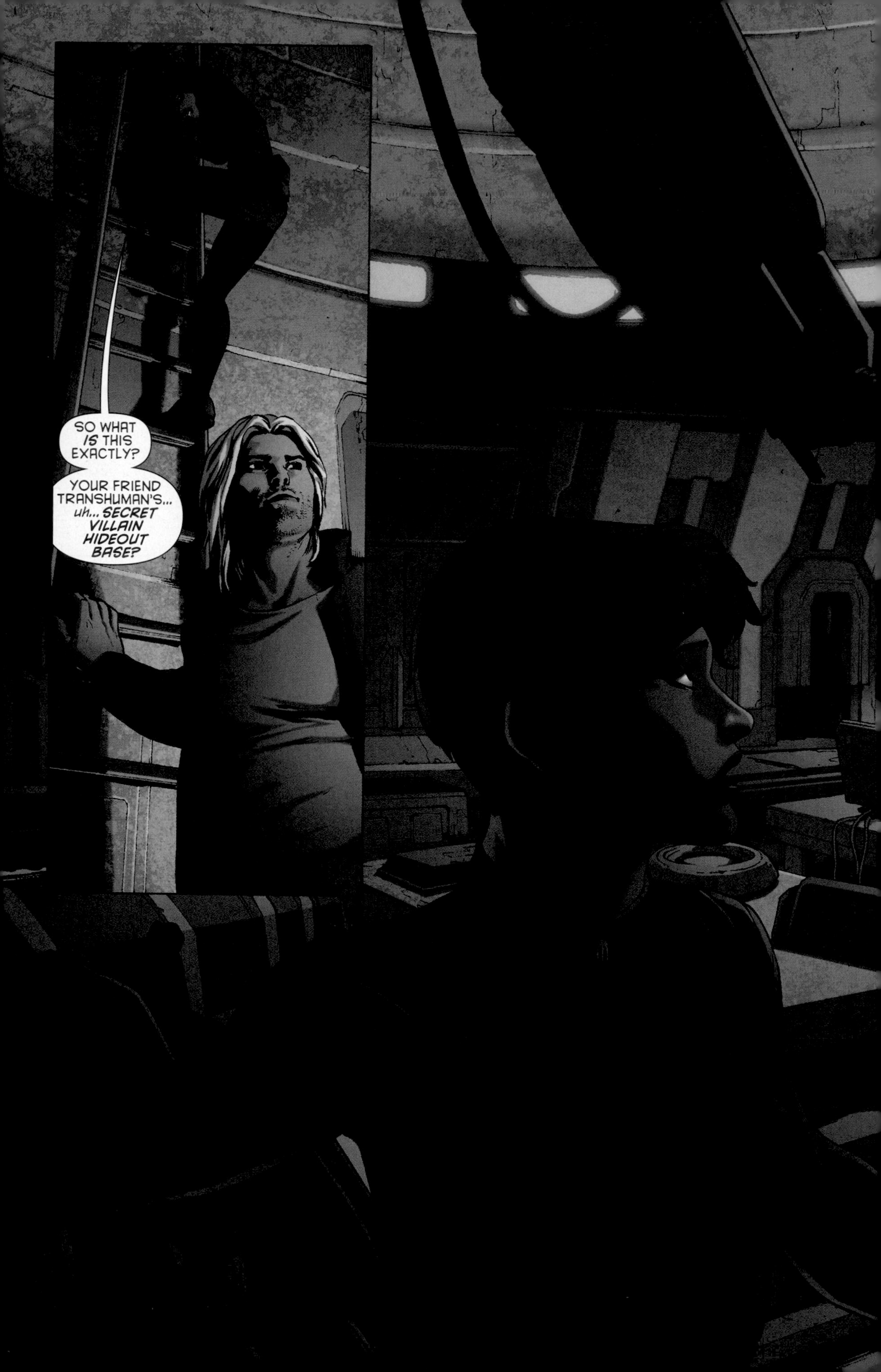
SO WHAT *IS* THIS EXACTLY?
YOUR FRIEND TRANSHUMAN'S... *uh*... ***SECRET VILLAIN HIDEOUT BASE?***

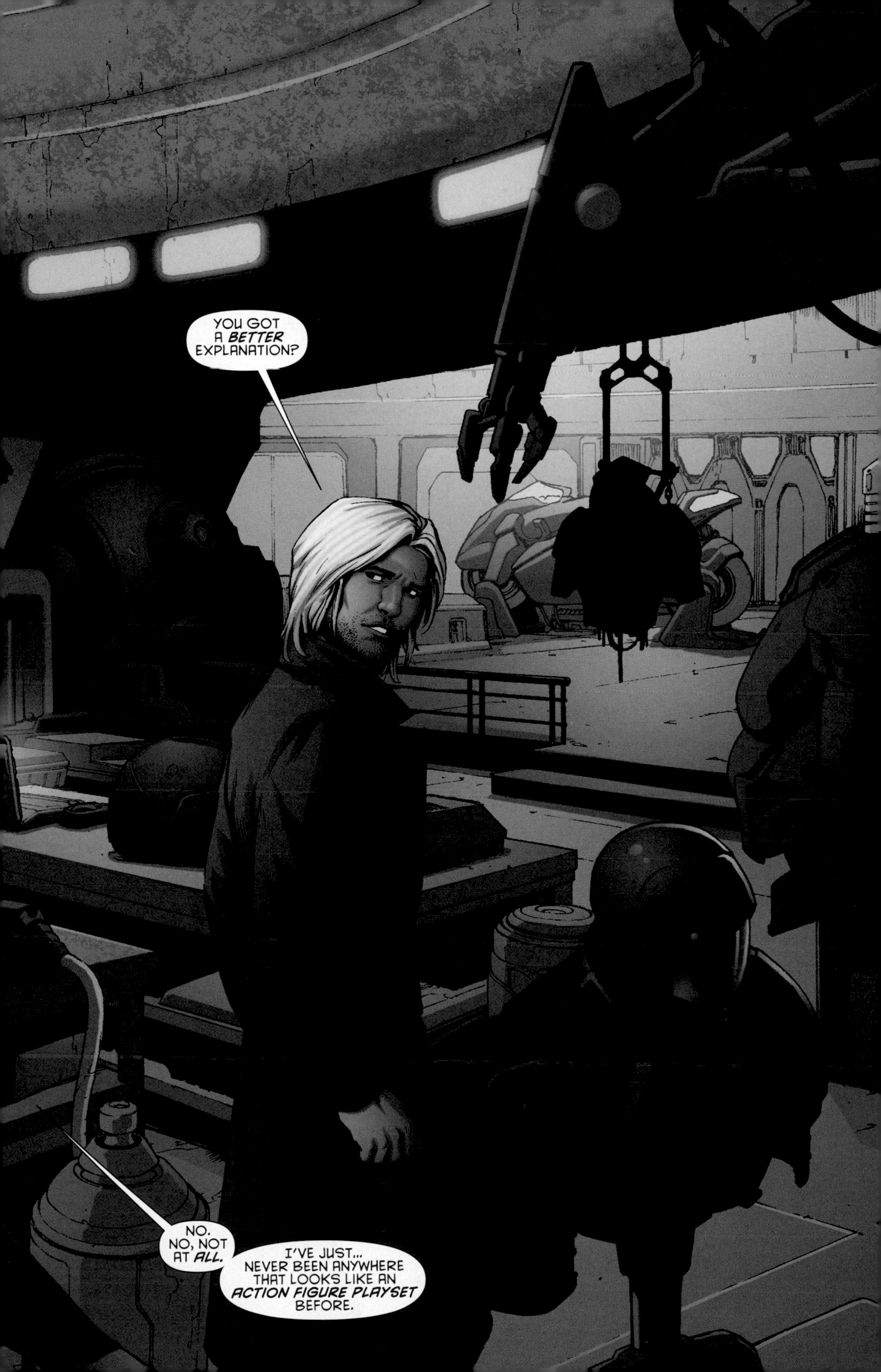
YOU GOT A *BETTER* EXPLANATION?
NO. NO, NOT AT *ALL*.
I'VE JUST... NEVER BEEN ANYWHERE THAT LOOKS LIKE AN *ACTION FIGURE PLAYSET* BEFORE.

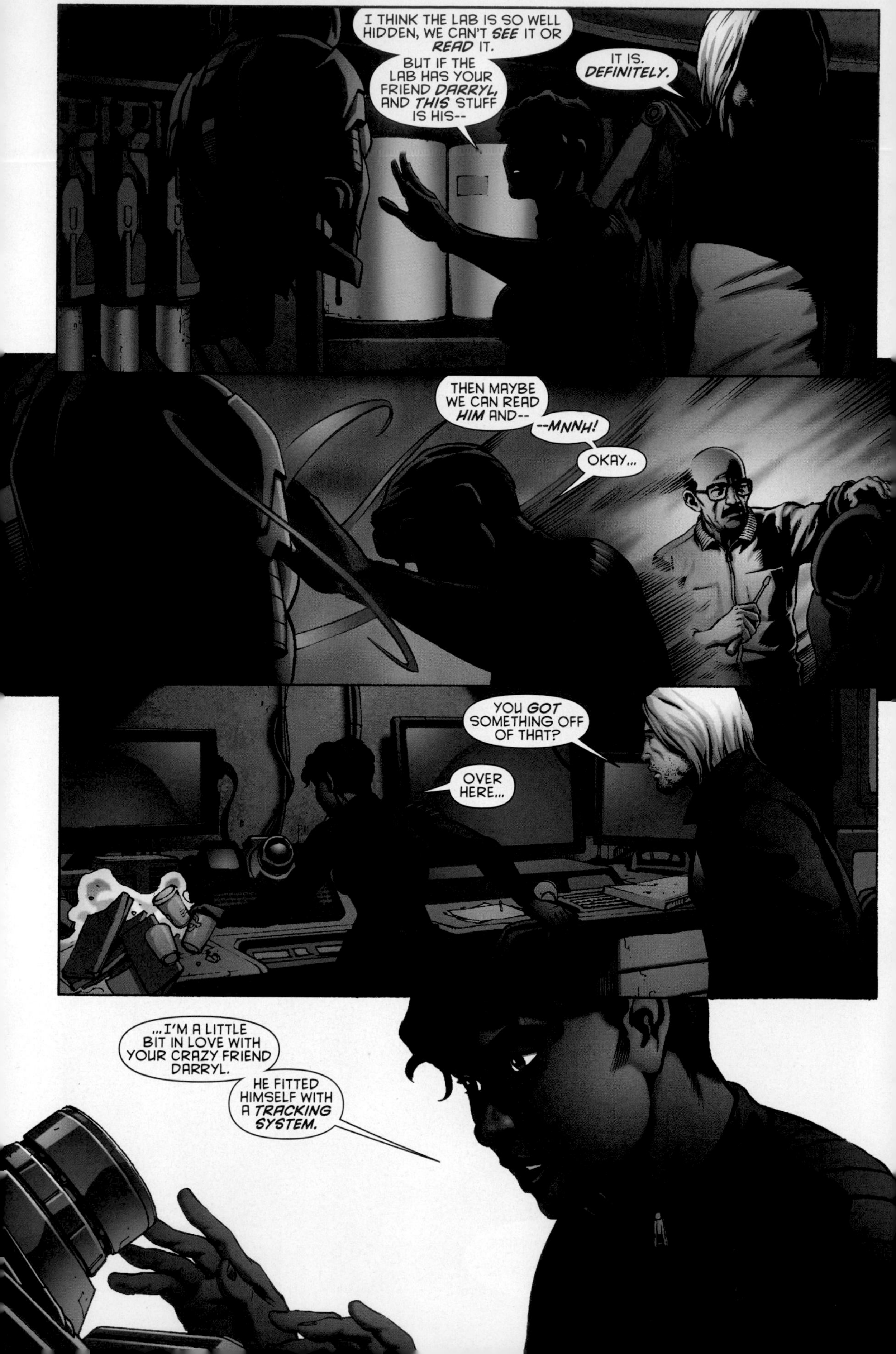
I THINK THE LAB IS SO WELL HIDDEN, WE CAN'T SEE IT OR READ IT.
BUT IF THE LAB HAS YOUR FRIEND DARRYL, AND THIS STUFF IS HIS--
IT IS. DEFINITELY.
THEN MAYBE WE CAN READ HIM AND--
--MNNH!
OKAY...
YOU GOT SOMETHING OFF OF THAT?
OVER HERE...
...I'M A LITTLE BIT IN LOVE WITH YOUR CRAZY FRIEND DARRYL.
HE FITTED HIMSELF WITH A TRACKING SYSTEM.

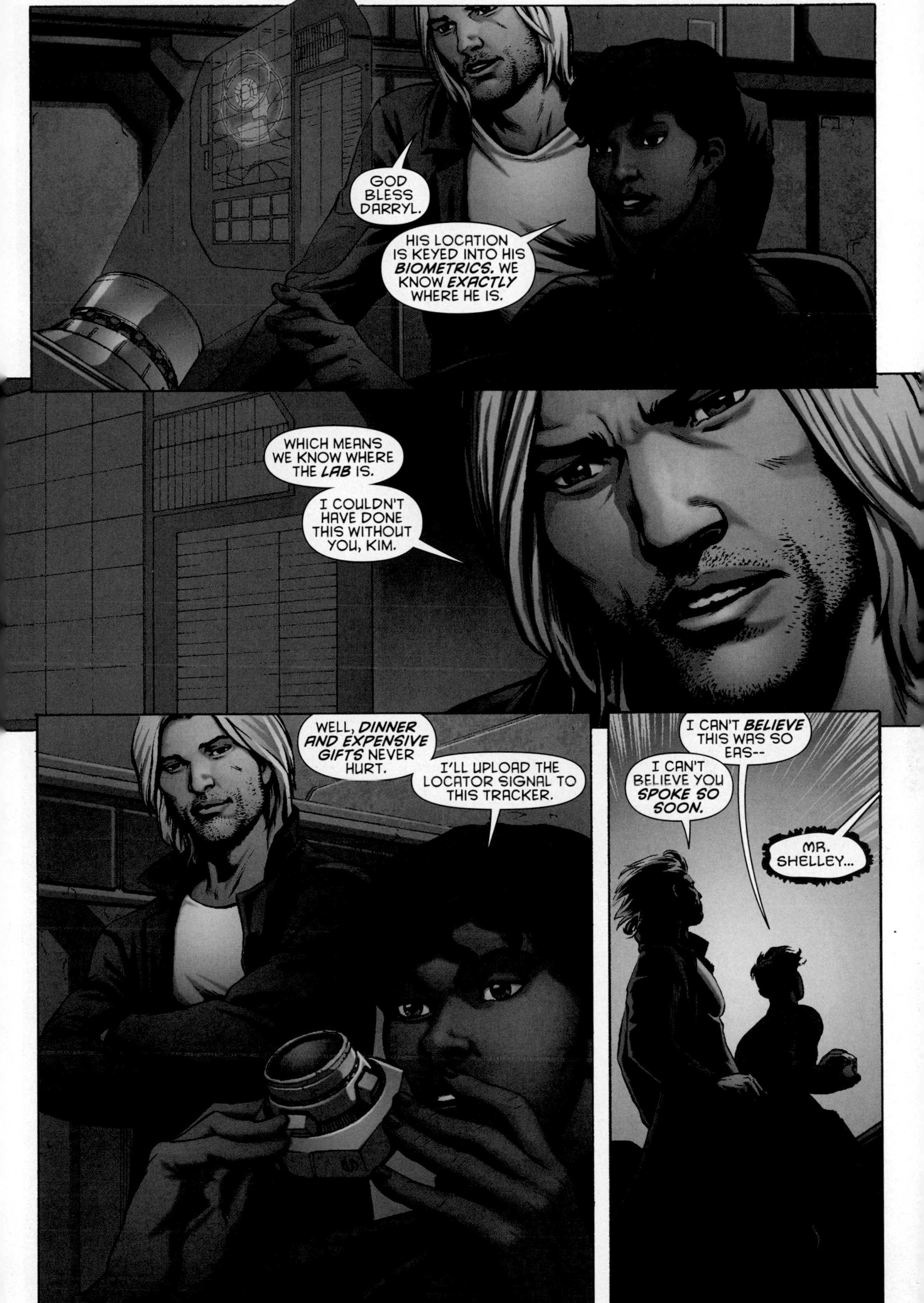
GOD BLESS DARRYL.
HIS LOCATION IS KEYED INTO HIS *BIOMETRICS.* WE KNOW *EXACTLY* WHERE HE IS.
WHICH MEANS WE KNOW WHERE THE *LAB* IS.
I COULDN'T HAVE DONE THIS WITHOUT YOU, KIM.
WELL, *DINNER AND EXPENSIVE GIFTS* NEVER HURT.
I'LL UPLOAD THE LOCATOR SIGNAL TO THIS TRACKER.
I CAN'T *BELIEVE* THIS WAS SO EAS--
I CAN'T BELIEVE YOU *SPOKE SO SOON.*
MR. SHELLEY...

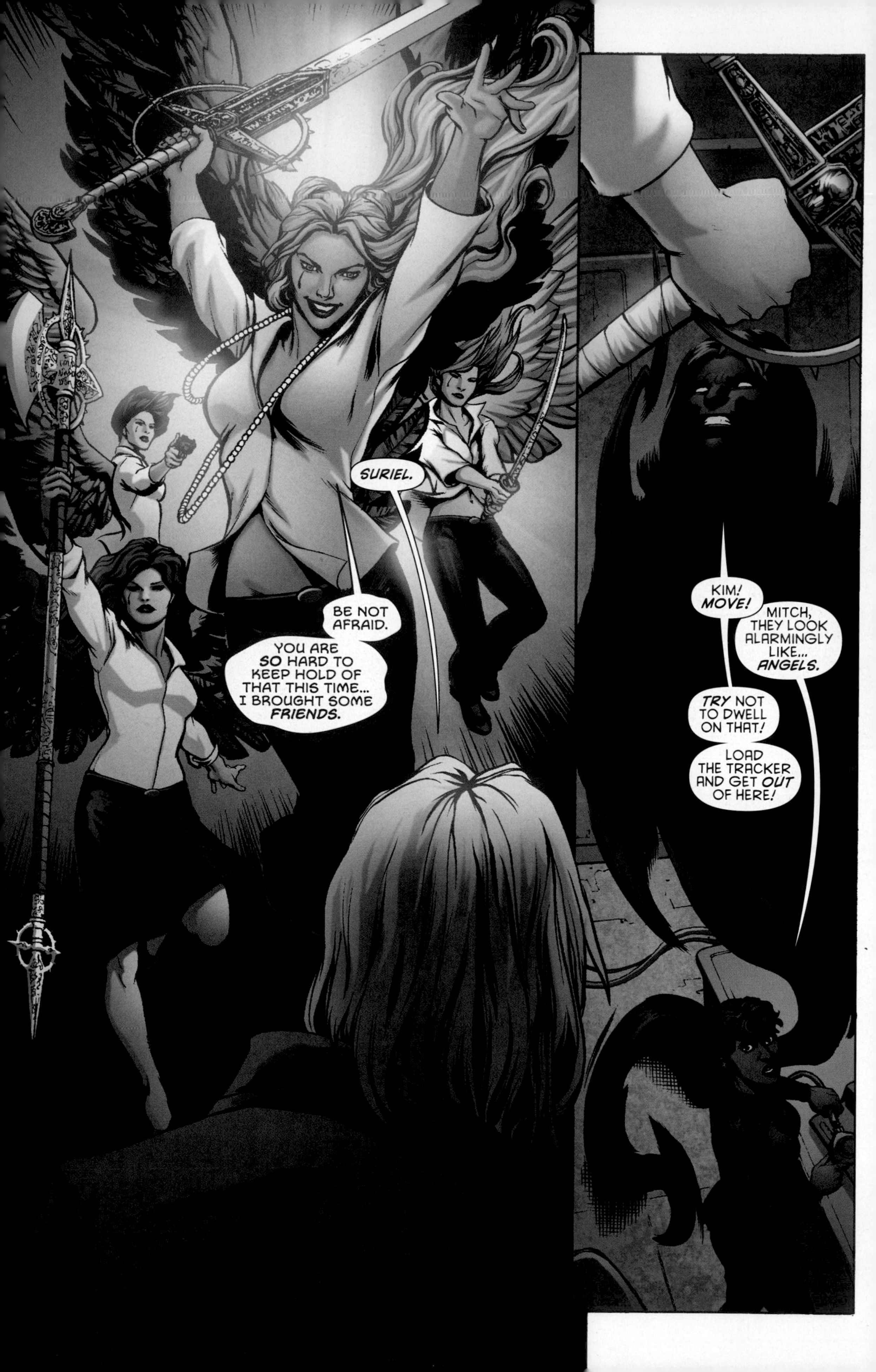
SURIEL.
BE NOT AFRAID.
YOU ARE SO HARD TO KEEP HOLD OF THAT THIS TIME... I BROUGHT SOME FRIENDS.
KIM! MOVE!
MITCH, THEY LOOK ALARMINGLY LIKE... ANGELS.
TRY NOT TO DWELL ON THAT!
LOAD THE TRACKER AND GET OUT OF HERE!

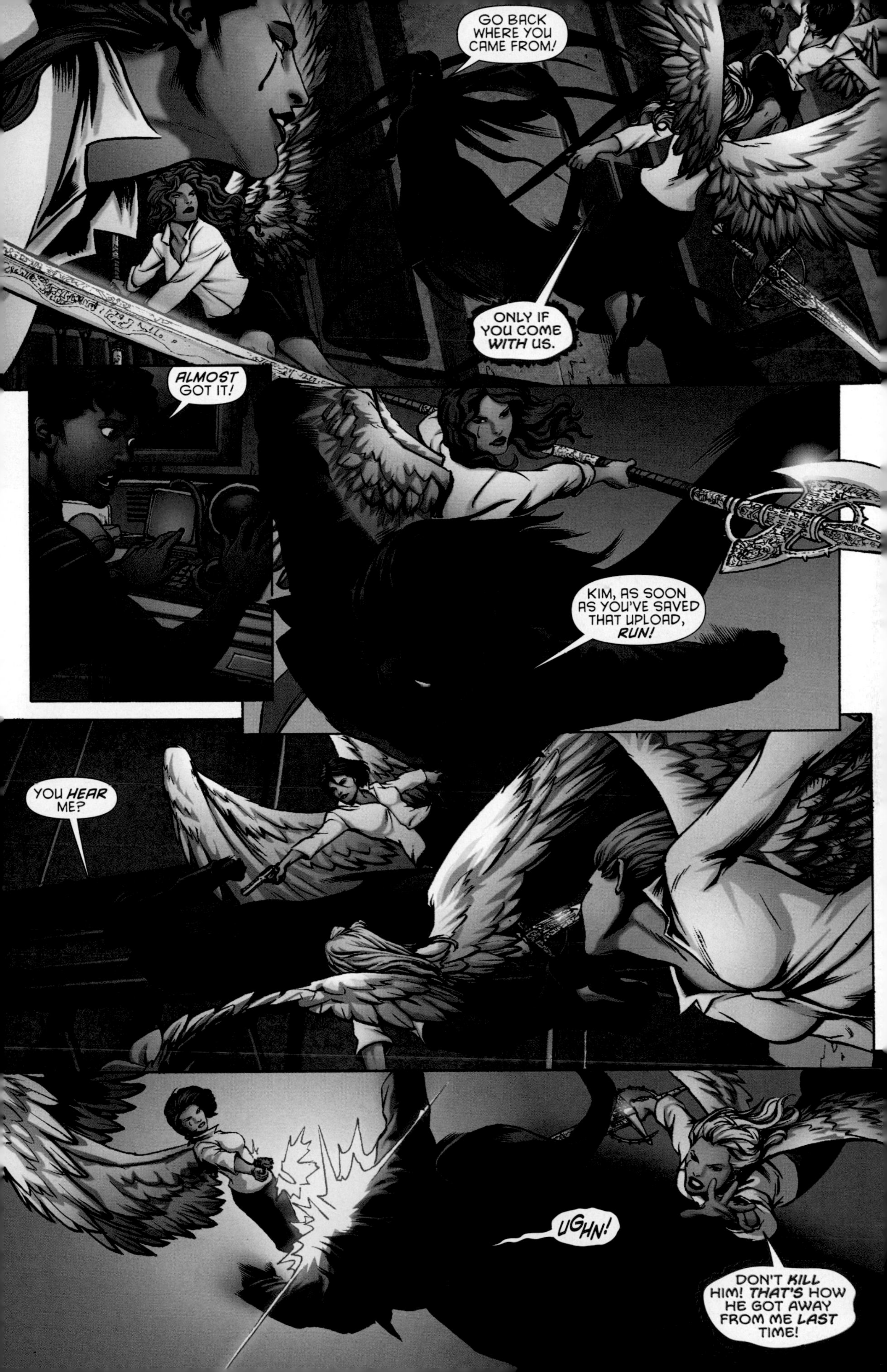
GO BACK WHERE YOU CAME FROM!
ONLY IF YOU COME WITH US.
ALMOST GOT IT!
KIM, AS SOON AS YOU'VE SAVED THAT UPLOAD, RUN!
YOU HEAR ME?
UGHN!
DON'T KILL HIM! THAT'S HOW HE GOT AWAY FROM ME LAST TIME!

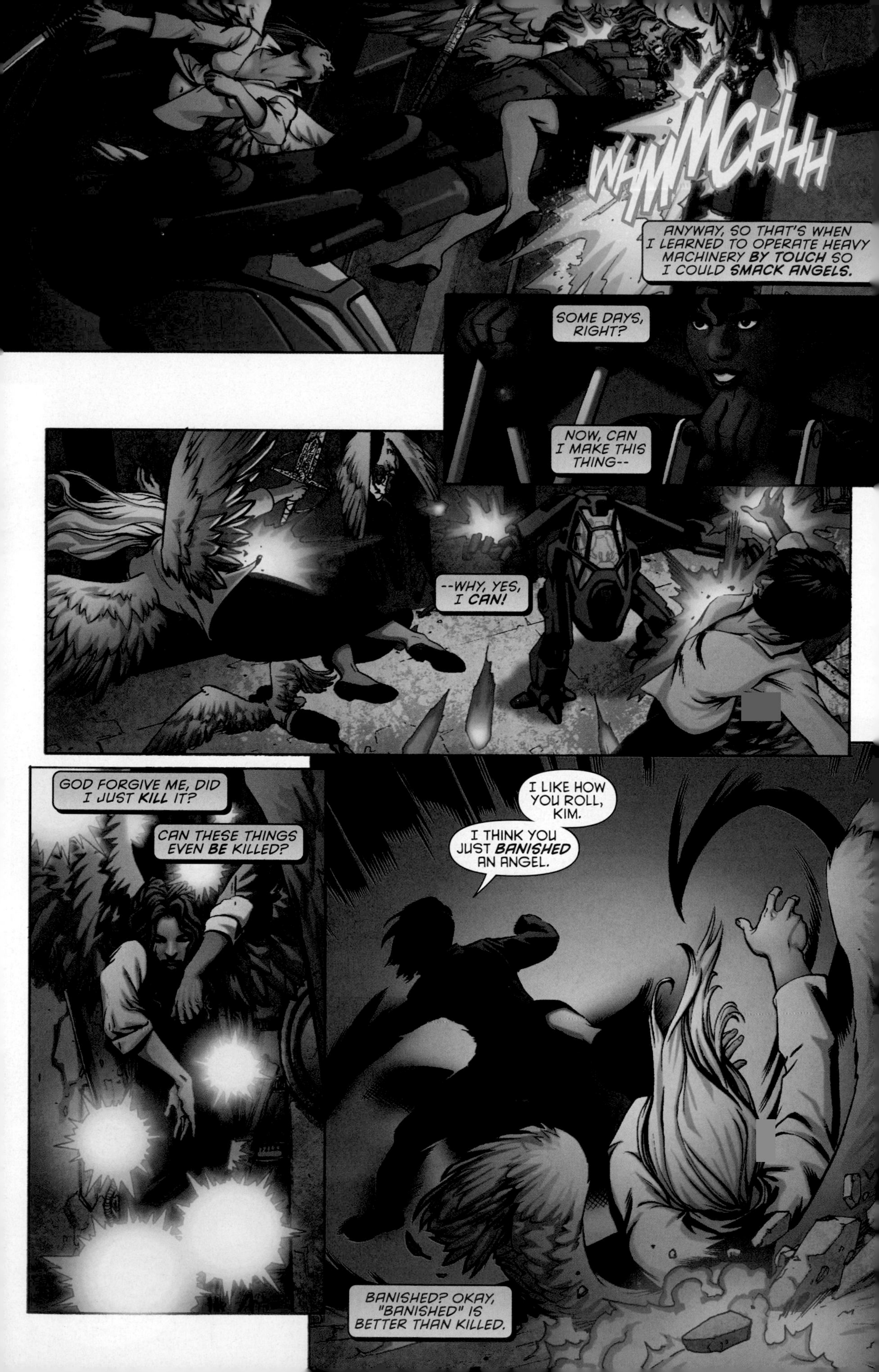
WHMMCHHH
ANYWAY, SO THAT'S WHEN I LEARNED TO OPERATE HEAVY MACHINERY BY TOUCH SO I COULD SMACK ANGELS.
SOME DAYS, RIGHT?
NOW, CAN I MAKE THIS THING--
--WHY, YES, I CAN!
GOD FORGIVE ME, DID I JUST KILL IT?
CAN THESE THINGS EVEN BE KILLED?
I LIKE HOW YOU ROLL, KIM.
I THINK YOU JUST BANISHED AN ANGEL.
BANISHED? OKAY, "BANISHED" IS BETTER THAN KILLED.

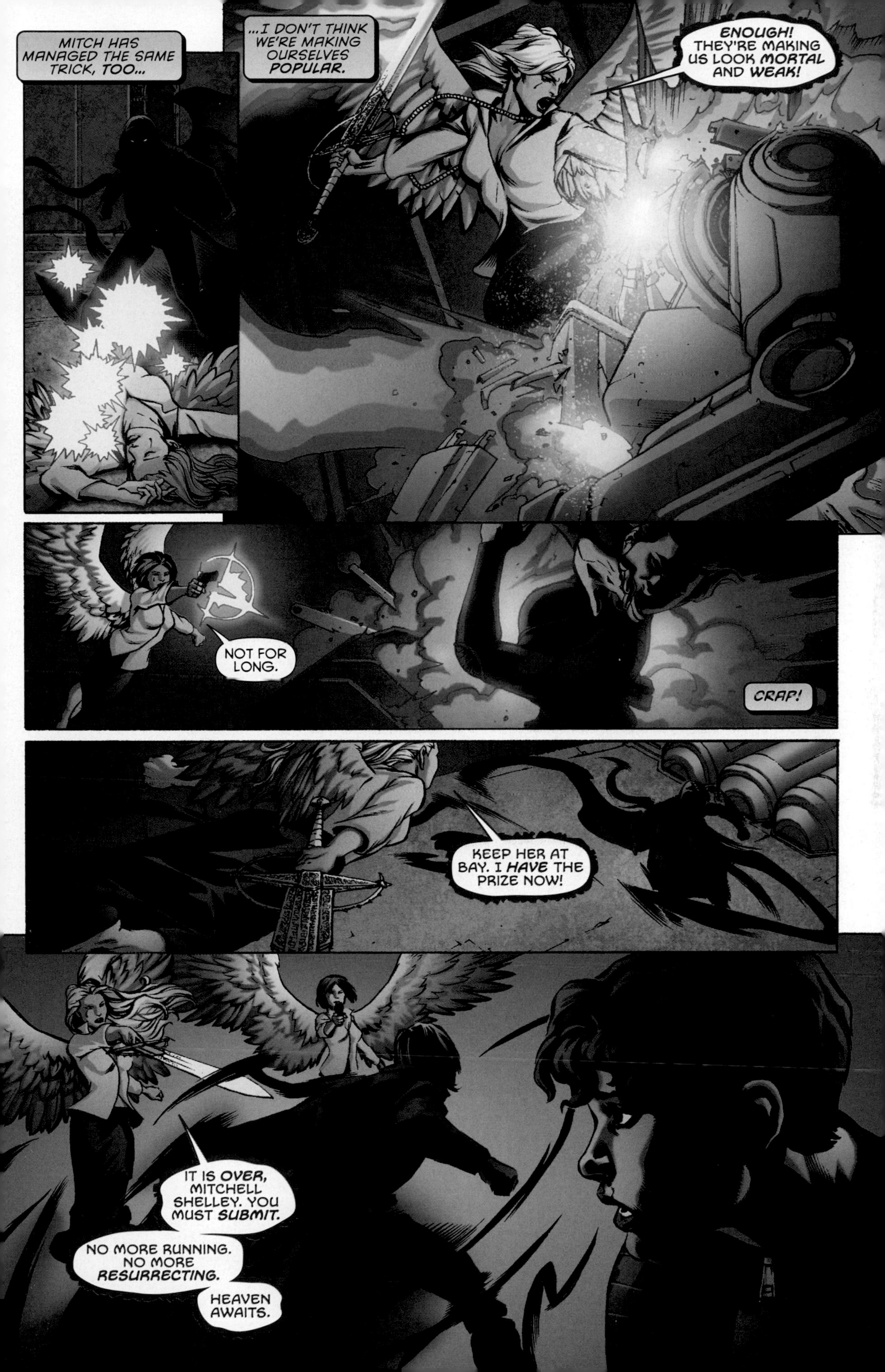
MITCH HAS MANAGED THE SAME TRICK, TOO...
...I DON'T THINK WE'RE MAKING OURSELVES POPULAR.
ENOUGH! THEY'RE MAKING US LOOK MORTAL AND WEAK!
NOT FOR LONG.
CRAP!
KEEP HER AT BAY. I HAVE THE PRIZE NOW!
IT IS OVER, MITCHELL SHELLEY. YOU MUST SUBMIT.
NO MORE RUNNING. NO MORE RESURRECTING.
HEAVEN AWAITS.

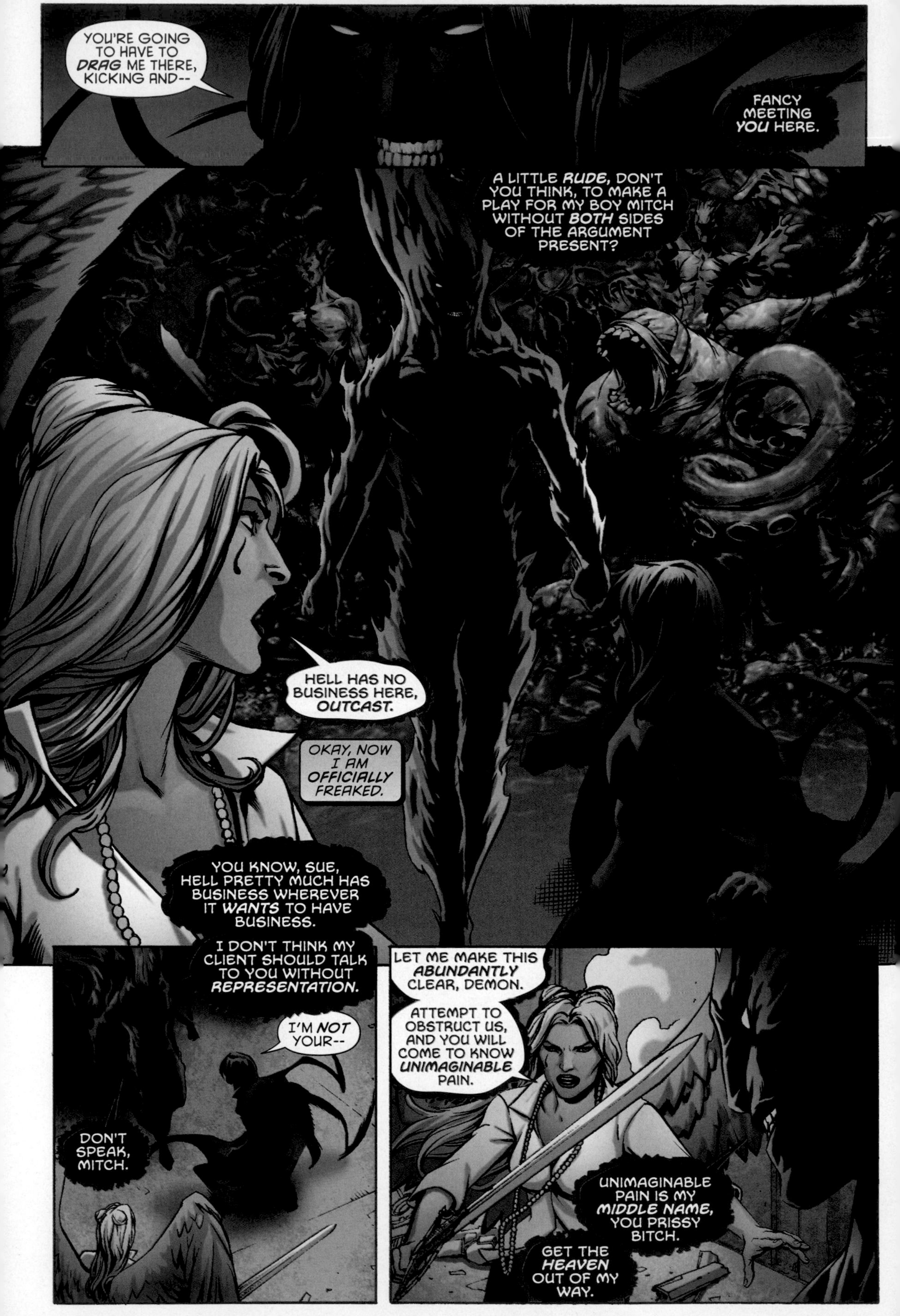
YOU'RE GOING TO HAVE TO DRAG ME THERE, KICKING AND--
FANCY MEETING YOU HERE.
A LITTLE RUDE, DON'T YOU THINK, TO MAKE A PLAY FOR MY BOY MITCH WITHOUT BOTH SIDES OF THE ARGUMENT PRESENT?
HELL HAS NO BUSINESS HERE, OUTCAST.
OKAY, NOW I AM OFFICIALLY FREAKED.
YOU KNOW, SUE, HELL PRETTY MUCH HAS BUSINESS WHEREVER IT WANTS TO HAVE BUSINESS.
I DON'T THINK MY CLIENT SHOULD TALK TO YOU WITHOUT REPRESENTATION.
I'M NOT YOUR--
DON'T SPEAK, MITCH.
LET ME MAKE THIS ABUNDANTLY CLEAR, DEMON.
ATTEMPT TO OBSTRUCT US, AND YOU WILL COME TO KNOW UNIMAGINABLE PAIN.
UNIMAGINABLE PAIN IS MY MIDDLE NAME, YOU PRISSY BITCH.
GET THE HEAVEN OUT OF MY WAY.

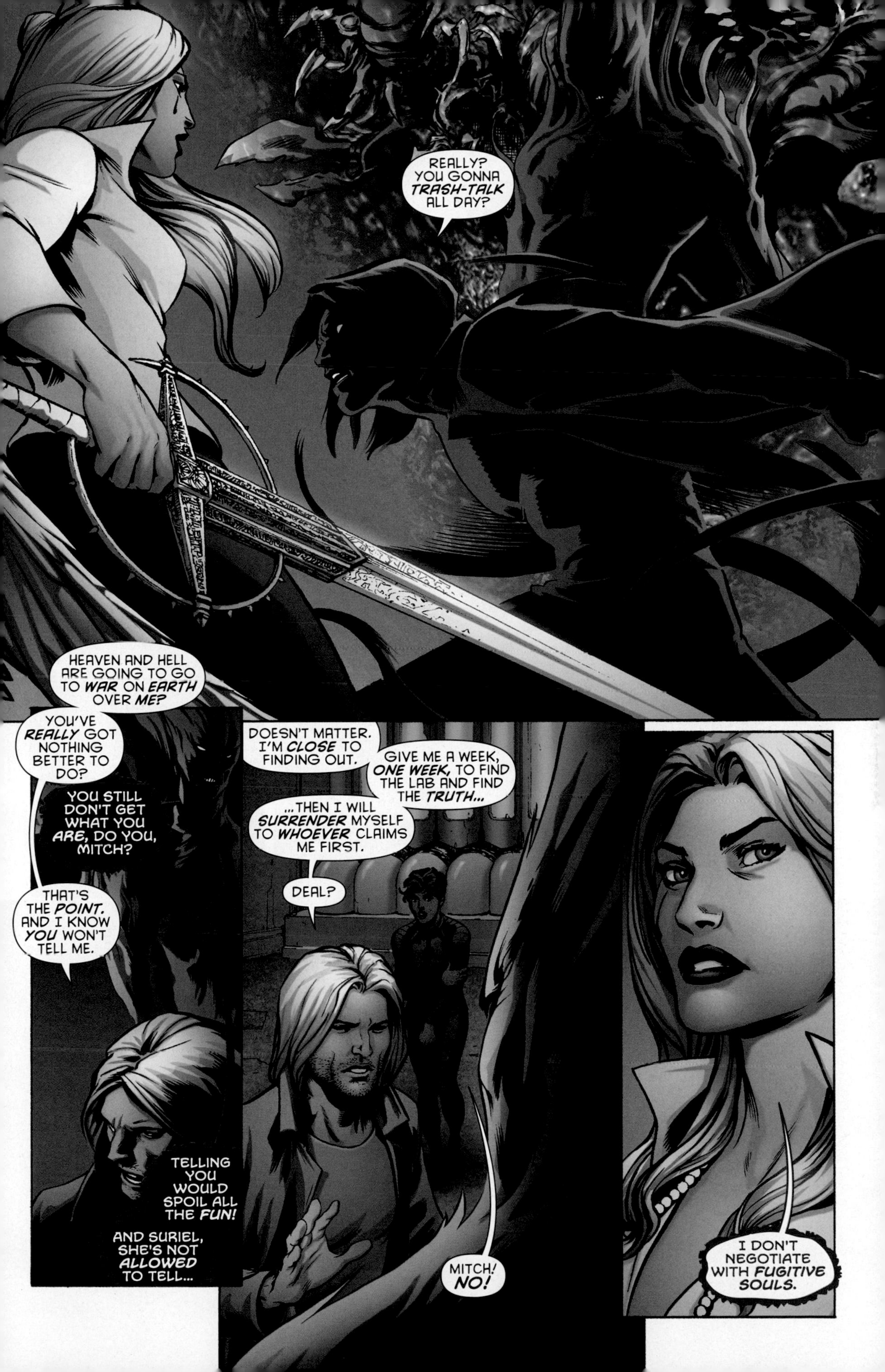
REALLY? YOU GONNA TRASH-TALK ALL DAY?
HEAVEN AND HELL ARE GOING TO GO TO WAR ON EARTH OVER ME?
YOU'VE REALLY GOT NOTHING BETTER TO DO?
YOU STILL DON'T GET WHAT YOU ARE, DO YOU, MITCH?
THAT'S THE POINT. AND I KNOW YOU WON'T TELL ME.
TELLING YOU WOULD SPOIL ALL THE FUN!
AND SURIEL, SHE'S NOT ALLOWED TO TELL...
DOESN'T MATTER. I'M CLOSE TO FINDING OUT.
GIVE ME A WEEK, ONE WEEK, TO FIND THE LAB AND FIND THE TRUTH...
...THEN I WILL SURRENDER MYSELF TO WHOEVER CLAIMS ME FIRST.
DEAL?
MITCH! NO!
I DON'T NEGOTIATE WITH FUGITIVE SOULS.

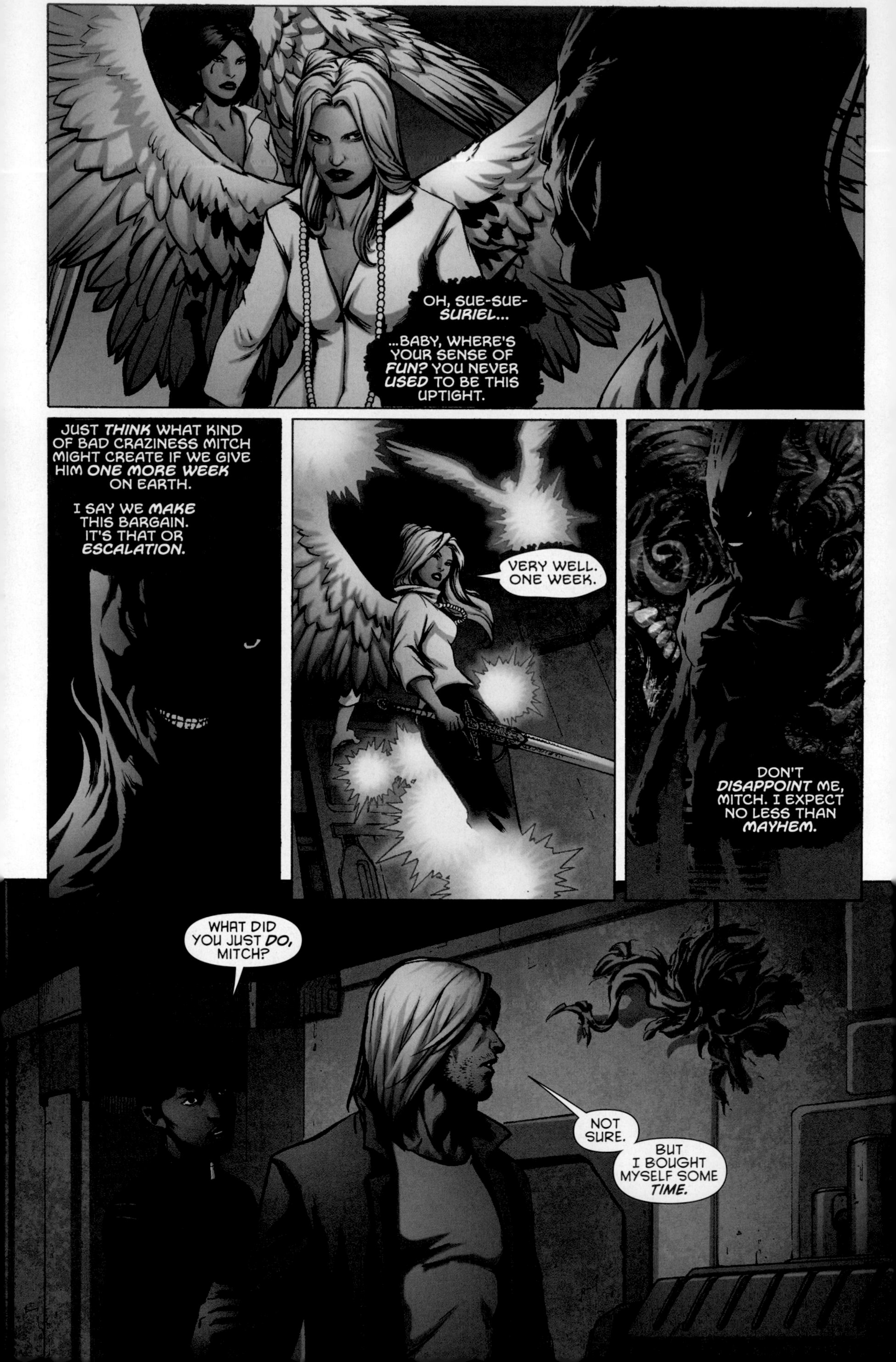
OH, SUE-SUE-SURIEL...
...BABY, WHERE'S YOUR SENSE OF FUN? YOU NEVER USED TO BE THIS UPTIGHT.
JUST THINK WHAT KIND OF BAD CRAZINESS MITCH MIGHT CREATE IF WE GIVE HIM ONE MORE WEEK ON EARTH.
I SAY WE MAKE THIS BARGAIN. IT'S THAT OR ESCALATION.
VERY WELL. ONE WEEK.
DON'T DISAPPOINT ME, MITCH. I EXPECT NO LESS THAN MAYHEM.
WHAT DID YOU JUST DO, MITCH?
NOT SURE.
BUT I BOUGHT MYSELF SOME TIME.

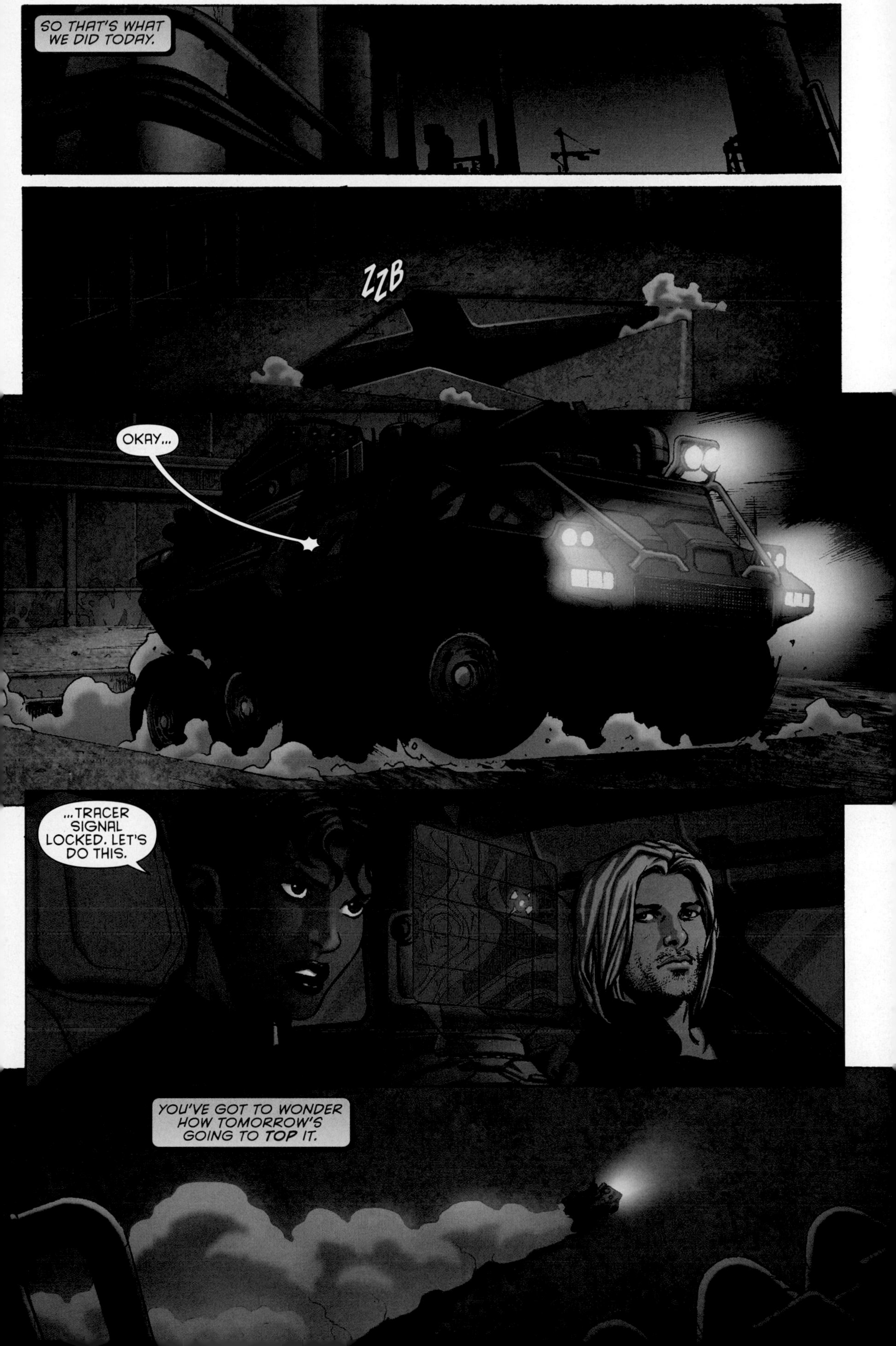
SO THAT'S WHAT WE DID TODAY.
ZZB
OKAY...
...TRACER SIGNAL LOCKED. LET'S DO THIS.
YOU'VE GOT TO WONDER HOW TOMORROW'S GOING TO TOP IT.

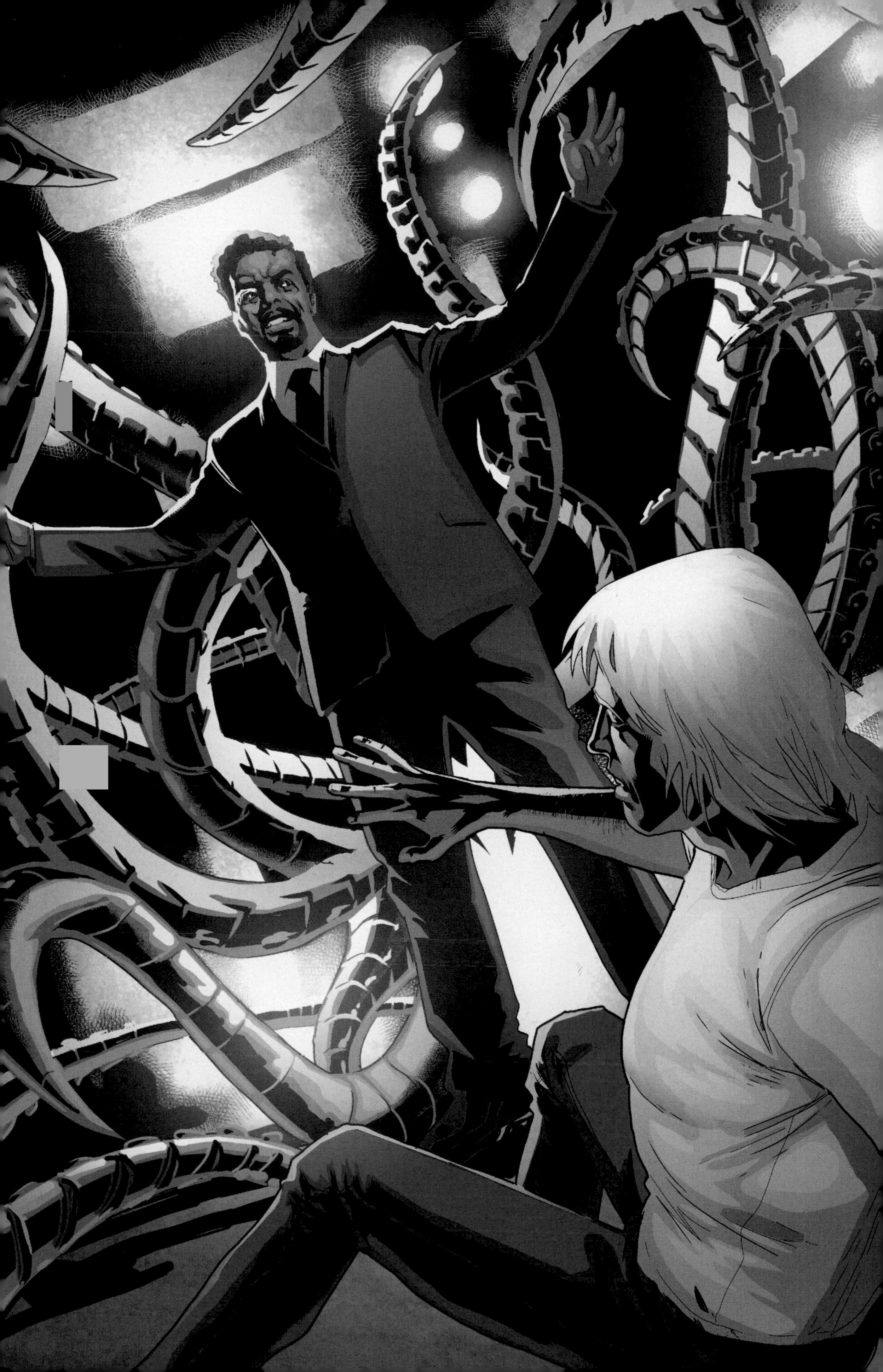

LAB RATS

DAN ABNETT & ANDY LANNING
writers

JESUS SAIZ & JAVIER PINA
artists

cover art by
PETE WOODS and JOHN KALISZ

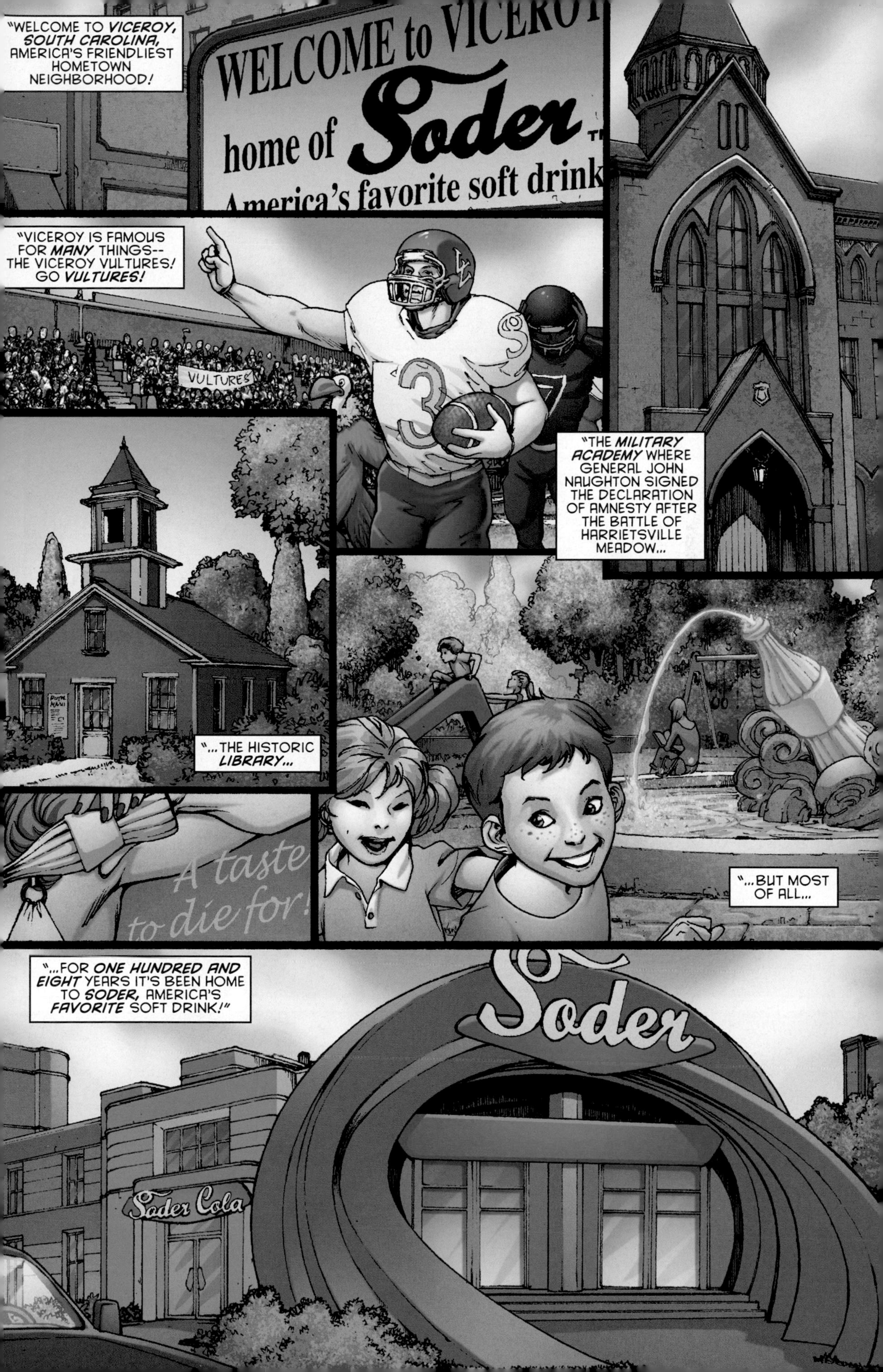

"WELCOME TO VICEROY, SOUTH CAROLINA, AMERICA'S FRIENDLIEST HOMETOWN NEIGHBORHOOD!
WELCOME to VICEROY
home of Soder™
America's favorite soft drink
"VICEROY IS FAMOUS FOR MANY THINGS-- THE VICEROY VULTURES! GO VULTURES!
VULTURES
"THE MILITARY ACADEMY WHERE GENERAL JOHN NAUGHTON SIGNED THE DECLARATION OF AMNESTY AFTER THE BATTLE OF HARRIETSVILLE MEADOW...
"...THE HISTORIC LIBRARY...
A taste to die for!
"...BUT MOST OF ALL...
"...FOR ONE HUNDRED AND EIGHT YEARS IT'S BEEN HOME TO SODER, AMERICA'S FAVORITE SOFT DRINK!"
Soder
Soder Cola

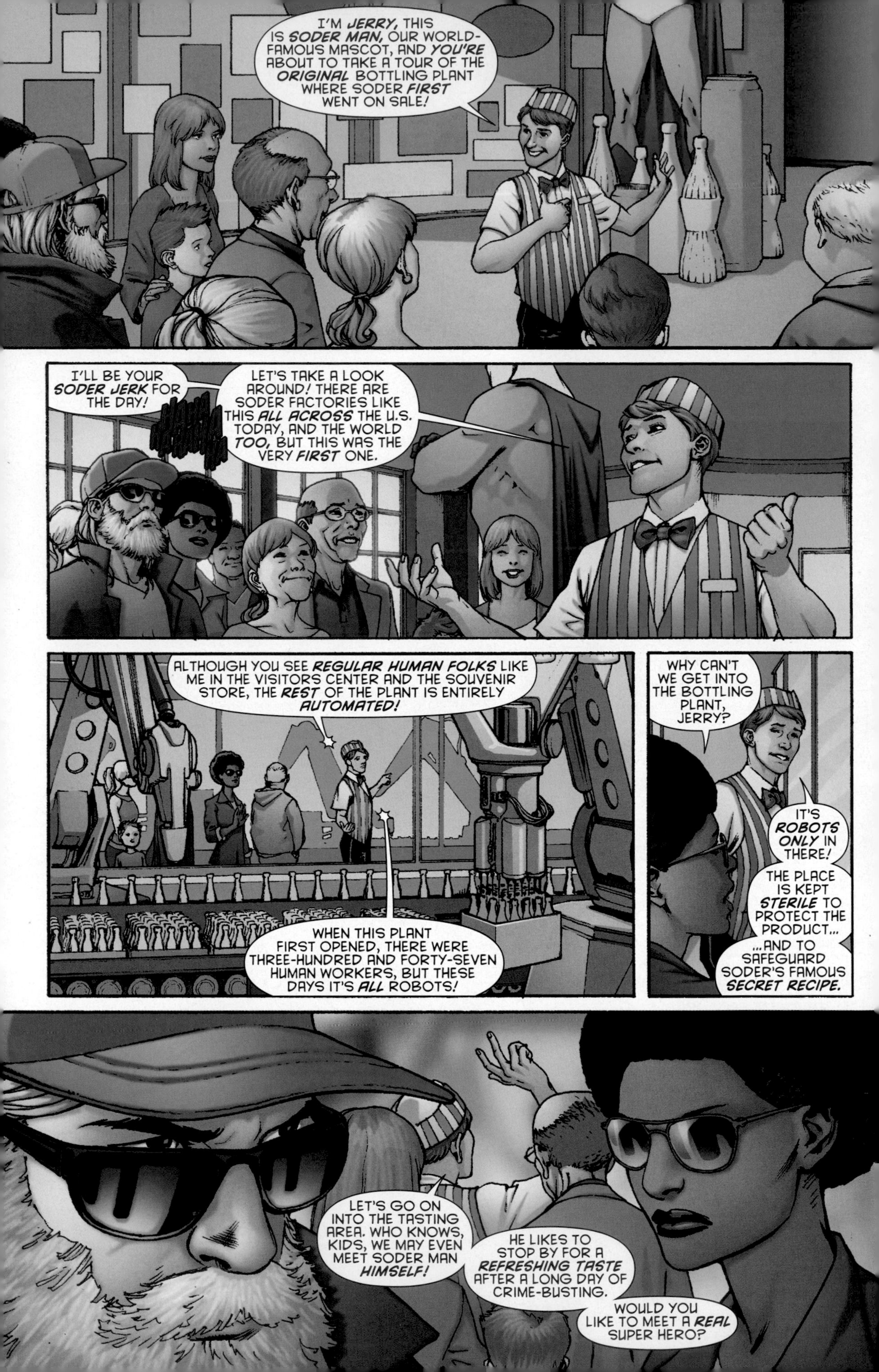
I'M JERRY, THIS IS SODER MAN, OUR WORLD-FAMOUS MASCOT, AND YOU'RE ABOUT TO TAKE A TOUR OF THE ORIGINAL BOTTLING PLANT WHERE SODER FIRST WENT ON SALE!
I'LL BE YOUR SODER JERK FOR THE DAY!
LET'S TAKE A LOOK AROUND! THERE ARE SODER FACTORIES LIKE THIS ALL ACROSS THE U.S. TODAY, AND THE WORLD TOO, BUT THIS WAS THE VERY FIRST ONE.
ALTHOUGH YOU SEE REGULAR HUMAN FOLKS LIKE ME IN THE VISITORS CENTER AND THE SOUVENIR STORE, THE REST OF THE PLANT IS ENTIRELY AUTOMATED!
WHEN THIS PLANT FIRST OPENED, THERE WERE THREE-HUNDRED AND FORTY-SEVEN HUMAN WORKERS, BUT THESE DAYS IT'S ALL ROBOTS!
WHY CAN'T WE GET INTO THE BOTTLING PLANT, JERRY?
IT'S ROBOTS ONLY IN THERE!
THE PLACE IS KEPT STERILE TO PROTECT THE PRODUCT...
...AND TO SAFEGUARD SODER'S FAMOUS SECRET RECIPE.
LET'S GO ON INTO THE TASTING AREA. WHO KNOWS, KIDS, WE MAY EVEN MEET SODER MAN HIMSELF!
HE LIKES TO STOP BY FOR A REFRESHING TASTE AFTER A LONG DAY OF CRIME-BUSTING.
WOULD YOU LIKE TO MEET A REAL SUPER HERO?

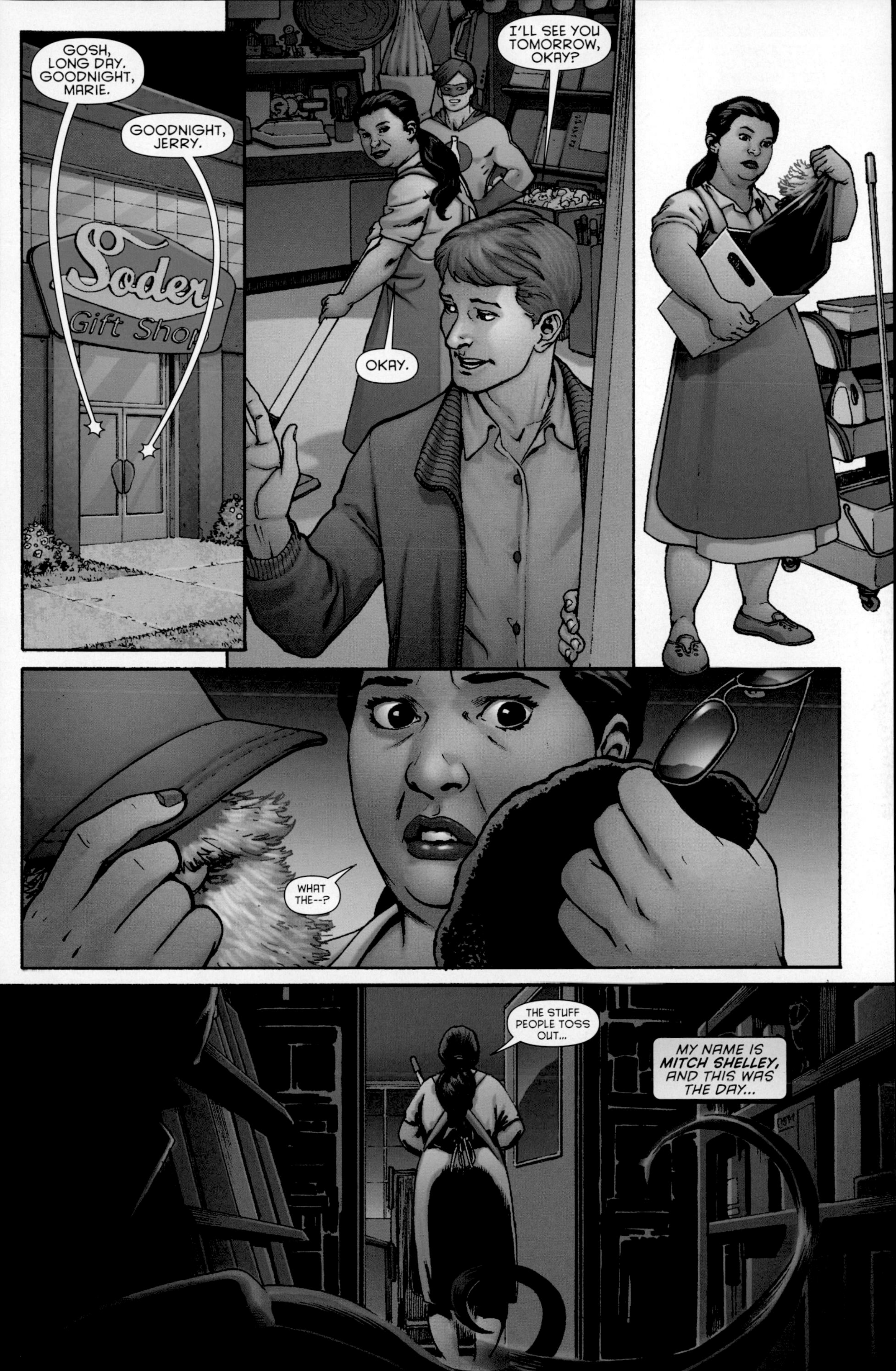
GOSH, LONG DAY. GOODNIGHT, MARIE.
GOODNIGHT, JERRY.
Soder Gift Shop
I'LL SEE YOU TOMORROW, OKAY?
OKAY.
WHAT THE--?
THE STUFF PEOPLE TOSS OUT...
MY NAME IS MITCH SHELLEY, AND THIS WAS THE DAY...

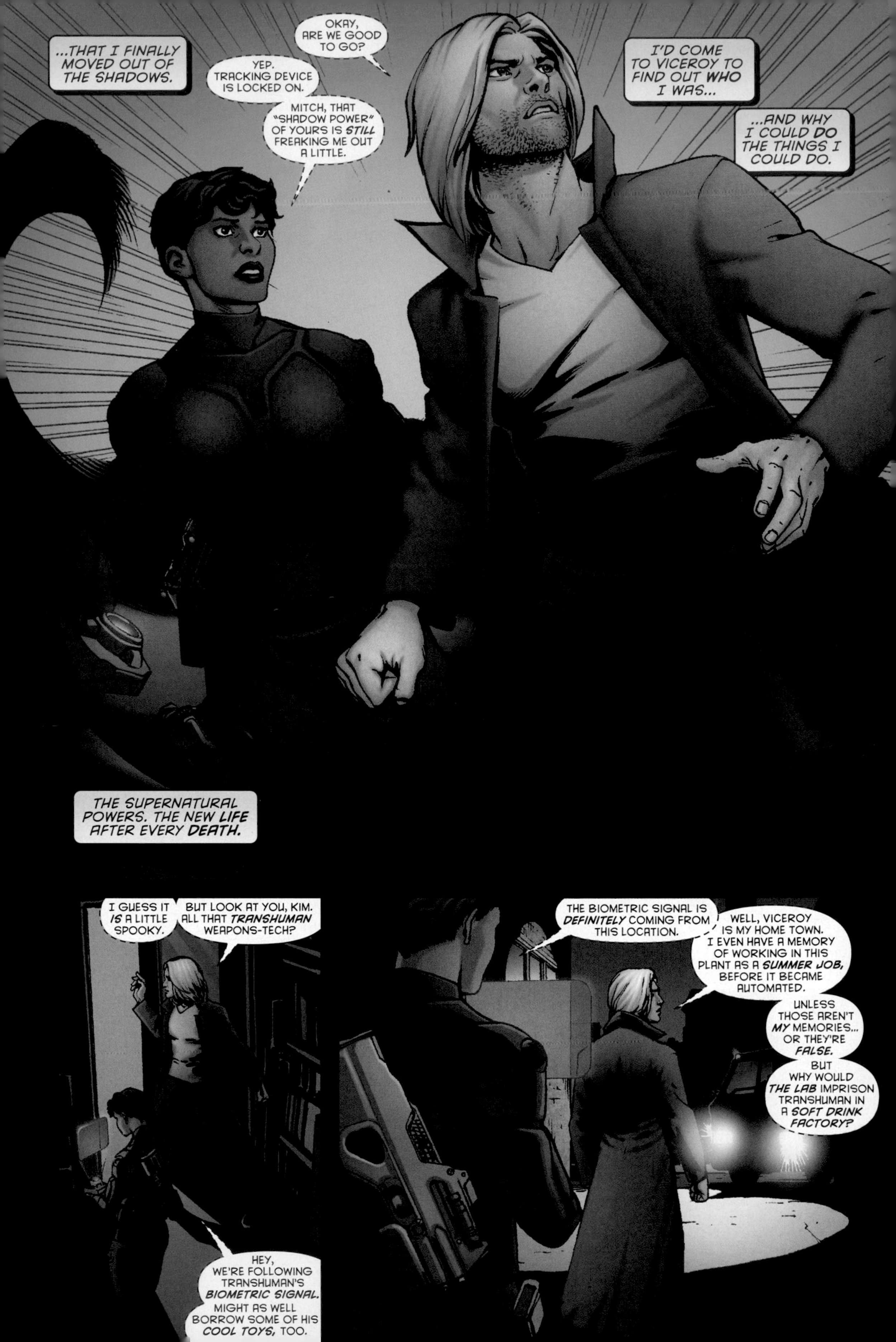

...THAT I FINALLY MOVED OUT OF THE SHADOWS.
OKAY, ARE WE GOOD TO GO?
YEP. TRACKING DEVICE IS LOCKED ON.
MITCH, THAT "SHADOW POWER" OF YOURS IS STILL FREAKING ME OUT A LITTLE.
I'D COME TO VICEROY TO FIND OUT WHO I WAS...
...AND WHY I COULD DO THE THINGS I COULD DO.
THE SUPERNATURAL POWERS. THE NEW LIFE AFTER EVERY DEATH.
I GUESS IT IS A LITTLE SPOOKY.
BUT LOOK AT YOU, KIM. ALL THAT TRANSHUMAN WEAPONS-TECH?
HEY, WE'RE FOLLOWING TRANSHUMAN'S BIOMETRIC SIGNAL. MIGHT AS WELL BORROW SOME OF HIS COOL TOYS, TOO.
THE BIOMETRIC SIGNAL IS DEFINITELY COMING FROM THIS LOCATION.
WELL, VICEROY IS MY HOME TOWN. I EVEN HAVE A MEMORY OF WORKING IN THIS PLANT AS A SUMMER JOB, BEFORE IT BECAME AUTOMATED.
UNLESS THOSE AREN'T MY MEMORIES... OR THEY'RE FALSE.
BUT WHY WOULD THE LAB IMPRISON TRANSHUMAN IN A SOFT DRINK FACTORY?

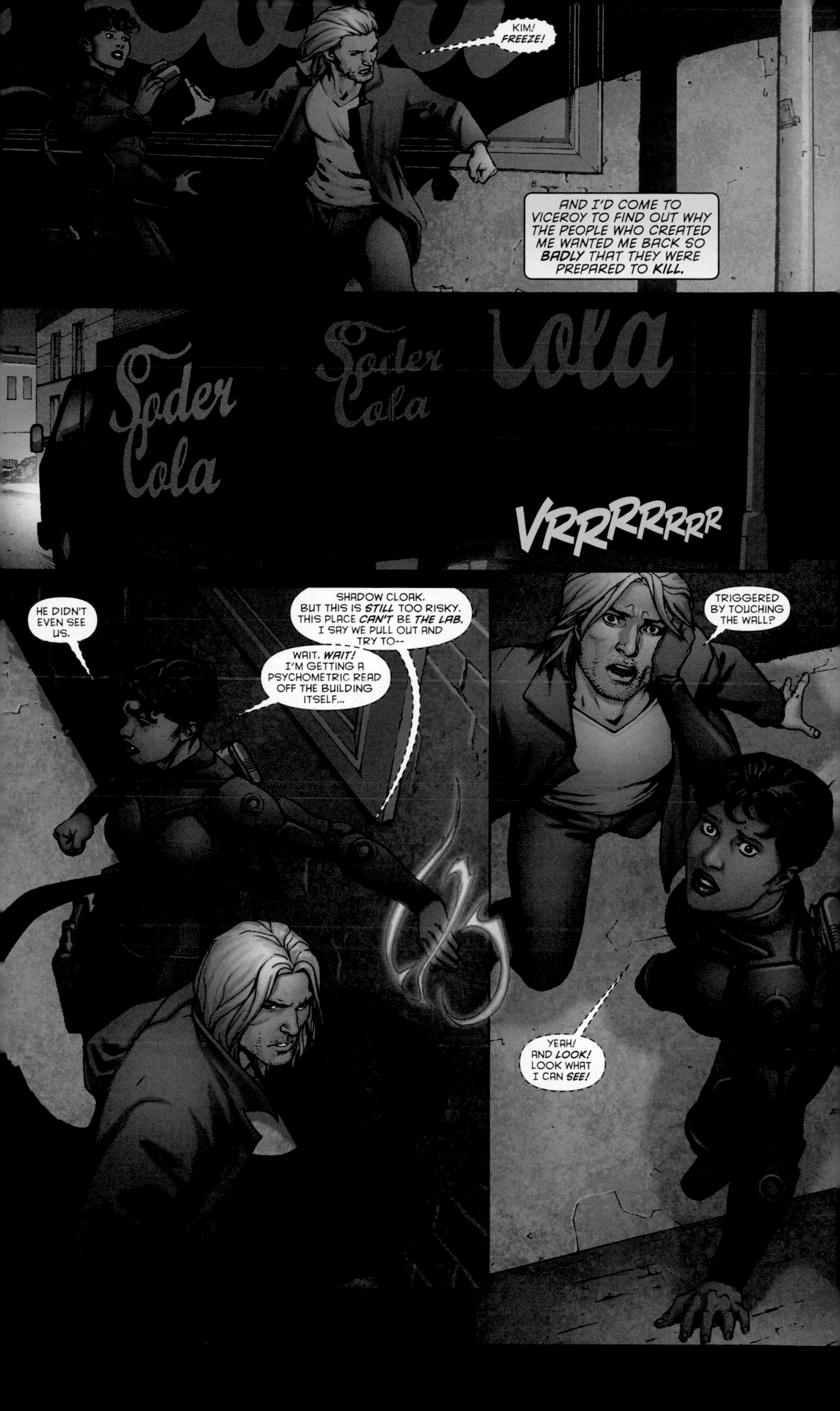
KIM! *FREEZE!*
AND I'D COME TO VICEROY TO FIND OUT WHY THE PEOPLE WHO CREATED ME WANTED ME BACK SO *BADLY* THAT THEY WERE PREPARED TO *KILL.*
Soder Cola
Soder Cola
VRRRRRRR
HE DIDN'T EVEN SEE US.
SHADOW CLOAK. BUT THIS IS *STILL* TOO RISKY. THIS PLACE *CAN'T* BE *THE LAB.* I SAY WE PULL OUT AND TRY TO--
WAIT. *WAIT!* I'M GETTING A PSYCHOMETRIC READ OFF THE BUILDING ITSELF...
TRIGGERED BY TOUCHING THE WALL?
YEAH! AND *LOOK!* LOOK WHAT I CAN *SEE!*

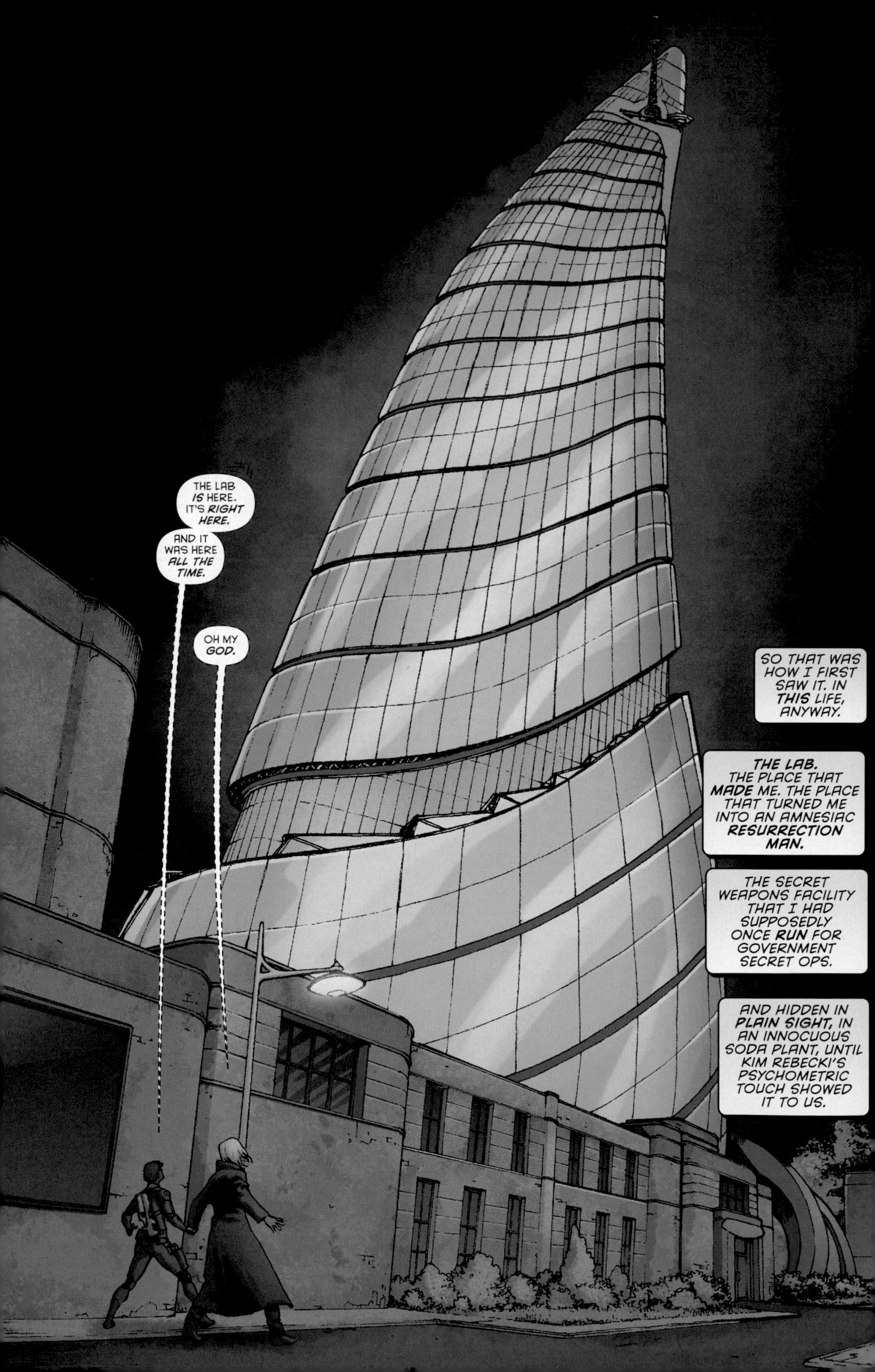
THE LAB *IS* HERE. IT'S *RIGHT HERE.*
AND IT WAS HERE *ALL THE TIME.*
OH MY *GOD.*
SO THAT WAS HOW I FIRST SAW IT. IN **THIS** LIFE, ANYWAY.
THE LAB. THE PLACE THAT ***MADE*** ME. THE PLACE THAT TURNED ME INTO AN AMNESIAC ***RESURRECTION MAN.***
THE SECRET WEAPONS FACILITY THAT I HAD SUPPOSEDLY ONCE **RUN** FOR GOVERNMENT SECRET OPS.
AND HIDDEN IN ***PLAIN SIGHT,*** IN AN INNOCUOUS SODA PLANT, UNTIL KIM REBECKI'S PSYCHOMETRIC TOUCH SHOWED IT TO US.

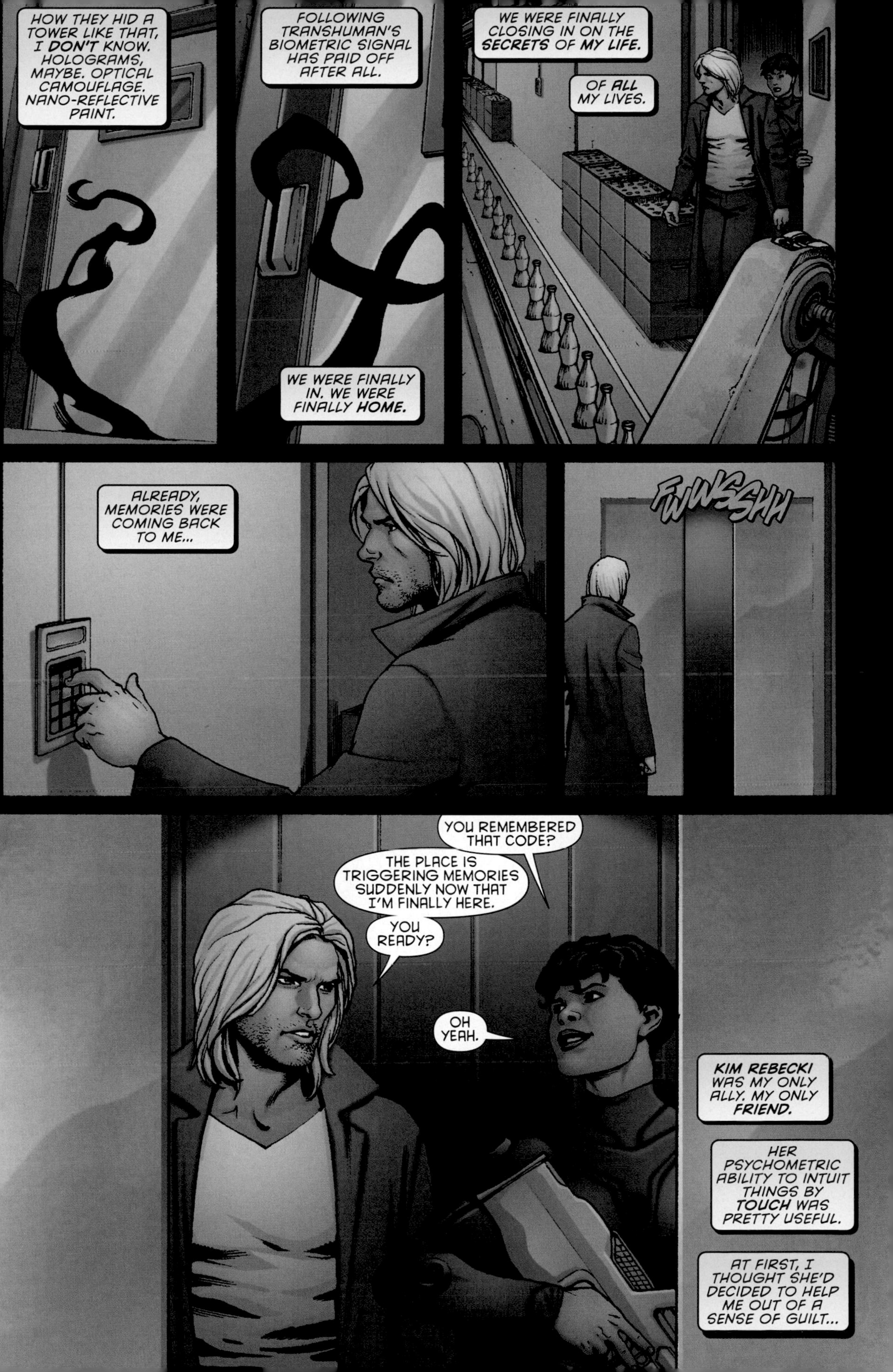

HOW THEY HID A TOWER LIKE THAT, I DON'T KNOW. HOLOGRAMS, MAYBE. OPTICAL CAMOUFLAGE. NANO-REFLECTIVE PAINT.
FOLLOWING TRANSHUMAN'S BIOMETRIC SIGNAL HAS PAID OFF AFTER ALL.
WE WERE FINALLY IN. WE WERE FINALLY HOME.
WE WERE FINALLY CLOSING IN ON THE SECRETS OF MY LIFE.
OF ALL MY LIVES.
ALREADY, MEMORIES WERE COMING BACK TO ME...
FWWSSHH
YOU REMEMBERED THAT CODE?
THE PLACE IS TRIGGERING MEMORIES SUDDENLY NOW THAT I'M FINALLY HERE.
YOU READY?
OH YEAH.
KIM REBECKI WAS MY ONLY ALLY. MY ONLY FRIEND.
HER PSYCHOMETRIC ABILITY TO INTUIT THINGS BY TOUCH WAS PRETTY USEFUL.
AT FIRST, I THOUGHT SHE'D DECIDED TO HELP ME OUT OF A SENSE OF GUILT...

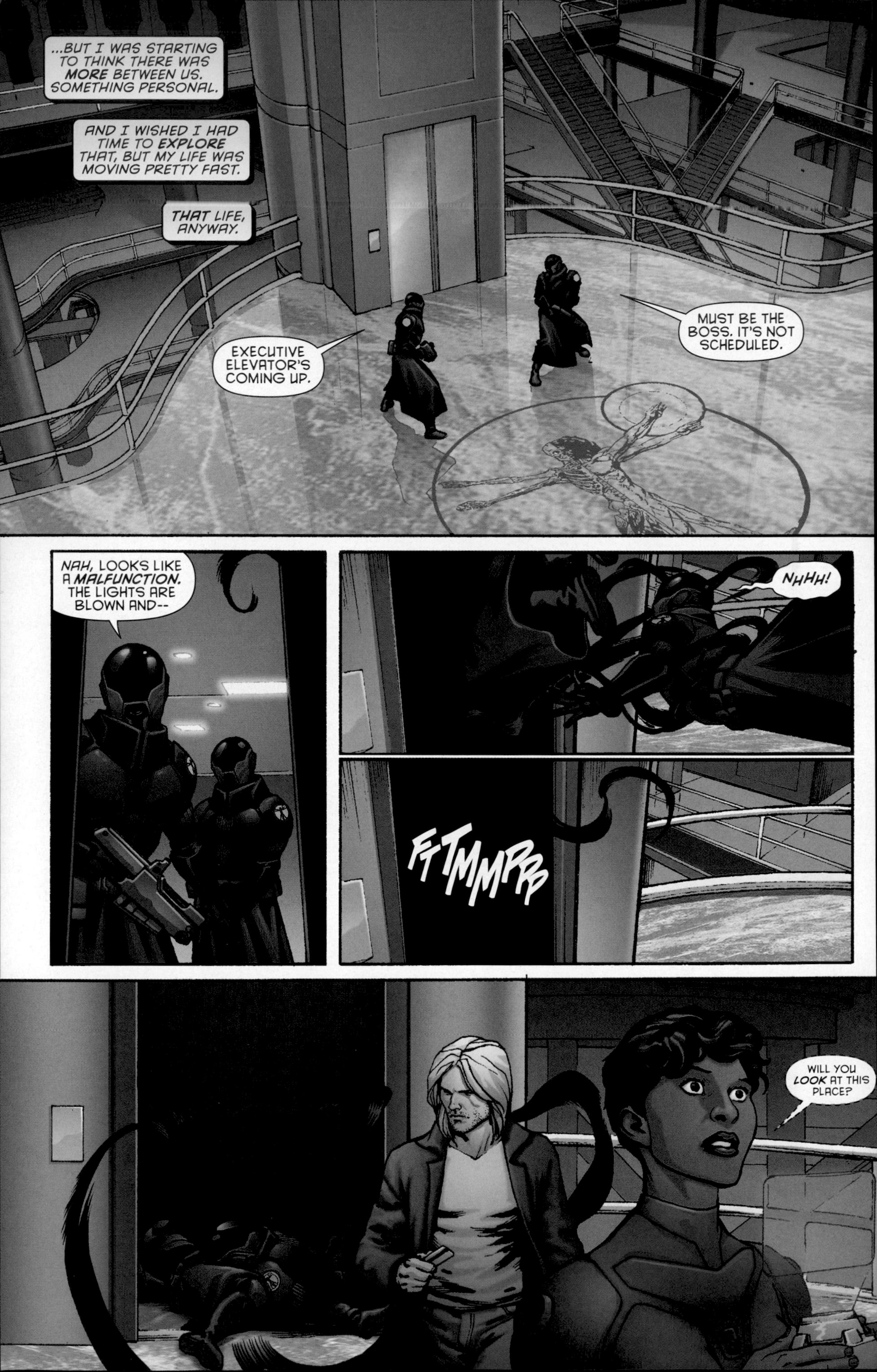
...BUT I WAS STARTING TO THINK THERE WAS MORE BETWEEN US. SOMETHING PERSONAL.
AND I WISHED I HAD TIME TO EXPLORE THAT, BUT MY LIFE WAS MOVING PRETTY FAST.
THAT LIFE, ANYWAY.
EXECUTIVE ELEVATOR'S COMING UP.
MUST BE THE BOSS. IT'S NOT SCHEDULED.
NAH, LOOKS LIKE A MALFUNCTION. THE LIGHTS ARE BLOWN AND--
NHHH!
FTTMMPPP
WILL YOU LOOK AT THIS PLACE?

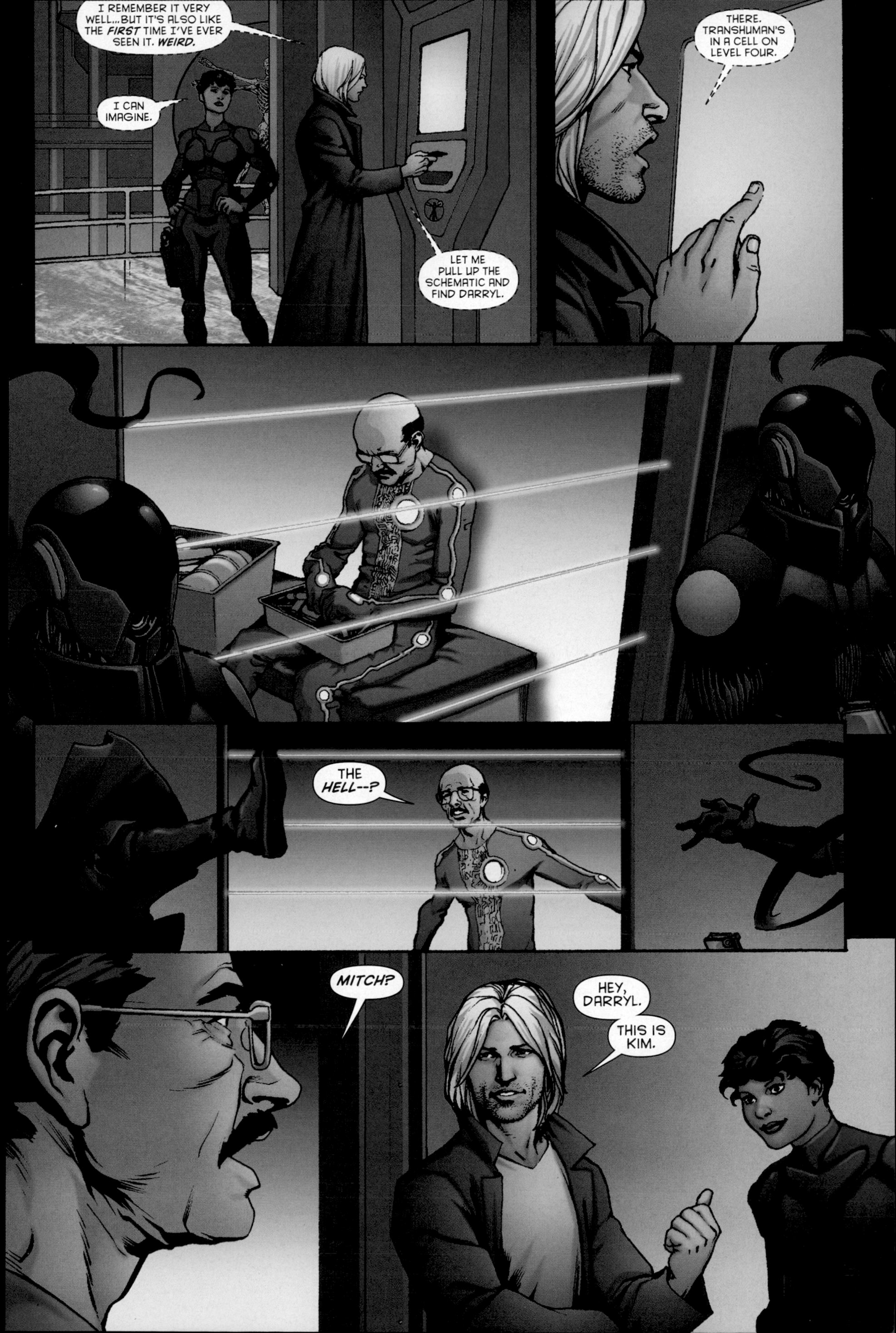
I REMEMBER IT VERY WELL...BUT IT'S ALSO LIKE THE *FIRST* TIME I'VE EVER SEEN IT. ***WEIRD.***
I CAN IMAGINE.
LET ME PULL UP THE SCHEMATIC AND FIND DARRYL.
THERE. TRANSHUMAN'S IN A CELL ON LEVEL FOUR.
THE *HELL*--?
MITCH?
HEY, DARRYL.
THIS IS KIM.

YOU CAME HERE TO BUST ME OUT? MITCH, THAT'S *SWEET*. BUT YOU *SHOULDN'T* HAVE DONE THAT.

DARRYL, I--

I SEE FROM THAT KIT YOUR *HOT FRIEND* IS WEARING THAT YOU FOUND MY *HIDEOUT*.

THEY *KNEW* YOU'D FIND IT AND TAKE SOMETHING.

DARRYL. COME ON.

THEY KNEW YOU'D COME FOR ME.

LOOK, I GOTTA GET MY ARMOR, OKAY?

DARRYL?

MITCH, I'M *SORRY*. THEY PROMISED ME A *CURE* IF I SAT HERE AND ACTED AS BAIT.

KLKK

AND, LIKE I TOLD YOU, I'M A *SUPER VILLAIN*.

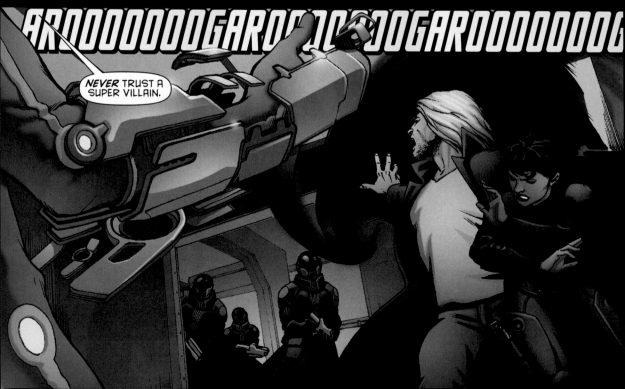

AROOOOOOOGAROOOOOOGAROOOOOOOG

NEVER TRUST A SUPER VILLAIN.

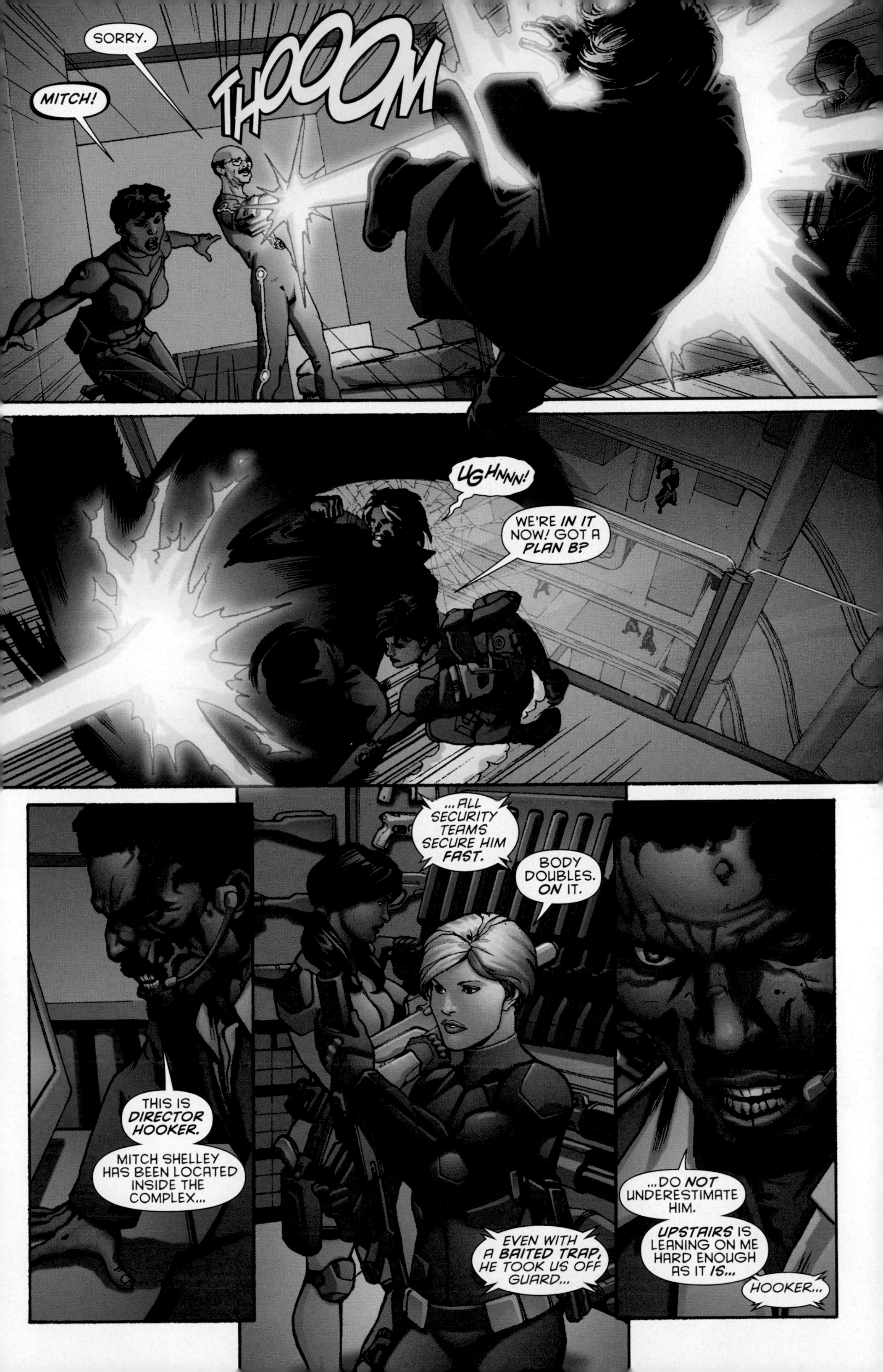
SORRY.
MITCH!
THOOOM
UGHNNN!
WE'RE IN IT NOW! GOT A PLAN B?
THIS IS DIRECTOR HOOKER.
MITCH SHELLEY HAS BEEN LOCATED INSIDE THE COMPLEX...
...ALL SECURITY TEAMS SECURE HIM FAST.
BODY DOUBLES. ON IT.
EVEN WITH A BAITED TRAP, HE TOOK US OFF GUARD...
...DO NOT UNDERESTIMATE HIM.
UPSTAIRS IS LEANING ON ME HARD ENOUGH AS IT IS...
HOOKER...

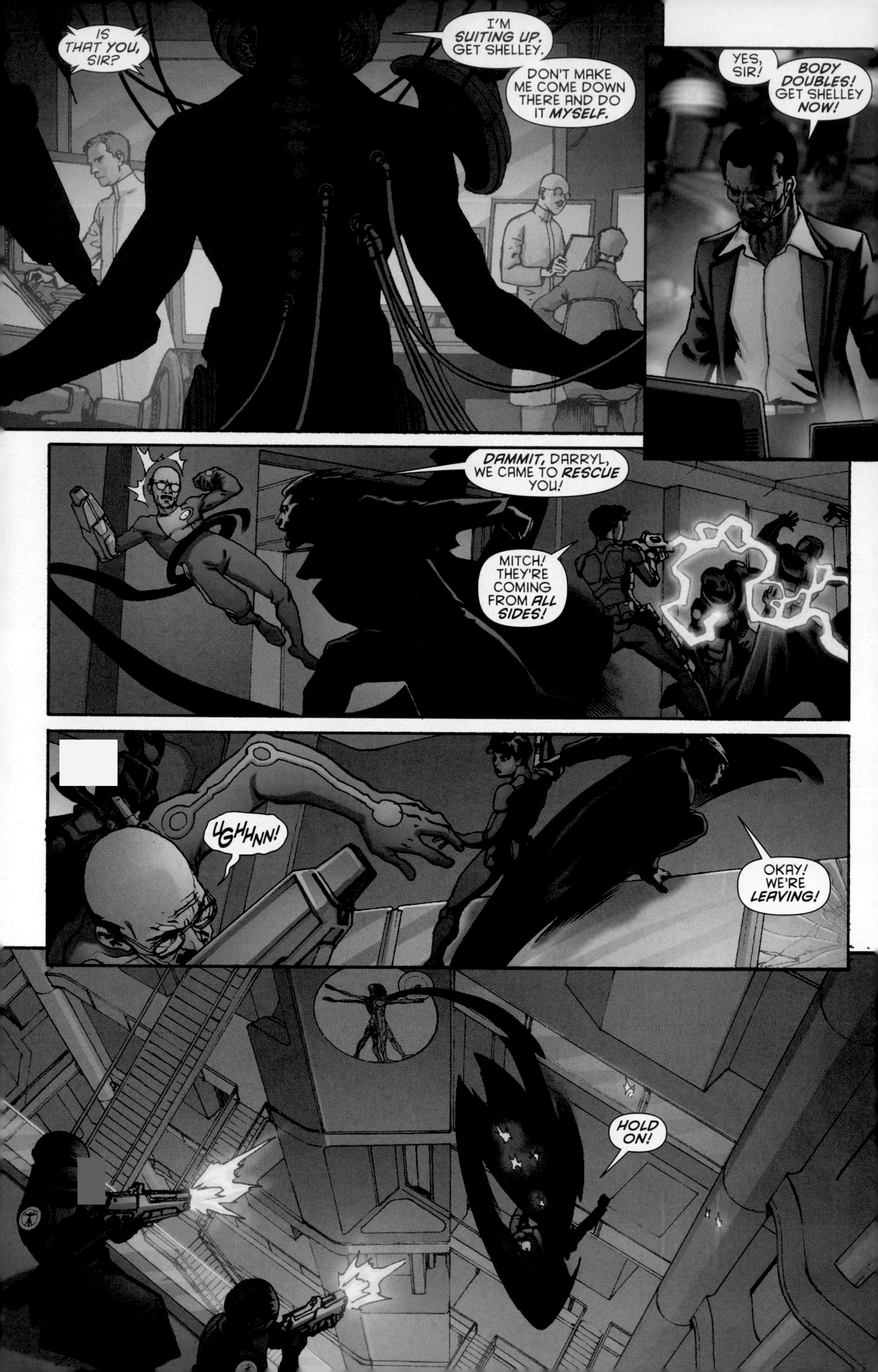
IS THAT YOU, SIR?
I'M SUITING UP. GET SHELLEY.
DON'T MAKE ME COME DOWN THERE AND DO IT MYSELF.
YES, SIR!
BODY DOUBLES! GET SHELLEY NOW!
DAMMIT, DARRYL, WE CAME TO RESCUE YOU!
MITCH! THEY'RE COMING FROM ALL SIDES!
UGHHNN!
OKAY! WE'RE LEAVING!
HOLD ON!

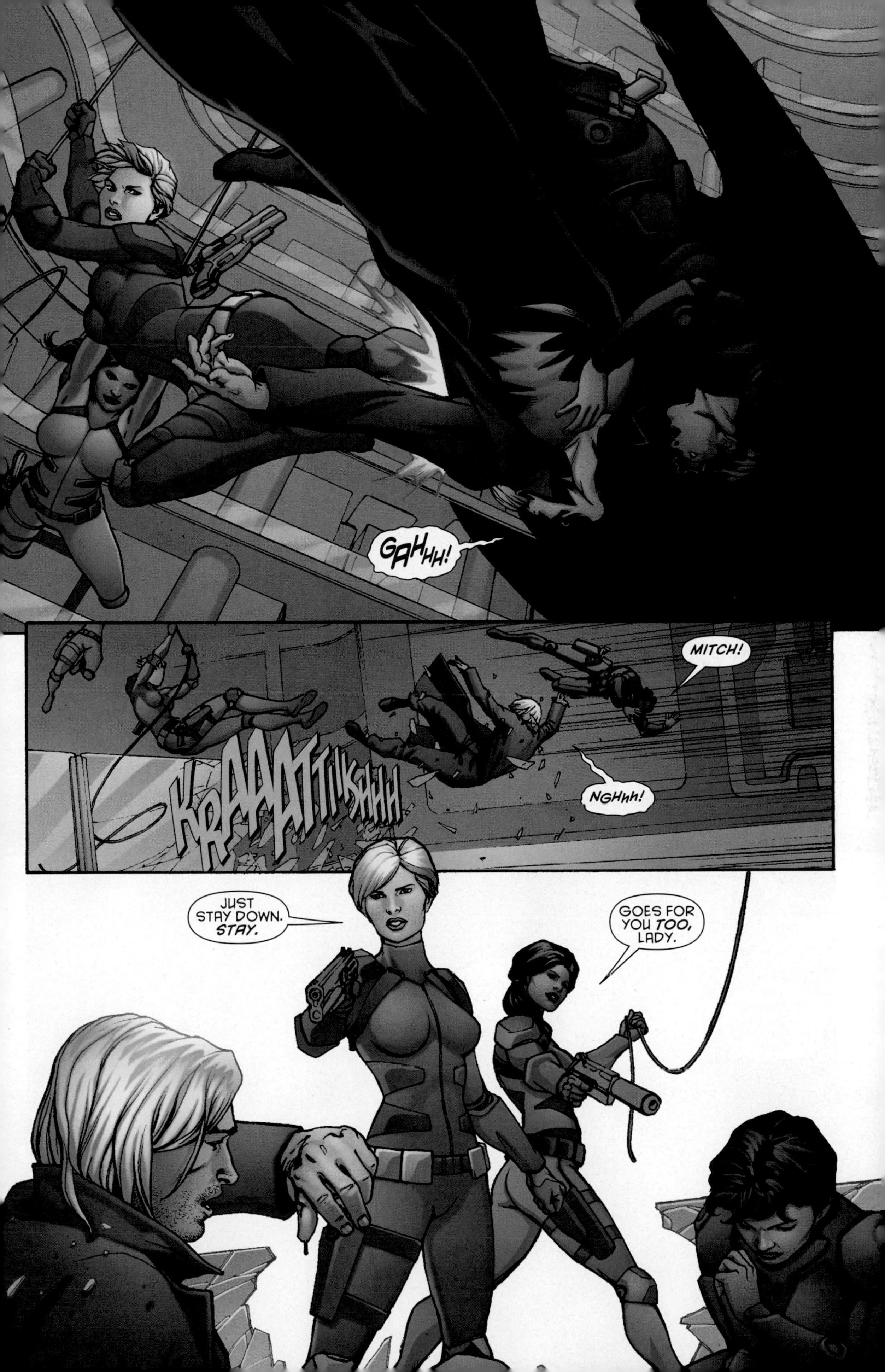
GAHHH!
MITCH!
KRAAATTIKSHHH
NGHhh!
JUST STAY DOWN. STAY.
GOES FOR YOU TOO, LADY.

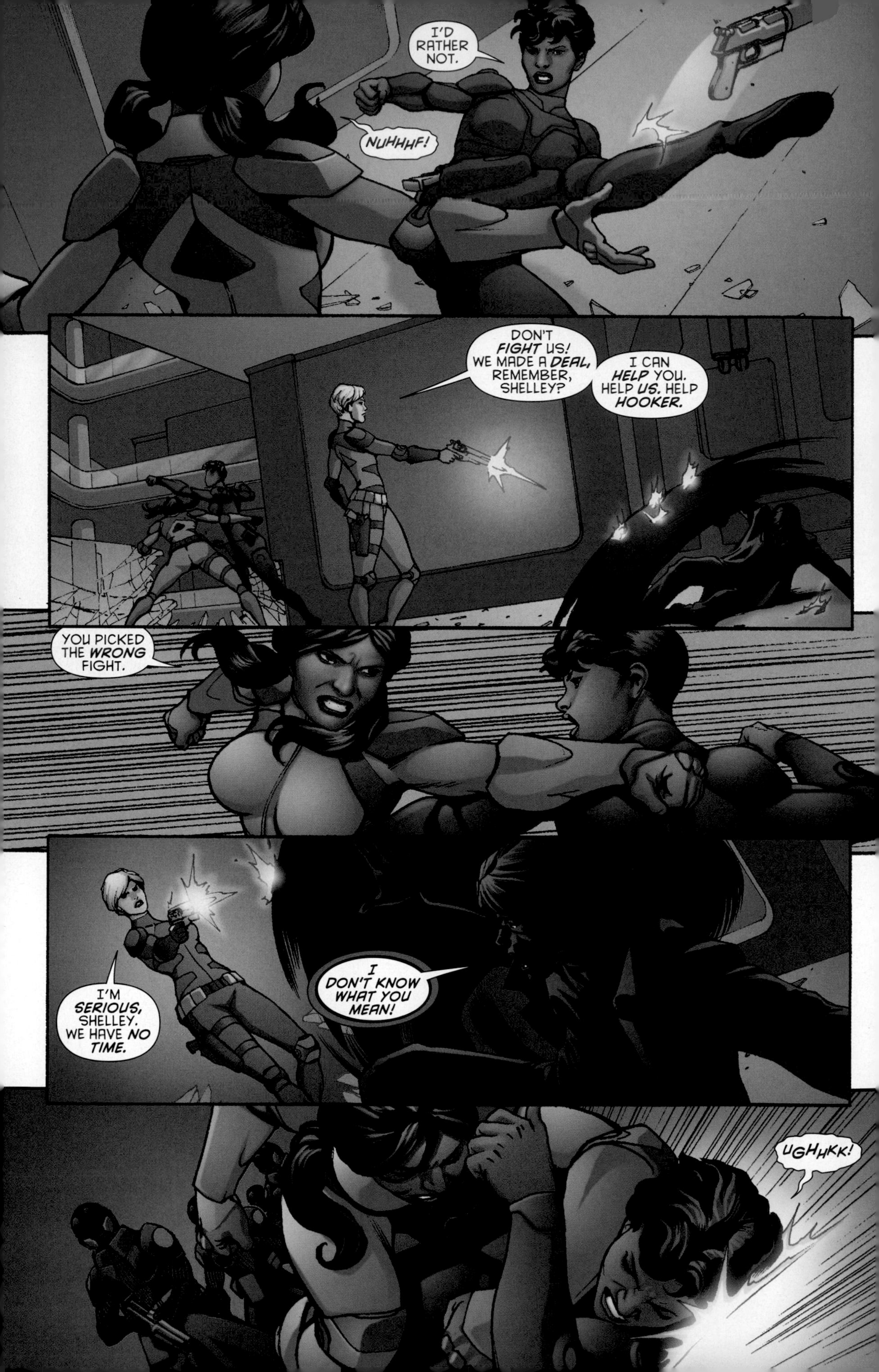
I'D RATHER NOT.
NUHHHF!
DON'T FIGHT US! WE MADE A DEAL, REMEMBER, SHELLEY?
I CAN HELP YOU. HELP US. HELP HOOKER.
YOU PICKED THE WRONG FIGHT.
I'M SERIOUS, SHELLEY. WE HAVE NO TIME.
I DON'T KNOW WHAT YOU MEAN!
UGHHKK!

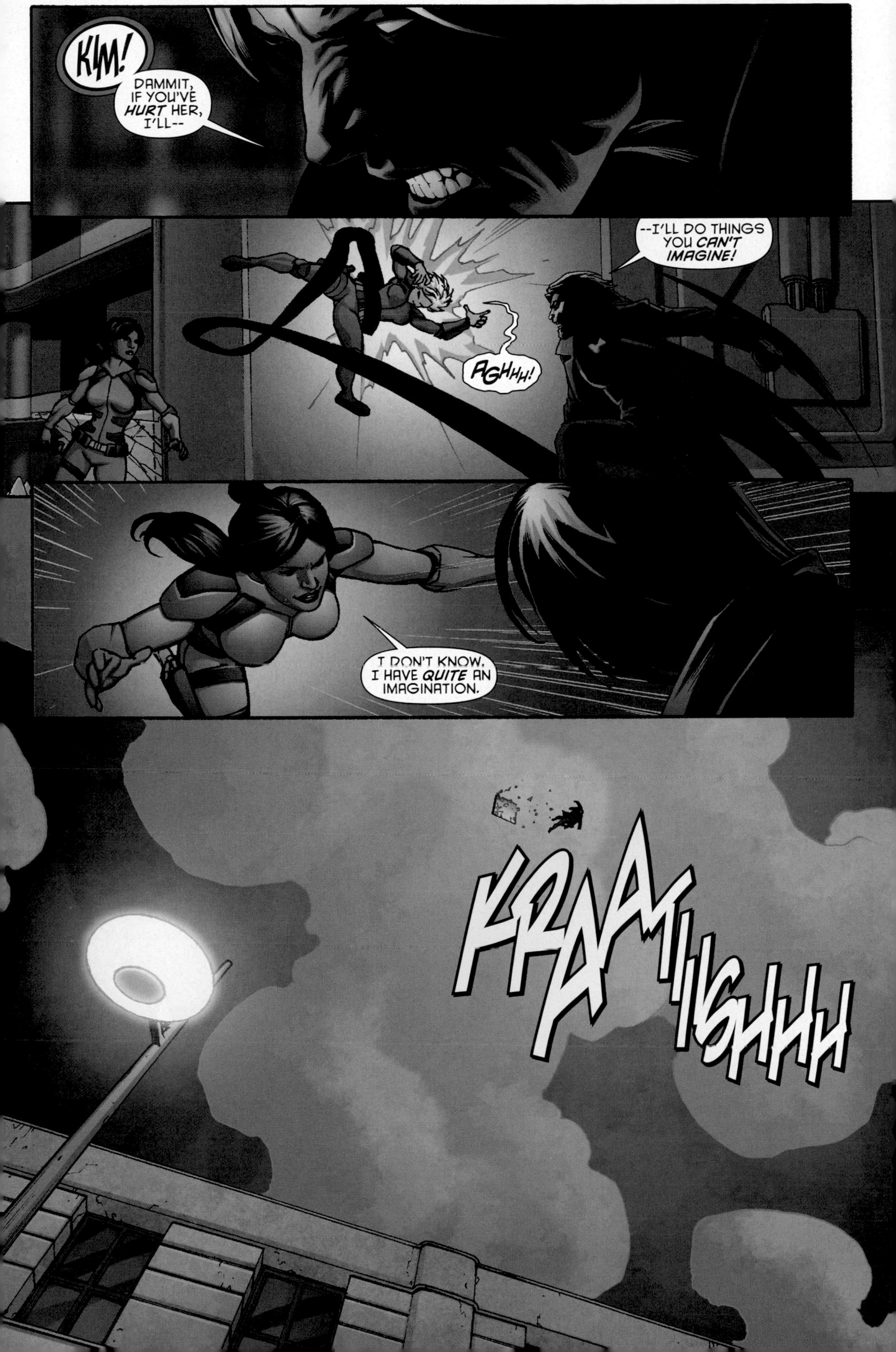
KIM!
DAMMIT, IF YOU'VE HURT HER, I'LL--
--I'LL DO THINGS YOU CAN'T IMAGINE!
AGHHH!
I DON'T KNOW. I HAVE QUITE AN IMAGINATION.
KRAAASHHH

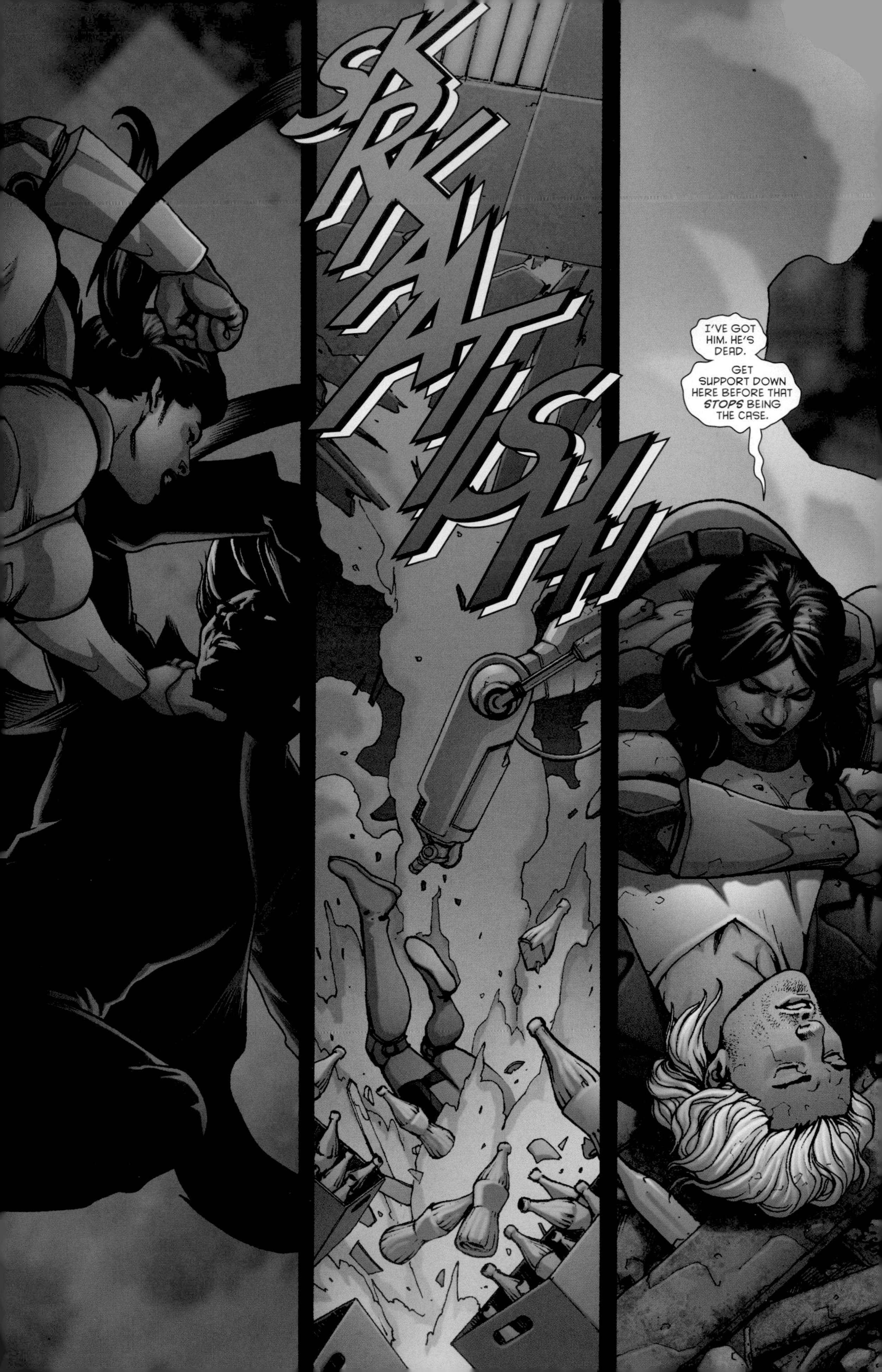
SKRRAKATTCHSSH
I'VE GOT HIM. HE'S DEAD.
GET SUPPORT DOWN HERE BEFORE THAT STOPS BEING THE CASE.

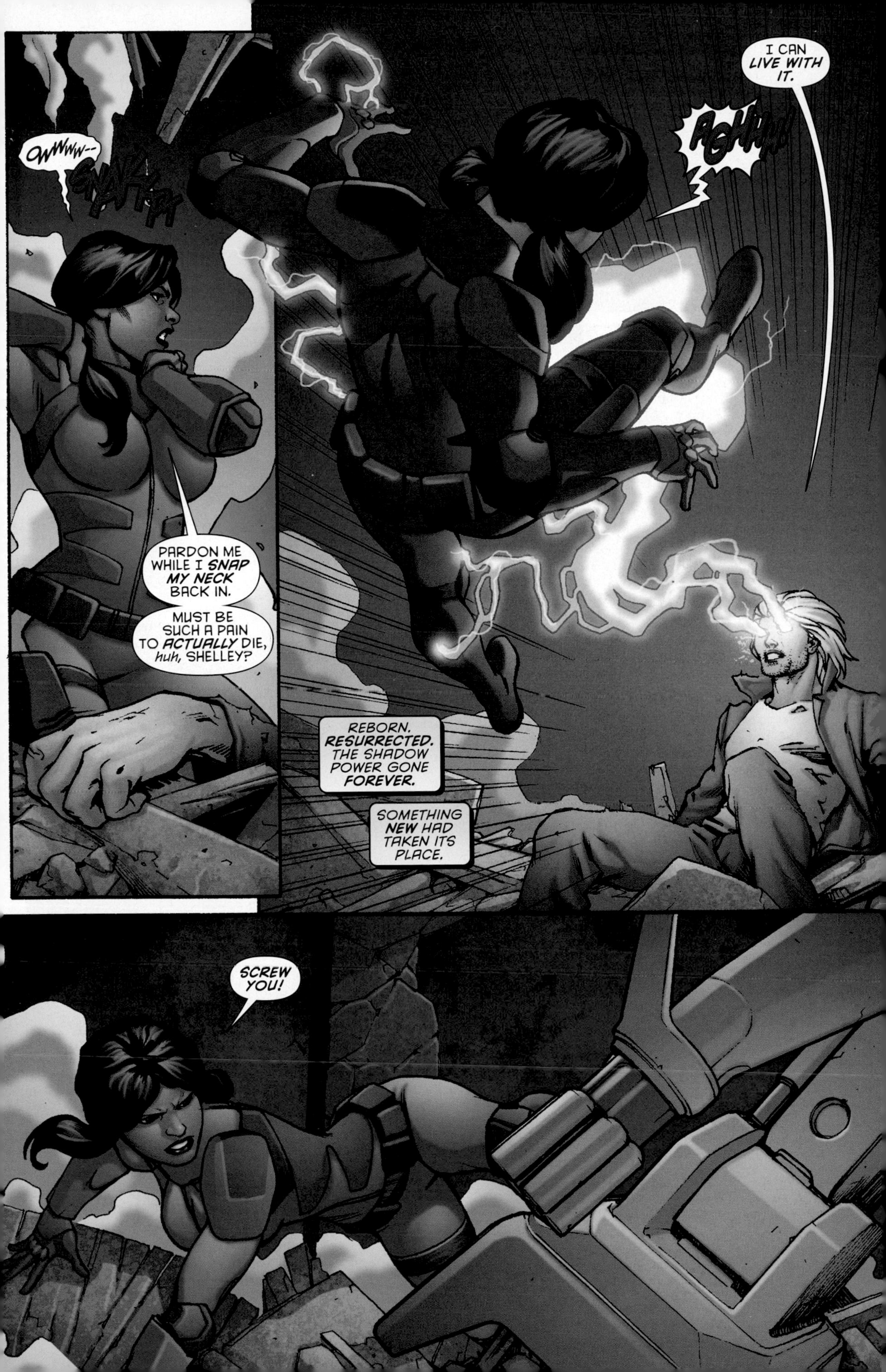
OWWWW--
SNAKKKT
PARDON ME WHILE I SNAP MY NECK BACK IN.
MUST BE SUCH A PAIN TO ACTUALLY DIE, huh, SHELLEY?
I CAN LIVE WITH IT.
AGHHH!
REBORN. RESURRECTED. THE SHADOW POWER GONE FOREVER.
SOMETHING NEW HAD TAKEN ITS PLACE.
SCREW YOU!

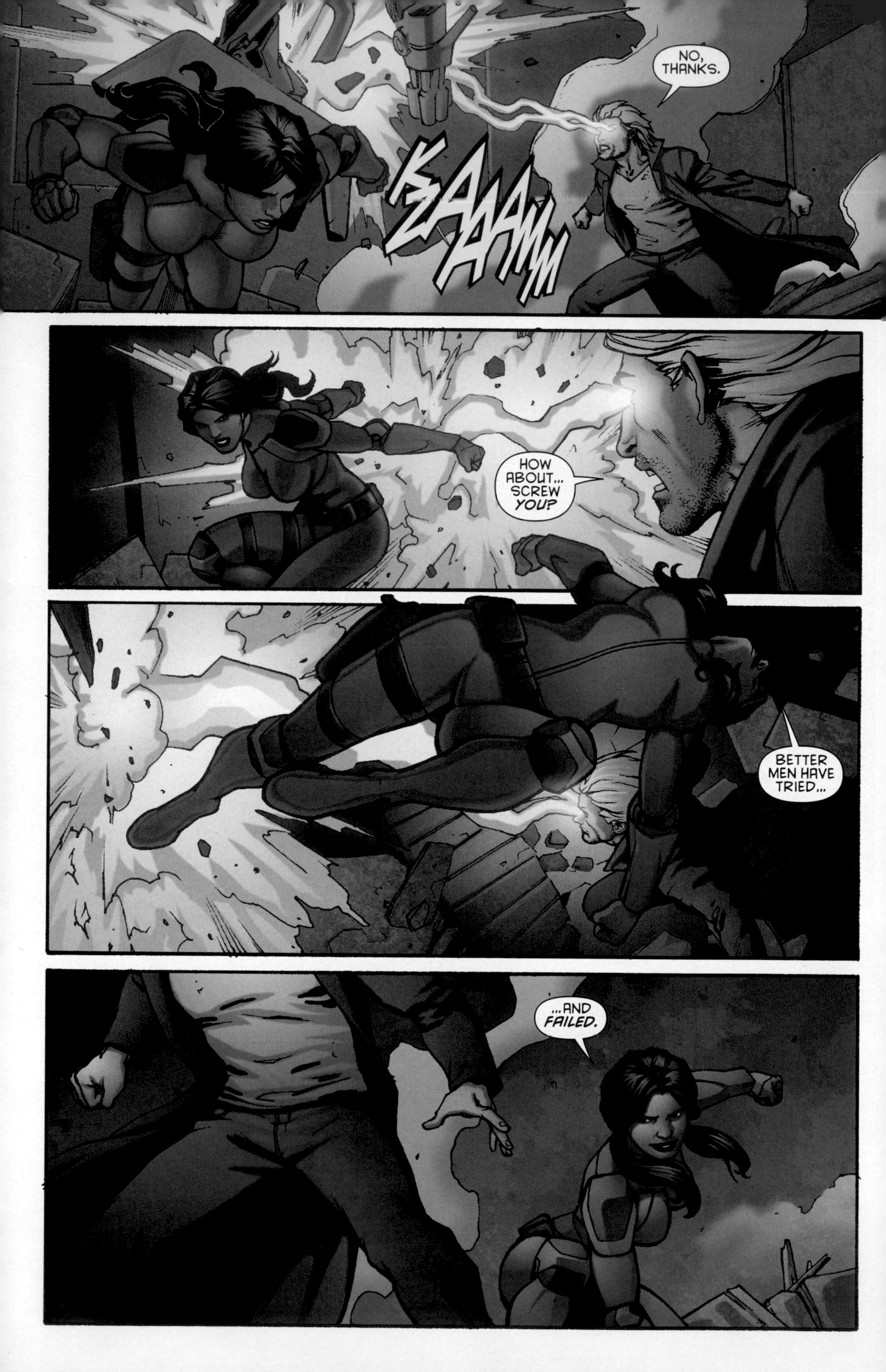
NO, THANKS.
KRAAAMM
HOW ABOUT... SCREW *YOU?*
BETTER MEN HAVE TRIED...
...AND *FAILED.*

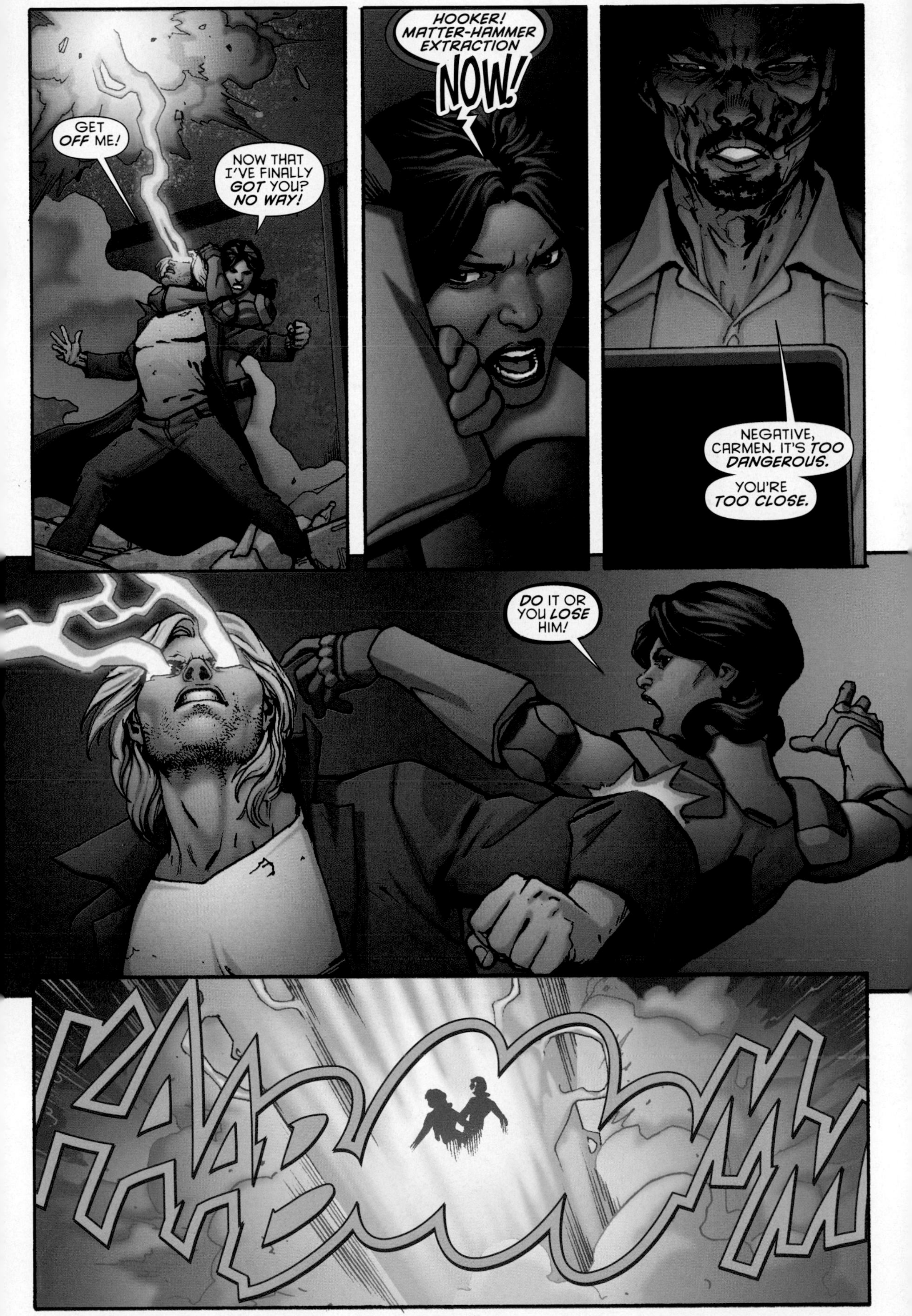
GET OFF ME!
NOW THAT I'VE FINALLY GOT YOU? NO WAY!
HOOKER! MATTER-HAMMER EXTRACTION NOW!
NEGATIVE, CARMEN. IT'S TOO DANGEROUS.
YOU'RE TOO CLOSE.
DO IT OR YOU LOSE HIM!
KABOOM

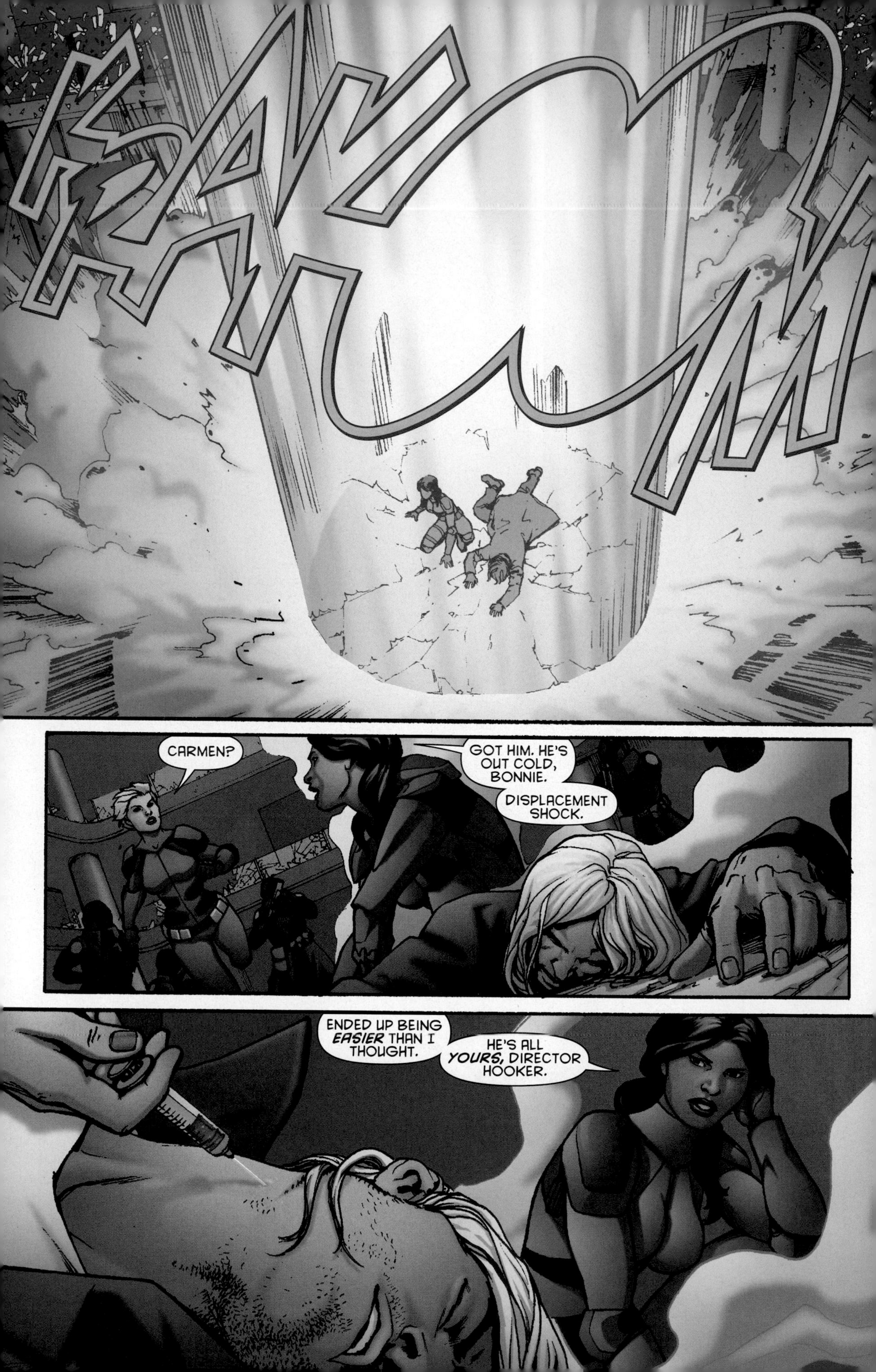
KRAKKOOM
CARMEN?
GOT HIM. HE'S OUT COLD, BONNIE.
DISPLACEMENT SHOCK.
ENDED UP BEING *EASIER* THAN I THOUGHT.
HE'S ALL *YOURS,* DIRECTOR HOOKER.

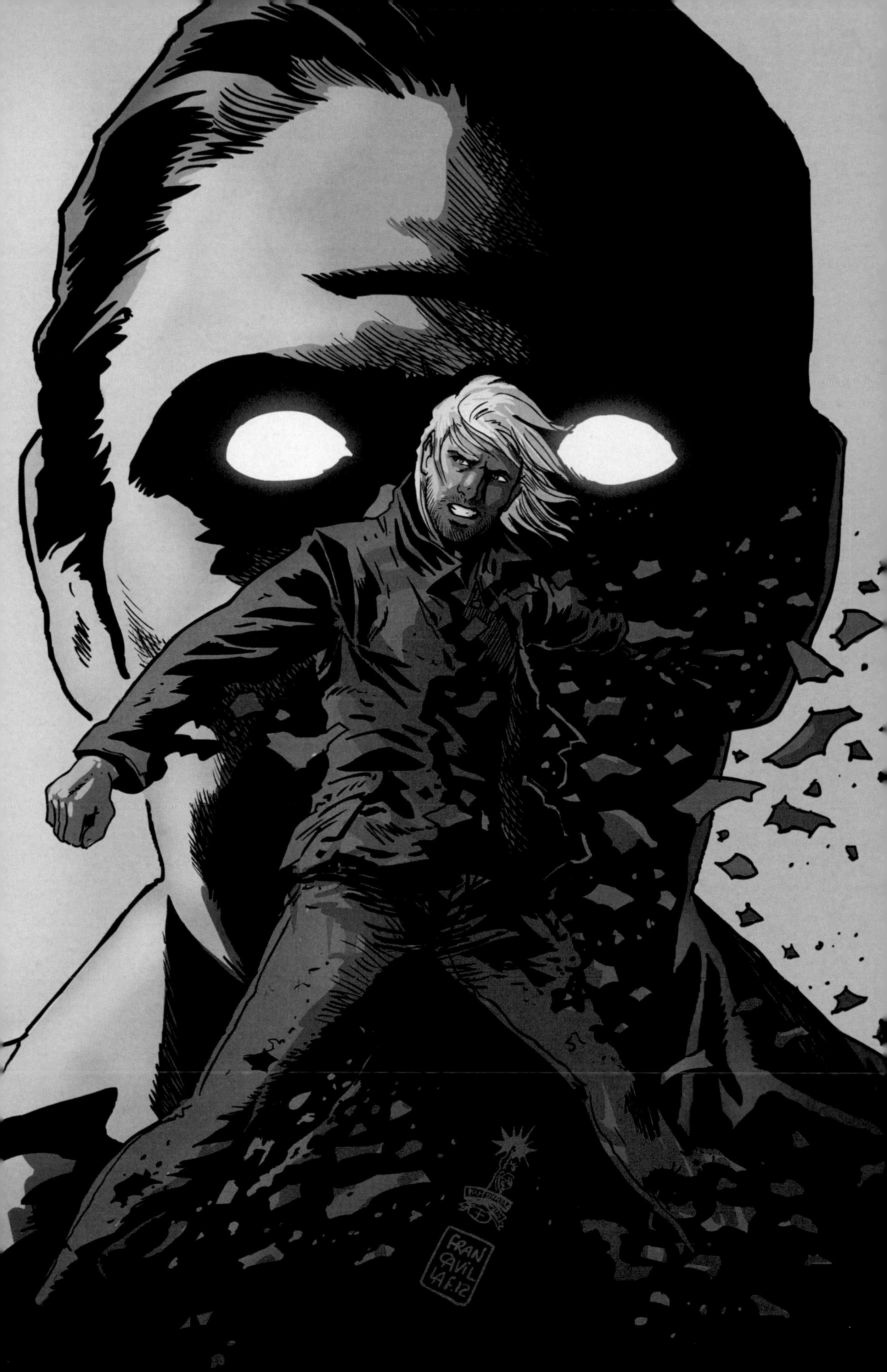
FRAN
CAVIL
LA F.12

THE REBORN IDENTITY

DAN ABNETT & ANDY LANNING
writers

JAVIER PINA
artist

cover art by
FRANCISCO FRANCAVILLA

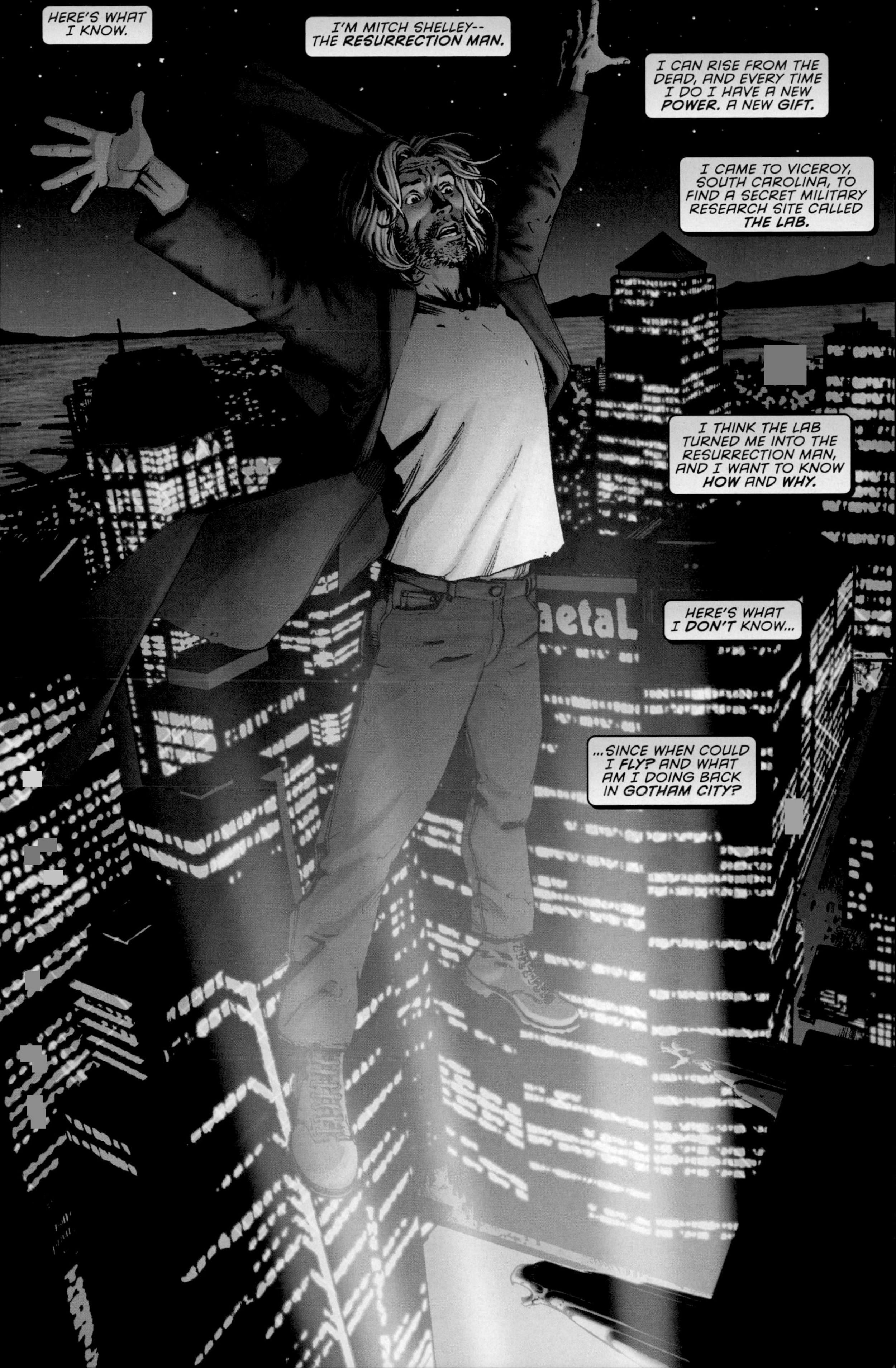
HERE'S WHAT I KNOW.
I'M MITCH SHELLEY-- THE RESURRECTION MAN.
I CAN RISE FROM THE DEAD, AND EVERY TIME I DO I HAVE A NEW POWER. A NEW GIFT.
I CAME TO VICEROY, SOUTH CAROLINA, TO FIND A SECRET MILITARY RESEARCH SITE CALLED THE LAB.
I THINK THE LAB TURNED ME INTO THE RESURRECTION MAN, AND I WANT TO KNOW HOW AND WHY.
aetal
HERE'S WHAT I DON'T KNOW...
...SINCE WHEN COULD I FLY? AND WHAT AM I DOING BACK IN GOTHAM CITY?

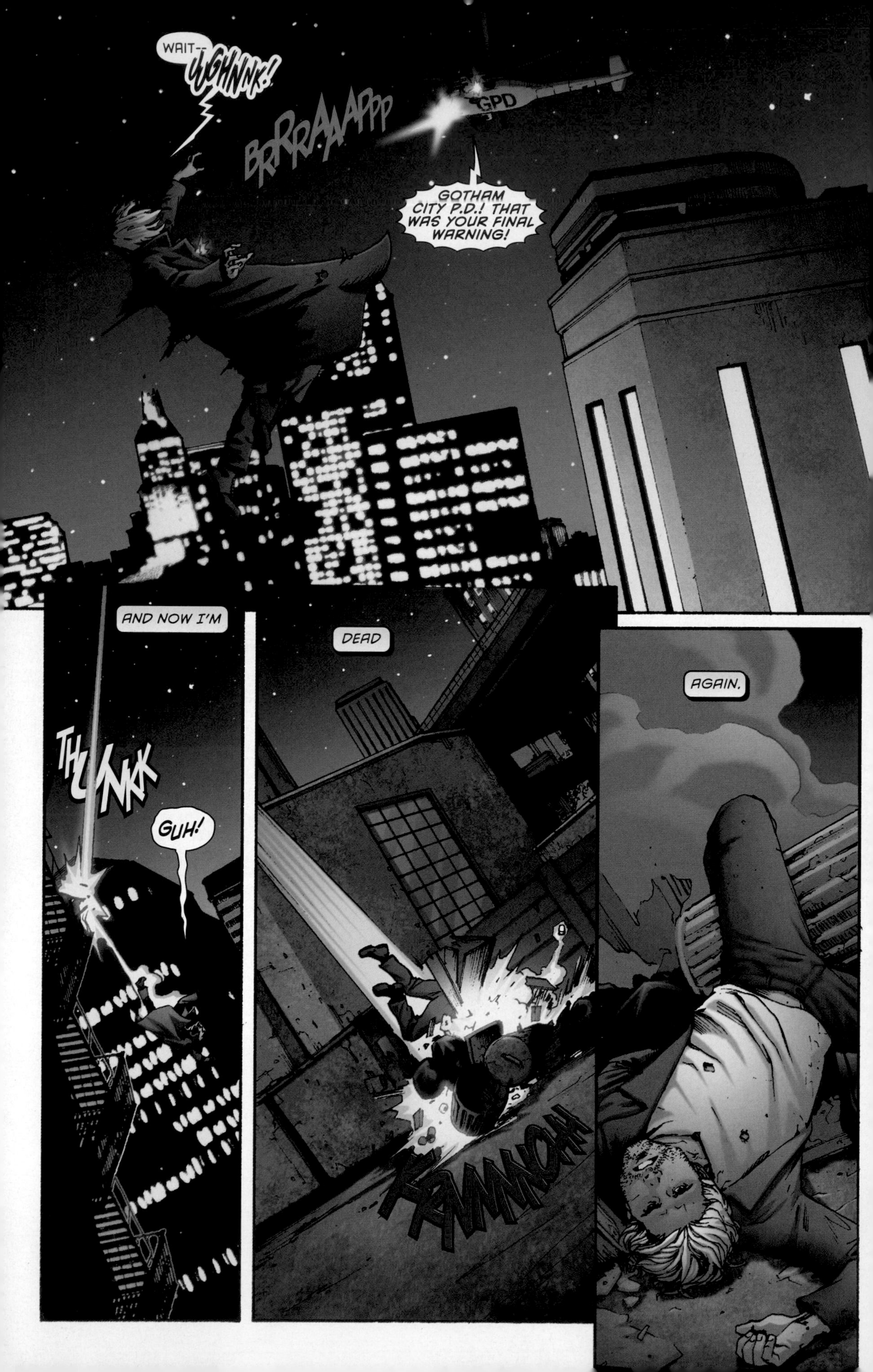
WAIT--
UGHNNK!
BRRRAAAPPP
GPD
GOTHAM CITY P.D.! THAT WAS YOUR FINAL WARNING!
AND NOW I'M
THUNKK
GUH!
DEAD
KRAMMOOM
AGAIN.

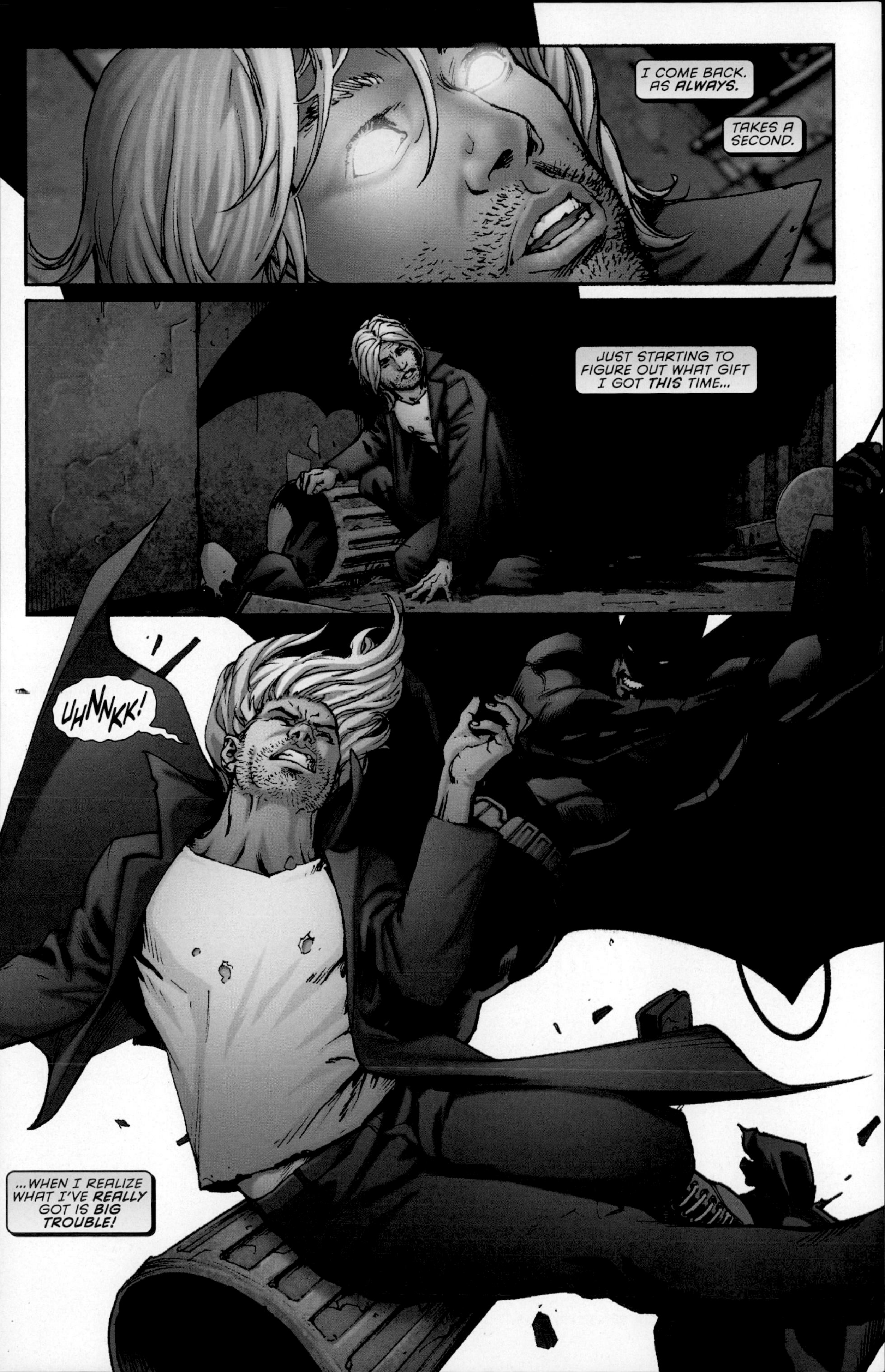
I COME BACK. AS ALWAYS.
TAKES A SECOND.
JUST STARTING TO FIGURE OUT WHAT GIFT I GOT THIS TIME...
UHNNKK!
...WHEN I REALIZE WHAT I'VE REALLY GOT IS BIG TROUBLE!

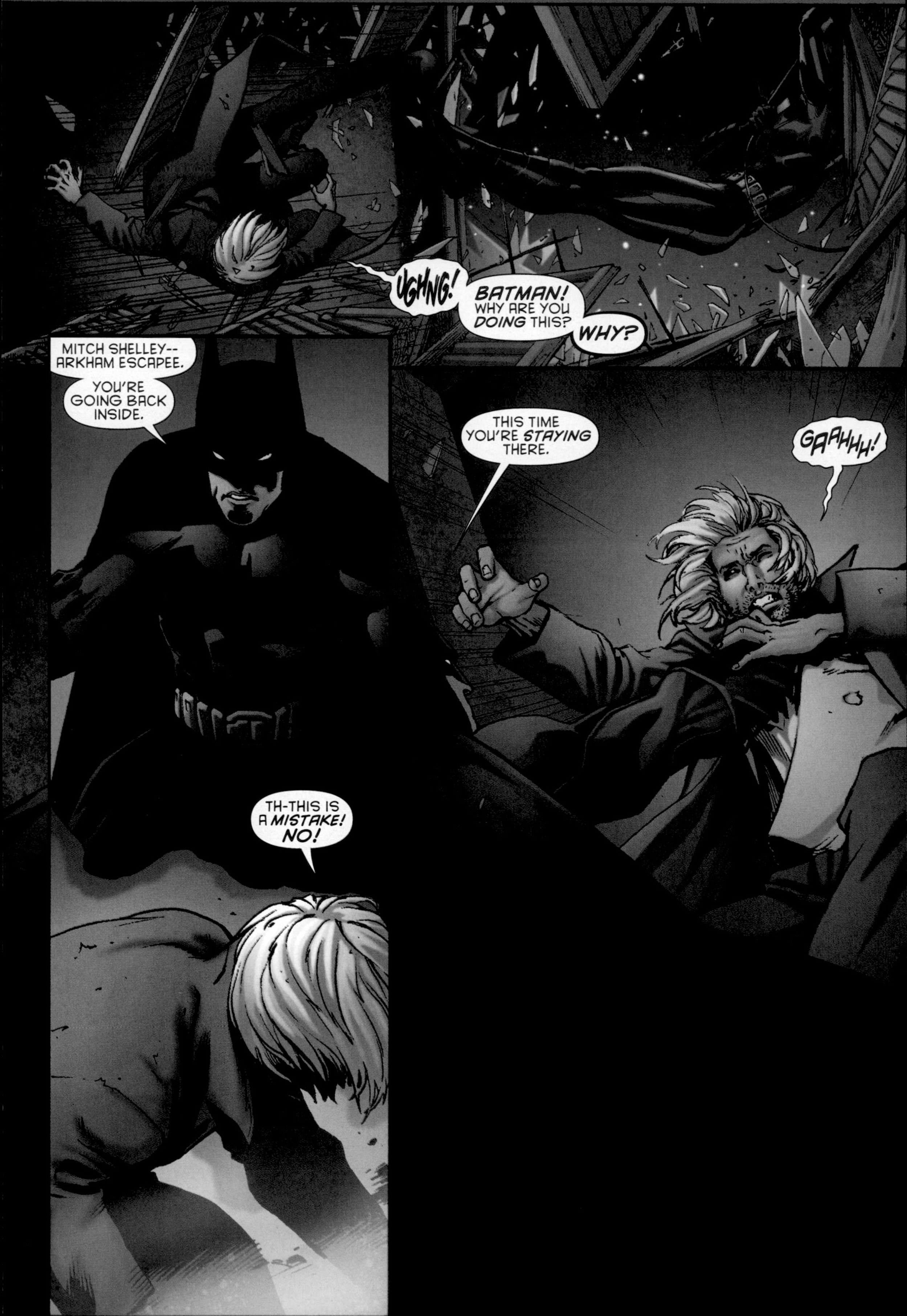
UGHNG!
BATMAN! WHY ARE YOU DOING THIS?
WHY?
MITCH SHELLEY-- ARKHAM ESCAPEE.
YOU'RE GOING BACK INSIDE.
THIS TIME YOU'RE STAYING THERE.
GAAHHH!
TH-THIS IS A MISTAKE! NO!

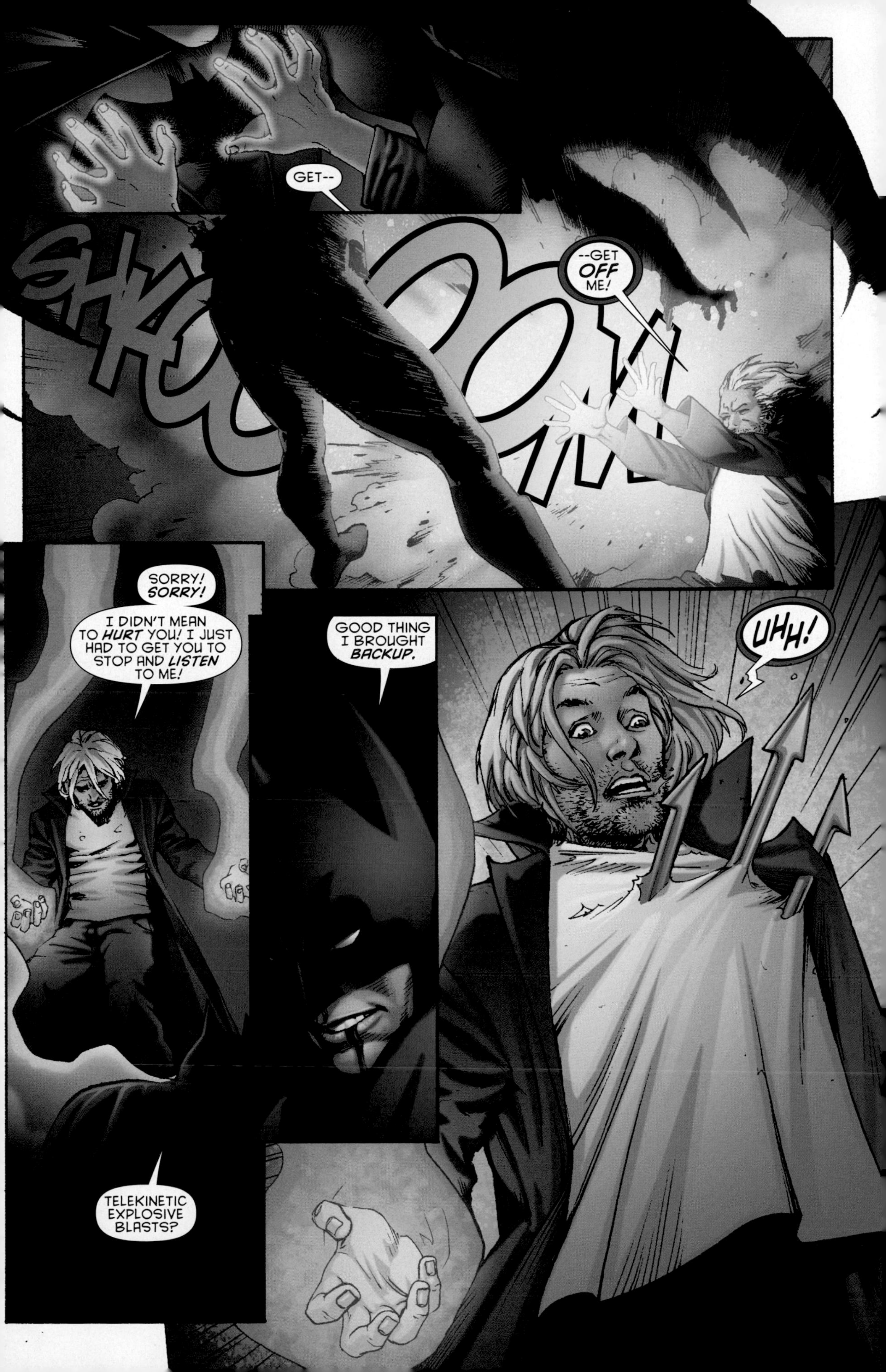
GET--
SHOOOM
--GET OFF ME!
SORRY! SORRY!
I DIDN'T MEAN TO HURT YOU! I JUST HAD TO GET YOU TO STOP AND LISTEN TO ME!
GOOD THING I BROUGHT BACKUP.
UHH!
TELEKINETIC EXPLOSIVE BLASTS?

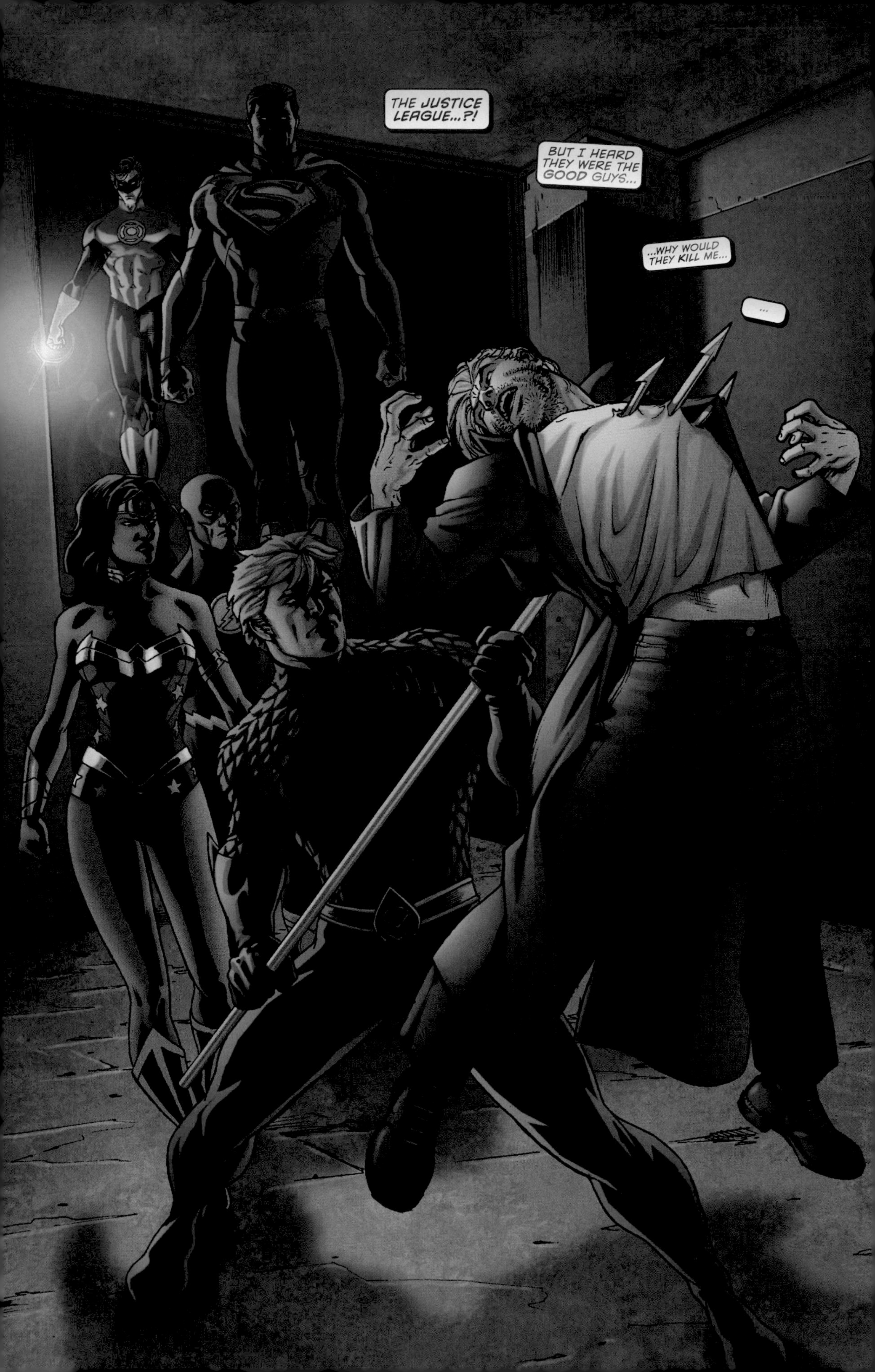
THE JUSTICE LEAGUE...?!
BUT I HEARD THEY WERE THE GOOD GUYS...
...WHY WOULD THEY KILL ME...
...

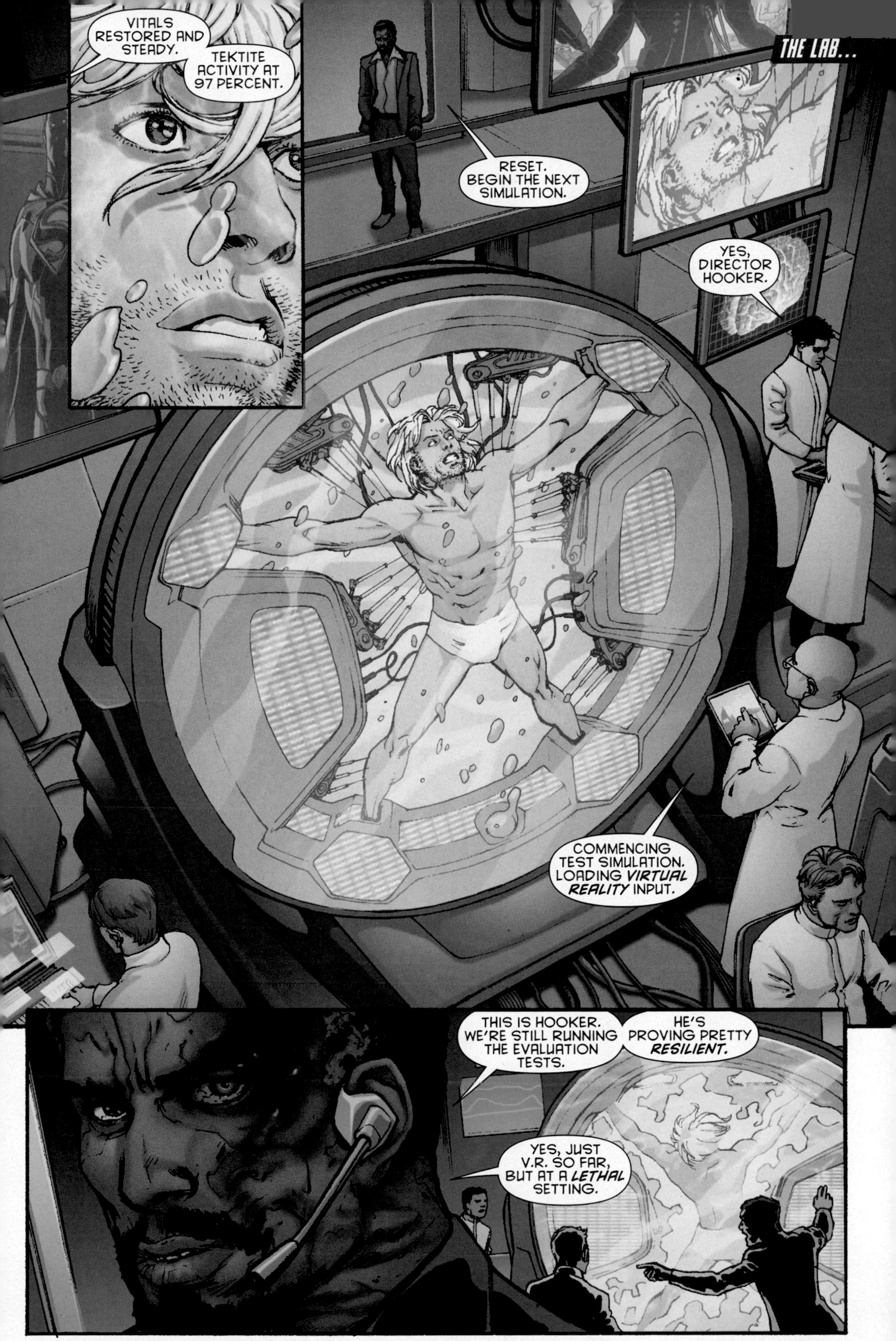
THE LAB...
VITALS RESTORED AND STEADY.
TEKTITE ACTIVITY AT 97 PERCENT.
RESET. BEGIN THE NEXT SIMULATION.
YES, DIRECTOR HOOKER.
COMMENCING TEST SIMULATION. LOADING *VIRTUAL REALITY* INPUT.
THIS IS HOOKER. WE'RE STILL RUNNING THE EVALUATION TESTS.
HE'S PROVING PRETTY *RESILIENT.*
YES, JUST V.R. SO FAR, BUT AT A *LETHAL* SETTING.

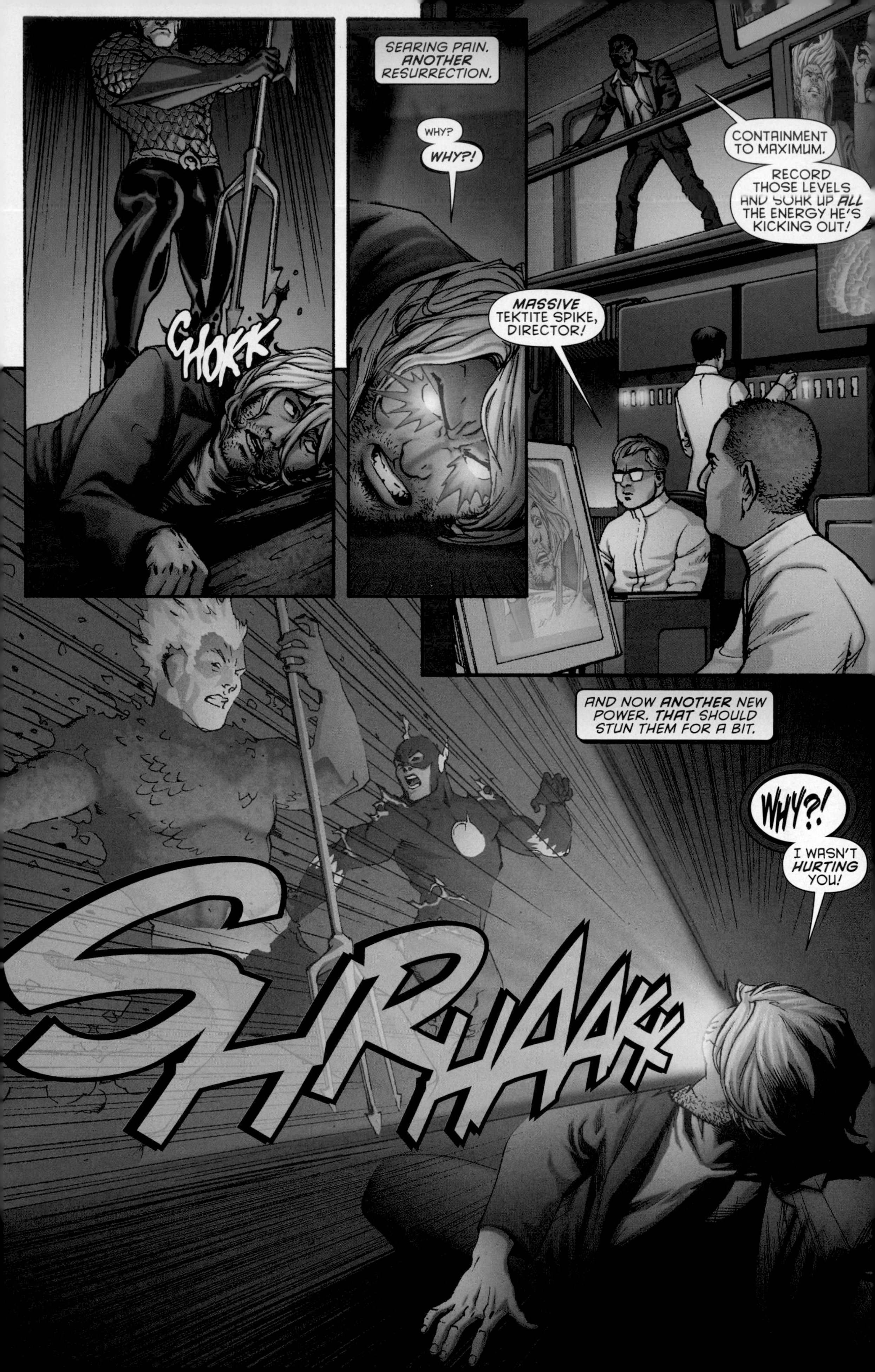
CHOKK
SEARING PAIN. ANOTHER RESURRECTION.
WHY? WHY?!
CONTAINMENT TO MAXIMUM.
RECORD THOSE LEVELS AND SUCK UP ALL THE ENERGY HE'S KICKING OUT!
MASSIVE TEKTITE SPIKE, DIRECTOR!
AND NOW ANOTHER NEW POWER. THAT SHOULD STUN THEM FOR A BIT.
WHY?!
I WASN'T HURTING YOU!
SHRAAAK

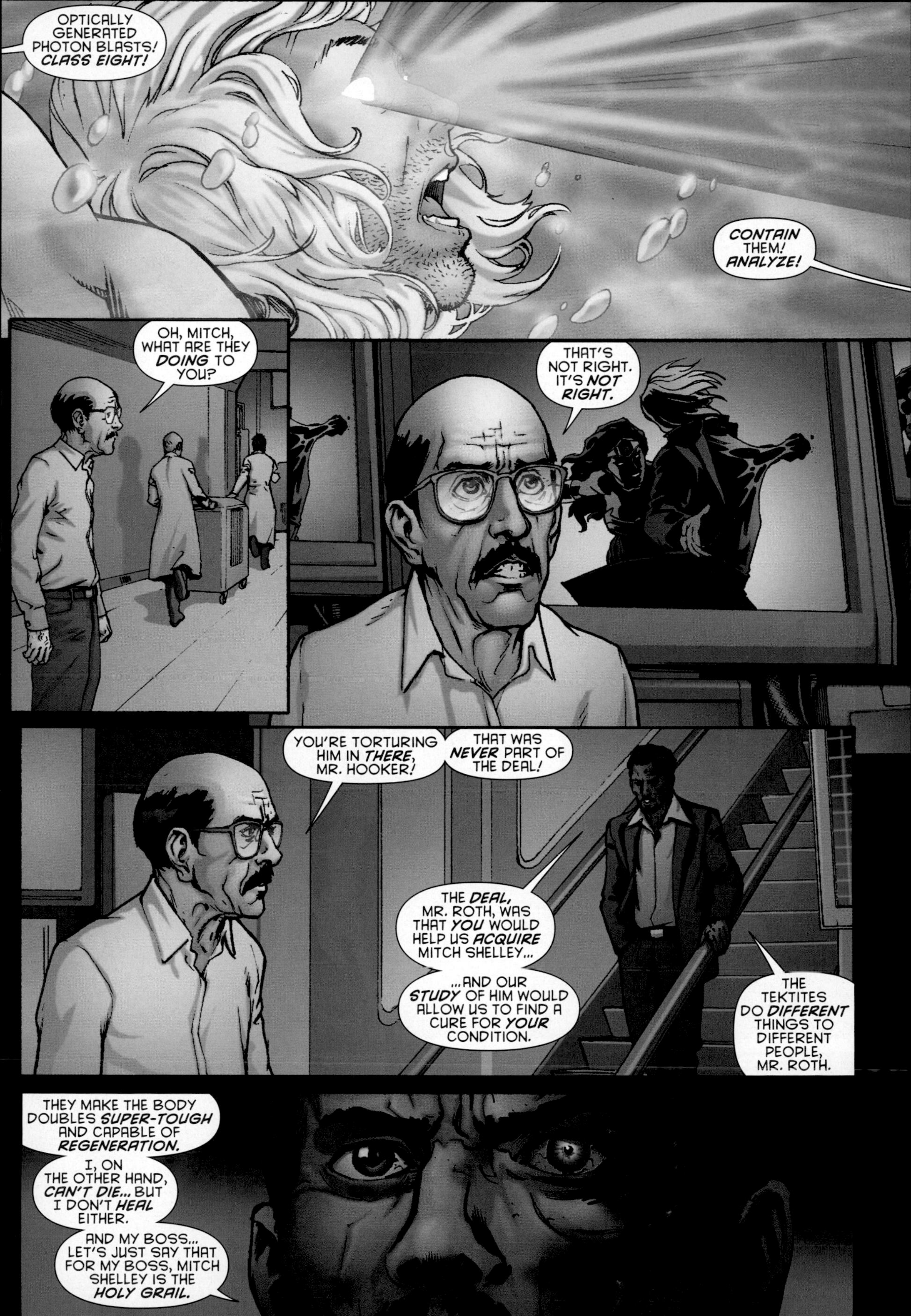
OPTICALLY GENERATED PHOTON BLASTS! CLASS EIGHT!
CONTAIN THEM! ANALYZE!
OH, MITCH, WHAT ARE THEY DOING TO YOU?
THAT'S NOT RIGHT. IT'S NOT RIGHT.
YOU'RE TORTURING HIM IN THERE, MR. HOOKER!
THAT WAS NEVER PART OF THE DEAL!
THE DEAL, MR. ROTH, WAS THAT YOU WOULD HELP US ACQUIRE MITCH SHELLEY...
...AND OUR STUDY OF HIM WOULD ALLOW US TO FIND A CURE FOR YOUR CONDITION.
THE TEKTITES DO DIFFERENT THINGS TO DIFFERENT PEOPLE, MR. ROTH.
THEY MAKE THE BODY DOUBLES SUPER-TOUGH AND CAPABLE OF REGENERATION.
I, ON THE OTHER HAND, CAN'T DIE... BUT I DON'T HEAL EITHER.
AND MY BOSS... LET'S JUST SAY THAT FOR MY BOSS, MITCH SHELLEY IS THE HOLY GRAIL.

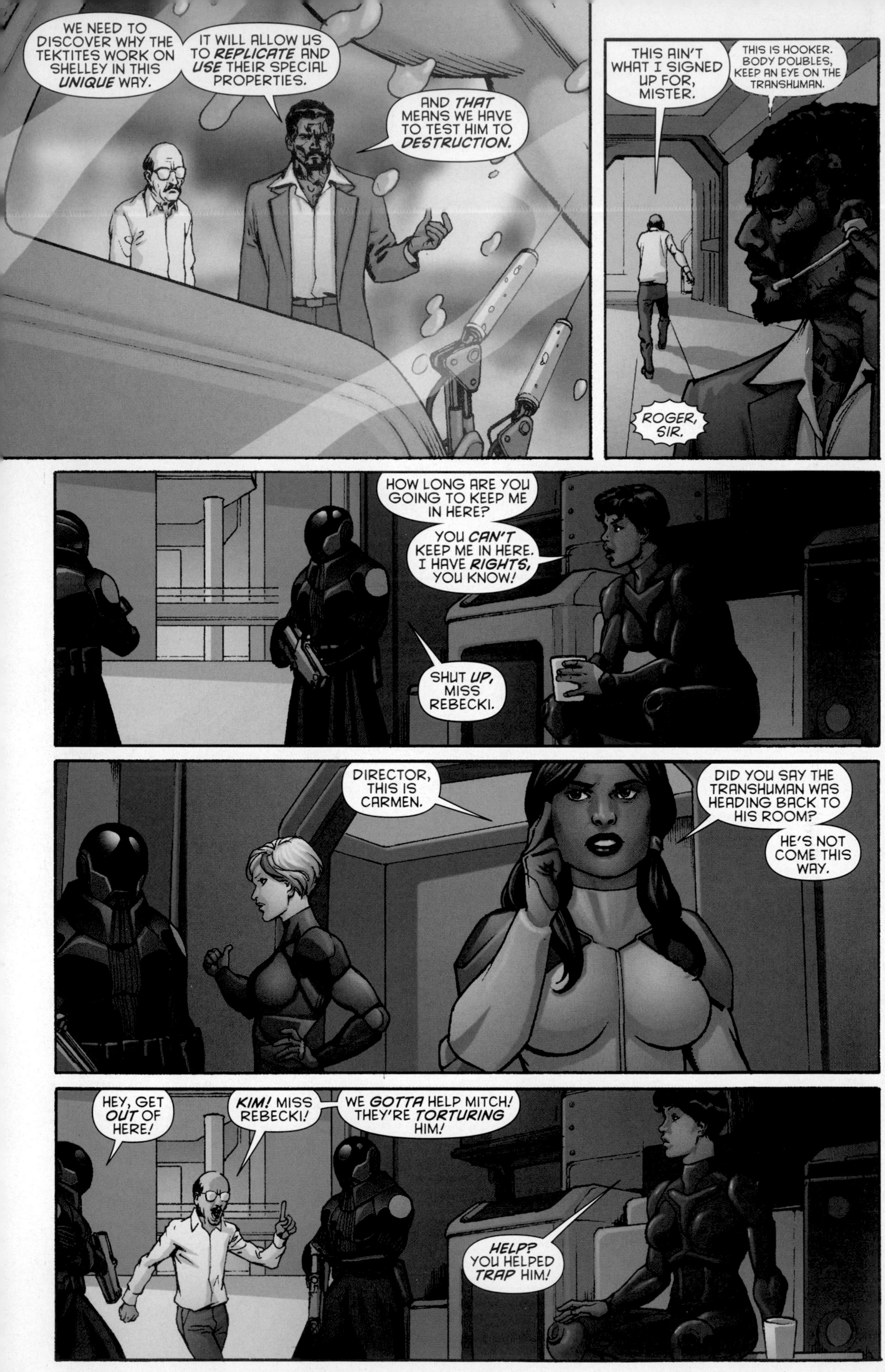
WE NEED TO DISCOVER WHY THE TEKTITES WORK ON SHELLEY IN THIS UNIQUE WAY.
IT WILL ALLOW US TO REPLICATE AND USE THEIR SPECIAL PROPERTIES.
AND THAT MEANS WE HAVE TO TEST HIM TO DESTRUCTION.
THIS AIN'T WHAT I SIGNED UP FOR, MISTER.
THIS IS HOOKER. BODY DOUBLES, KEEP AN EYE ON THE TRANSHUMAN.
ROGER, SIR.
HOW LONG ARE YOU GOING TO KEEP ME IN HERE?
YOU CAN'T KEEP ME IN HERE. I HAVE RIGHTS, YOU KNOW!
SHUT UP, MISS REBECKI.
DIRECTOR, THIS IS CARMEN.
DID YOU SAY THE TRANSHUMAN WAS HEADING BACK TO HIS ROOM?
HE'S NOT COME THIS WAY.
HEY, GET OUT OF HERE!
KIM! MISS REBECKI!
WE GOTTA HELP MITCH! THEY'RE TORTURING HIM!
HELP? YOU HELPED TRAP HIM!

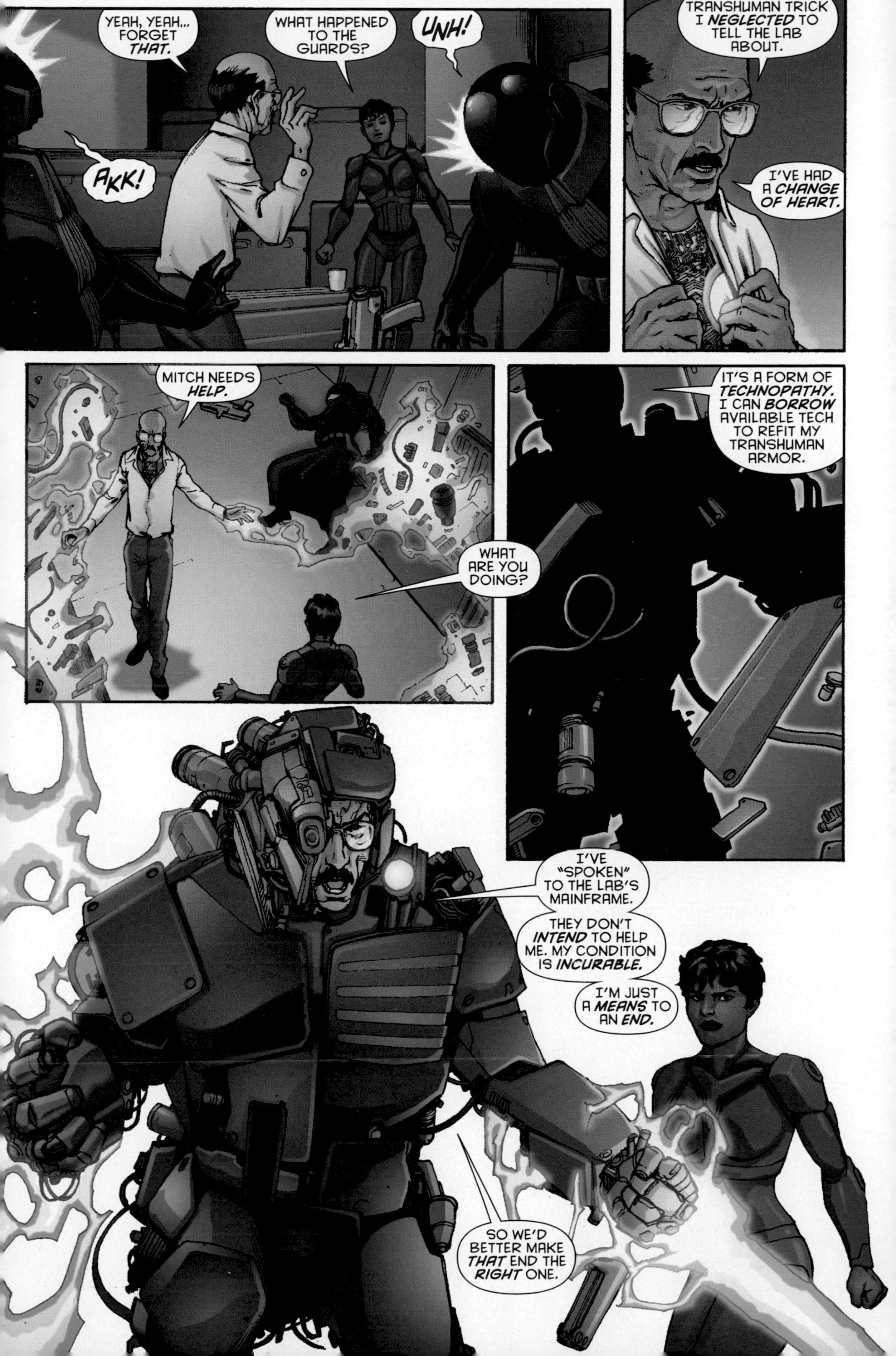
YEAH, YEAH... FORGET *THAT.*
AKK!
WHAT HAPPENED TO THE GUARDS?
UNH!
A LITTLE TRANSHUMAN TRICK I *NEGLECTED* TO TELL THE LAB ABOUT.
I'VE HAD A *CHANGE OF HEART.*
MITCH NEEDS *HELP.*
WHAT ARE YOU DOING?
IT'S A FORM OF *TECHNOPATHY.* I CAN *BORROW* AVAILABLE TECH TO REFIT MY TRANSHUMAN ARMOR.
I'VE "SPOKEN" TO THE LAB'S MAINFRAME.
THEY DON'T *INTEND* TO HELP ME. MY CONDITION IS *INCURABLE.*
I'M JUST A *MEANS* TO AN *END.*
SO WE'D BETTER MAKE *THAT* END THE *RIGHT* ONE.

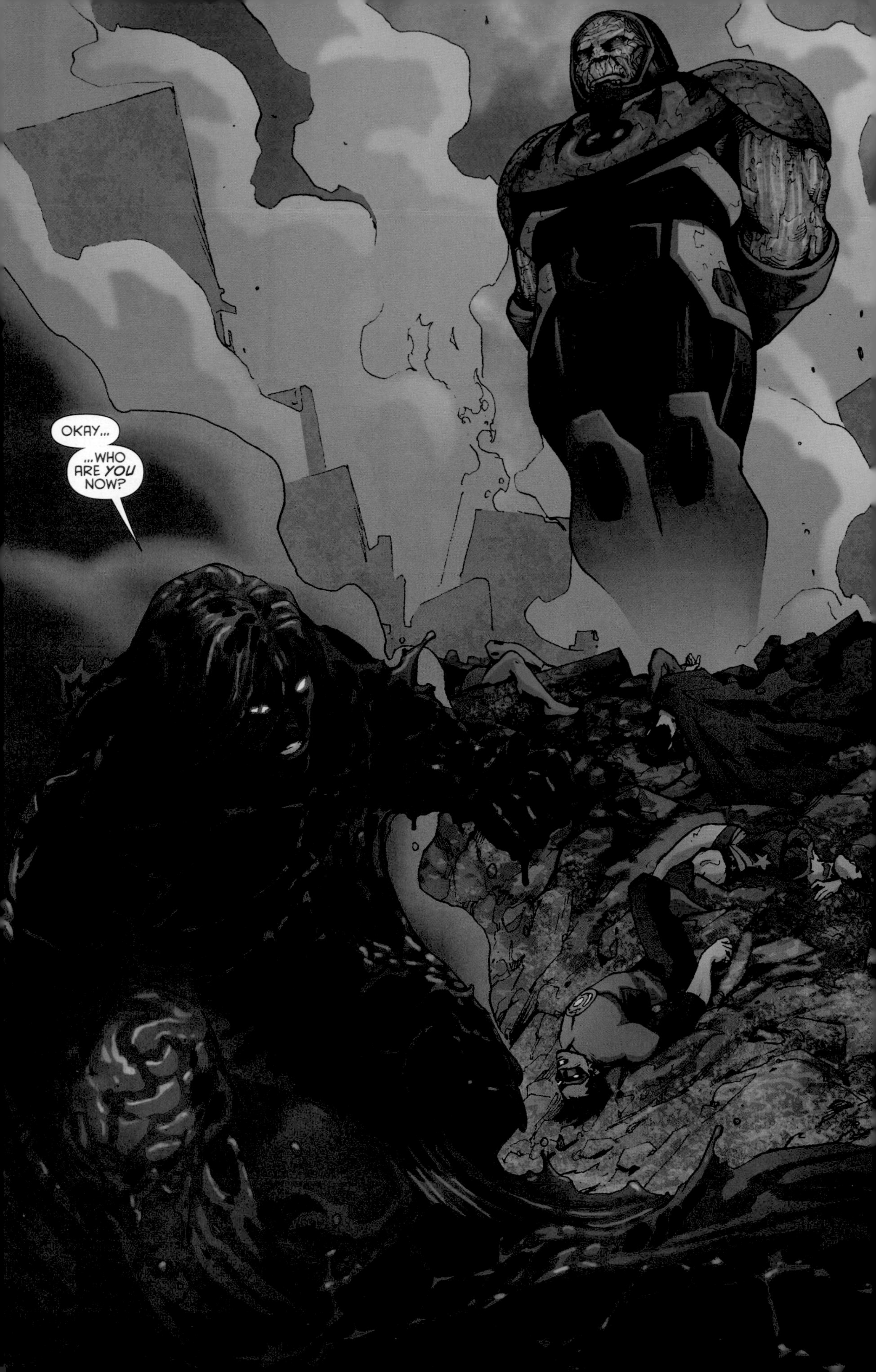
OKAY...
...WHO ARE *YOU* NOW?

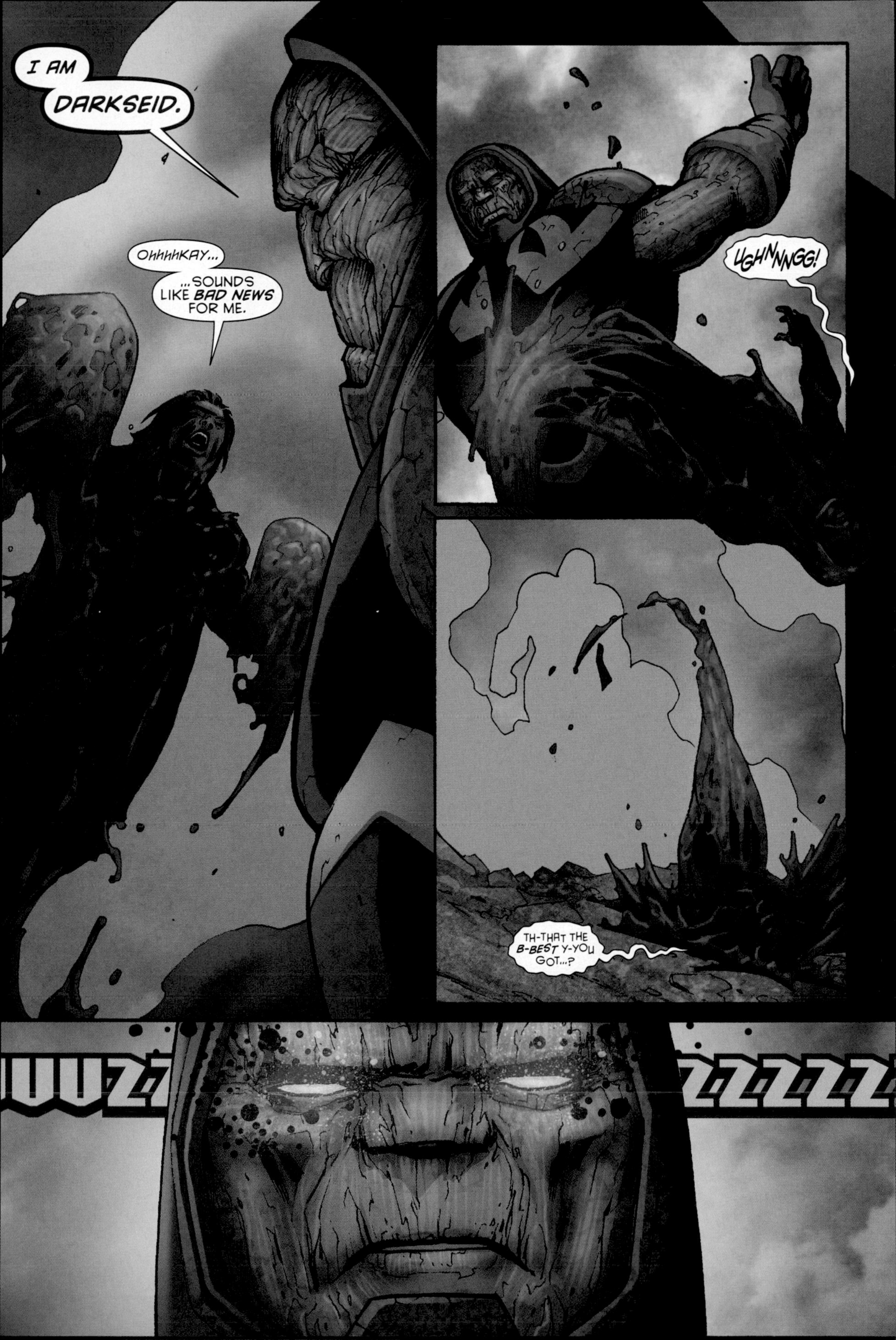
I AM DARKSEID.
OHHHHKAY... ...SOUNDS LIKE BAD NEWS FOR ME.
UGHNNNGG!
TH-THAT THE B-BEST Y-YOU GOT...?
VUUZZZZZZZ

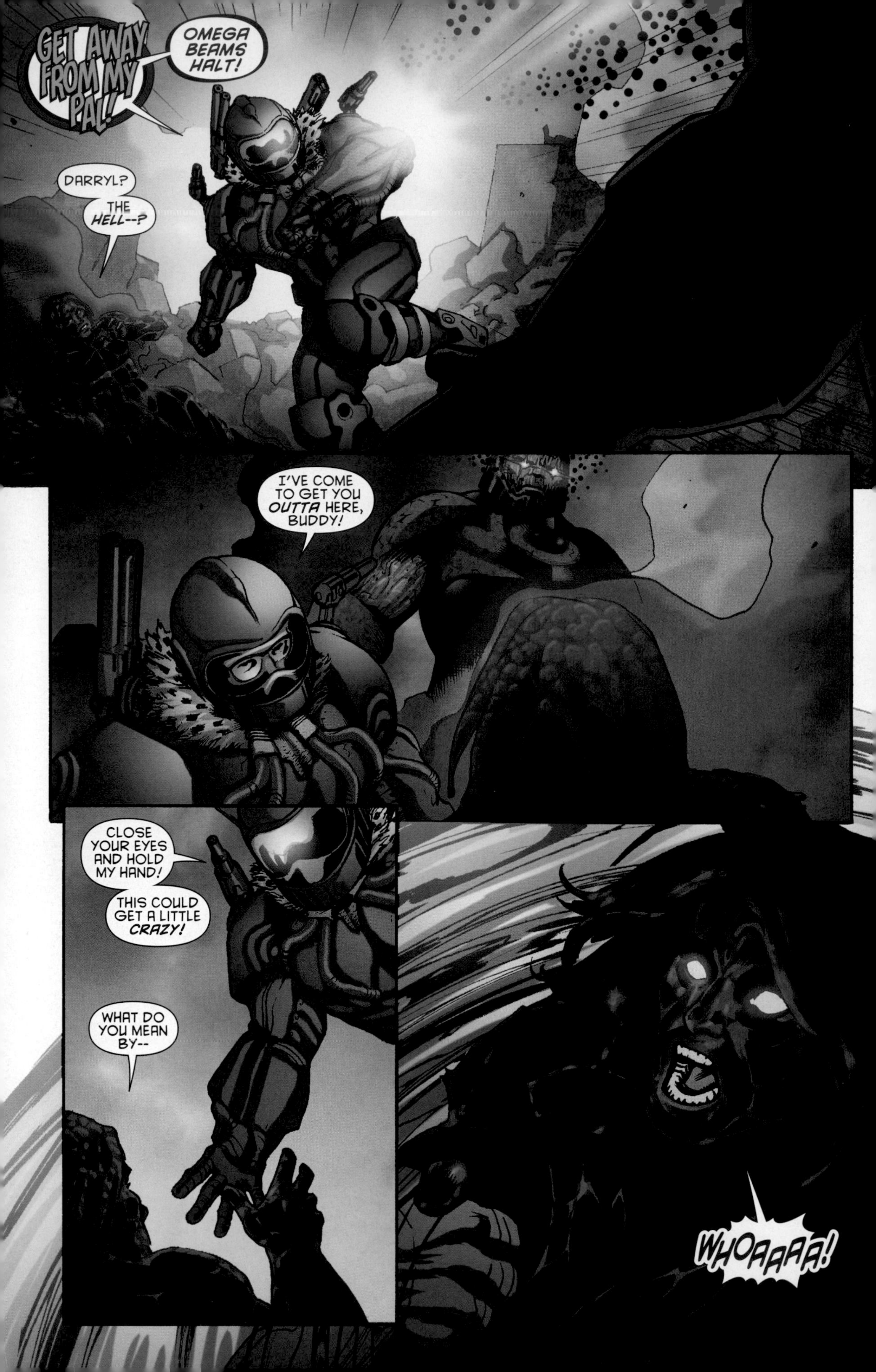
GET AWAY FROM MY PAL!
OMEGA BEAMS HALT!
DARRYL?
THE HELL--?
I'VE COME TO GET YOU OUTTA HERE, BUDDY!
CLOSE YOUR EYES AND HOLD MY HAND!
THIS COULD GET A LITTLE CRAZY!
WHAT DO YOU MEAN BY--
WHOAAAAA!

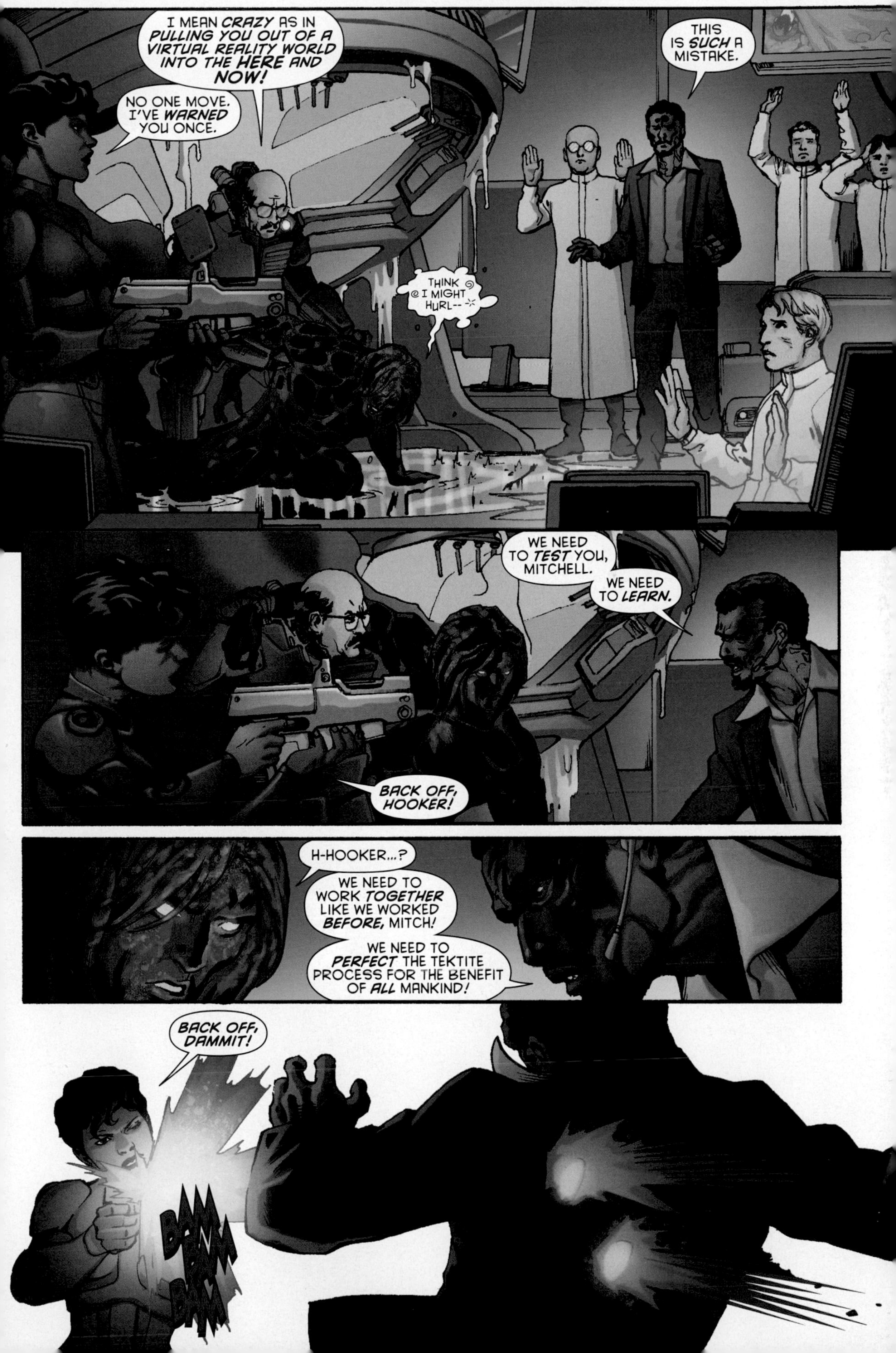

I MEAN CRAZY AS IN PULLING YOU OUT OF A VIRTUAL REALITY WORLD INTO THE HERE AND NOW!
NO ONE MOVE. I'VE WARNED YOU ONCE.
THIS IS SUCH A MISTAKE.
THINK I MIGHT HURL--
WE NEED TO TEST YOU, MITCHELL.
WE NEED TO LEARN.
BACK OFF, HOOKER!
H-HOOKER...?
WE NEED TO WORK TOGETHER LIKE WE WORKED BEFORE, MITCH!
WE NEED TO PERFECT THE TEKTITE PROCESS FOR THE BENEFIT OF ALL MANKIND!
BACK OFF, DAMMIT!
BAM BAM BAM

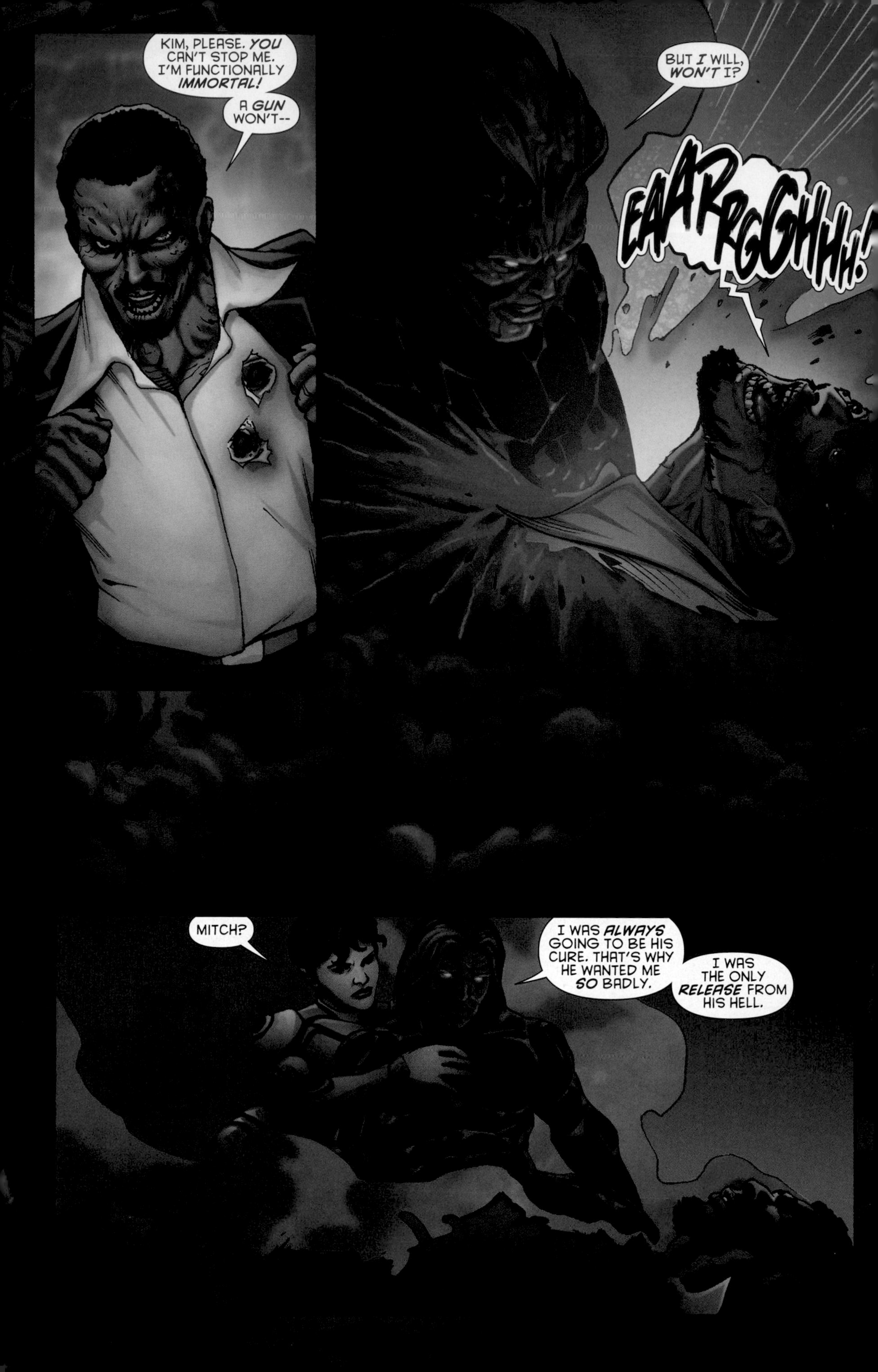
KIM, PLEASE. YOU CAN'T STOP ME. I'M FUNCTIONALLY IMMORTAL!
A GUN WON'T--
BUT I WILL, WON'T I?
EAARRGGHHH!
MITCH?
I WAS ALWAYS GOING TO BE HIS CURE. THAT'S WHY HE WANTED ME SO BADLY.
I WAS THE ONLY RELEASE FROM HIS HELL.

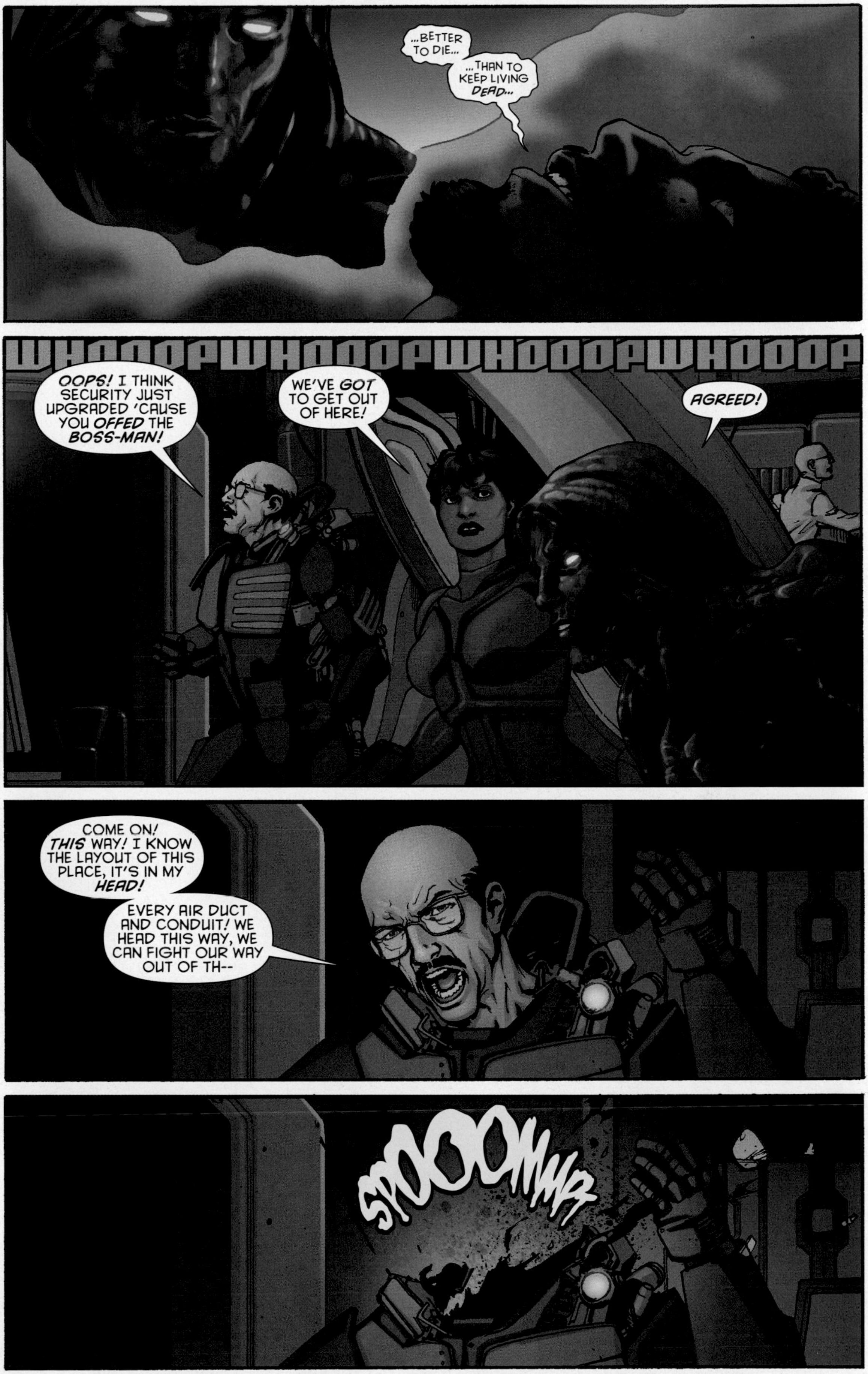

...BETTER TO DIE...
...THAN TO KEEP LIVING DEAD...
WHOOOPWHOOOPWHOOOPWHOOOP
OOPS! I THINK SECURITY JUST UPGRADED 'CAUSE YOU OFFED THE BOSS-MAN!
WE'VE GOT TO GET OUT OF HERE!
AGREED!
COME ON! THIS WAY! I KNOW THE LAYOUT OF THIS PLACE, IT'S IN MY HEAD!
EVERY AIR DUCT AND CONDUIT! WE HEAD THIS WAY, WE CAN FIGHT OUR WAY OUT OF TH--
SPOOOMMR

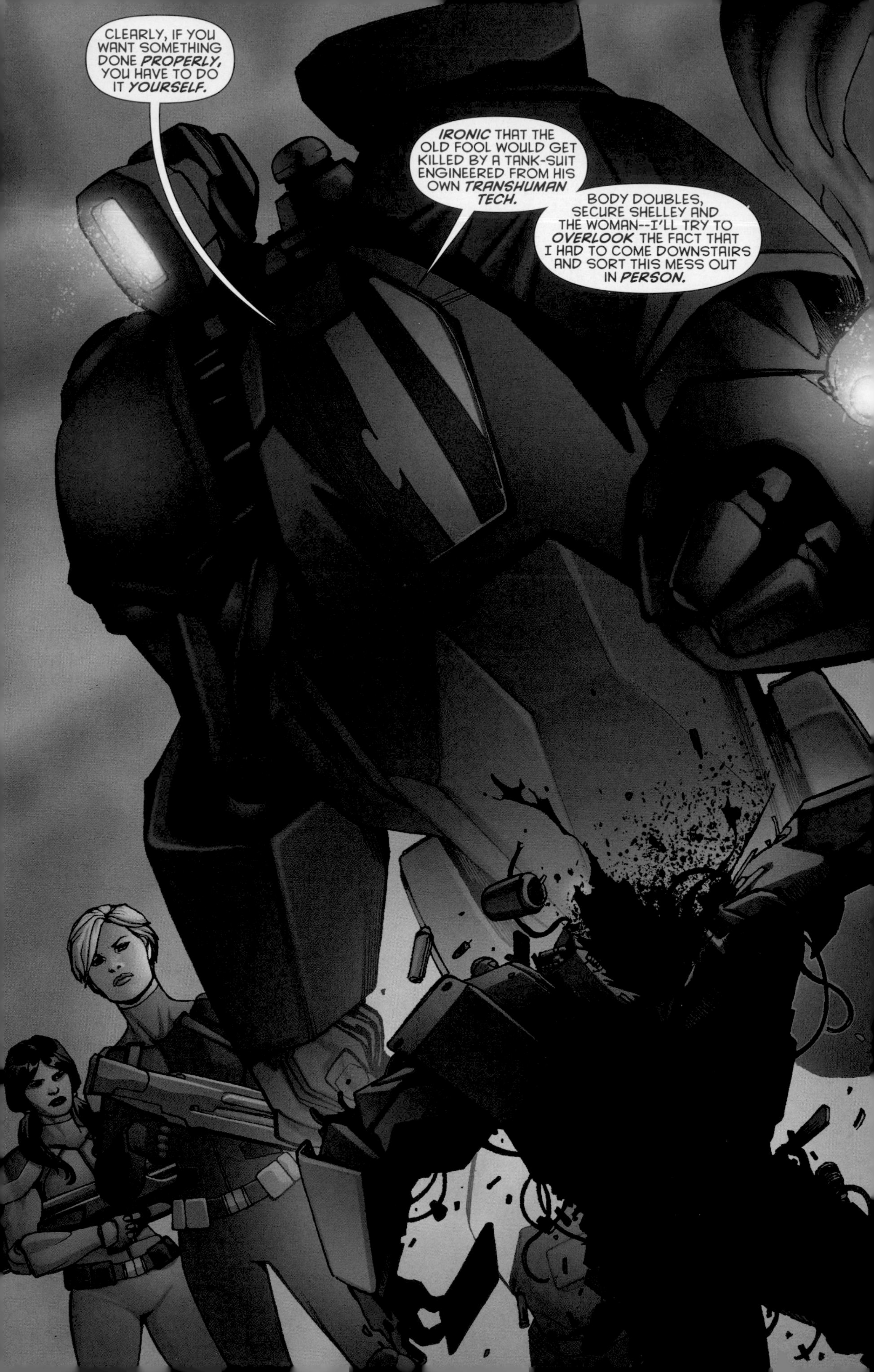
CLEARLY, IF YOU WANT SOMETHING DONE *PROPERLY,* YOU HAVE TO DO IT *YOURSELF.*
IRONIC THAT THE OLD FOOL WOULD GET KILLED BY A TANK-SUIT ENGINEERED FROM HIS OWN *TRANSHUMAN* *TECH.*
BODY DOUBLES, SECURE SHELLEY AND THE WOMAN--I'LL TRY TO *OVERLOOK* THE FACT THAT I HAD TO COME DOWNSTAIRS AND SORT THIS MESS OUT IN *PERSON.*

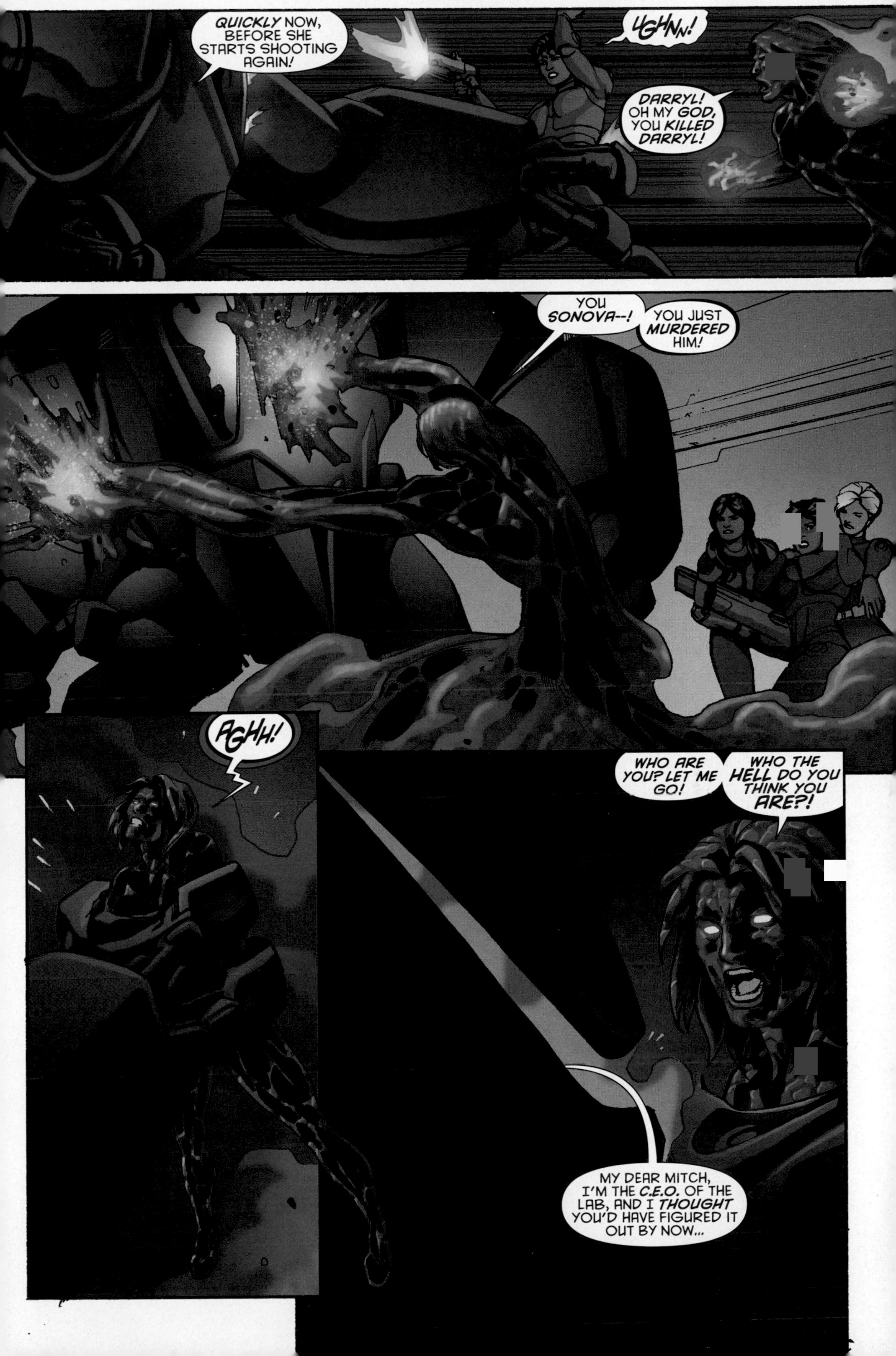
QUICKLY NOW, BEFORE SHE STARTS SHOOTING AGAIN!
UGHNN!
DARRYL! OH MY GOD, YOU KILLED DARRYL!
YOU SONOVA--!
YOU JUST MURDERED HIM!
AGHH!
WHO ARE YOU? LET ME GO!
WHO THE HELL DO YOU THINK YOU ARE?!
MY DEAR MITCH, I'M THE C.E.O. OF THE LAB, AND I THOUGHT YOU'D HAVE FIGURED IT OUT BY NOW...

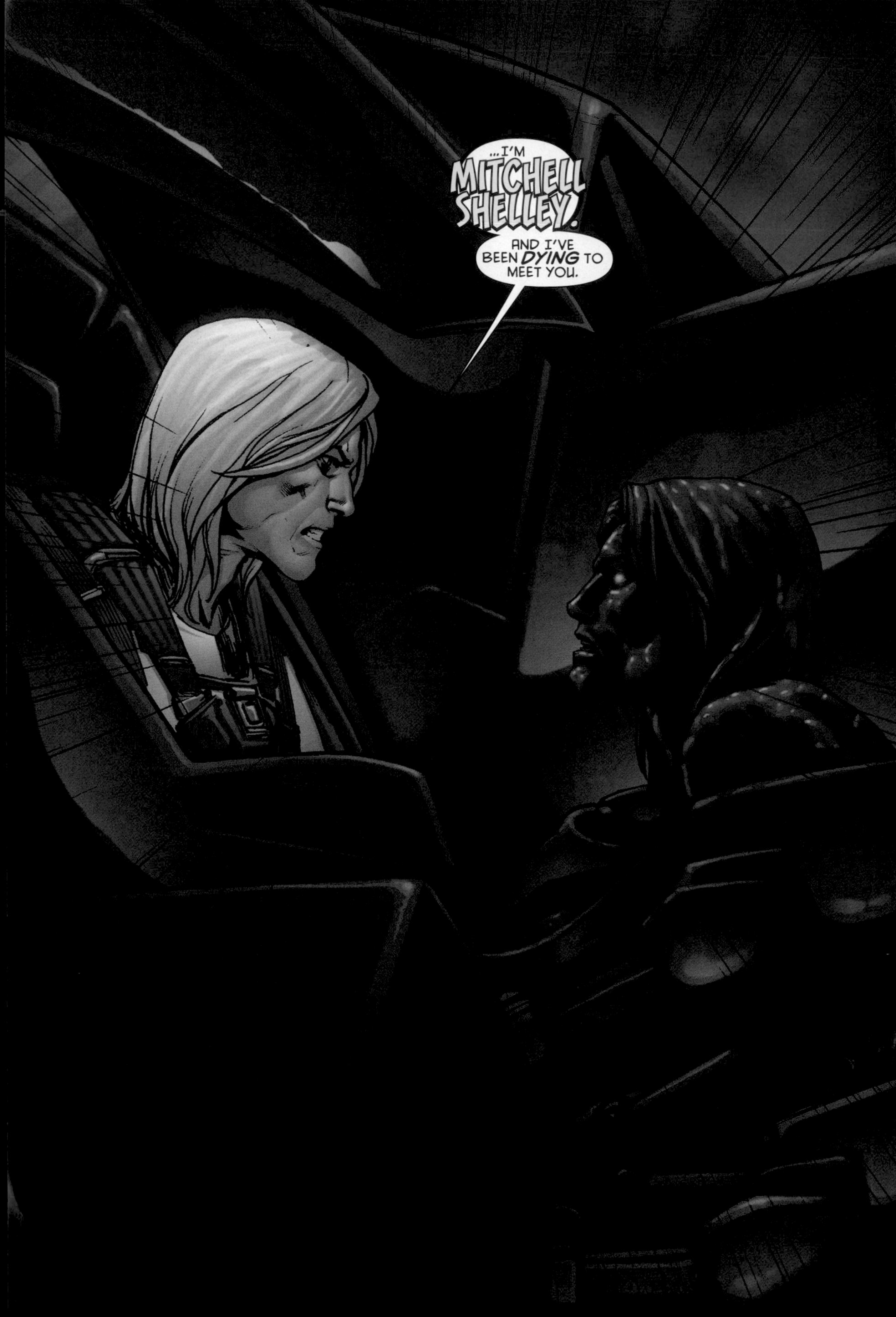
...I'M MITCHELL SHELLEY.
AND I'VE BEEN DYING TO MEET YOU.

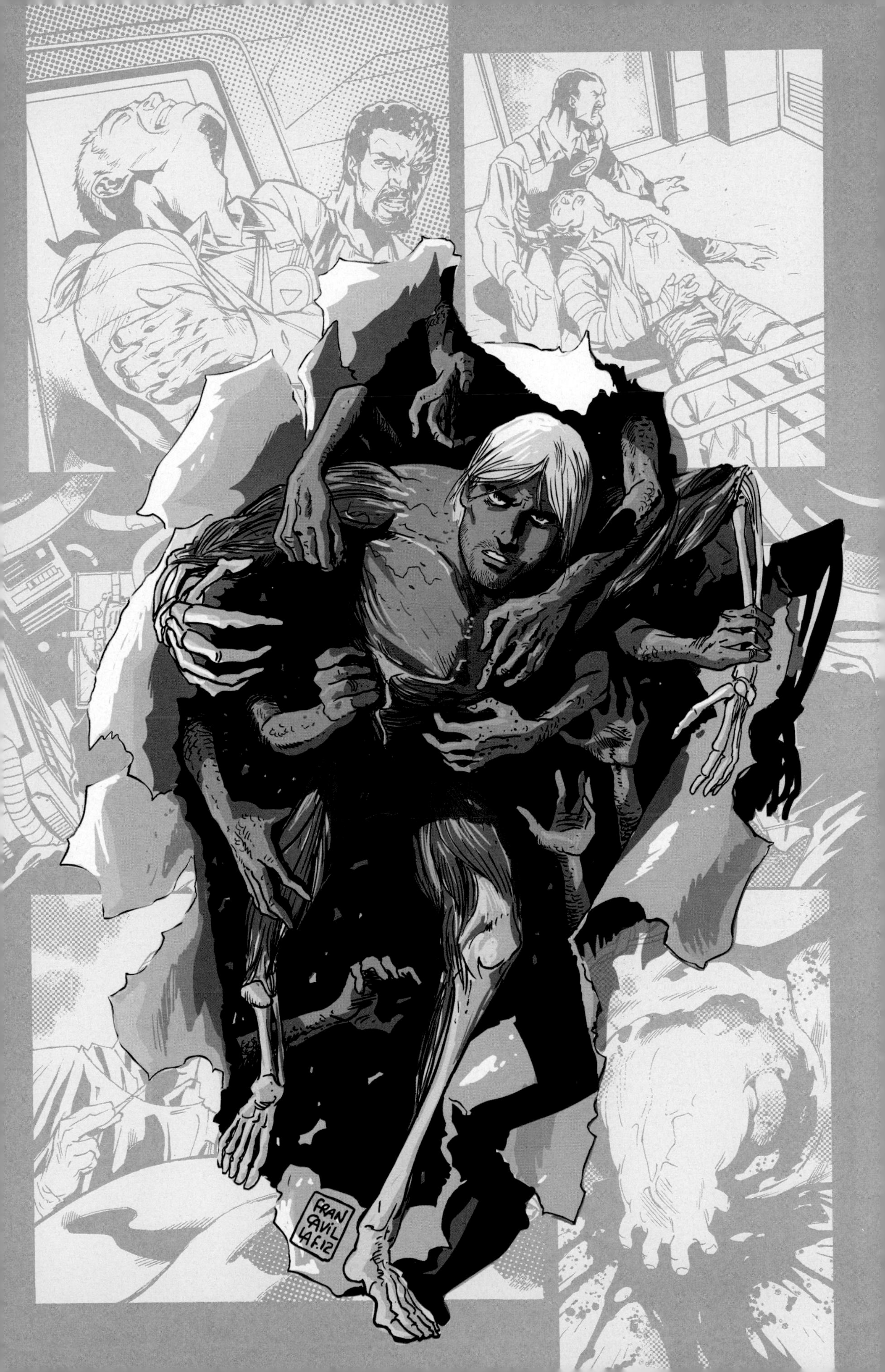
FRAN
CAVIL
LA F.12

FACE THE TRUTH

DAN ABNETT & ANDY LANNING
writers

RAMON BACHS & JESUS SAIZ (page 20)
artists

cover art by
FRANCESCO FRANCAVILLA

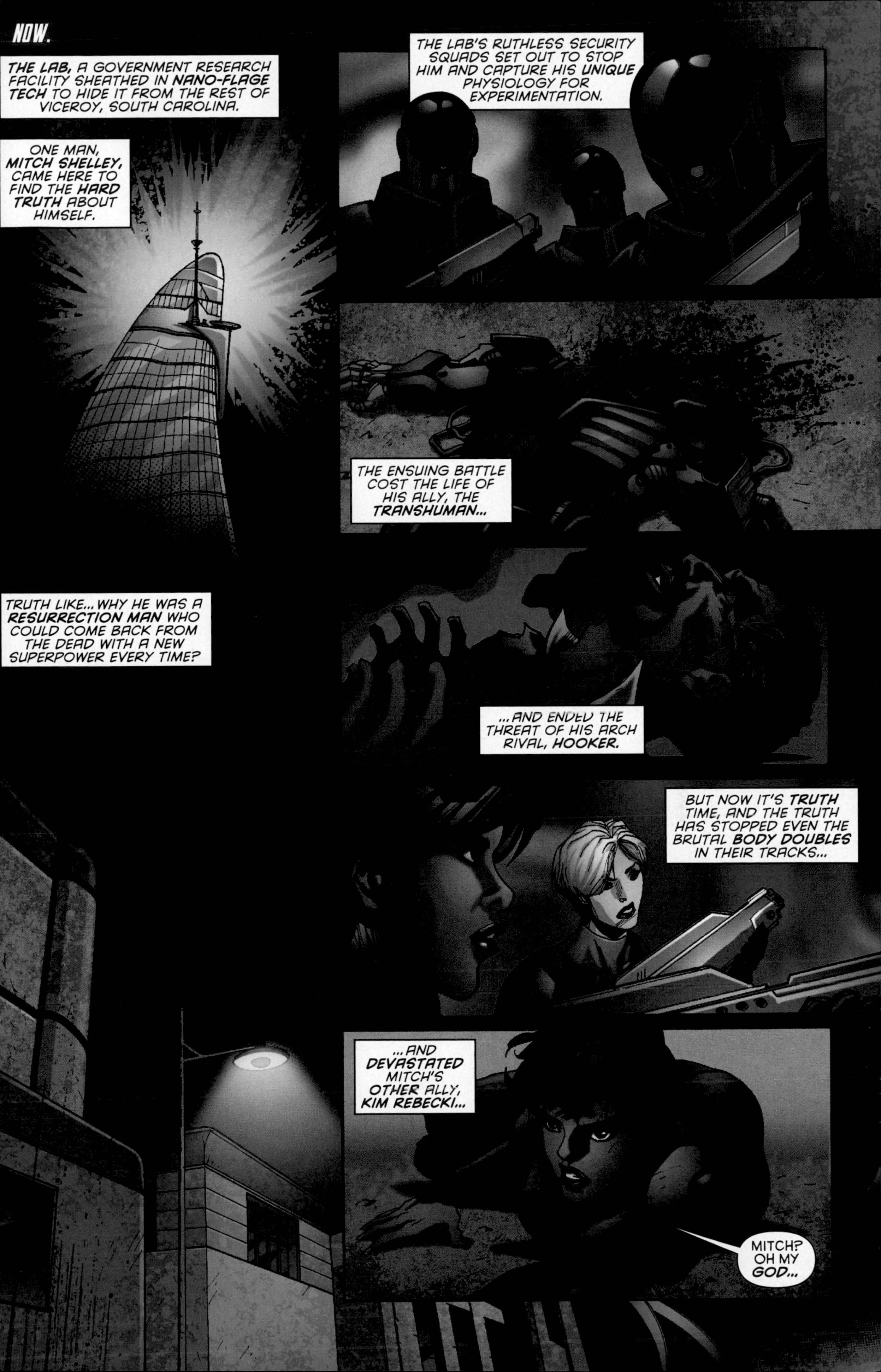
NOW.
THE LAB, A GOVERNMENT RESEARCH FACILITY SHEATHED IN NANO-FLAGE TECH TO HIDE IT FROM THE REST OF VICEROY, SOUTH CAROLINA.
ONE MAN, MITCH SHELLEY, CAME HERE TO FIND THE HARD TRUTH ABOUT HIMSELF.
TRUTH LIKE... WHY HE WAS A RESURRECTION MAN WHO COULD COME BACK FROM THE DEAD WITH A NEW SUPERPOWER EVERY TIME?
THE LAB'S RUTHLESS SECURITY SQUADS SET OUT TO STOP HIM AND CAPTURE HIS UNIQUE PHYSIOLOGY FOR EXPERIMENTATION.
THE ENSUING BATTLE COST THE LIFE OF HIS ALLY, THE TRANSHUMAN...
...AND ENDED THE THREAT OF HIS ARCH RIVAL, HOOKER.
BUT NOW IT'S TRUTH TIME, AND THE TRUTH HAS STOPPED EVEN THE BRUTAL BODY DOUBLES IN THEIR TRACKS...
...AND DEVASTATED MITCH'S OTHER ALLY, KIM REBECKI...
MITCH? OH MY GOD...

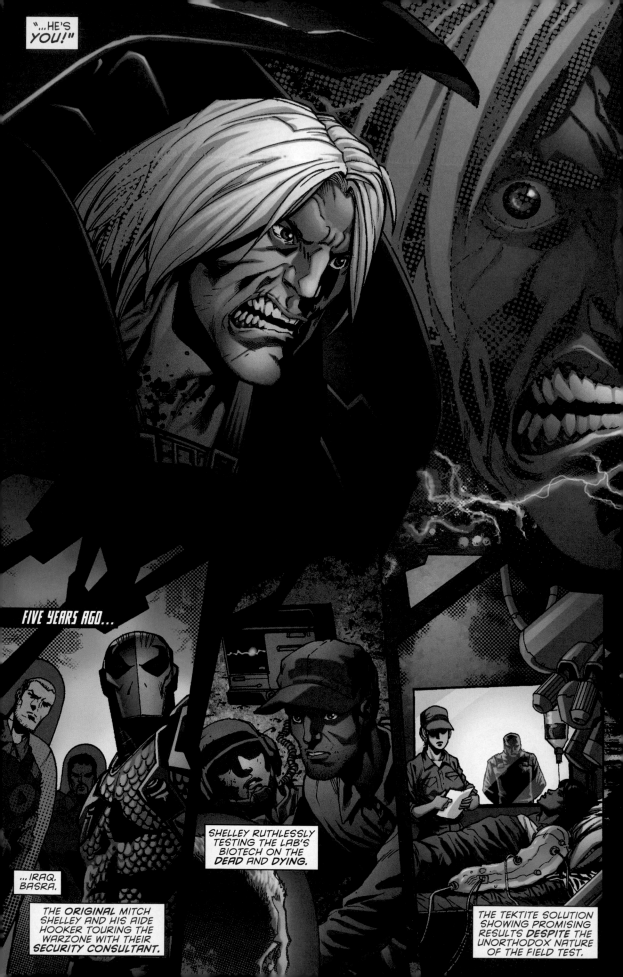

"...HE'S YOU!"

FIVE YEARS AGO...

...IRAQ. BASRA.

THE ORIGINAL MITCH SHELLEY AND HIS AIDE HOOKER TOURING THE WARZONE WITH THEIR SECURITY CONSULTANT.

SHELLEY RUTHLESSLY TESTING THE LAB'S BIOTECH ON THE DEAD AND DYING.

THE TEKTITE SOLUTION SHOWING PROMISING RESULTS DESPITE THE UNORTHODOX NATURE OF THE FIELD TEST.

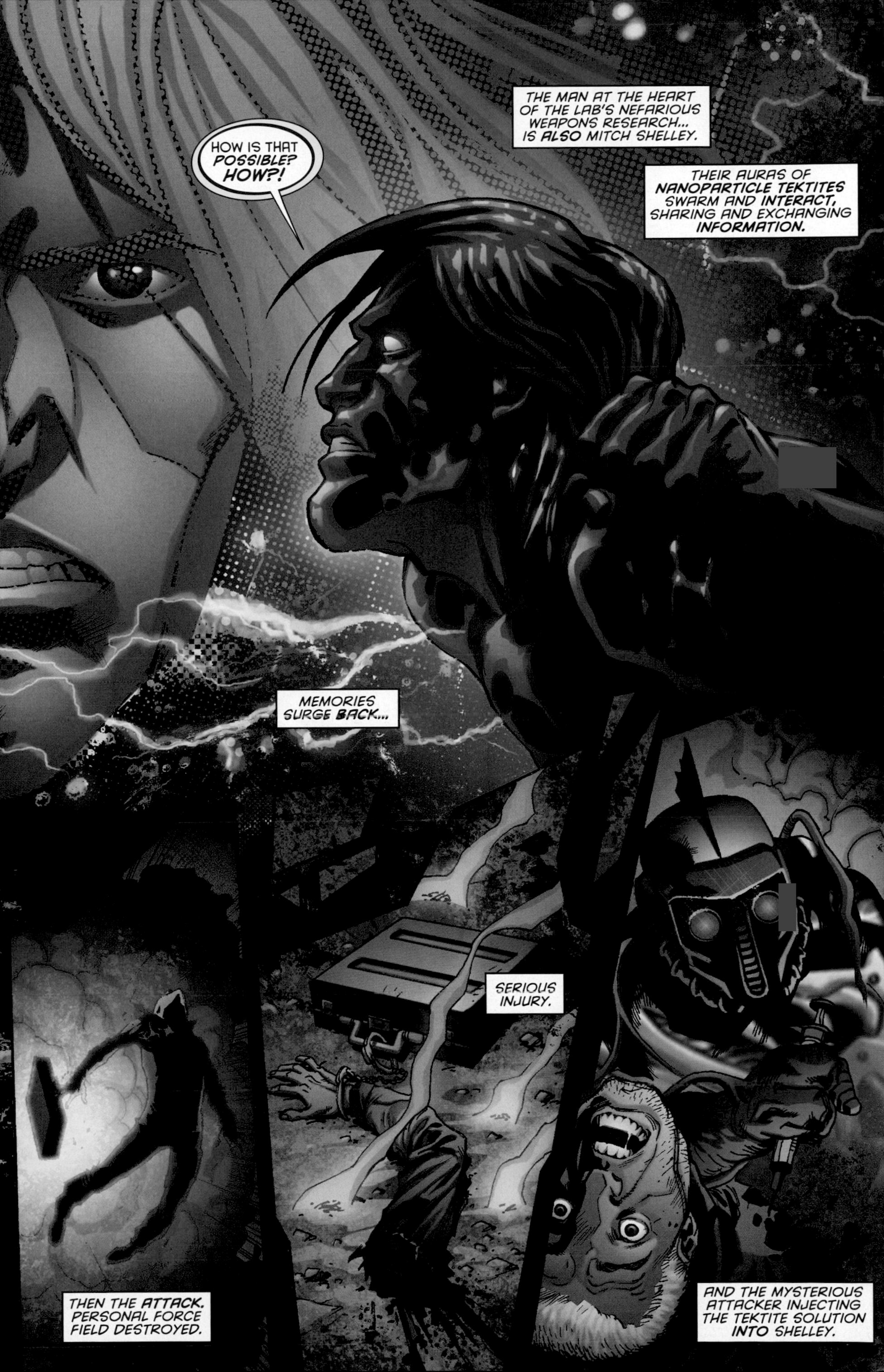
THE MAN AT THE HEART OF THE LAB'S NEFARIOUS WEAPONS RESEARCH... IS ALSO MITCH SHELLEY.
HOW IS THAT POSSIBLE? HOW?!
THEIR AURAS OF NANOPARTICLE TEKTITES SWARM AND INTERACT, SHARING AND EXCHANGING INFORMATION.
MEMORIES SURGE BACK...
SERIOUS INJURY.
THEN THE ATTACK. PERSONAL FORCE FIELD DESTROYED.
AND THE MYSTERIOUS ATTACKER INJECTING THE TEKTITE SOLUTION INTO SHELLEY.

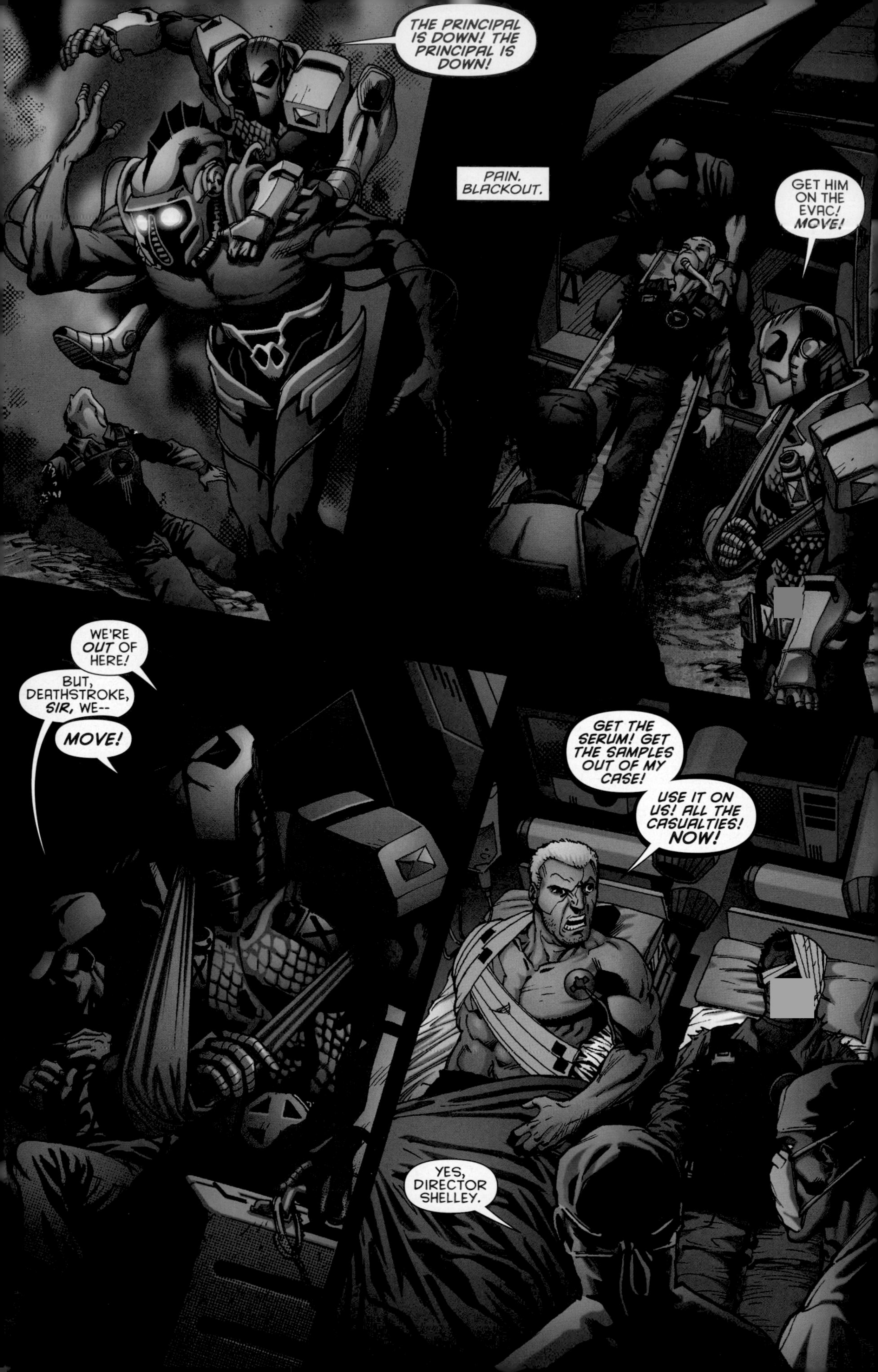
THE PRINCIPAL IS DOWN! THE PRINCIPAL IS DOWN!
PAIN. BLACKOUT.
GET HIM ON THE EVAC! MOVE!
WE'RE OUT OF HERE!
BUT, DEATHSTROKE, SIR, WE--
MOVE!
GET THE SERUM! GET THE SAMPLES OUT OF MY CASE!
USE IT ON US! ALL THE CASUALTIES! NOW!
YES, DIRECTOR SHELLEY.

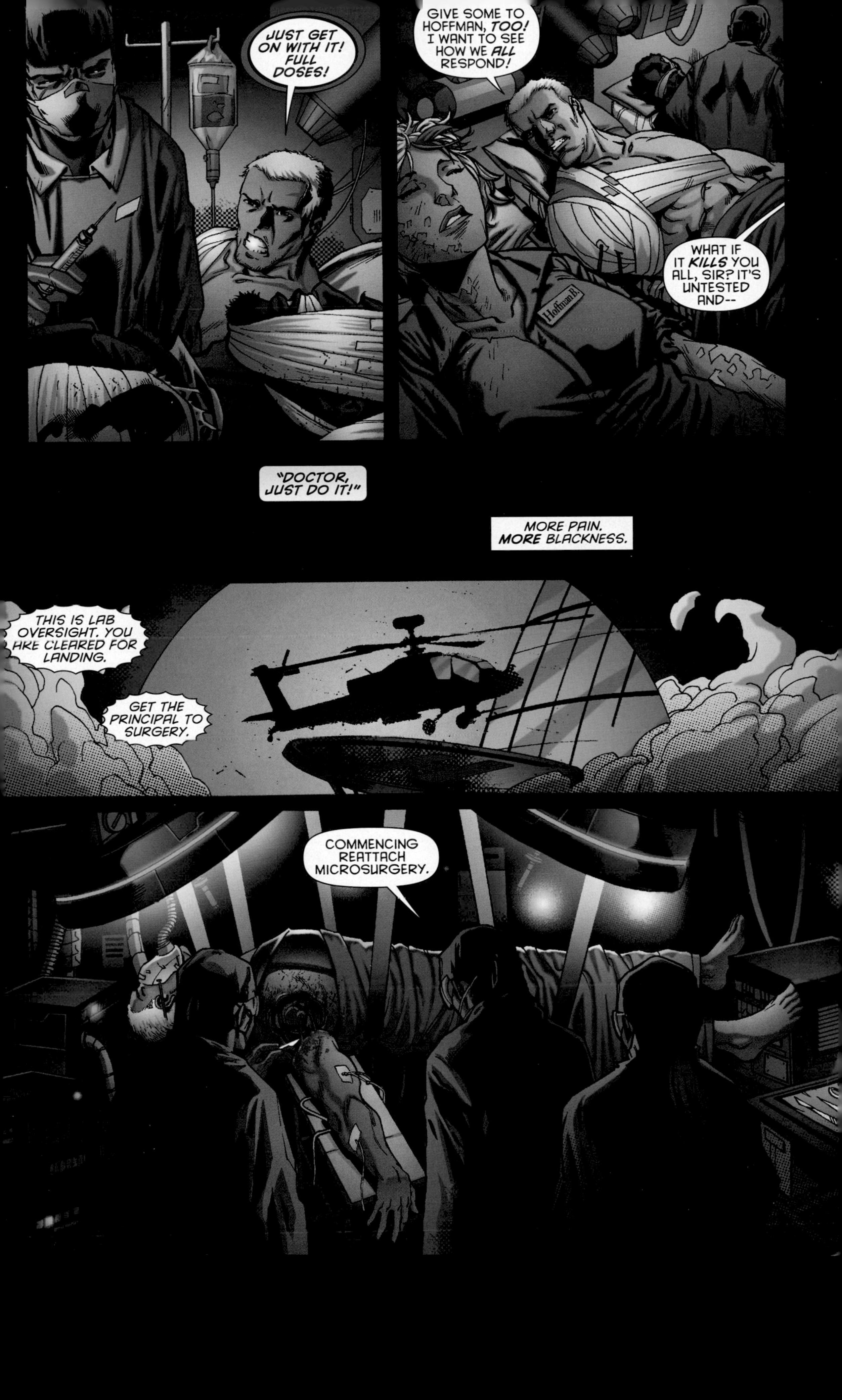
JUST GET ON WITH IT! FULL DOSES!
GIVE SOME TO HOFFMAN, TOO! I WANT TO SEE HOW WE ALL RESPOND!
Hoffman B.
WHAT IF IT KILLS YOU ALL, SIR? IT'S UNTESTED AND--
"DOCTOR, JUST DO IT!"
MORE PAIN. MORE BLACKNESS.
THIS IS LAB OVERSIGHT. YOU ARE CLEARED FOR LANDING.
GET THE PRINCIPAL TO SURGERY.
COMMENCING REATTACH MICROSURGERY.

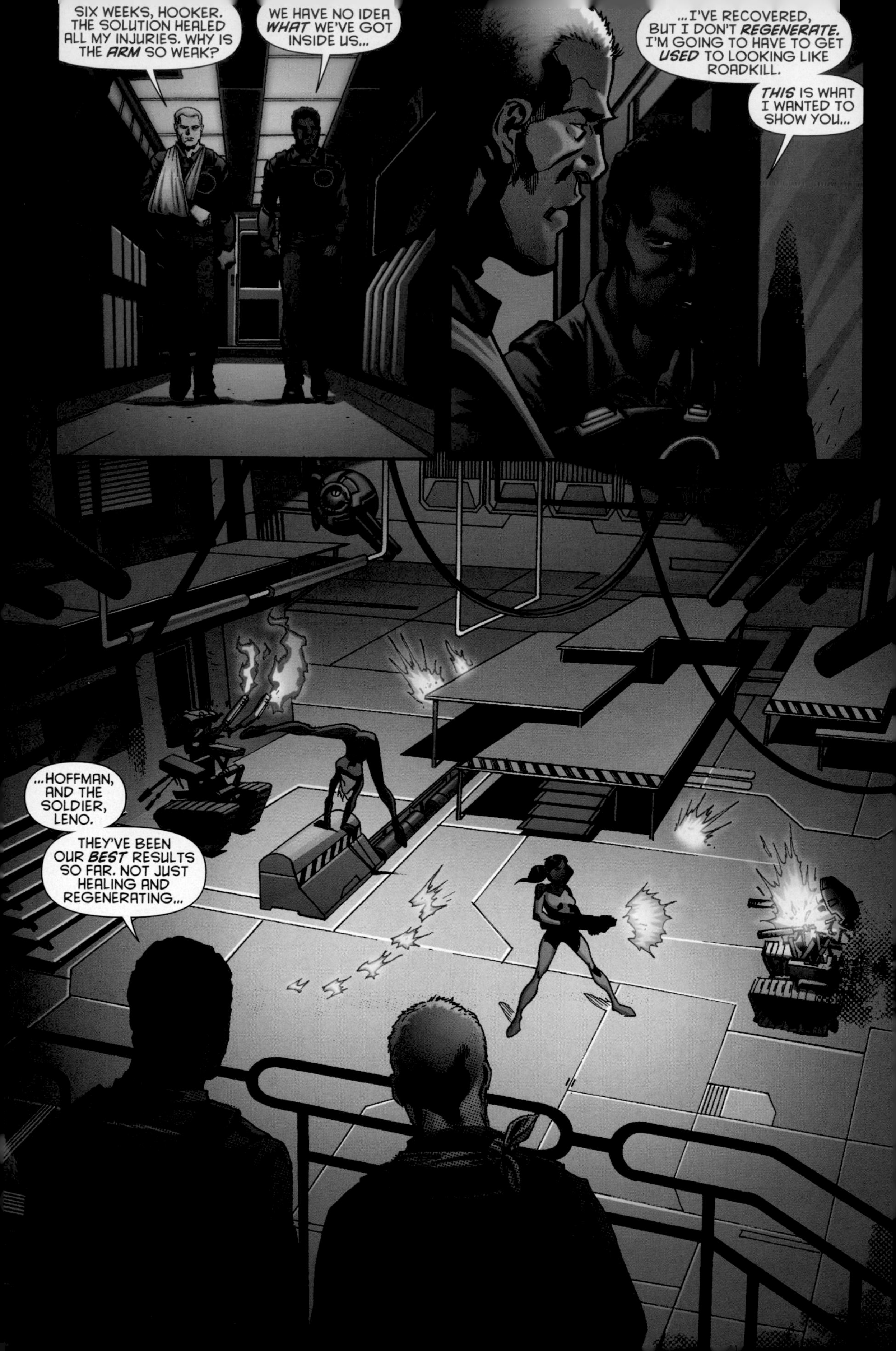
SIX WEEKS, HOOKER. THE SOLUTION HEALED ALL MY INJURIES. WHY IS THE *ARM* SO WEAK?
WE HAVE NO IDEA *WHAT* WE'VE GOT INSIDE US...
...I'VE RECOVERED, BUT I DON'T *REGENERATE.* I'M GOING TO HAVE TO GET *USED* TO LOOKING LIKE ROADKILL.
THIS IS WHAT I WANTED TO SHOW YOU...
...HOFFMAN, AND THE SOLDIER, LENO.
THEY'VE BEEN OUR *BEST* RESULTS SO FAR. NOT JUST HEALING AND REGENERATING...

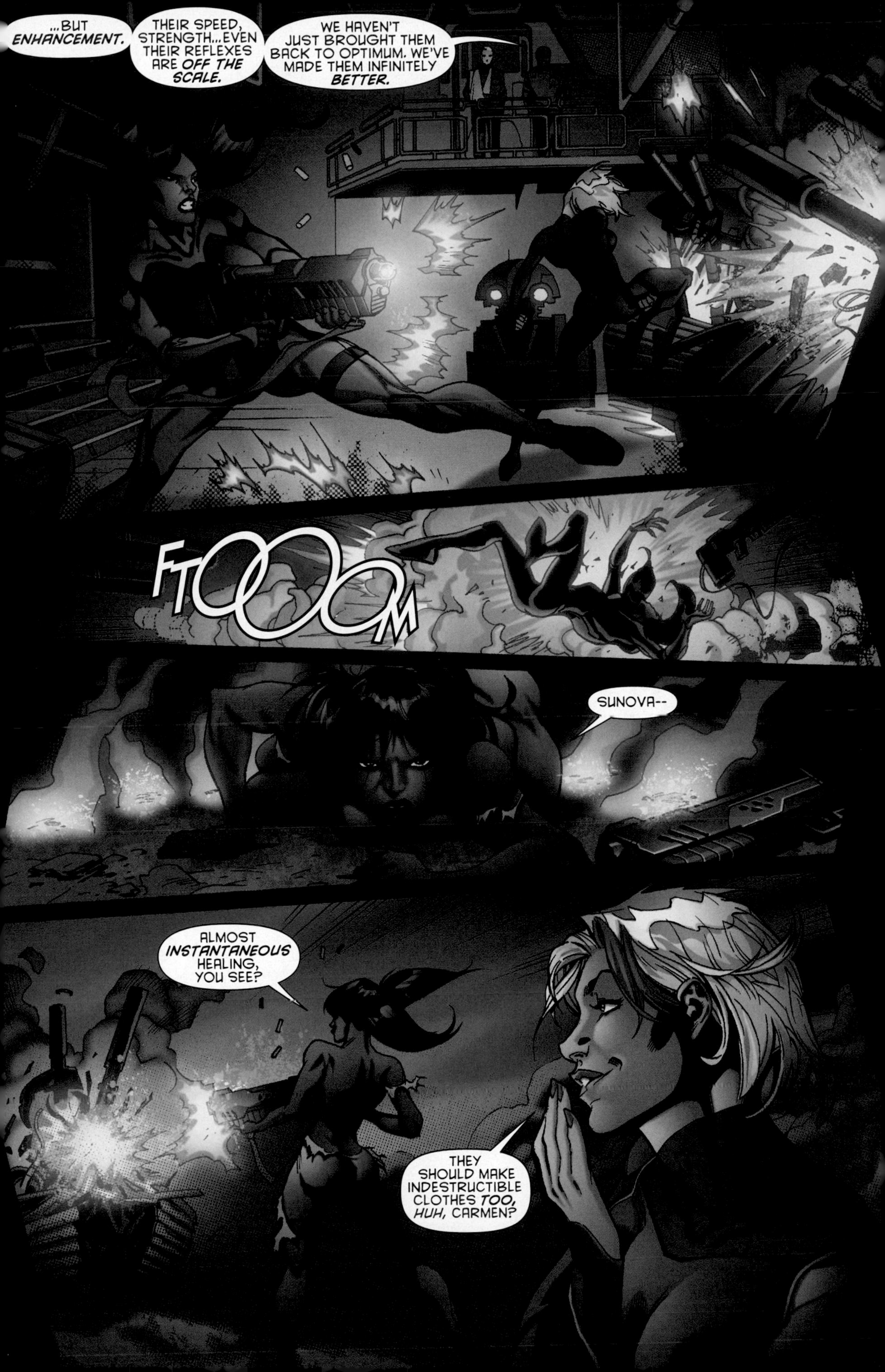
...BUT ENHANCEMENT.
THEIR SPEED, STRENGTH...EVEN THEIR REFLEXES ARE OFF THE SCALE.
WE HAVEN'T JUST BROUGHT THEM BACK TO OPTIMUM. WE'VE MADE THEM INFINITELY BETTER.
FTOOOM
SUNOVA--
ALMOST INSTANTANEOUS HEALING, YOU SEE?
THEY SHOULD MAKE INDESTRUCTIBLE CLOTHES TOO, HUH, CARMEN?

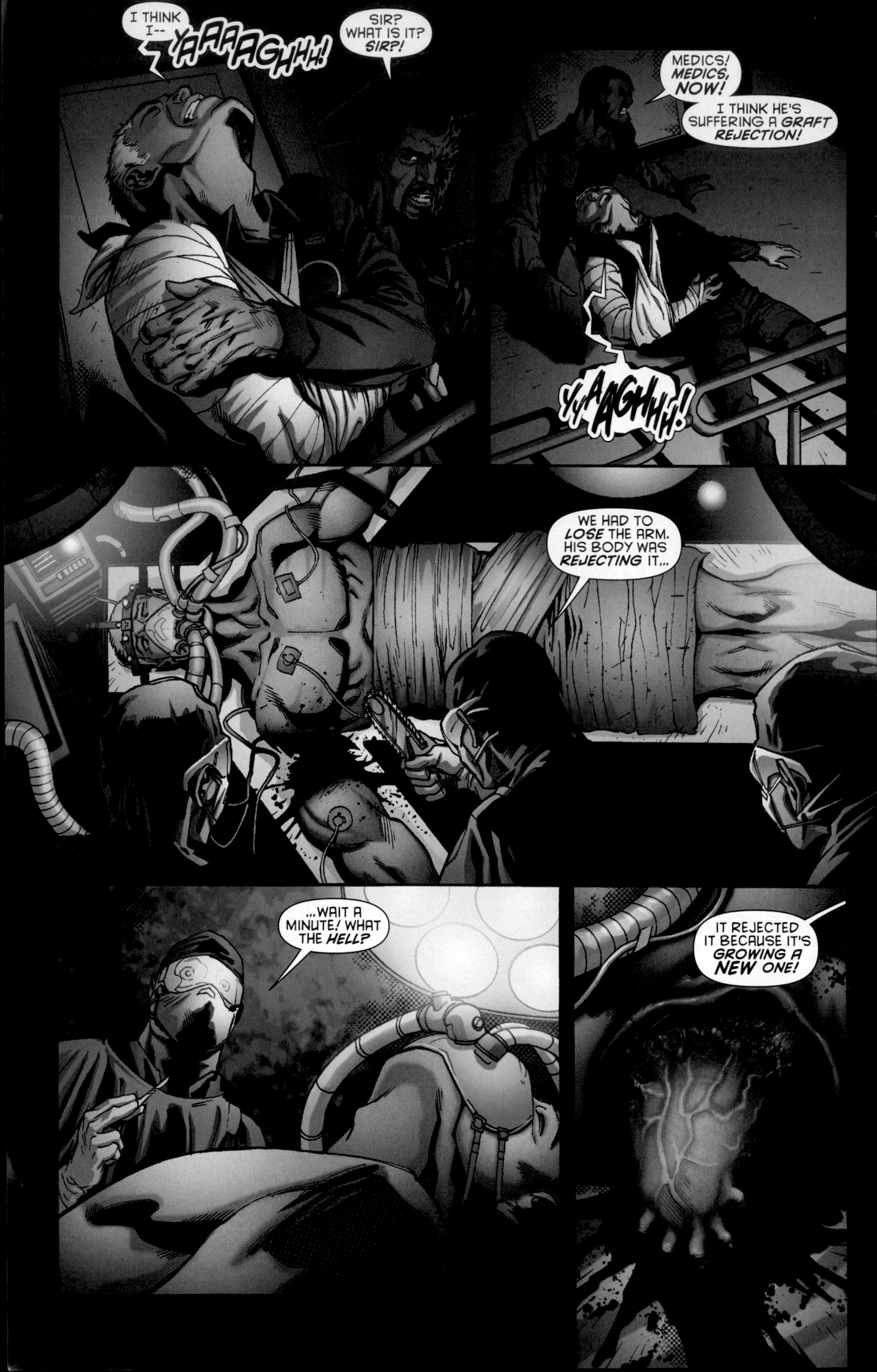
I THINK I--
YAAAAAGHHH!
SIR? WHAT IS IT? SIR?!
MEDICS! MEDICS, NOW!
I THINK HE'S SUFFERING A GRAFT REJECTION!
YYAAAGHHHH!
WE HAD TO LOSE THE ARM. HIS BODY WAS REJECTING IT...
...WAIT A MINUTE! WHAT THE HELL?
IT REJECTED IT BECAUSE IT'S GROWING A NEW ONE!

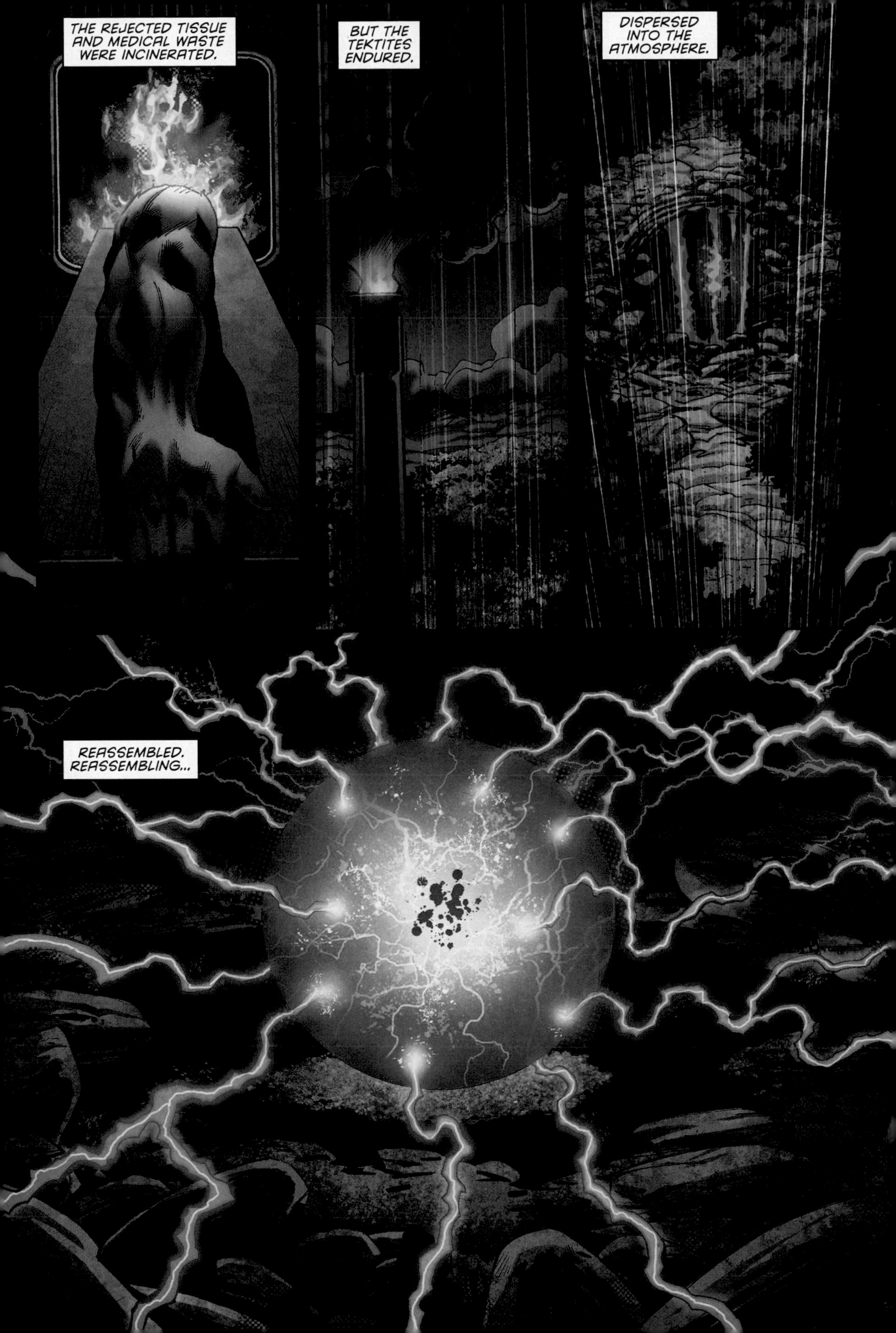
THE REJECTED TISSUE AND MEDICAL WASTE WERE INCINERATED.
BUT THE TEKTITES ENDURED.
DISPERSED INTO THE ATMOSPHERE.
REASSEMBLED. REASSEMBLING...

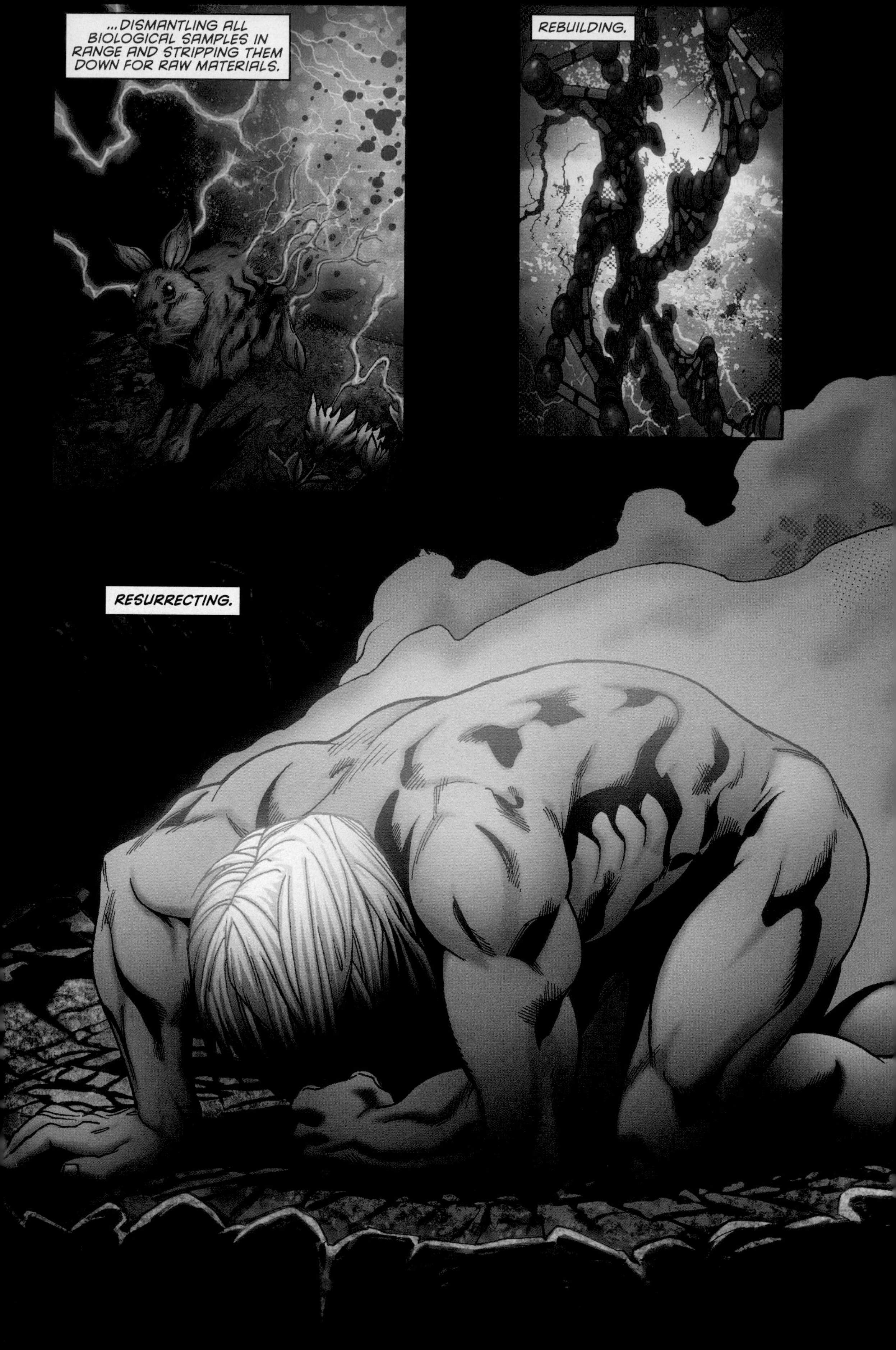
...DISMANTLING ALL BIOLOGICAL SAMPLES IN RANGE AND STRIPPING THEM DOWN FOR RAW MATERIALS.
REBUILDING.
RESURRECTING.

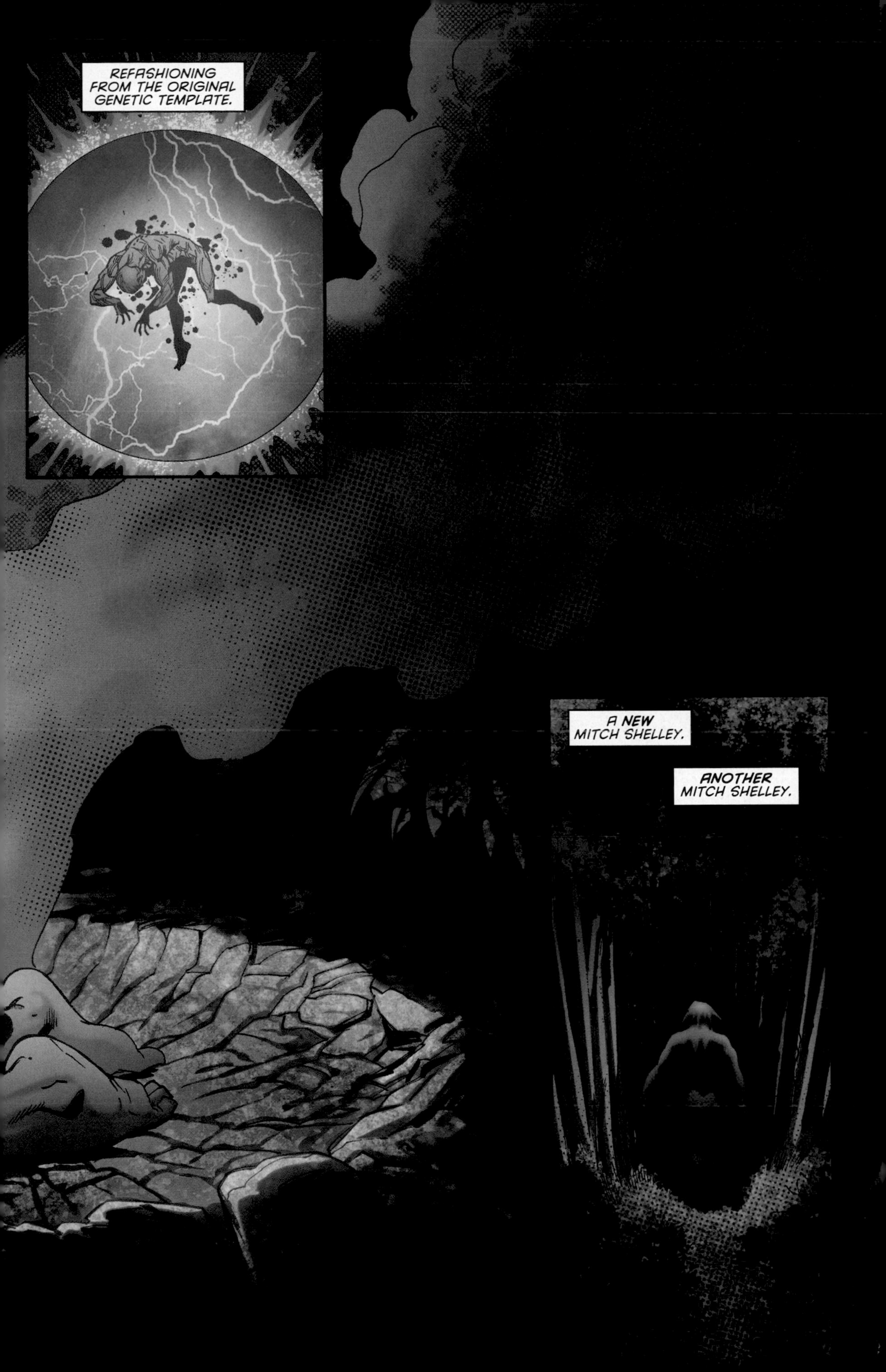
REFASHIONING FROM THE ORIGINAL GENETIC TEMPLATE.
A NEW MITCH SHELLEY.
ANOTHER MITCH SHELLEY.

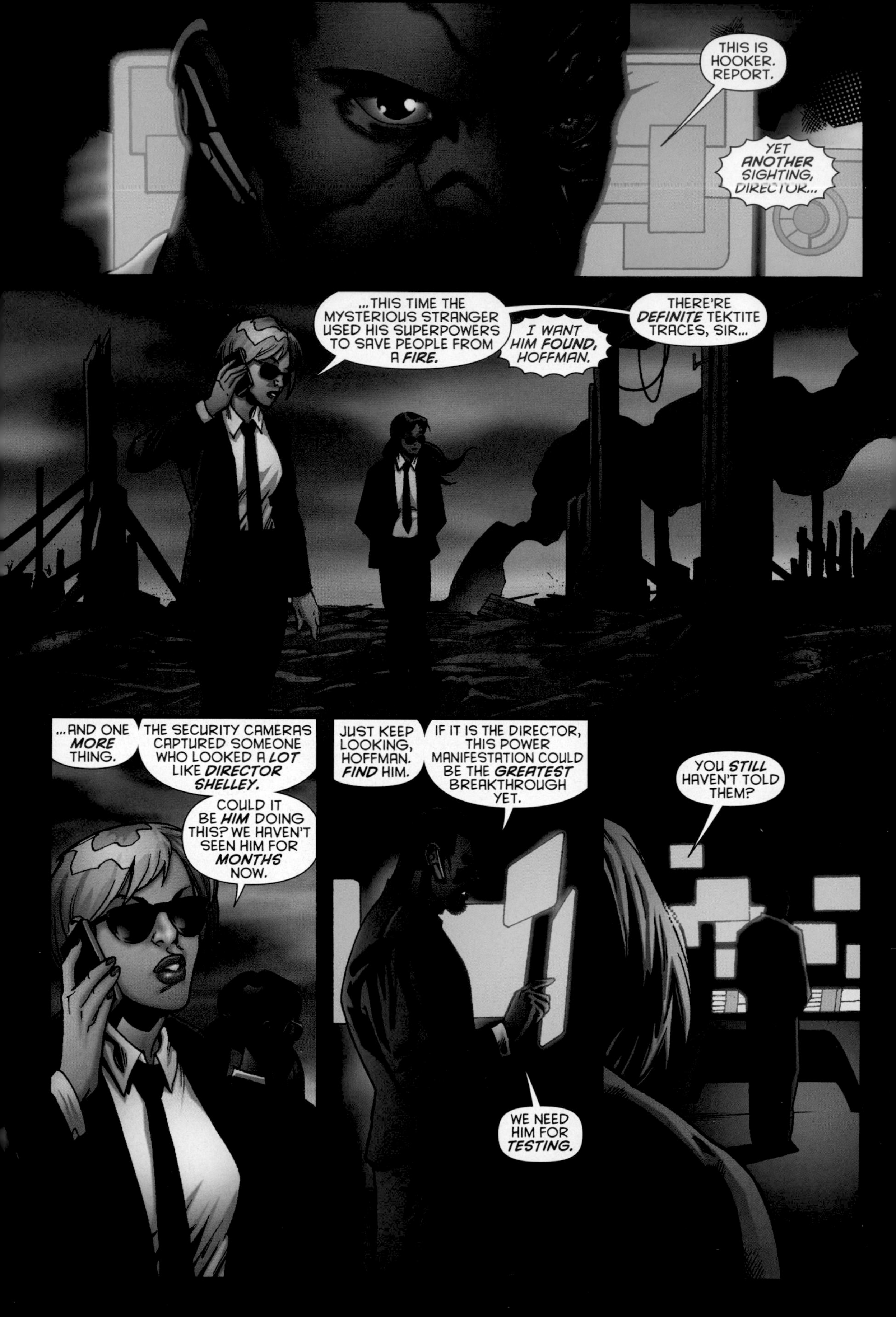
THIS IS HOOKER. REPORT.
YET ANOTHER SIGHTING, DIRECTOR...
...THIS TIME THE MYSTERIOUS STRANGER USED HIS SUPERPOWERS TO SAVE PEOPLE FROM A FIRE.
THERE'RE DEFINITE TEKTITE TRACES, SIR...
I WANT HIM FOUND, HOFFMAN.
...AND ONE MORE THING.
THE SECURITY CAMERAS CAPTURED SOMEONE WHO LOOKED A LOT LIKE DIRECTOR SHELLEY.
COULD IT BE HIM DOING THIS? WE HAVEN'T SEEN HIM FOR MONTHS NOW.
JUST KEEP LOOKING, HOFFMAN. FIND HIM.
IF IT IS THE DIRECTOR, THIS POWER MANIFESTATION COULD BE THE GREATEST BREAKTHROUGH YET.
WE NEED HIM FOR TESTING.
YOU STILL HAVEN'T TOLD THEM?

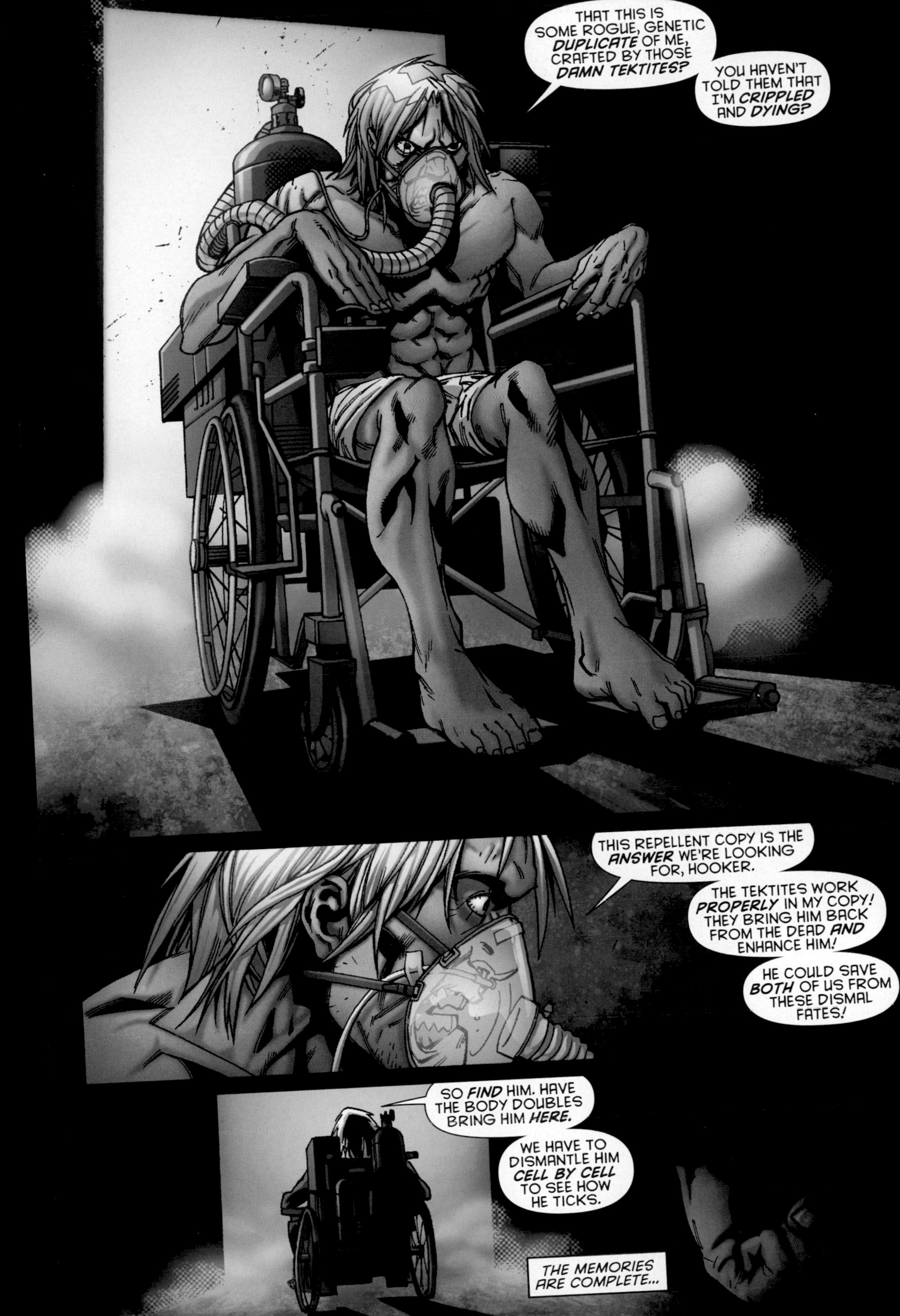
THAT THIS IS SOME ROGUE, GENETIC DUPLICATE OF ME, CRAFTED BY THOSE DAMN TEKTITES?
YOU HAVEN'T TOLD THEM THAT I'M CRIPPLED AND DYING?
THIS REPELLENT COPY IS THE ANSWER WE'RE LOOKING FOR, HOOKER.
THE TEKTITES WORK PROPERLY IN MY COPY! THEY BRING HIM BACK FROM THE DEAD AND ENHANCE HIM!
HE COULD SAVE BOTH OF US FROM THESE DISMAL FATES!
SO FIND HIM. HAVE THE BODY DOUBLES BRING HIM HERE.
WE HAVE TO DISMANTLE HIM CELL BY CELL TO SEE HOW HE TICKS.
THE MEMORIES ARE COMPLETE...

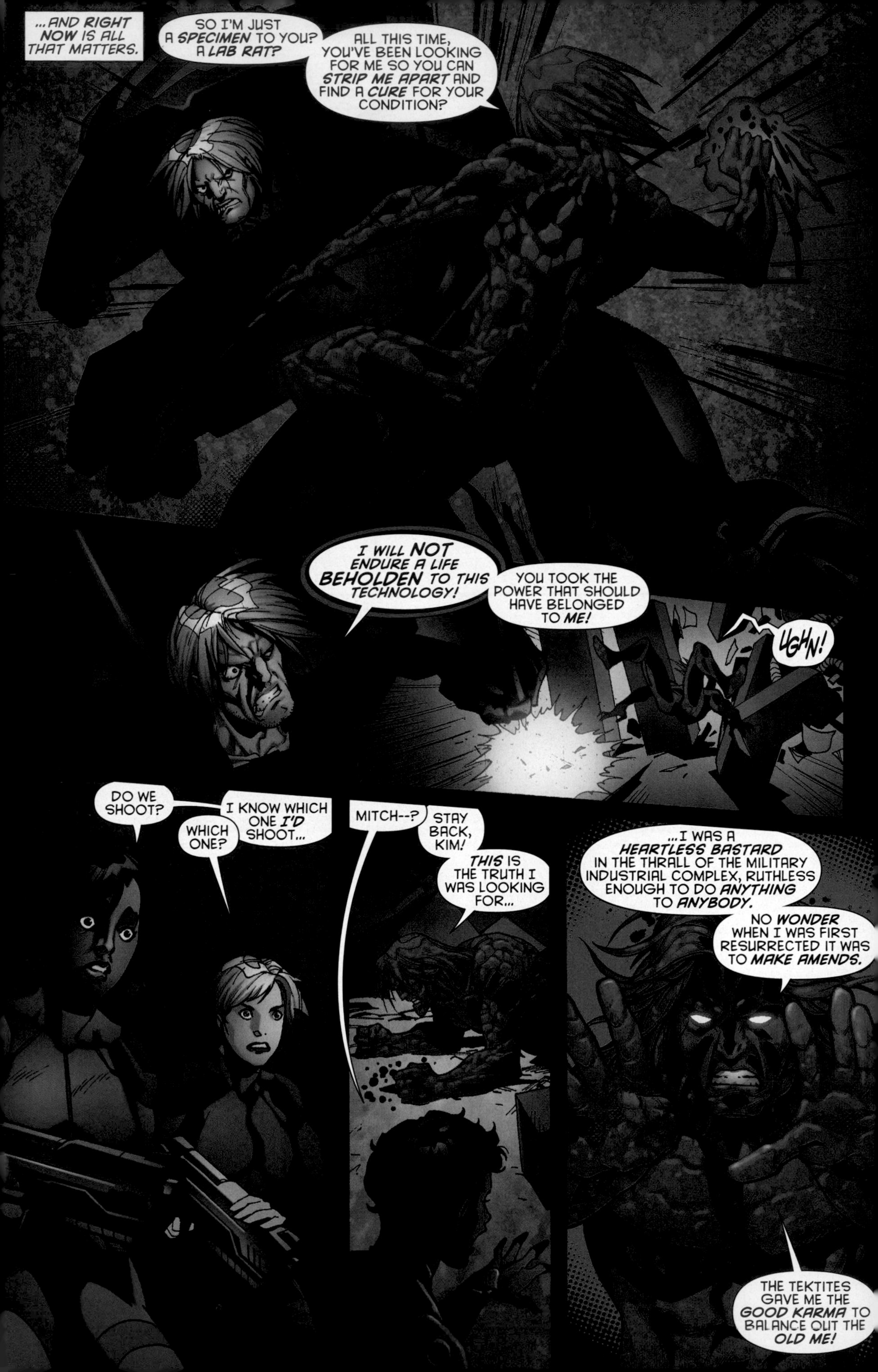
...AND RIGHT NOW IS ALL THAT MATTERS.
SO I'M JUST A SPECIMEN TO YOU? A LAB RAT?
ALL THIS TIME, YOU'VE BEEN LOOKING FOR ME SO YOU CAN STRIP ME APART AND FIND A CURE FOR YOUR CONDITION?
I WILL NOT ENDURE A LIFE BEHOLDEN TO THIS TECHNOLOGY!
YOU TOOK THE POWER THAT SHOULD HAVE BELONGED TO ME!
UGHN!
DO WE SHOOT?
I KNOW WHICH ONE I'D SHOOT...
WHICH ONE?
MITCH--?
STAY BACK, KIM!
THIS IS THE TRUTH I WAS LOOKING FOR...
...I WAS A HEARTLESS BASTARD IN THE THRALL OF THE MILITARY INDUSTRIAL COMPLEX, RUTHLESS ENOUGH TO DO ANYTHING TO ANYBODY.
NO WONDER WHEN I WAS FIRST RESURRECTED IT WAS TO MAKE AMENDS.
THE TEKTITES GAVE ME THE GOOD KARMA TO BALANCE OUT THE OLD ME!

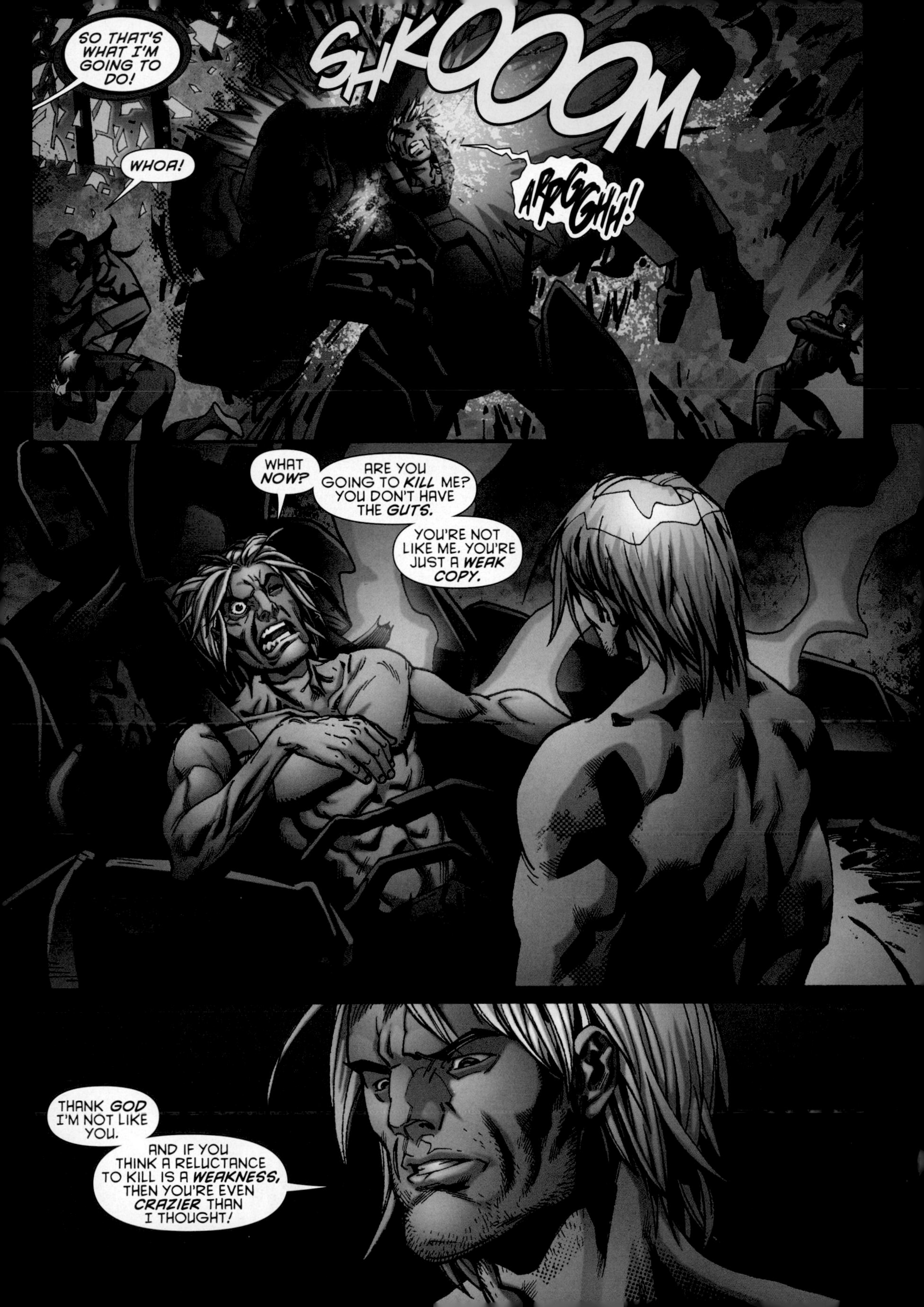
SO THAT'S WHAT I'M GOING TO DO!
SHKOOOOM
WHOA!
ARRGGGHH!
WHAT NOW?
ARE YOU GOING TO KILL ME? YOU DON'T HAVE THE GUTS.
YOU'RE NOT LIKE ME. YOU'RE JUST A WEAK COPY.
THANK GOD I'M NOT LIKE YOU.
AND IF YOU THINK A RELUCTANCE TO KILL IS A WEAKNESS, THEN YOU'RE EVEN CRAZIER THAN I THOUGHT!

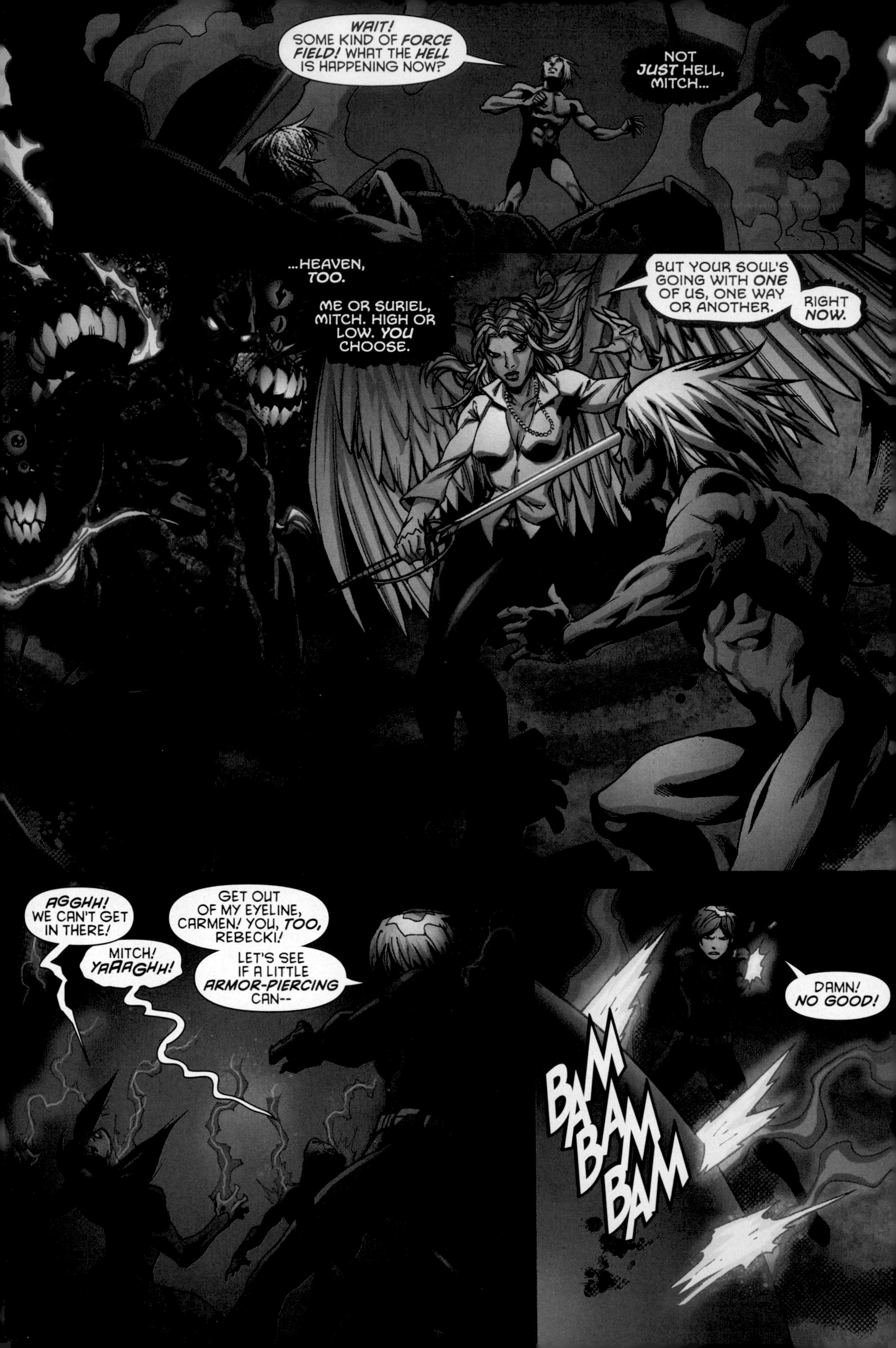
WAIT! SOME KIND OF FORCE FIELD! WHAT THE HELL IS HAPPENING NOW?
NOT JUST HELL, MITCH...
...HEAVEN, TOO.
ME OR SURIEL, MITCH. HIGH OR LOW. YOU CHOOSE.
BUT YOUR SOUL'S GOING WITH ONE OF US, ONE WAY OR ANOTHER.
RIGHT NOW.
AGGHH! WE CAN'T GET IN THERE!
MITCH! YAAAAGHH!
GET OUT OF MY EYELINE, CARMEN! YOU, TOO, REBECKI!
LET'S SEE IF A LITTLE ARMOR-PIERCING CAN--
BAM BAM BAM BAM
DAMN! NO GOOD!

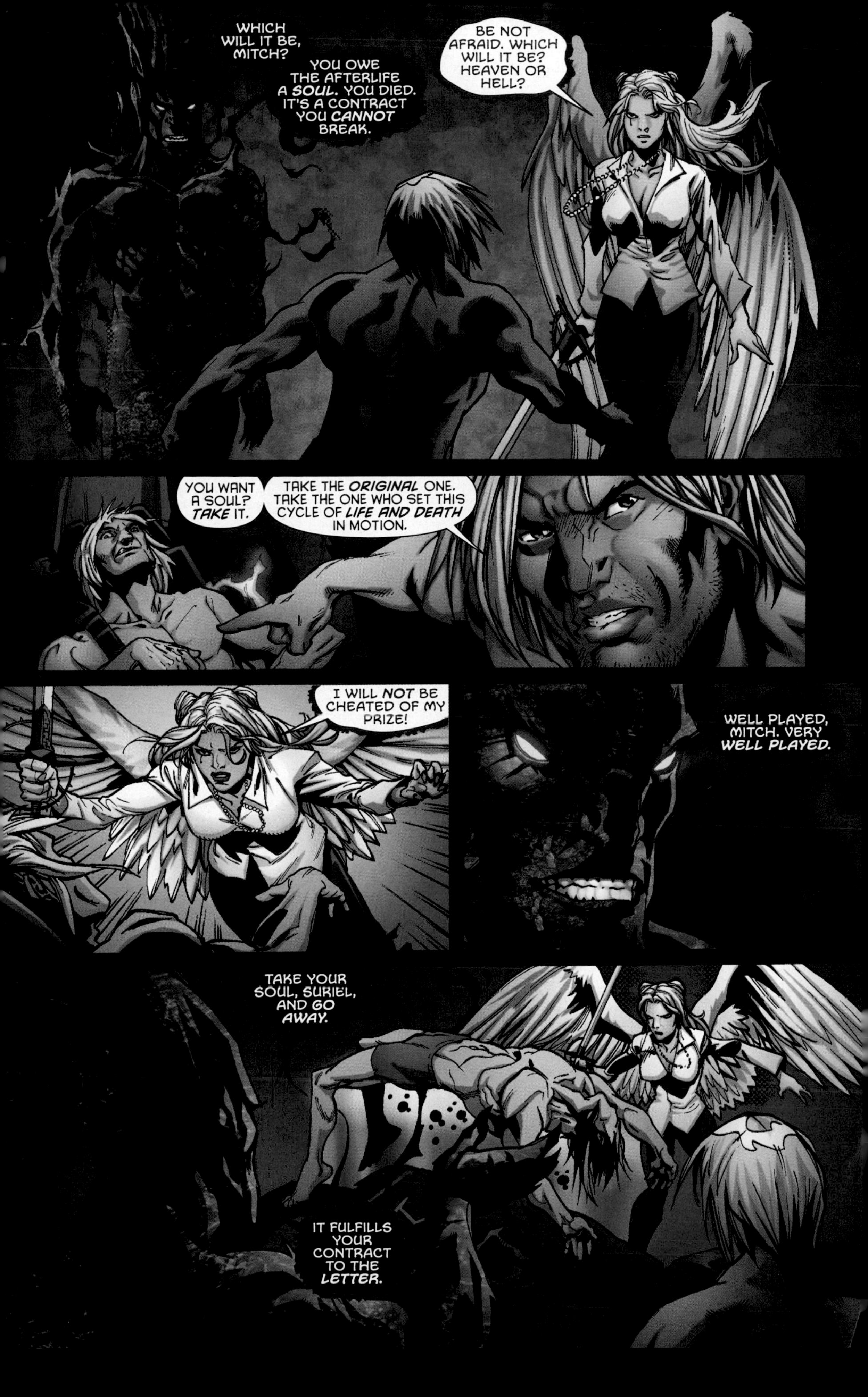
WHICH WILL IT BE, MITCH?
YOU OWE THE AFTERLIFE A SOUL. YOU DIED. IT'S A CONTRACT YOU CANNOT BREAK.
BE NOT AFRAID. WHICH WILL IT BE? HEAVEN OR HELL?
YOU WANT A SOUL? TAKE IT.
TAKE THE ORIGINAL ONE. TAKE THE ONE WHO SET THIS CYCLE OF LIFE AND DEATH IN MOTION.
I WILL NOT BE CHEATED OF MY PRIZE!
WELL PLAYED, MITCH. VERY WELL PLAYED.
TAKE YOUR SOUL, SURIEL, AND GO AWAY.
IT FULFILLS YOUR CONTRACT TO THE LETTER.

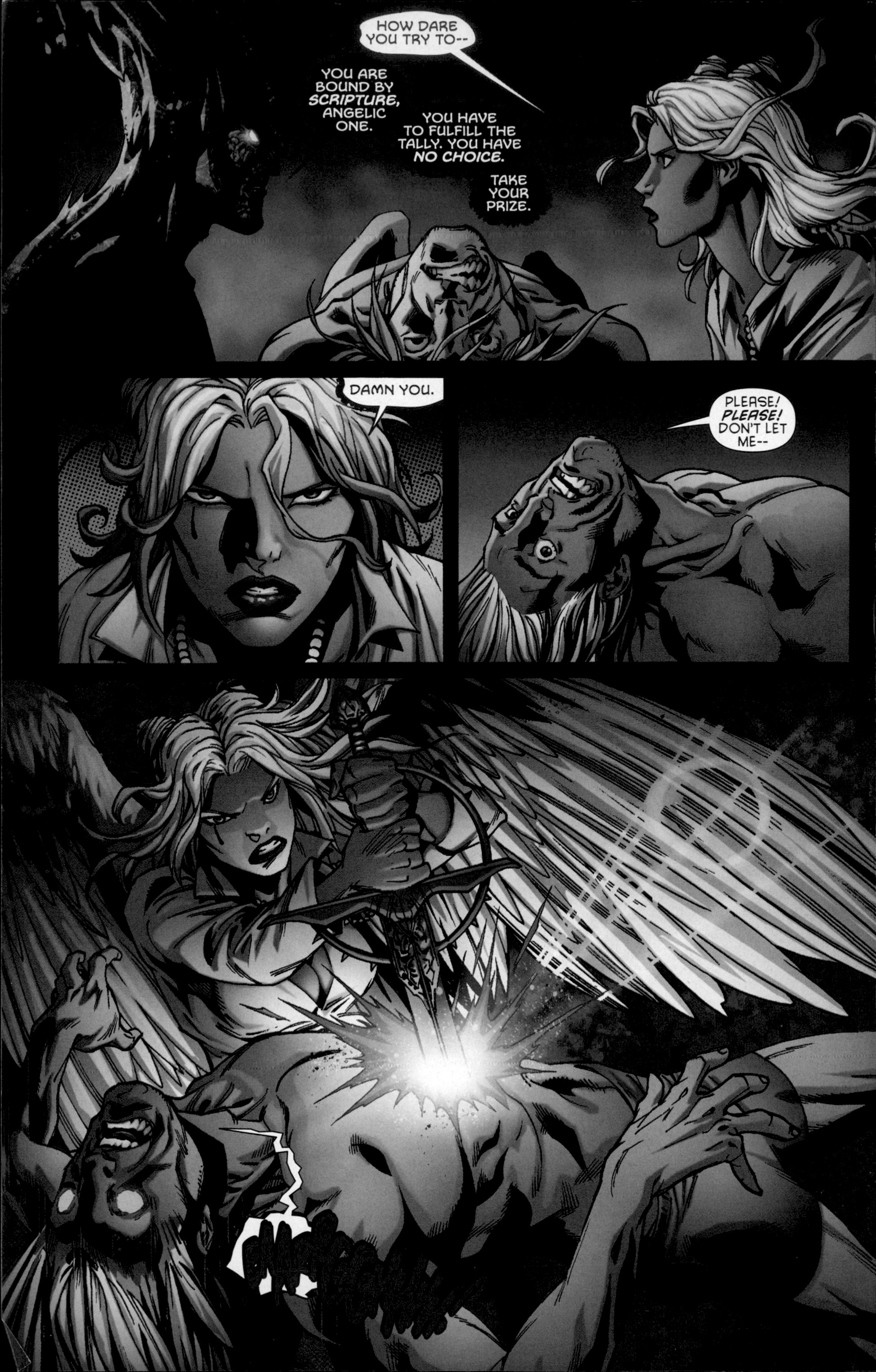
HOW DARE YOU TRY TO--
YOU ARE BOUND BY SCRIPTURE, ANGELIC ONE.
YOU HAVE TO FULFILL THE TALLY. YOU HAVE NO CHOICE.
TAKE YOUR PRIZE.
DAMN YOU.
PLEASE! PLEASE! DON'T LET ME--

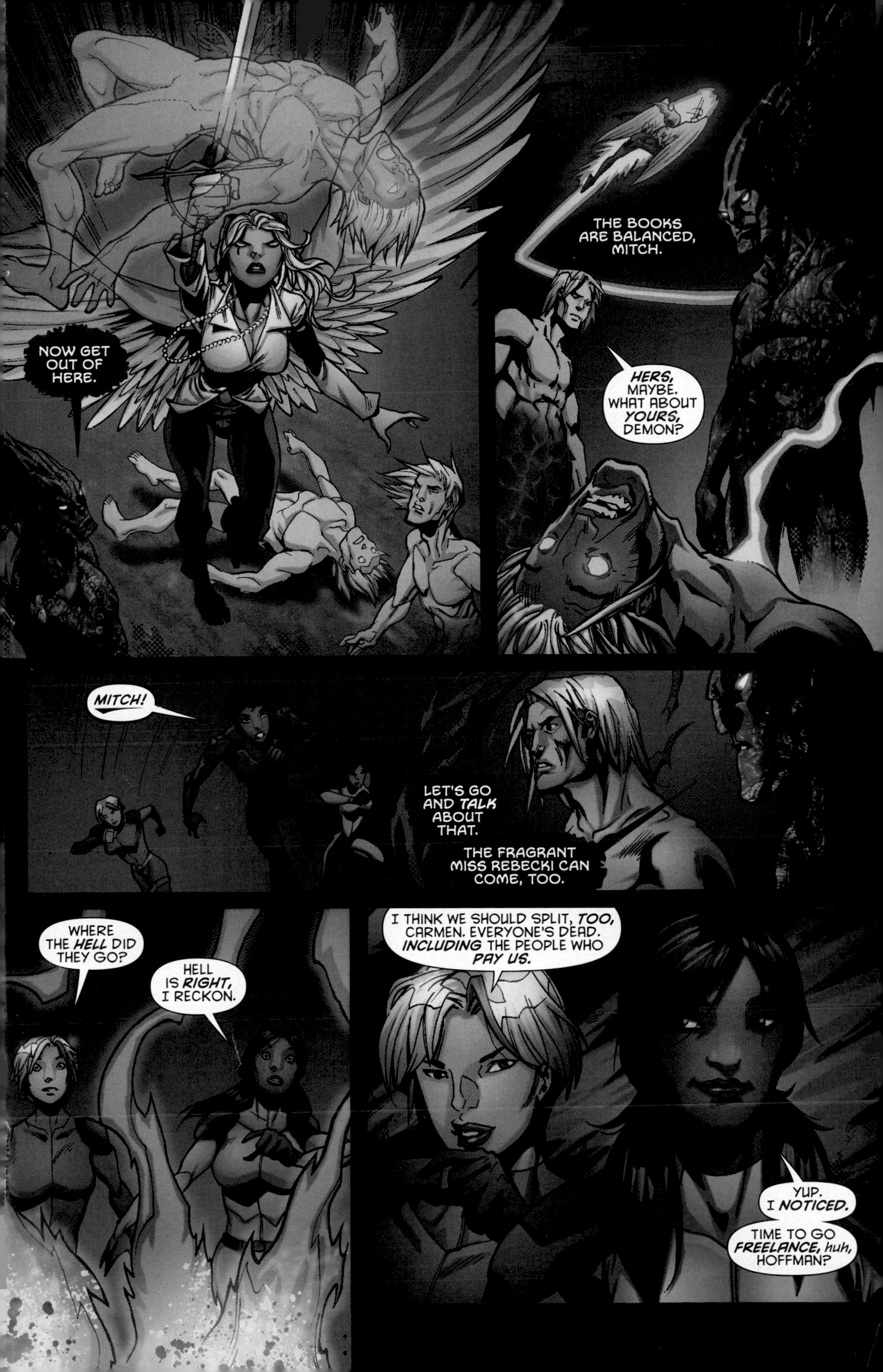
NOW GET OUT OF HERE.
THE BOOKS ARE BALANCED, MITCH.
HERS, MAYBE. WHAT ABOUT YOURS, DEMON?
MITCH!
LET'S GO AND TALK ABOUT THAT.
THE FRAGRANT MISS REBECKI CAN COME, TOO.
WHERE THE HELL DID THEY GO?
HELL IS RIGHT, I RECKON.
I THINK WE SHOULD SPLIT, TOO, CARMEN. EVERYONE'S DEAD. INCLUDING THE PEOPLE WHO PAY US.
YUP. I NOTICED.
TIME TO GO FREELANCE, huh, HOFFMAN?

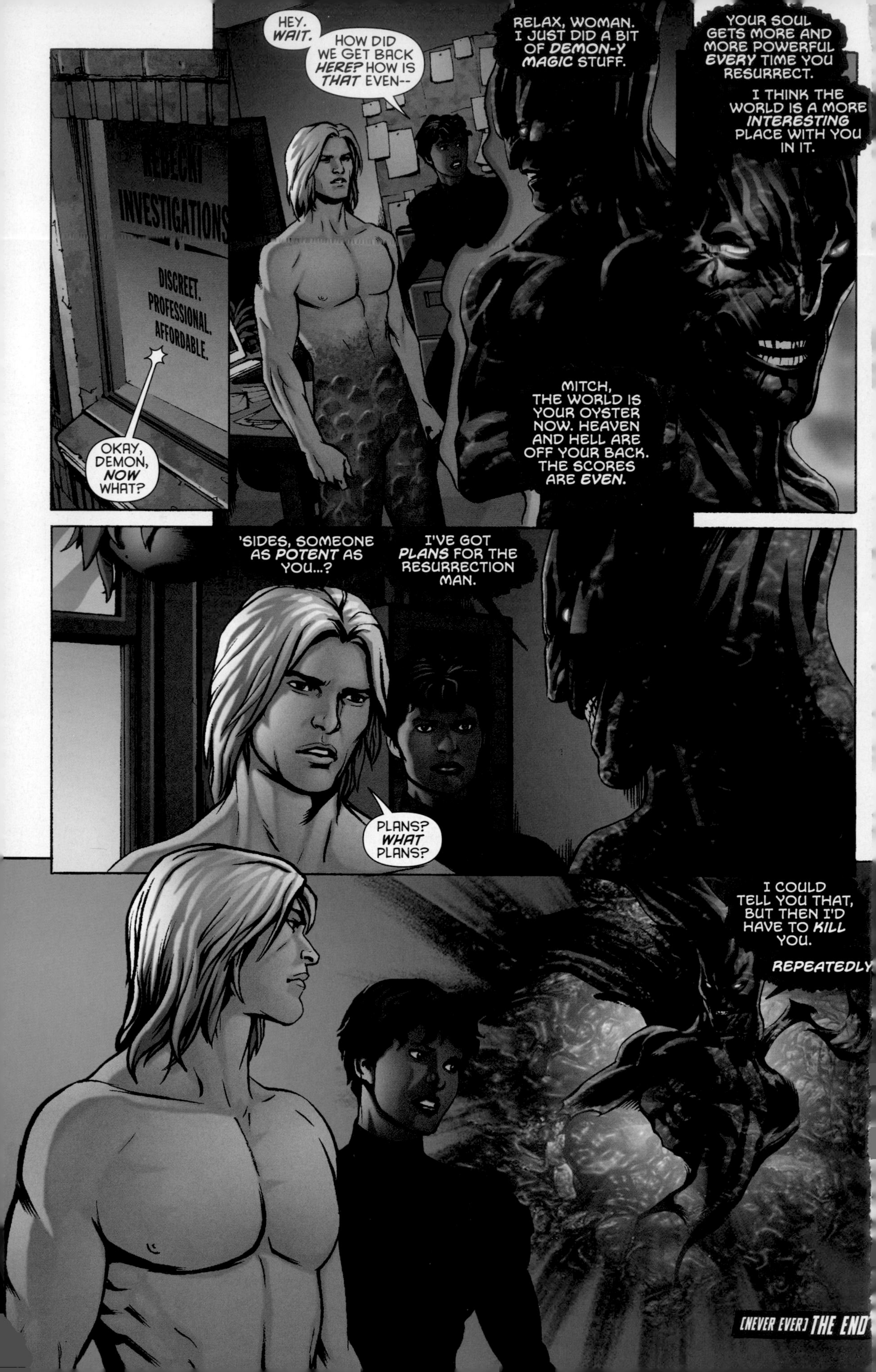
HEY. WAIT.
HOW DID WE GET BACK HERE? HOW IS THAT EVEN--
RELAX, WOMAN. I JUST DID A BIT OF DEMON-Y MAGIC STUFF.
YOUR SOUL GETS MORE AND MORE POWERFUL EVERY TIME YOU RESURRECT.
I THINK THE WORLD IS A MORE INTERESTING PLACE WITH YOU IN IT.
REBECKI INVESTIGATIONS
DISCREET. PROFESSIONAL. AFFORDABLE.
OKAY, DEMON, NOW WHAT?
MITCH, THE WORLD IS YOUR OYSTER NOW. HEAVEN AND HELL ARE OFF YOUR BACK. THE SCORES ARE EVEN.
'SIDES, SOMEONE AS POTENT AS YOU...?
I'VE GOT PLANS FOR THE RESURRECTION MAN.
PLANS? WHAT PLANS?
I COULD TELL YOU THAT, BUT THEN I'D HAVE TO KILL YOU.
REPEATEDLY
[NEVER EVER] THE END